MW00453202

Life among the Ordinary

Completing Our Nation's
Great Unfinished Business

Michael D'Angelo

Cari Burkard and Jackie Garnett, Co-Editors

First Edition: June 2014

Printed in the United States of America

Suncoast Digital Press, Inc.

ISBN: 978-1-939237-23-1

Library of Congress Cataloging-In-Publication Data
Library of Congress Control Number: 2014940025

"No matter how loyal the different members of a national body may be to one another, their mutual good faith will bleed to death, unless some among them have the intelligence to trace their national ills to their appropriate causes, and the candid courage to advocate the necessary remedial measures."

- Herbert Croly, <u>The Promise of American Life</u> (1909)

Contents

Introduction

You don't know me, but there are millions of people in the United States of America who are just like me. Millions. I am an ordinary citizen, a common man.

Life among the Ordinary presents a rare kind of voice, independent and not owned, free of and unmuted by the influence of any party or commercial allegiance. [1] This permits the freedom to tell a story through a different lens, using the eyes of an ordinary citizen within our imperfect yet predictable human nature. Thus empowered, the lens possesses a natural ability to capture the essence of American democracy—and identify the cause of its unrest.

The story celebrates the journey of the ordinary citizen in the pursuit of happiness. Ordinary status permits some simple yet universal observations about the fascinating role which ordinary people and human nature play in coming together to make history.

The theme is guided by a moral compass which embraces a sense of humanity's purpose—that we are here not merely to collect things and change money—but to serve. How can America apply this ancient principle in a practical way to meet the challenge of our time and complete the *great unfinished business of the nation*—achieving meaningful equality of opportunity?

As we attempt to aim higher, there is good reason for optimism. The final destination is of course important. But the journey supplies the richness by which our lives come to be defined. What is it about adherence to an incorruptible, disinterested "ethical obligation" that distinguishes the unselfish citizen from the mere hoarder of gold?

***

Nature is simple in its essence, and seemingly perfect in every way. Man is a simple product of nature, but human nature is, as we have come to know, imperfect. The intersection of nature with the birth of a human being constitutes life in its simplest form.

Good parents typically say that all a baby really needs are three things: food, warmth and love. That's it. Do we recognize just how tiny is the traditional hospital blanket, which covers the newborn infant for baby's first picture? It's slightly larger, perhaps, than an ordinary dish cloth.

But then, the hospital blanket begins to grow larger, and so do the problems. And somehow, it gets complicated. A single, precipitous event can complicate things, like a child's poor performance in school, the loss of a parent's job, an ill-conceived marriage, ugly divorce, illness, or untimely death. Other times, complication arrives through seemingly incongruous events: the birth of a child into poverty with no father, no parents, no adult role model at all. After all, not even a few of us can be fortunate enough to have the opportunity to grow up the privileged child of the rich man. As a matter of pure numbers, it's just not reality.

Somewhere along the line, however, we may recognize how something that started off so simple could get complicated. Those with the special twin gifts of inner strength and mental toughness are able to navigate these choppy waters with great discipline. And, through a healthy measure of self-examination, they begin to simplify. Hopelessly lost for a time in a race whose value has come into question, for a variety of reasons, they find their way back to basics. They prioritize, and through this process the journey of life begins anew.

The tricky part is just how to go about the process of simplifying. For some, great comfort and solace are found and nurtured within the social fabric of the bedrock institutions upon which we lean. These lie mainly in the realm of religion and politics. It is interesting in our American democracy that each of these institutions, although sacred in its own right, is kept separate and distinct. There can be neither politics in religion, nor religion in politics. It has been the law of the land since 1791.

Despite the imperfections inherent in each of these institutions (after all, they are creatures conceived by the work of man, and man is by nature a simple yet imperfect creature), when we begin to peel back the onion and reveal the essence, we react quite differently. As it should be, since there is no instruction manual for such things.

Some choose to accept the inherent flaws, whether perceived as minor or major is of little consequence. They voluntarily submit to the structure of the nominal authorities. Further, they acquiesce to the fact that while these old friends may be far from perfect, somehow we *need* them.

Others drink the Kool-Aid, no questions asked, seemingly oblivious to the flaws. Here the word "brainwashed" seems appropriate, although perhaps it is more diplomatic to settle on the word "dependent." The politics of fear is deployed, ideally on the weaker minded of our brethren, in an indoctrination that is both intensive and forcible. The aim is to destroy our basic convictions and attitudes and replace them with an alternative set of fixed beliefs. Through this transformative process we can be controlled and manipulated as necessary to promote the self-serving goals of the leaders.

Still others see through the self-interest component, reject the various rules and regulations as both arbitrary and artificial mechanisms, and choose to go it alone. Their independent path less traveled is guided not by man-made lenses, filters or walls but only by the voice in their inner bosom. These individuals understand that while these institutions started off well, continue to mean well and do an awful lot of good things for an awful lot of people, sometimes they are corrupted. These individuals understand that there is a higher authority than both the law and man-made religious institutions.

Which is the preferred or more correct path? All are reasonable. There is no right or wrong answer. There's only *us*, and the quality of our daily existence, such as we ordinary citizens make of it. But the path less traveled has higher upside for greater understanding. Prudently navigated, this path alone has the capacity to identify and suspend the limiting self-interest component of politics and religion. The complicated can thus become simplified, permitting the underlying message to shine through.

***

Some brief background will be useful. Any street sense is likely owed to formative years in Brooklyn, New York. Take the poster entitled *A New Yorker's View of the World*, New York featured prominently in the center. Moving west, New Jersey is an alien place, still somewhat pronounced. Next lies California, its thought stimulating the imagination, in significantly smaller lettering. Lastly, Russia is crammed in tiny letters, wherever that is. Moving east of New York in the opposite direction is the Atlantic Ocean, "the pond" which leads to England. And that's it. This poster conveys a message.

People from Brooklyn believe that the world contains only two types of people: those from Brooklyn—and everybody else. They do not consider themselves to be the world's smartest people, as long as it is understood they are smarter than people not from Brooklyn.

To be sure, there is daily fighting and disagreement among them, as would befit a tiny island sand bar packed with people. However, in disputes with outsiders, even mortal enemies have each other's backs. This conveys another message.

Gainful pursuit over the years has required many hats in various capacities. This has included work as a landscaper, fast food line worker, dishwasher, busboy, water meter reader, gas station attendant, cement mixer and a house packer for a moving company.

Law school is intellectually stimulating, and the legal profession remains noble. The idea of *practicing* law may sound enchanting. But the reality tends to be mundane. Once learned, even a monkey can be trained to perform many lawyerly tasks which are in reality basic and routine.

The life of a W-2 employee as an attorney with a major national insurance company, in the culture of "old boy" white Anglo-Saxon protestant (WASP) men, was an out of place experience. Corporate America is not the place for a second generation Italian-American kid from Brooklyn. How many others continue to face the same obstacles?

After toiling for others for a number of years, a long, successful run as a principal in private law practice followed. There would be one law partner, who remains a dear friend.

Running a business does have its benefits, like setting your own hours. Typically that means working most of the time, but one can take some odd time off during the middle of a work day to attend to important things, like family stuff. This permits spending much quality time with activities like coaching in the local Little League baseball program, one of the joys of family and hometown community life.

To experience a son within the setting of his childhood friends is priceless and irreplaceable. Any success along the way is pure gravy. But success there was. His travel teams won back to back county championships for the first time in our town's 30-year affiliation with the program.

Little League underscored an important lesson on the value of a well-run organization. Everyone worked together, but within a hierarchy and with a particular role, subordinating self-interest to the interest of the team concept. We spoke with one voice, under the direction of Brian Zychowski, our team manager and head coach. While the group was not the most talented, our staff took pride in hearing feedback that our teams were supremely disciplined, well coached and fun to watch.

Coach Z is a school teacher, administrator and district superintendent by professional training. He became a mentor in countless ways, many unforeseeable when we were first innocently paired together. As a father of 6 children, he was extremely busy. Yet he was always the one to approach to get things done. He fit the old cliché perfectly: "If you want to get something done, asks a busy person."

Our close relationship of trust facilitated the alignment of our thinking such that we could finish each other's sentences. To this day it remains a special friendship.

***

Seeds of discontent with law practice, however, were sprouting. It had become obvious that work life had become disconnected with purpose. Coach Z helped put feelings in proper perspective. His challenge was to find a way to re-introduce intellectual stimulation, though easier said than done.

Innocently enough, he suggested that together we read a biography on John Adams, while coaching the kids. In the midst of teaching the nuts and bolts of the grand old game, we simultaneously rattled off interesting quotes. Parents who were watching must have thought we were crazy. A favorite was John Adams' declaration that "Facts are stubborn things." [2] Its application contained much potential.

One biography's lead into another revealed an interesting pattern. Many of the subjects were also professing to be less than completely enamored with law practice. For example, there was Adams' son, John Quincy, who would become an American statesman. After experiencing life after law practice as a diplomat in Holland, the younger Adams stressed that life in Holland provided

> A situation in itself much preferable to that of eternal expectation in a lawyer's office for business, which when it comes, is scarcely sufficient to give bread, and procures one more curses than thanks.

Pledging that he would accept any honorable employment before that of an attorney, son told father bluntly that "I shall not be willing to go through it again," adding that "my feelings on this subject become daily more strongly confirmed." [3]

Theodore Roosevelt offered an interesting perspective on lawyers, who maintain contrary positions on important issues as their interests bid them. But an independent voice labors under no such limitation, charged only with conviction for the side of the right:

> Personally I have not the slightest sympathy with debating contests in which each side is arbitrarily assigned a given proposition and told to maintain it without the least reference to whether those maintaining it believe in it or not. I know that under our system this is necessary for lawyers, but I emphatically disbelieve in it as regards general discussion of political, social and industrial matters. What we need is to turn out of our colleges young men with ardent convictions on the side of the right; not young men who can make a good argument for either right or wrong as their interest bids them. There is no effort to instill sincerity and intensity of conviction. On the contrary, the net result is to make the contestants feel that their convictions have nothing to do with their arguments. [4]

Harry Truman encouraged his understudies to study the law but felt that just knowing the law wasn't enough. Truman felt the trouble with far too many lawyers was that they knew the law but did not know much of anything else. Consequently, he also encouraged study concerning the nature of man and the culture and heritage of Western Civilization in general. [5] This observation was an epiphany.

Meanwhile, as an embedded observer of interaction with kids on the field, Coach Z also suggested a stint at classroom teaching. Some great Americans had wanted to be teachers, but for the turn of events outside their control. Harry Truman, for one, had always wanted to be a history teacher. But Truman never had the opportunity, since his father had traded away his college education money. U.S. Grant, for another, had wanted simply to become a math teacher. In their time, both were self-described ordinary men, although history would now seem to judge them differently.

What made Harry Truman so indispensable to then-President Franklin D. Roosevelt in the election of 1944? Their backgrounds couldn't have been more different. F.D.R. was from "old money," Ivy League pedigree. Truman was a common farmer from Missouri with no more than a high school education. F.D.R. knew he was dying and was not likely to complete his 4th term in office. Why, then, did F.D.R. want Harry Truman as his running mate? Surely he must have known that Truman would become President.

Fortunately, Providence had other plans for great Americans like Harry Truman and U.S. Grant, their dreams of rewarding teaching careers being dashed by external events. It was U.S. Grant, who reminded us at the opening of his memoirs that

'Man proposes and God disposes.' There are but few important events in the affairs of men brought about by their own choice. [6]

Practically speaking, some additional sentiment from Theodore Roosevelt provided further encouragement: "Do what you can, with what you've got, where you are." [7]

There had been little interest in history. And now nearing mid-life, both formal teacher training and experience were noticeably lacking. But Dr. Mark Lender, the history department chair at Kean University, a respected public institution which produces tomorrow's K-12 public school teachers, offered an adjunct position, teaching US History. Through his kind consideration, a frantic search to locate an educator's hat ensued.

***

Most universities place a premium on writing. If you haven't published a book, you simply will not be considered for a full-time teaching position. This is a curious policy. Seeking to execute academic reform, Woodrow Wilson, the young President of Princeton University, would only let go of a faculty member "because of failure to *teach* properly, not for failure to publish or specialize." [8] He felt that private prep school teachers were more effective than their university counterparts, for the simple reason that they taught better. This was inspirational.

In his Princeton inaugural address, Wilson also stated that "every concrete thing (America) has done has seemed to rise out of some abstract principle, some vision of the mind." He believed that students

Should be taught a broad citizenship ... and prepared for the duties and challenges of public life wherever they happened to be, a general serviceableness. Rather than know one subject minutely, they should be enlightened ... . They should study American history in particular, so they could plan the future. Broad training would help them relate to all types and see their point of view. [9]

The learning process begins with asking questions, which promotes and inspires critical thinking. An effective platform evolves through the telling of stories. When one story is begun, it starts out clear and linear, like anyone's family tree.

But then it branches out, loops back and links up with others, until what students think is a simple piece of cloth is suddenly a more complex tapestry. The classroom is a place so full of curiosity that, through storytelling, we can see their lessons and connections to one another.

Core topics in addition to history are developed—philosophy, geography, the role and influence of religion, social science, economics, language and word origin. What are the elusive qualities and high ideals necessary for true leadership? Thorny topics do not escape the lens—immigration and its impact, racism, discrimination and civil rights' development. By comparing to current events through life experience, students gain a better understanding of the historical connections between then and now.

The goal is to enable students to master the art of critical thinking, to learn how to "walk a mile in the other person's shoes" with empathy for others. Once able to identify the recurring themes and tendencies prevalent in human nature, students are at once more aware. Consequently, they are empowered to make responsible, informed decisions and become active, alert citizens in their adult daily life. Sometimes, one can actually see the light bulb go on.

The final classes—on the topic of *America in Our Time*—typically spin heads. If they didn't get it before, here students come to understand it is not so simple. It is complicated. They come to appreciate that there are many more questions than there are answers. Students learn that one thread cannot so easily be removed without affecting the tapestry's overall integrity. In the end, they are better prepared to assume their rightful place in the national conversation.

***

This narrative will proceed in similar fashion, digression facilitating a chance to see the bigger picture.

We will begin by learning about the "science of human nature" and why many have characterized it as being most useful. Its variety of behaviors is constant and predictable. Its elements have changed little through time. So if one were to recognize the patterns in these behaviors, then plug in an assortment of random ordinary people, places and dates, one would unlock forever the mystery of understanding history. That being the case, can there ever be anything really *new* in the world?

Alexander Hamilton actually used the forces of human nature to secure the economic system of capitalism in this country. But Thomas Jefferson objected. What was his basis? And why did George Washington decide the question in favor of Hamilton?

Theodore Roosevelt said our country's history has faced two great crises: first when it was formed, and then again when it was perpetuated. In 1912 T.R. identified the substance of Jefferson's objection as the basis of our third great crisis, bringing it back to life if only for a time. A hundred years later, America is still confounded by the nation's great unfinished business. In truth, all roads still lead to this place.

There are but 4 important lessons of US History, and we will discover each of them. What is the pursuit of happiness, and why is it important yet elusive? Why is it difficult to define and so hard to hold onto? Are we alone in its pursuit, or can we also learn a thing or two from Eastern meditations? Can we find happiness under a bush, or must we step out into the arena to fight for it?

We will travel together as ordinary citizens on a diversion into how we see things, what we are seeing, and who, in particular, permits access to the video room.

We will learn about lenses, filters and walls. Why do we have them? What benefits and detriments may they provide? We will learn to appreciate the difficulty in distinguishing what is real from what only appears to be real. We will come to better identify "needs" in the pursuit of happiness and distinguish from what are merely "wants." Understanding the powerful forces that permit access to the video room is essential to determine what may be necessary to preserve the American Dream.

Students of US History *do* appear to be in a preferred position to best plan the future, at least when measured alongside those who choose to neglect its study. But there are legitimate concerns that *opportunities* afforded to students of US History are not favorable for the development of their genius. The prospects to exercise opportunities and capitalize on their intellectual position are equally unfavorable. While the US Constitution guarantees ordinary citizens the "equal protection of the laws," there is no known guarantee of an opportunity to plan America's future.

Statistics show that 20% of all Americans control 85% of all wealth, and a full 40% of all Americans possess absolutely no wealth to speak of. [10] What appears to be lacking is not intellectual capacity (for even an ordinary citizen can achieve a significant measure of intellectual achievement), but equal access to America's economic opportunity structure.

And while the lack of equal access has traditionally been more acute among America's people of color, it is not strictly limited to that particular demographic. Women are and have been vulnerable too, having been denied the right to vote until almost a full 60 years after the black man. Imagine then, being both black *and* a woman? America's white population, the vast majority of ordinary citizens, has also become increasingly vulnerable in recent years.

Some of the causes are obvious. The US Constitution is said to be an organic, flexible document. But since its enactment in 1789, economic forces have concentrated in ways that were perhaps not foreseeable then. Among the culprits are the financial interests of capitalism, the resulting onset of the spirit of party or political factions, large corporations, unions, lobby groups and political action committees. Each shares a large, economic, private self-interest component.

Thomas Jefferson identified certain hereditary, artificial and arbitrary privileges which flow from principles adverse to liberty and are undesirable in a democratic society. Their beneficiaries use these privileges to amass wealth unfairly, and to secure and maintain their status, at the expense of ordinary citizens, by exerting an "influence" over lawmakers. But when the umpire is corrupted, our national institutions and constitutional guarantees of equal opportunity are impeded.

Likewise, corporate boardrooms and public legislatures alike confer "benefits" which many perceive to be unconscionable. But when the short-term view runs into the long-term commitment and the money runs out, has each been shown to have given merely expectations?

Corporations use the private bankruptcy laws to shed employee legacy costs, downsize and recapitalize. But the case of workers in the public sector is different. Historically, legislatures have stood behind public unions, extremely reluctant to disturb their contractual rights. But that is changing.

Some lawmakers have chosen to eliminate the collective bargaining process, thereby effectively eliminating the union. But is it wisdom to kill the union, which may be only a *symptom* of the problem? Or might it be preferable to provide lawmakers with effective insulation from economic pressures which tend to corrupt them? And might improved transparency also provide a better means to a desirable end?

Central to everything mentioned thus far is a discussion of the need for change balanced against the obligation to protect the powerful status quo. Is one more important than the other? Can we implement change merely by flying under the radar, or must we be more aggressive? How hard do we fight—and how much risk must we assume? Do property rights deserve a continuing higher societal priority than human welfare? Or should the two work together?

We will reflect on the issue whether, and to what extent, *moral* issues are said to be "secondary." We will consider how Americans attempt to juggle the difficult concepts of tolerance and inclusion in their daily lives, often merely *saying* one thing but *doing* another. Finally, we will conclude with a discussion which centers on Paris 1919, or tomorrow. How did we arrive at this mysterious thing we call the status quo which encapsulates today's problems? Are there any realistic, practical solutions?

***

At times, those who ask serious questions expose themselves to criticism from a group which claims legitimacy as the sole defenders of the faith of the American spirit. Dissenters, arguing that while they love what America represents it can still be made better, are seen as un-American. Challenges posed to majority rule and the status quo are viewed as unpatriotic. Sometimes, the voices of dissent are silenced by the ruling party through various means. This is as unfortunate as it is dangerous to our civil liberties.

While the acquiescence of the minority and defeated candidates is a necessary maxim of self-governing society, there is a real, quantifiable danger of the "tyranny of the majority."

In his 1801 Inaugural Address the nation's new third president, Thomas Jefferson, sought to assure his defeated foes by proclaiming a sacred principle:

> that though the will of the majority is in all cases to prevail, *that will, to be rightful, must be reasonable*; that the minority possess their equal rights, which equal laws must protect, and to violate would be oppression. [11]

Jefferson understood that an "error of opinion may be tolerated where reason is left free to combat it." In other words, we are all loyal Americans, whose patriotism should not be questioned and who should not be at another's throats.

> But every difference of opinion is not a difference of principle. We have been called by different names brethren of the same principle. We are all republicans: we are all federalists. [12]

Jefferson's tolerance for differences of opinion is admirable. We all make mistakes. The wisdom of an old proverb conveys a hope that others will have better luck: "A wise man learns from his mistakes, but a wiser man learns from somebody else's mistakes." What can the ordinary citizen learn from this lesson as we attempt to plan America's future?

The USA is the greatest country on earth. It remains the envy of the world for the core principles and values for which we stand, such as the freedom to utter dissent. We are one nation, under God, with liberty and justice for all. We are ordinary *American* citizens through and through.

This introduction concludes with another John Adams' quote, offered with gentle humility. You may know someone who has claimed it more recently, as surely one had said it before: "The longer I live, the more I read, the more patiently I think, and the more anxiously I inquire, the less I seem to know." [13]

Chapter 1
An Important Lesson in the Most Useful "Science of Human Nature"

What then to do about Jesus of Nazareth
Miracle wonderman – hero of fools?
No riots, no army, no fighting, no slogans
One thing I'll say for him – Jesus is cool.
...

I see bad things arising – the crowd crown him king
Which the Romans would ban.
I see blood and destruction, our elimination
Because of one man.
...

What then to do about this Jesusmania?
How do we deal with the carpenter king?
Where do we start with a man that is bigger
Than John was when John did his Baptism thing?

Fools! You have no perception!
The stakes we are gambling are frighteningly high!
We must crush him completely –
So like John before him, this Jesus must die.
For the sake of the nation this Jesus must die.

- from the song, *This Jesus Must Die,*
from the Broadway musical, *Jesus Christ Superstar* (1970)

***

More than a few people say they "hate" history, until coming to relate its relevance to events in their own lives. Why is the subject of history emphasized as extensively as it is in our K-12 secondary schools? Why is it maintained as a core discipline in many of the nation's public universities and most, if not all, of the nation's elite liberal arts institutions of higher learning? Why is history taught so poorly, with an excruciating emphasis on memorizing reams of facts and figures, absent any particular context or personal relevance? More simply stated, why do we bother to study history? What exactly is the point?

Let's begin with a discussion of human nature. In the early 1960s Harry Truman was still a familiar figure, if not a household name. Dad used to refer to grandpa simply as "Harry S," because, we were told, grandpa looked like Harry S. Truman. Both men were short, appeared physically frail, their gray hair closely cropped, and sported funny looking top hats. No matter that grandpa was of Italian descent and had come to this country with millions of immigrants similarly situated in the early 20ᵗʰ century. When grandpa received this greeting, he just smiled. Looking back, it is likely that grandpa had no idea who Harry S. Truman was.

In the early 1970s the popular rock band, Chicago, recorded a song called "Harry Truman" on its *Chicago VIII* album. The song began, *"America needs you, Harry Truman. Harry won't you please come home."* Here was another clue.

Perhaps it was just mere coincidence that the Watergate scandal was about to break, compelling President Nixon to resign the presidency in disgrace. This was the same Nixon who grew up in the shadow of the infamous Joseph McCarthy, US Senator, R-WI, one of the key proponents of the communist "Red Scare." This was the same Nixon who, as Vice President to then-President Eisenhower, had attempted to label Harry Truman as "soft" on communism. It was a futile charge simply to advance Nixon's own personal cause.

Some may be surprised to learn that Harry Truman was the last American President who did not attend college. Nor did grandpa, for that matter. But Truman did have some good teachers along the way, perhaps the finest of whom was his mother. Mattie Truman's philosophy had been simple. "You knew right from wrong, you always tried to do right, and you did your best. That's all there was to it." [14]

One of Truman's many biographers described the little farming town of Independence, Missouri, where Truman had grown up, as a town where people live a long time and have long memories. Moreover, the people there all seemed to have something in common with Truman. They had character. Can we say that about the community in which we live?

Perhaps this background would help to explain an incident, in which a national women's group was discussing Mr. Truman and his attitudes and saying some very harsh things about him. One of his former school teachers, since retired, was in the group. She took it as long as she could, then got up and said, "Now I don't know anything about the issues, but

I know that Harry Truman is honest, and whatever he says will stand the test of time." [15] The school teacher then sat down, and the group moved on to another topic.

Despite his lack of formal education, Truman was one of our smartest leaders, self taught in the mold of Abraham Lincoln. Truman had gained his considerable knowledge from a passion to study history. Even during his presidency, he could be found reading, his library filled only with biography and history. Like most intelligent people, he criticized lawyers, in that they knew the law but not much of anything else. "Gotta read your history," Harry was known to say, for a viewpoint of whatever the present issue happened to be within the context of the bigger picture. Above all, Truman encouraged the study of the nature of man and the culture and heritage of Western Civilization in general.

This presented another set of clues about human nature. Harry Truman was proficient in his reading of an old, classic series, entitled *Plutarch's Lives*, a bound set of which he possessed from his childhood days. The work was written in the late 1st century and consisted of a series of biographies of famous men. The surviving work, more commonly known as the *Parallel Lives*, consists of 23 pairs of biographies, each pair consisting of one Greek and one Roman. It is a work of considerable historical importance, arranged to illuminate the common moral virtues or failings of the subjects of the biographies.

From his reading of history, Truman concluded its elements of continuity were most striking, including, above all, human nature, which had changed little if any through time. [16]

> When I was in politics, there would be times when I tried to figure somebody out, and I could always turn to Plutarch, and 9 times out of 10 I'd be able to find a parallel in there. In 1940, when I was running for re-election in the Senate, there was this big apple grower named Stark trying to beat me. I'd started him out in politics, but in 1940 he was out to lick me, and I couldn't figure it out.

> But the more I thought about him, the more he reminded me of what Plutarch said about Nero. I'd done a lot of thinking about Nero. What I was interested in was how having started as well as he did, he ended up in ruin. And Plutarch said the start of his troubles was when he began to take his friends for granted and started to buy his enemies.

> And I noticed some of those same traits in old Starks. That's how I decided I could lick him, and I did, of course. Nobody thought I could, but I did.
> …
> But about Plutarch. It was the same with those old birds in Greece and Rome as it is now. I told you. The only thing new in the world is the history you don't know. [17]

3

Harry Truman was thus deftly suited to apply the lessons learned to the problems of his time–which were in abundance. One of his favorite lines, "The only thing new in the world is the history you don't know," was no doubt invaluable in dealing with the ominous strongmen of the era. These were people like Germany's Adolph Hitler, the Soviet Union's Joseph Stalin and China's Mao Tse-tung, finding similar connections with other despots and historical figures that had come before.

The formula was really not very complicated. Essentially, while the names, the dates and the places may change, as well as the arbitrary lines and national boundaries on a map and the reign of great empires, human nature does not change. So, if one were to study and comprehend the workings of human nature, one would be able to juxtapose the names, the dates and the places from one era to another, and pretty well figure out not only the course but also the direction of events.

America loved, needed—and misses—Harry Truman, for many reasons. First and foremost, America loved his honesty and candor. Somehow, those are ingredients that seem to have been missing in our national leaders, say, over the last 50 years or so. America also loved Harry Truman because he was an underdog, who always seemed to snatch victory from the jaws of defeat, and staunchly defended the rights of the common man. "Give 'em hell, Harry" was the familiar phrase used by the people to show their support for his unbending principles.

In fact, Truman didn't see how it made much sense for one to enter politics and not be the proponent of the common man. [18] To be sure, he was known to review applications for appointments to West Point from Missouri boys. Bypassing folders thick with recommendations from judges, state legislators, mayors, etc., Truman would favor an application consisting of a single page, written in pencil on a sheet of cheap, rough paper.

Lastly, Harry Truman seemed to know his place in the natural order and that his role, although very important, was essentially fleeting. He never considered himself to be the President. Rather, Truman viewed himself as he was, the trustee of the Office of the President of the United States. And he knew that his time was merely temporary. On the former point, when asked the secret of his success, Truman cited to Oliver Wendell Holmes, Civil War soldier and US Supreme Court Justice. Old Holmes answered: "The secret of my success is that at a very early age I discovered that I am not God."

And similarly, Truman said that he never forgot where he came from, and would go back to: Independence, Missouri. All he had to recollect was the story of Cincinnatus, the Roman hero, who was compelled to give up his plow when called into service to save the empire in its time of dire need. When Truman's work was successfully completed in 1952, the man who arguably held the most power ever concentrated in any one single man to that moment in history, voluntarily gave up the power, put down the sword and returned to his farm country origins, like Cincinnatus before him.

***

The constancy of human nature is persuasive authority for the proposition that it must be set apart as its own science. A keen understanding of this science can be most useful in light of its predictability. And among the recurring patterns of predictable human behavior, both good and bad, the most useful science of human nature contains an important lesson.

My law partner, Michael Blythe, frequently says that *one can expect reasonable men to act reasonably in their own best interest.* This is a simple statement. However, it is rendered meaningless, absent some context. In fact, when the message is repeated over and over by the same voice, one naturally begins to tune it out. But it is provocative in light of Truman's experiences regarding the constancy of human nature.

There's a familiar story about an expectation of reasonable men acting reasonably in their own best interest. Some say it is the greatest story ever told, the story of Jesus Christ. As the story goes, Christ voluntarily chooses to forego his immortality to take on human form, that is, an imperfect form. His purpose is to provide ordinary people a working model as to how to set the main priorities of human existence.

We don't have a lot of detail on Christ's day to day life, unfortunately. But one scene depicts Christ in the temple. There he overturns the tables of the money changers who had infiltrated its halls, casting them out with a rare display of anger. [19] It seems that economics had gained an undesirable preference over morality.

"Love one another" is the main message recalled from the old Catholic grammar school days. And, coupled with that idea, the greatest gift a human can give to another is to sacrifice one's own life for that of another.

But the greatest story ever told also contains a very interesting and important message about how the *other* humans in the story behaved themselves.

The preamble to this chapter from the popular Broadway musical, *Jesus Christ Superstar*, illustrates the basic story. Christ's popular following and the threat to the authority of Rome that it represented reached a critical mass upon his riding into Jerusalem on Palm Sunday. Whether Christ meant it or not, the act was seen as an act of extreme provocation.

For the Jewish people, who were Roman subjects, the physical protection of Rome's economic and military might could be relied upon, only if they adhered to two simple (yet at the same time complicated) rules. Those rules were, first, pay your taxes (hence the phrase "Give to Caesar that which is Caesar's"), and second, don't rebel. The violation of either was sure to bring trouble.

In Christ's case, his ride to Jerusalem on Palm Sunday would surely rouse the masses and thereby constitute a clear violation of Rome's second rule. And so, the Jewish people had to confront a serious problem, sooner rather than later, or face the reality that the Romans would solve the problem for them.

The names Pharisees and Sadducees were the fancy old terms for the lawyers and priests of the day. Together, they constituted a powerful leadership body that claimed greater moral authority and righteousness than the rest of the Jewish society of Christ's time. Setting themselves up as models of what was right and "godly," they were hyper-zealous to preserve and protect the name of God on earth and his laws. While we may detect the obvious strain of self-interest in this arrangement, they did not see themselves as bad people.

Being in a position of authority, these leaders were now faced with a serious dilemma. If Christ could lead a rebellion which would culminate in the overthrow of Roman authority with their assistance, then they could conveniently ride Christ's coattails. Their own authoritative status within the new power structure would at least remain intact, if not likely increase. However, should the rebellion be crushed, then their fate would certainly be the same. The stakes could not have been higher for them. So, they questioned Christ.

"Where is your army?" they wanted to know, out of more than just mere curiosity.

"I have no army" was Christ's succinct reply. "My kingdom is not of this earth. My kingdom is the kingdom of heaven." This response was dubious, failing to inspire confidence in the Pharisees and Sadducees, who could not rest easily.

In the interim, the devil would tempt Christ, offering anything he desired to reject his Father's plan for man's salvation. Rejecting this supreme temptation, in what can only be labeled a sheer test of will, Christ continued: "I will tear down the temple in one day, and re-build it in three." Christ was, of course, referring to his upcoming crucifixion, death and resurrection, to follow during the course of events over the ensuing week. But the Pharisees and Sadducees were yet to know this.

They quickly summed up the earthly situation and concluded that Christ was probably out of his mind. The Pharisees and Sadducees were certainly reasonable men and made a fateful decision. They *said* they must choose the military power of Rome over the popular yet enigmatic and army-less Christ, "for the sake of the nation." Left unsaid was the fact that they were simply acting reasonably in their own best interest—in *self*-interest.

In human terms, the decision was not difficult. They were not going to do something silly like risk their exalted place in Jewish society. They were not going down with the ship. In reality, they were sacrificing Christ to preserve their *own* status. It was convenient. It was expedient. It's what human beings typically do. It's an important lesson in the most useful science of human nature. Pilate would not interfere with an internal decision of the Jewish people.

Christ was also aware that one of his own 12 disciples, Judas, accepted money to betray him. Moreover, when the heat was really turned up, the situation still fluid, Peter, the rock upon which Christ would subsequently build his Christian church, denied knowing him on 3 separate occasions in rapid sequence. After all, Peter had reasonably concluded that Christ's fate would be his as well, had he simply admitted knowing him. Again, here was an example of a reasonable man, acting reasonably in his own best interest. The rest, as they say, is history.

But then there was that remarkable close: "Forgive them, Father, for they know not what they do." Christ did not blame them, as we mere mortals are prone to do. He forgave them instead. For a proven model of leadership, the ordinary citizen doesn't have to look beyond the example

7

of Christ: deny yourself, to advance a just cause, by the example of your actions. In other words, live toward the service of others.

Sounds simple, doesn't it?

***

This analysis of human behavior tends to be perplexing, sobering, yet predictable nonetheless. Might there be other recurring patterns of human behavior, both good and bad, which can be readily identified and typed, as well?

It's an impossible act to follow the incredible story of Jesus Christ, but in terms of famous people in US History, at this point Benjamin Franklin will have to do. If George Washington was the Father of our Country, then it can also be said that Benjamin Franklin was the Grandfather of our Country.

In 1776, at the time of independence from Great Britain, Franklin was 70 years of age, which was on the old side. He was 81-years-old at the time of the 1787 convention gathering in Philadelphia, which was instrumental to the ratification of our present constitution two years later. As such, although he was a founding father (or, grandfather), Benjamin Franklin did not fight in the Revolutionary War, was never elected president, and never served in the US Congress.

Most people are familiar with the story of Ben Franklin only in general terms. We are aware that he came from Philadelphia, had something significant to do with the adoption of the Declaration of Independence and was somehow related to the famous liberty bell. Beyond that, the ordinary citizen cannot point to much more. "Writing has been of Great Use to me in the Course of my Life," Franklin stated with characteristic calculated understatement. He himself credited a lifetime of enormous and varied successes to "my having learnt a little to scribble." [20]

Most people are also surprised to learn that Ben Franklin was not, in fact, *from* Philadelphia. Rather, he was from Philadelphia by way of Boston, where his parents resided and he had been born in 1706 and raised in his early years.

Upon his immigration to America, Franklin's father had begun a business as a Boston candle maker. At age 10, young Ben was apprenticed to the business, but he didn't much like it. At age 12, he was bound to his older brother's printing business, which was to run to his 21st birthday.

8

Franklin found this arrangement to be totally unacceptable, but in those days, that was to be his plight. At age 17, unhappy with what he referred to as his brother's "harsh and tyrannical" treatment, he sought to leave his brother's employ and join with another printer. However, both his brother and father bad mouthed him around town, ending any effective attempt at what we refer to today as upward social mobility.

But Franklin was undeterred, and persevered. He had bigger ideas, albeit ideas which involved great risk. Risky business was better than the alternative though. So he secretly left his family and traveled a distance of some 300 miles by boat to New York, with no knowledge of any person or the place and very little money in his pocket. Finding that no printing work could be found there, Franklin continued 100 miles further to Philadelphia, where he found work with a journeyman printer.

Pennsylvania's governor promised to lend young Ben money to open his own printing shop. The governor further suggested that Franklin go to London to buy printing materials and arrange for supplies on letters of credit also promised by the governor. On the strength of these promises, Franklin set off for London, a sea voyage which would take a full 50 days. He was 18 at the time. Arriving in London, Franklin quickly learned that he had been duped by the governor, who had no credit to give, and summed up the situation thus:

> But what shall we think of a Governor's playing such pitiful Tricks, and imposing so grossly on a poor ignorant Boy! It was a Habit he had acquired. He wish'd to please every body; and having little to give, he gave expectations. [21]

Here was a young man, even at such a tender age, who had an extraordinary awareness of the tendencies of human nature. He would require every morsel of that awareness to survive in a foreign land. But not only did Franklin survive, he flourished. He quickly found work in his field as a printer, knowing that it would improve him such that, upon returning to America, he would be able to set up to greater advantage. Franklin worked in London for two years before returning to America.

His instinct had been correct, and his career subsequently took off. By age 24, Franklin was named the official printer for Pennsylvania. And at age 26 came the first publication of his popular *Poor Richard's Almanac*, which he considered "a proper Vehicle for conveying Instruction among the common People, who bought scarce any other book." [22]

Most interesting among his many varied endeavors in a rich, multi-faceted life was an attempt to arrive at moral perfection. In his reading, he had enumerated and catalogued 13 moral virtues. Arranged in order of importance, the previous acquisition of some perhaps facilitating the acquisition of others, they were as follows:

1. TEMPERANCE.
Eat not to Dullness.

Drink not to Elevation.

2. SILENCE.
Speak not but what may benefit others or yourself.

3. ORDER.
Let all Things have their Places. Let each Part of your Business have its Time.

4. RESOLUTION.
Resolve to perform what you ought. Perform without fail what you resolve.

5. FRUGALITY.
Make no Expense but to do good to others or yourself: i.e., Waste nothing.

6. INDUSTRY.
Lose not time.—Be always employ'd in something useful.—Cut off all unnecessary actions.

7. SINCERITY.
Use no hurtful deceit.

8. JUSTICE.
Wrong none, by doing Injuries or omitting the Benefits that are your Duty.

9. MODERATION.
Avoid Extreams. Forbear resenting Injuries so much as you think they deserve.

10. CLEANLINESS.
Tolerate no Uncleanness in Body, Cloaths or Habitation.

11. TRANQUILITY.
Be not disturbed at Trifles, or at Accidents common or unavoidable.

12. CHASTITY.
Rarely use Venery but for Health or Offspring; Never to Dullness, Weakness, or the Injury of your own or another's Peace or Reputation.

13. HUMILITY.
Imitate Jesus and Socrates. [23]

Franklin's intention was to attempt, systematically, a plan for self-examination, seeking somewhat ambitiously to acquire *all* the virtues at once. But he quickly judged that this would be an impractical distraction. So, he lowered the bar, beginning to focus his attention on just one virtue at a time, in the arranged order. When the first had been mastered,

Franklin would proceed to another, until he had successfully gone through all 13. He allotted 1 week to each venture, and consequently he could complete a full course in 13 weeks, and 4 courses in a year.

He continued the plan for some time, with occasional intermissions, achieving satisfaction in seeing his faults diminish. But he was also alarmed to some degree in learning that he found himself so much fuller of faults than he had imagined. Business, travel and a multiplicity of affairs also interfered, however, stretching a single 13 week course to a full year, or longer. Strength and progress in one virtue would cause a relapse in another, vexing him to consider giving up the attempt altogether.

In the end, Franklin found that his undertaking was akin to a man who brought his ax to the grind stone to be sharpened. As the wheel ground on, the ax had become *speckled*, that is, very sharp and shiny at one turn, yet a bit duller nor as bright at another. No matter how much the wheel ground on, and the ax turned to a point of physical fatigue, the speckled ax still looked the same. He concluded that although he had fallen short, he was better and happier than had he not attempted it, and contented that perhaps a speckled ax was best.

***

The Declaration of Independence is perhaps the one document which best identifies the American spirit among the nation's of the world and is consequently what makes us unique. The 1776 writing has been described as "an expression of the American mind," as painted by its author, Thomas Jefferson.

In pertinent part it states that among the "certain and inalienable rights" which all men possess are "life, liberty and the pursuit of happiness." Interestingly, however, the word "happiness" is without definition. Neither are the words "property," the ownership thereof, or "bank" anywhere mentioned. Nor is a particular economic system contemplated either here or in the US Constitution that was subsequently enacted in 1789. What, then, is the pursuit of happiness?

The answer to that question in the annals of American History begins with the figure of Alexander Hamilton, the nation's first Secretary of the Treasury serving under President George Washington.

Importantly, like Franklin before him, Hamilton was also a superb student of human nature, even going so far as to elevate its status to its own "science." [24] Hamilton approached and studied history to determine the nature of the laws which controlled human affairs, seeking to extract a moral and thereby useful lesson, to chart the course of human events. [25]

Hamilton saw the "pursuit of happiness" in the form of the physical greatness of the state as being above the happiness of its citizens. To the extent that the two were at odds, Hamilton would choose the former, since

> there was no hope of combining order with liberty until the people were prevented from giving free reign to their passions. The people sober might be trusted, but when they became drunk—and history proved that they went on such binges with distressing frequency—they behaved like tyrants. It was the peculiar merit of the Federal (US) Constitution … that under its benign auspices the people, even when they lost possession of their faculties, were constrained from running amuck. [26]

His financial plan, though highly controversial, was set forth on the successful British model of capitalism. It specified, among other things, the creation of a central banking system under one supreme National Bank. This bank was to be in corporation form, chartered under the authority of the new federal government of the US (seen in the form of the Federal Reserve, headed in 2014 by Janet Yellen).

Good thing Hamilton was armed with a keen understanding of certain predictable patterns of human nature which did not change over time. In this instance, knowledge was power. Hamilton well knew that the plan alone, sound as it may have been, was insufficient to guarantee its passage in the republic with the new constitution. Something more was needed, some human incentive.

And so Hamilton used the forces of human nature, in their uninterrupted forms both good and bad as they were observed to exist, to successfully implement and solidify his plan. Noting perhaps the greatest human vice to be greed, he surmised that if this passion could be harnessed in service to the state, "the nation was on its way to power, opulence and greatness." [27] So he incentivized the speculative interest, prevalent on the dark side of human nature and especially among the moneyed class, to provide the support vital to its success.

Yes, Hamilton's plan conceived a new class of speculative wealth and money-making, created out of thin air and to be endorsed by the full faith and credit of the US government. Members of Congress, as well as the bankers and speculators, all more or less positioned on the inside, were the earliest plan subscribers and beneficiaries. By and through its undertaking the new federal government created a system of preference for the so-called moneyed class over the remaining classes of society that were not moneyed.

Nevertheless, understanding that this model had achieved unsurpassed economic dominance on the world stage through the British, Hamilton's financial plan placed the new nation upon a solid economic foundation. Moreover, the plan placed the new nation on a course for more than two centuries worth of unprecedented economic growth and prosperity for the masses of ordinary citizens. Hamilton's efforts earned him his deserving place on the $10 bill.

But almost immediately upon enactment, Hamilton's financial plan was the subject of intense criticism and attack. On the one hand, there could be little doubt that it was a practical plan. The nation needed a stable, secure banking system, without which the established European powers would supply neither loans nor credit. It was also expedient. Its proponents pointed for validation to a proven model.

But on the other hand, it was self-serving, Hamilton being a resident of New York with a multitude of personal and professional connections in the financial arena. It unfairly and disproportionately rewarded Northern bankers at the expense of Southern farmers, thereby heightening sectional differences. It created a preference for two distinct economic classes: the haves – and have nots.

It may come as no surprise then, that Jefferson himself was the primary objector to what he viewed as Hamilton's perversion of the idyllic pursuit of happiness. But his objection had little to do either with numbers, economics or speculation.

Although a fuller reflection on Jefferson's own particular views must await subsequent discussion, suffice here to consider the following. The author of the document which set forth that "all men are created equal" viewed with consternation a plan which would not treat all men equally under the law. Such a plan violated the unfettered freedom of the individual citizen to pursue happiness.

In a later period, Andrew Jackson would declare war on and victory over Hamilton's federal banking system. In the throes of battle, Jackson astutely observe that "If the people only understood the rank injustice of our money and banking system there would be a revolution before morning." [28]

***

While capitalism may have achieved a monopolistic grip over Western Civilization, scarcely can it be said that Western Civilization maintains such sway over the pursuit of happiness. Or the ways of human nature. It should come as little surprise then, that criticism of Hamilton's financial plan, ominous and foreboding as it was, could well have been predicted.

The ordinary citizen may recognize the same moral in a parallel story from the realm of *Eastern* Civilization. More specifically, ancient Taoist thought also addresses the workings of human nature, dwelling in its unity. Therein lay the same timeless, uncontroverted truths, offering merely a hint of the opposition attacks Hamilton's plan would later face.

Cracking the Safe

For security against robbers who snatch purses, rifle luggage, and crack safes,
One must fasten all property with ropes, lock it up with locks, bolt it with bolts.
This (for property owners) is elementary good sense.
But when a strong thief comes along he picks up the whole lot,
Puts it on his back, and goes on his way with only one fear:
That ropes, locks and bolts may give way.
Thus what the world calls good business is only a way
To gather up the loot, pack it, make it secure
In one convenient load for the more enterprising thieves.
Who is there, among those called smart,
Who does not spend his time amassing loot
For a bigger robber than himself? [29]

Taoist thought is also consistent with its Western counterpart in acknowledging the unfortunate fact of life that the world values money, reputation, long life. Similarly, what the world counts as joy are health and bodily comforts, good food, beautiful things to look at. Misfortune involves the opposite: lack of money, bodily discomfort, labor, no chance to get your fill of the finer things.

14

This concern for happiness creates anxiety and makes life unbearable.

The rich make life intolerable, driving themselves in order to get more and more money which they cannot really use. In so doing they are alienated from themselves, and exhaust themselves in their own service as though they were the slaves of others.

The ambitious run day and night in pursuit of honor, constantly in anguish about the success of their plans, dreading the miscalculation that may wreck everything. Thus, they are alienated from themselves, exhausting their real life in service of the shadow created by their insatiable hope.

Taoist thought teaches us that happiness is illusory, inasmuch as we as mere mortals are destined to die some day. And so, we tend to expend all of our energies worrying, obsessed about it, trying to do what we can to delay this particular eventuality. We don't live in the present, where life is to be lived. Instead, we squander the present, living in a precarious state of worry regarding a future, over which we have little control.

By contrast to the rich or ambitious man, or his counterpart the poor man,

Take the case of the minister who conscientiously and uprightly opposes an unjust decision of his king! Some say, 'Tell the truth, and if the King will not listen, let him do what he likes. You have no further obligation.'

On the other hand, Tzu Shu continued to resist the unjust policy of his sovereign. He was consequently destroyed. But if he had not stood up for what he believed to be right, his name would not be held in honor.

So there is the question, Shall the course he took be called "good" if, at the same time, it was fatal to him?

I cannot tell if what the world considers 'happiness' is happiness or not. All I know is that when I consider the way they go about attaining it, I see them carried away headlong, grim and obsessed, in the general onrush of the human herd, unable to stop themselves or to change their direction. All the while they claim to be just on the point of attaining happiness. [30]

In the end, as with most things, it is supposed that the beauty of the pursuit of happiness lies in the eyes of the beholder.

Perhaps the closest expression of the pursuit of happiness comes in the form of an inspirational poem, related by Bill Maione, a wise and dear friend. Titled *Desiderata*, its prose offers a simple positive credo for our ordinary yet hectic lives.

The common myth is that the poem was found in a Baltimore church in 1692 and is centuries old, and of unknown origin. It is said that Desiderata was in fact written around 1920 (although some say as early as 1906), and certainly copyrighted in 1927, by lawyer Max Ehrmann (1872-1945) based in Terre Haute, Indiana.

It is reproduced here below in its entirety, with gratitude to its long deceased author:

Desiderata

Go placidly amid the noise and haste,
and remember what peace there may be in silence.

As far as possible, without surrender, be on good terms with all persons.
Speak your truth quietly and clearly; and listen to others,
even to the dull and the ignorant; they too have their story.
Avoid loud and aggressive persons; they are vexations to the spirit.

If you compare yourself with others, you may become vain and bitter,
for always there will be greater and lesser persons than yourself.
Enjoy your achievements as well as your plans.
Keep interested in your own career, however humble;
it is a real possession in the changing fortunes of time.

Exercise caution in your business affairs, for the world is full of trickery.
But let this not blind you to what virtue there is;
many persons strive for high ideals, and everywhere life is full of
heroism.
Be yourself. Especially, do not feign affection.
Neither be cynical about love, for in the face of all aridity and
disenchantment,
it is as perennial as the grass.

Take kindly to the counsel of the years, gracefully surrendering the
things of youth.
Nurture strength of spirit to shield you in sudden misfortune.
But do not distress yourself with imaginings.
Many fears are born of fatigue and loneliness.

Beyond a wholesome discipline, be gentle with yourself.
You are a child of the universe
no less than the trees and the stars;
you have a right to be here.
And whether or not it is clear to you,
no doubt the universe is unfolding as it should.

Therefore be at peace with God, whatever you conceive Him to be.
And whatever your labors and aspirations,
in the noisy confusion of life,
keep peace in your soul.

With all its sham, drudgery and broken dreams,
it is still a beautiful world.
Be cheerful. Strive to be happy.

***

It is compelling to begin each semester's new US History I (colonial period) class with the first (of what are only four) important lesson of US History. This lesson is not found in any textbook on US History. It comes to us by way of the classic 1966 movie, *The Good, The Bad and The Ugly*. The movie stars Clint Eastwood, among others, in one of his early, featured roles.

The setting is the state of Texas during the Civil War 1860s. Texas, as some may recall, was a slave state at the time in the fledgling Confederate States of America. For the better part of the movie, Clint Eastwood (the "Good") and Tuco, his Mexican counterpart (the "Ugly," played by Eli Wallach), engage in a systematic series of Western, small town robberies.

The script did not deviate from the following. Tuco would get himself arrested for the commission of a serious capital offense, which called for his hanging in the public square. Customarily, the town residents would come out to witness the hanging. While the noose was being prepared, and the prisoner brought forth, Eastwood would rob all of the vacant homes. But then, just before the noose would tighten, Eastwood would appear on horseback. With his excellent aim, he would shoot through the rope from a distance, freeing Tuco. Simultaneously, Eastwood would ride through the square, displaying perfect timing to snatch him up and ride off. The two would repeat the sequence in the next town.

Although very different and caring little for the welfare of the other, each is compelled to keep the other alive, because each has half a secret. Together, they know that a large stash of money, containing exactly 8 bags of gold, is buried in a cemetery. Eastwood knows the name of the grave under which the stash is buried, and Tuco knows the name of the cemetery. But neither knows the other's secret. Lacking a corresponding bond of trust, each guards his half of the secret with his life. A third player, a corrupt Union Army officer (the "Bad," played by Lee Van Cleef), sheds his military uniform for civilian clothes and secretly follows the two for what he hopes will be his own private payoff.

Toward the movie's climax, Tuco finally gives up his share of the secret, reluctantly disclosing the name of the cemetery. The three then come together at the cemetery circle, near the grave site where the gold is buried. But since Eastwood will not voluntarily divulge the name on the grave, they engage in a final stand off.

After some tense moments that seem like hours, Eastwood draws first, killing Van Cleef (the "Bad"). Eastwood then admits to Tuco that he had secretly removed the bullets from Tuco's gun the previous night, which had rendered harmless Tuco's stand off threat.

Viewers are left with the "Good" and the "Ugly." With a loaded gun, the entire loot at his disposal and Tuco absent any weapon and defenseless, Eastwood now faces a moral dilemma. Does he take all the gold, and run? In the process, what does he do with Tuco? Kill him? Wound him? If he allows Tuco to live, does he leave Tuco his full share? Or does he leave just a portion, in Eastwood's sole but arbitrary discretion?

The dilemma is interesting, not appreciably different from the one which the early Old World European settler to the continent of North America faced toward his brethren, the American Indian.

In the end, Eastwood rides off into the sunset, with his own 4 bags of gold, exactly half the loot, securely mounted to his saddle bags. He leaves Tuco stranded and thirsty in the sweltering Texas sun, without a horse, and with a difficult situation in which to make his way back to civilization. But importantly, Eastwood leaves Tuco with his entire share, fully 4 gold bags. For when one thinks about it, how much of the gold do any of us really need?

The New World was a land of plenty, so called, but its historical relationship with the native American Indian culture was marked by contact, conquest and catastrophe; the three "C's." Simple contact was the predominant destructive force. The Old World germs to which the settler had become immune effectively wiped out 90% of the indigenous Indian population, whose systems were not similarly protected. Second was the idea of forced "removal" of the Indians from their lands. And, of course, there were mass killings. But this was the side show.

We all learned the first lesson of US History by the time of kindergarten. There is more than enough to go around. The lesson, of course, is to share.

Chapter 2
Flying Under the Radar

Nobody loves you when you're down and out
Nobody sees you when you're on cloud nine
Everybody's hustlin' for a buck and a dime
I'll scratch your back and you scratch mine

I've been across to the other side
I've shown you everything, I got nothing to hide
And still you ask me do I love you, what it is, what it is
All I can tell you is it's all show biz
All I can tell you is it's all show biz

Nobody loves you when you're down and out
Nobody knows you when you're on cloud nine
Everybody's hustlin' for a buck and a dime
I'll scratch your back and you knife mine

- from the song, *Nobody Loves You (When You're Down and Out)*,
by John Lennon (1974)
available on the *Walls and Bridges* collection

***

Standing in a familiar position, belly up to the bar, a young lawyer attempts to let off some steam after work, enjoying a couple of beers during happy hour. Wearing blue jeans, a t-shirt and sneakers, though he had come with a friend, the lawyer was anonymous, relaxed and very comfortable in his clothes and in his own skin.

Invariably, he got to talking with the fellow next to him. The substance of the conversation was unimportant, for it was essentially two guys engaged in enjoyable small talk. Enjoyable, that is, until the fellow asked the lawyer what he did for a living. Then, the tone of the conversation changed.

Typically, the lawyer avoided occupational "shop" talk during such times, which included discussion of means of livelihood. Through experience, he had found that it both diminished the interactive encounter and was also distracting. Nor was it fun, with the negative perception of lawyers being what it was, when one was simply trying to relax.

The lawyer tried to deflect the question on several successive occasions, trying to change the conversation as subtly as possible. But that fellow was undeterred.

"Come on! What's the big deal? What do you do for a living?" the fellow persisted.

Temporarily, the young lawyer weakened, and in a flash it was out: "Okay, I'm a lawyer," he responded. And there it was.

The fellow seemed somehow surprised, and there was a brief pause. As if he hadn't heard the first time, the fellow persisted: "This conversation's great. I've never met *anybody* who dressed like you, or talked like you, who was a lawyer." He pressed on: "So, *really*, what do you do for a living?"

Much to the lawyer's chagrin, this went on for awhile. Despite repeated assurances, the fellow could not believe his bar mate was a lawyer. "Let me see one of your business cards." There! He figured he had the lawyer trapped. If a card couldn't be produced, the fellow would know for sure the lawyer was pulling his leg.

The lawyer begged for a conclusion to this folly: "Fair enough. If I show you my card, will you leave it alone and we move on to another topic?"

"Okay," said the fellow, with the hint of a sinister smile creasing his face, which made the lawyer feel more than slightly uncomfortable.

But the lawyer was also relieved. So he relaxed again, sighed, took a deep breath and reached into his pocket for the evidence that would shut this guy up. Suddenly, though, the lawyer's eyes widened, as he scrambled through his pockets, which were empty. Typically, he did not carry business cards in his jeans. After all, he was relaxing, not working. What did he need business cards for? The lawyer's spirits sunk, however, as he was forced to admit, meekly to this strange man, that he had failed to bring any cards along. He threw up his hands for some compassion and leniency.

"Sure, you're a lawyer," the fellow mocked. "Actually, it's just as I suspected. You're not a lawyer. You're just another lying a-hole." With that, he turned abruptly and moved to another spot at the bar. His trust for the lawyer was obviously breached, irreparably. The conversation was concluded.

Part of that was the lawyer's own fault. In his subsequent days, when he combined law practice with teaching, he would find it absolutely amazing that people would treat him in a completely different manner, depending on whether he told them he was a lawyer—or a school teacher. If it was the former, like the gentleman from the story above, typically they couldn't get far enough away from him (if they believed his story, that is). But if it was the latter, then the lawyer couldn't get them to shut up. The more he threw out some conversational facts, typically about pertinent events in US History, the more they talked. In both settings, the lawyer was the same person, but the results were drastically different.

To be sure, one cannot fly under the radar if one cannot communicate effectively. And one cannot communicate effectively if there is insufficient understanding of the nature of the listener. Put another way, one must take the necessary steps to "know your audience." Conversely, it is equally important to understand where the speaker is coming from, as well as what is to be gained or lost, if anything, by the message being conveyed.

The board game of Trivial Pursuit provides an effective illustration of the above point. It was a hot game when it first came out. But as experience showed, the questions were too hard for some, and too easy for others. For still others, some of the categories were either irrelevant or impossible. Kids would be required in certain instances to answer questions better framed for adults, and vice versa, all at the luck of the draw of a card. Consequently, the game lost its mystique, and its popularity. It failed to know its audience.

***

Some people hear it time and again. Friends routinely lament their very existence (or so it seems) in a rant that goes something like this: "What is it with you? You live right in amongst us. You're accessible most of the time. You show up at enough social events to conclude that you're still alive and in the loop. Yet no one truly *knows* what you're doing." For mass effect, a colleague leaves the following voice message: "You have a new nickname: 'The Phantom,' who is mysterious, who comes and goes."

"That's because I fly under the radar," comes the typical response. But what does it mean? These people are individuals known to set their own itinerary. Acting upon their own instincts and accountable for their actions to themselves only, they typically do not worry about what the crowd is doing or choose to fly in formation with the other birds.

Why is it important to fly under the radar? In a commercial setting, radar is a device typically used to locate and map the direction of airplanes, travelling in different directions or flight paths and at different speeds and altitudes. This facilitates safe, efficient civilian air travel.

But consider the concept of radar in its more ominous, military application. The radar operator uses the device to locate and lock on a target, typically an enemy plane, to deliver information to a weapons system designed to bring the plane down. These days, the weapons system is guided by radar actually affixed to the weapon. During the Persian Gulf War in the early 1990s, military briefers reveled in public briefings to display the devastatingly accurate effect of radar guided bombs on their intended military targets.

So if one flies under the radar, as the expression goes, one may go about the business of daily, ordinary life with fewer distractions and minimal detection. This enables sharper focus with corresponding productivity gains and a higher quality of individualized life. It also neatly avoids the swing of the hammer to set the protruding nail on the carpenter's punch list.

Another way to minimize the glare of the spotlight in one's life is to keep it simple, or, if it is overly complicated, to learn to simplify. US History is replete with examples of exceptional men who had begun their lives as merely ordinary men, flying under the radar and keeping it simple. But due to a sudden change of circumstances beyond their control, these men would become forever immortalized by historians, academics and ordinary citizens.

A primary example is Robert E. Lee, the great Civil War military general, and certainly one of the most admired and revered heroes of Southern lore. Robert E. Lee was a Virginia native, a top student at West Point, a born leader by all accounts—tall, handsome, spirited, yet reserved in many ways, and honorable to a fault.

In a letter to his son in 1860, a copy of which Mattie Truman also gave to her son, Harry, on his 10th birthday in 1894, Lee counseled:

> You must be frank with the world; frankness is the child of honesty and courage. Say just what you mean to do on every occasion, and take it for granted you mean to do right. ... Never do anything wrong to make a friend or keep one; the man who requires you to do so, is dearly purchased at a sacrifice. Deal kindly, but firmly with all your classmates; you will find it the policy that wears best. Above all do not appear to others what you are not. [31]

Few will recall, however, what was predicted to be the greatest mistake of Lee's life, as foretold by his then commanding officer. At the outset of the Civil War, Gen. Lee would decline the offer of the most powerful military position in the nation, that being, the head of all Union armies. Instead, Gen. Lee would resign from the Union army and then join the Confederate forces, all in loyal deference to his family and the secession vote of his cherished Virginia homeland. [32]

Few others will recall that the lasting message of Gen. Lee was *not* his legendary generalship against great numbers in numerous acts of courage on the battlefield. Rather, the enduring message of Robert E. Lee was the way in which he handled defeat. Perhaps you could say that Gen. Lee's message has flown under the radar.

The issues which had brought on military hostilities could not be solved politically. Consequently, they were submitted to the battlefield, and then resolved on the side of the Union. Gen. Lee was aware of the script that had to follow. On that fateful day in April 1865, he agreed to a meeting with Gen. U.S. Grant at Appomattox to negotiate the terms of surrender, like the gentlemen that he was. Lee accepted his fate and the fate of his fiercely loyal troops, put down his sword and returned to peaceful civilian life.

But what would Lee do, now as a *former* general? After declining several more lucrative financial opportunities, he finally settled on what he felt was an appropriate position which would permit him to set a low key example in a new civilian role. He agreed to accept the presidency of Washington College, a small Southern school located in rural Virginia (better known today as Washington and Lee University). Lee understood the implications of his enormous influence as a role model to his devoted people that they likewise must bury the ax and carry on peacefully. [33]

Perhaps it is best to appreciate that Lee's greatest reverence was reserved for the common foot soldier, the infantryman (or GI, standing for government infantry, as these soldiers are called today). According to Lee, these soldiers did what they were ordered to do without complaint, without question, and without regard for what might be in it for them. Lee's men would perform any act; endure virtually any hardship, of which there were many, if Lee would only say the word. Fight hard and spirited, endure incredible deprivation, and usually prevail in battle against the overwhelming material and numerical superiority of the North. This would be proven time and again. His common foot soldiers were totally selfless, according to Lee, who took care of his men. Not flashy, perhaps, nor even newsworthy, they flew under the radar. But Lee loved his men, and they loved him. So they performed for him. [34]

U.S. Grant presents another interesting, yet entirely different, flying under the radar story. The eventual head of all Union armies during the Civil War, Grant's name is linked for eternity in military terms with his adversary, Lee. For one thing, Grant *looked* more like a common foot soldier, rather than the man who at the Civil War's end had grown to become the most trusted Northern man in the Southern Confederacy. But Grant did not receive the title until a series of Northern generals had failed miserably before him.

U.S. Grant's background had also included graduation from West Point, but unlike Lee, he was no better than an average student in the classroom. He was an uncomplicated man from humble beginnings in small town Ohio, with a pleasant and straight forward disposition and a plain writing style to match. His most noteworthy talent during his school days was a legendary proficiency in the handling of horses. Even the most rambunctious, wild and stubbornly resistant to authority were brought to him and in short order these horses were broken and became obedient. Grant consistently demonstrated the uncanny ability to become seamless with the four legged equine. This would serve him well in his ensuing military career.

U.S. Grant's journey to greatness, however, was neither direct nor without controversy. After graduation from West Point, he was stationed in the West Coast territory above the new state of California, lonely and separated from his wife and family. Bored and despairing, he began to drink more than what was good for him, and it began to affect his performance.

Having reached the degree of Captain, things began to unravel. His commanding officer, a consummate military man, had found him inebriated during a visit to the remote outpost and gave Grant a choice. Grant could either resign the military without further inquiry into his conduct or face a damaging military court martial trial, during which all of the dirty laundry would be aired in public. Grant abruptly chose to resign without giving reason, but the involvement of alcohol was confirmed. Years later, Grant stated that "the vice of intemperance had not a little to do with my decision to resign." [35]

Returning home to Illinois, a subsequent attempt at farming failed. When the Civil War broke out in 1861, Grant was broke and destitute, found peddling firewood on a street corner in St. Louis. However, a premium was placed on men who had officer's training and experience, which fortunately Grant had, thus enabling him to re-enlist and entertain a command. [36]

In 1863 President Lincoln summoned Gen. Grant to Washington, D.C. to attend the official ceremony commemorating Grant's appointment to the rank of lieutenant-general in the Army of the United States. The ceremony truly was an historic occasion, since it marked the first such appointment since Gen. George Washington's ascension to the same rank generations before.

Grant traveled to the nation's capital with typical understatement, in the company of his 13-year-old son. A welcoming committee to meet the train and escort him to his hotel failed to materialize. He was inconspicuous and unrecognized, most of his uniform hidden by mud and travel stains. When the pair entered the hotel, the desk clerk, bored and accustomed to dealing with the capital city's most distinguished guests, saw no one in particular. The clerk suggested there might be a small room, if agreeable. Grant politely accepted and signed the register.

However, when the clerk twirled the book around and saw the name, "U.S. Grant and son, Galena, Illinois," suddenly everything clicked. Recognizing the magnitude of his error, the stunned clerk was transformed into a model of hospitality. The previously offered small room was forgotten, and instead the clerk suggested the best suite in the hotel, where President Lincoln had stayed the week before his inauguration. Grant accepted the change without comment, not wanting to call attention to himself.

As he saw it, any room would do. His ordinary, pedestrian disposition provided the perfect cover from which to fly under the radar. [37]

To be sure,

> Not a sign about him suggested rank or reputation or power. He discussed the most ordinary themes with apparent interest, and turned from them in the same quiet tones, and without a shade of difference in his manner, to decisions that involved the fate of armies, as if great things and small were to him of equal moment. In battle, the sphinx awoke. The outward calm was even then not entirely broken; but the utterance was prompt, the ideas were rapid, the judgment was decisive, the words were those of command. The whole man became intense, as it were, with a white heat. [38]

One of the enduring legacies of U.S. Grant, his rightful place as the face on the $50 bill aside, is the trust and respect, if not the love, which the South had developed for him. These accolades were earned largely on account of his having given Gen. Lee "honorable terms" of surrender at Appomattox. They were also largely responsible for his accession to his place as the nation's 18th president during the turbulent Reconstruction era following the Civil War.

More than any other single factor, perhaps, the presidential administration of U.S. Grant set a more constructive, flying under the radar tone for Reconstruction, which could have been much bloodier than it already figured to be.

***

Despite the obvious advantages of flying under the radar, however, its primary criticism is highlighted by the old adage that "talk is cheap." Anyone can talk, but *doing* is the hard part. In truth, there is something most favorable to infer from the image of the gladiator in the ring, as opposed to the spectator on the sidelines. As Theodore Roosevelt reminds us:

> It is not the critic who counts, nor the man who points out how the strong man stumbled or where the doer of deeds could have done them better. The credit belongs to the man who is actually in the arena, whose face is marred by dust and sweat and blood, who strives valiantly, who errs and comes short again and again, who knows the great enthusiasms, the great devotions, and spends himself in a worthy cause, who at the best knows the triumph of high achievement, and who at the worst, if he fails, at least fails while daring greatly, so that his place shall never be with those cold and timid souls who know neither victory nor defeat. [39]

T.R.'s famous *Man in the Arena* quote was meant as an attack on skeptics "of lettered leisure" who, cloistered together in academia, "sneered" at anyone who tried to make the real world better. [40]

And then there is the following directive from Christ, which appears in the Holy Gospel of Matthew:

> Neither do men light a candle, and put it under a bushel, but on a candlestick; and it giveth light unto all that are in the house.
>
> Let your light so shine before men, that they may see your good works ... [41]

It's both easy and convenient to sit back and criticize, rather than take action. This is because human nature is such that ordinary people are naturally averse to change. Change involves the unknown, which generates the fear response in human nature. Certain individuals have figured out that wth the knowledge that the unknown is feared, the ordinary citizen can be controlled en masse simply through use of scare tactics.

This phenomenon helps to explain, in part, both the power and depth of Franklin D. Roosevelt's famous words, during the very depths of the Great Depression of the early 1930s:

> So, first of all, let me assert my firm belief that *the only thing we have to fear is fear itself*–nameless, unreasoning, unjustified terror which paralyzes needed efforts to convert retreat into advance. [42]

F.D.R. was speaking of the effects of the Great Depression on the morale of ordinary Americans. He was saying, essentially, that if the mass of ordinary citizens could not shake out of their pessimistic economic outlook, then it would be difficult, if not impossible, to turn things around. In the election that brought F.D.R. to the presidency, his adversary had campaigned on a platform which called for no change from the status quo. This despite economic conditions that had brought record and, in fact, staggering national unemployment numbers, bread lines, and the virtual elimination of the classic dividing lines between rich and poor. For as a result of the Great Depression, virtually everyone's wealth had been wiped out.

More recently, former President George W. Bush 43 [43] seemed to deftly transform the tragic events of September 11, 2001 ("9/11") into a successful politics of fear campaign. Many have said that his successful exploitation of this particular vice of human nature assured his re-election to a second term. National security was said to be at risk. Whether it was or was not involves another discussion.

But consequently, many of the personal freedoms to which ordinary citizens had become accustomed, including the right to free speech, were curtailed under the provisions of the Patriot Act. [44] While there are other examples of this in US History, President Bush reduced the tactic to an art form, deploying familiar "Listen to me, or we're all doomed" politics of fear rhetoric.

Here is seemingly yet another useful lesson in the science of human nature. Staying the course, and *avoiding* change, even at seemingly exorbitant cost, is the easier and preferred method. Human beings are imitative creatures of habit, by nature, comfortable with the routine they know. Life outside the box (of accepted knowledge or practice), so to speak, is unsettling, even troubling. Content with the world they know, most ordinary citizens rarely challenge themselves even with minimal risk, perceived to be inordinate and thus unacceptable.

We've all heard the familiar expression that "the devil is in the details." Implementing change involves many details that involve experiment and thus can be worked out neither in advance nor easily. Absent some precedent that provides a known comfort level that ordinary citizens can latch on to, the devil we know is typically preferable to the devil we don't. This helps to explain why many ordinary citizens will decline the prospect of a new job. Even though the potential reward may be greater, the details are unclear, and the risk of the unknown is consequently too great and therefore unacceptable.

But framed in a more constructive light, if you want something you've never had before, you have to do something you've never done before.

***

Oddly enough, the college student of US History who would be tomorrow's K-12 public school teacher is not required to take a class in philosophy. This is unfortunate, since an influential lesson derives from this standard liberal arts offering. Owing to its important foundation upon which an understanding of human nature as a "most useful science" is based, the underlying story has become a core lesson of the first "half" of US History. No ordinary citizen should leave home without it.

The story is familiarly known as Plato's *Allegory of the Cave* (an allegory being a fancy term for a short moral story). Given the title, the setting takes place within the confines of a cave, within which there are prisoners. The prisoners are chained and bound to the ground so

28

that they are unable to turn their heads to see what is going on behind them. Behind the prisoners a candle is set, and behind the candle some puppeteers. The motions of the puppeteers before the candle cast a series of shadows on the walls in front of the prisoners. The prisoners can see only the shadows, which are likened to the "reality" they are perceiving.

Subsequently, one of the prisoners is able to free himself from the bonds and is thus able, if not forced, to look upon and understand the spectacle that once dictated his *perception* of reality. The prisoner is able to realize that these new images in front of him are now the *new* accepted forms of reality. When these visions of the "real truth" are told to the other prisoners, they are accepted painfully in such a way as to be "aching" to their eyes. Naturally, they would be inclined to return to the comfort of what they have always seen as a pleasant and painless acceptance of truth. Their beliefs have been challenged. The prisoner is further emboldened to face the fear of the unrecognized outside world. He is compelled to climb the steep ascent of the cave and step outside into the bright sun.

Once outside the cave, and fully immersed in the sun's rays, the prisoner's natural reaction is bewilderment, fear, and blindness to the objects he is now being told is real. But in time, his eyes adjust to the sun, and he recognizes and now understands it as the cause of all that is around him, as a source of good. Should he go back to his prior life in the cave? It is quickly agreed that the prisoner would rather suffer any fate than returning to his previous life and primitive understanding. But what of the other prisoners?

Upon returning to the cave, the released prisoner is ridiculed by the other prisoners for taking the useless climb out of the cave in the first place. The others cannot understand something they have yet to experience, so it's up to this prisoner to discharge a duty to share his knowledge with the others, while not being contemptuous of those who do not choose to share his enlightenment. The progress of human development represents our own path to complete awareness as guided by virtue and enlightenment.

It is not over then. The released prisoner who had achieved the state of enlightenment and undertook the commitment to distribute it to others, in advocacy of change to a new, improved way of doing things, or condition of existence, or simply a better order, is heavily scrutinized. This is simply because he is first.

Plato, the Greek philosopher, also provides us with a critical reminder of the importance of the one who would come first:

> You know that the beginning is the most important part of any work, especially in the case of a young and tender thing; for that is the time at which the character is being formed and the desired impression is more readily taken. ... Shall we just carelessly allow children to hear any casual tales which may be devised by casual persons, and to receive into their minds ideas for the most part the very opposite of those which we should wish them to have when they are grown up?
>
> We cannot. Anything received into the mind at that age is likely to become indelible and unalterable; and therefore it is most important that the tales which the young first hear should be models of virtuous thoughts ...
>
> Then will our youth dwell in a land of health, amid fair sights and sounds, and receive the good in everything; and beauty, the effluence of fair works, shall flow into the eye and ear, like a health giving breeze from a purer region, and insensibly draw the soul from the earliest years into likeness and sympathy with the beauty of reason.
>
> There can be no nobler training than that. [45]

Consider our great leader and founding father, George Washington. In US History, Washington played the critical character role and undertook the painful burden of being the first. Anyone who has the distinction of being the oldest child in the family is well aware of this unenviable rite of passage.

***

Flying under the radar also has its place within the great tradition of the New York Yankees of major league baseball. The financial juggernaut that its franchise and success represent to some, evil empire to others, the Yankee franchise has at its core four homegrown players: Derek Jeter, the captain and team's iconic franchise figure; Mariano Rivera, the smooth, effortless, ice-in-his-veins closer; Jorge Posada, the catcher; and his battery mate, Andy Pettitte, the starting pitcher.

The identity of the franchise is forged by these four players, who came up together in the mid 1990s. In the present economic environment, it is an indisputable fact that no other team in major league baseball, even those with considerable means, has held on to its core of players as have the Yankees.

But the collective identity of the Yankees, while powerful, is somewhat different than what one might presume, given the perceived glamour of New York City and the glitz of the lights on Broadway. The adjectives sometimes used for these four players are professional, undemonstrative, dignified, and arguably a bit colorless. [46] Even in the glare of that exceedingly difficult spotlight, might it be that these players are also flying under the radar?

Each is also extremely humble. Take Derek Jeter, for example. A friend relates a great story about Derek Jeter. She had been on vacation, working out at the fitness center, which was generally available to the patrons of the resort where she was a guest. Standing by one of the weight machines, tired, sweaty, smelly, and admittedly not particularly motivated, she suddenly spotted Derek Jeter, working out anonymously at a nearby station. There were no reporters or crowds or anyone for that matter within sight.

Immediately, she brightened. But faced with the prospect of actually *meeting* Derek Jeter, she became nervous. Her heart began to race, and then thump. Finally, she mustered the nerve to go over to him and strike up a conversation, which she prayed would not be awkward. After exchanging greetings, she asked if she could take his picture.

"Sure," Jeter replied.

She wished she had a real camera, but her cell phone camera would now have to do. As she pointed the camera toward Jeter, he suddenly put up his hand, and in the process imposed a simple condition. The condition instantly demonstrated the requisite selflessness which makes him such a great leader of men: "You can take my picture, but *only* if you're in it, too!"

Flustered, she attempted to press him, but Derek Jeter would have none of it. She was sweaty, essentially mortified, but this was Derek Jeter, and this was a once in a lifetime opportunity. She relented. Fortunately, she found another volunteer patron, who was happy to oblige. She handed over the cell phone camera, and took up a position next to Jeter. Standing side by side, she was not even as tall as his shoulder. Jeter put his arm around her shoulder, and he smiled. Over the ensuing days, the picture was texted to just about everyone she knew, her beaming smile standing out noticeably against her slight posture and sweaty t-shirt.

Baseball umpires, if they're good, also have an understanding that they are supposed to be selfless and fly under the radar. Those who go to the trouble of obtaining formal certification to umpire high school varsity baseball and softball understand that there are few greater experiences than the view from behind home plate.

It is the best seat in the house. And the seat is *free*! There is hardly a better feeling than shouting the words "play ball" at exactly 4:00 pm on a high school field, while pointing to the pitcher and inviting play to begin.

The object is simply to record outs, as quickly and reasonably as possible, and then get out of there. Make the calls firmly yet fairly, don't vacillate and move the game along at a brisk pace. In other words, don't vacillate like a squirrel perched in the road, when a car happens to be coming. The game is supposed to be about the players and the plays—not the umpires. Let the players play, and fly under the radar.

Occasionally, a pitch which is a good foot off the plate—and called a "ball," draws ire and the invariable heckling that goes with it. Typically, the defensive team's manager, coaches or even a random fan down the foul line yells: "Come on, ump. What are you—blind? That pitch was a strike!" In that instance, a good umpire says nothing and doesn't dare engage or react even slightly. The umpire thinks to himself that critics would be of a different opinion, had they just been better *informed*—had they just had a superior view of things.

Serving as an umpire, referee or other official is a lonely vocation. Upon making a particular call, the umpire plainly observes half the spectators howling their upset almost instantaneously at a perceived blown call. Meanwhile, the other half is notoriously silent, evidencing the fact that the umpire simply made the call he was supposed to make.

The analogy is obviously not limited to the baseball diamond. The other major sports of football, basketball and hockey are just the same. Judges inside a courtroom also fit the criteria nicely. It is true that occasionally the hand of an authority figure is needed for such legitimate purposes as maintaining control, regulating the flow, and providing the sometimes necessary penalty for detrimental conduct. But the best compliment that can be paid to each—is that they let the players play, such that in simple terms the spectator didn't even know they were there. After the game, while filing out of the stadium, when the fans talk about what a great *game* it was, and not the *officiating*, they surely provide validity to this point.

***

Consider the objective of keeping the game and its players functioning smoothly and separate from the officiating—all while flying under the radar—in the context of our democratic system. In 1787 the founding fathers were faced with quite a predicament. A low key, unassuming approach would appear to have been rather impossible then, given the scope and magnitude of the crisis which was upon the young nation and their proposed remedial social science project. Today, however, this seems lost on the ordinary citizen. But it is worth remembering.

The young, fledgling democracy was in danger of failing, just 11 years into the experiment. Under our then and first constitution, known as the Articles of Confederation, each state (there were 13 at the time) retained its own individual sovereignty and the corresponding power to veto *any* law with which it happened to disagree. Given the diversity of regional and economic interests, this meant that no truly uniform or effective law could reasonably be enacted. An effective army could not well be raised for national defense, nor taxes either levied or collected to pay for it. Nor could the commerce of the national economy be effectively regulated.

Unfortunately, the setting did not make provision for a team bus. Rather, there were to be essentially 13 separate cab rides to the ballpark, and social chaos was the potential imminent consequence. The experiment in democracy was in acute danger of failure, the patient on life support. Accordingly, there was an urgent sense to maintain a state of order and control, or as it has been couched in political terms, to preserve internal political stability.

But what if there were *too much* order and control? The corresponding fear in that instance was that the mass of ordinary citizens would be left with a one man wrecking ball, serfs to what we otherwise know as a dictator. The people of France were to learn this lesson painfully, when their popular revolution, corresponding in time more or less with our own American Revolution, degenerated into mob rule and then eventually the dictatorship of Napoleon. The French Revolution would later conclude with the anomalous result of the near ruin of Europe in continental military conquest and its people subjected to a military tyrant.

Either extreme presented the founding fathers with vexatious concern for the survival and continuation of the great American experiment in democracy. The situation was analogous to harnessing the desirable properties of light. On the one hand, the founding fathers viewed the shortcomings of the Articles of Confederation as the futile attempt to illuminate the path with a flashlight which contains failing batteries.

This light simply had neither power nor strength sufficient to provide even minimal let alone adequate illumination.

On the other hand resided the "It was the best of times, it was the worst of times" comparison with the ongoing French Revolution, as described in Charles Dickens' novel, *The Tale of Two Cities*. In that situation, the light of democracy had become so supremely concentrated in strength as to represent the immense power of a pure, unfiltered laser beam. That is to say, if anyone were to fix a gaze directly into the beam or somehow end up in its path, the result would conceive a wrecking ball of disaster.

From this dilemma, it was clear that a delicate yet efficient balancing act was necessary. What was needed was something in between the two undesirable extremes. The flashlight had to be strengthened, its batteries replaced with new, more powerful ones. Its light had to be made strong enough to provide clear illumination of the path forward, of the path to continued enlightenment. At the same time, the light had to be kept weak enough to avoid injury or plunder and filtered to counter its extreme direct effect. Somehow, the strengthening of the flashlight had to match the gentle diffusing of the laser beam. What was needed perhaps, was "a government that was too weak to aid the wolves, and yet strong enough to protect the sheep." [47]

James Madison devised his great doctoral thesis from this vantage point. Here, of course, we are speaking of his authorship of the US Constitution, America's second and latest attempt at true democratic self rule: a solemn, permanent, social compact among the states to operate with individual sovereignty but within the framework of a collective federal system. The creation of the US Constitution was molded, set forth and argued in Philadelphia at the Constitutional Convention in 1787.

Madison's review of all such prior human efforts at harnessing effective democratic rule, coupled with a series of compromises as a result of the founders' debate, forged a system of checks and balances. The result was creation of our present system of government, with three equal branches, each independent of, yet answerable to, the others. The legislative branch would make the laws, the executive branch would enforce them and the judicial branch would provide interpretation where necessary. No one branch, nor the people themselves, would be able to grab all the light at any one time. However, a sufficient concentration of light would still be permitted to protect the rule of law and permit progressive social change to occur.

34

In the legislative branch, a compromise denied the big states (House of Representatives) the ability to swallow up the small states (Senate). That is, the legislature itself would be split into two distinct branches, creating what was referred to as a bicameral chamber. The assent of *both* would be required to enact a new law. Even the president, the one direct representative of *all* the citizens, would be elected not directly by a majority vote of the citizens but rather indirectly by what would become known as an electoral college.

Seeking to ensure that a lone rogue state or small minority of states could not stalemate the process, the founders also made a shrewd agreement for implementation of the new US Constitution. When the affirmative vote of 9 of the original 13 states had been given, the new constitution would become the law of the land in all 13 states. The necessary ratification figure was thus accomplished two years later in 1789, and in the end, all 13 states would vote unanimously to ratify the new constitution. It was a bloodless revolution, or, as the French might say, a coup d'état. Compared to the way things had been done previously, it could be said that the revolution to create a new US Constitution turned our old system of government on its head.

But just how does our system of government relate to the idea of flying under the radar? In other words, who would we identify as the umpire? Thomas Jefferson, for one, argued that it was the legislature, working in unison with the executive, which was best suited to play the unassuming, under-appreciated role of umpire. On the important condition that proper policy was in place by the combined efforts of this pair, working together, then thereafter,

> The path we have to pursue is so quiet that we have nothing scarcely to propose to our Legislature. A noiseless course, not meddling with the affairs of others, unattractive of notice, is a mark that society is going on in happiness. If we can prevent the government from wasting the labors of the people, under the pretense of taking care of them, they must become happy. [48]

To this,

> It must be added, however, that unless the President's mind in a view of everything which is urged for and against (a particular bill) is tolerably clear that it is unauthorized by the Constitution; if the pro and the con hang so even as to balance his judgment, a just respect for the wisdom of the legislature would naturally decide the balance in favor of their opinion. It is chiefly for cases where they are clearly misled by error, ambition or interest, that the Constitution has placed a check on the negative (i.e.: veto) of the President. [49]

So, it is the legislative branch that serves the role of the baseball umpire, calling balls and strikes, letting the citizens "play" and using its authority to maintain a level playing field. Examples of the legislative process, working for the common good and not so common good are replete throughout US History and need not concern us here. But the ordinary citizen must be mindful that the "science of human nature" will always be silently at work in the democratic process. Furthermore, the ordinary citizen can be reasonably assured that the democratic process will of necessity involve an expectation of reasonable men acting reasonably in their own best interest.

***

This chapter on flying under the radar should conclude with a few brief words.

Lawyers utilize a familiar expression that "a good prosecutor can indict a ham sandwich." That is, if an ordinary citizen looks at anything either long enough, or closely enough, one is bound to find some inherent flaw, which must then become the subject of greater scrutiny.

The founding fathers knew that their effort was not perfect, that nothing conceived on such a scale and magnitude could ever hope to achieve perfection. But it was finally agreed after much debate to put small differences aside and come together for the greater good, to accept the new constitution as an excellent starting point, and amend it where necessary down the road. This would be the only clear path to the continuation of the great American experiment in democracy.

Finally, let's look at this another way. If one were to place a cell under the microscope, and increase the magnification power by a factor of 10 in successive individual increments, the viewer would invariably experience the following visual progression. One would begin by observing a simple, fuzzy blur. Then, with each successive magnification, the blur would gradually take on definition, coming into focus. Eventually, the focus would be clear to the finest level of detail. Finally there would be over-magnification, causing the view to return to the fuzzy blur, where it began.

If, at the same time, one were to point a telescope to the stars and heavens above, and follow the same progression as with the microscope, the end result would be similar. [50] Perhaps, there is a lesson to be taken from that.

Achieving the pinnacle. By doing the job right. Being humble and selfless, yet independent. Eschewing the whim of the crowd. Simplifying—in the model of Henry David Thoreau, the 19th century American author, poet and philosopher. [51] Staying below the radar. Attributes which make ordinary leaders of ordinary people tasteless to hungry predators and opposing critics, and consequently immune from successful or coordinated attack. In the quest for virtue and enlightenment, on the path to human progress.

Chapter 3
A Few of My Favorite Things: US History (Part 1)

She came from Providence,
the one in Rhode Island
Where the old world shadows hang
heavy in the air
She packed her hopes and dreams
like a refugee
Just as her father came across the sea

She heard about a place people were smilin'
They spoke about the red man's way,
and how they loved the land
They came from everywhere
to the Great Divide
Seeking a place to stand
or a place to hide
...
Who will provide the grand design?
What is yours and what is mine?
'Cause there is no more new frontier
We have got to make it here
We satisfy our endless needs
And justify our bloody deeds,
in the name of destiny
and in the name of God

- from the song, *The Last Resort,*
by The Eagles (1976)
available on the *Hotel California* collection

***

"I wonder why we are made so that what we really think and feel we cover up," confided Harry S. Truman, the 33rd President of the United States, to his wife, Bess, looking back. Mr. Truman felt that it was one of his greatest limitations that he had withheld too much of himself from public view. But in contrast to his predecessor, Franklin D. Roosevelt (and it would become part of Truman's destiny to be forever contrasted with F.D.R.), he was truly uncomplicated, open and genuine.

39

Importantly, this was even more pronounced after it was clear that he was destined to be a figure in history, as well. [52]

Typically, students are in agreement that the Truman quote is true in their own lives. Otherwise, at least in the context of relationships, they would be left exposed, vulnerable and perhaps, ultimately, rejected. Better, and *safer*, to hide what we truly feel. In the context of business relationships, divulging too much information is also felt to be far from the best policy. In so doing, profits might be eroded or the enjoyment or even maintenance of a hard fought competitive advantage put at risk. And so today, rather than being open or transparent, ordinary citizens and business organizations choose to mask their true intentions.

"Good God, Truman will be President," it was being said everywhere on the news of the passing of F.D.R. in April 1945 and the realization that Harry Truman was President. The news struck like massive earth tremors in quick succession. "If Harry Truman can be President, so could my next door neighbor." People were fearful about the future of the country and that the war (World War II) would drag on even longer now. "What a great, great tragedy. God help us all." F.D.R.'s death and the thought of Truman in the White House came as a shock wave and actually made some people feel physically ill. "The country and the world don't deserve to be left this way . ...." [53]

***

Ancient Lineage

It wasn't *supposed* to be "this way," certainly not in the *natural* order of things. When the path is not well marked or its direction uncertain, it can be helpful to view things in an historical context, which permits a "big picture" perspective.

Presently, Western Civilization generally acknowledges the great, continuing American experiment in democracy to be the "keeper of the light." America traces its lineage and draws its inspiration from ancient times. More specifically, the lineage begins first from the hand of God, through Moses to the Biblical Covenants, which were the earliest traces of the idea of a covenant to form a people. Advances were derived from the ancient Egyptians, whose building of monumental pyramids, temples and obelisks, and systems of math, medicine, irrigation and agriculture, have stood the test of centuries.

The ancient Greeks contributed the likes of Aristotle, Socrates, Plato and Plutarch. Aristotle is generally credited with providing the origin of some of the earliest thoughts on democratic principles and "politics," that dreaded word. He tutored Alexander the Great, creator of one of the largest empires in ancient history, around 335 BC. Socrates, by his astute listening and questioning skills, would leave his subjects to find the answers themselves. His example remains the preferred teaching "Socratic method" in American law schools. Plato's aforementioned *Allegory of the Cave*, is among many invaluable philosophy lessons. *Plutarch's Lives* provides a timeless lesson of history, the essays persuasive authority for the proposition that names, dates and national boundaries change, but human nature does not.

The ancient Romans followed in impressive fashion. Julius Caesar, one of the great, early military generals, was credited for laying the groundwork of the Roman Empire. In "crossing the Rubicon" (River), the so-called point of no return, Caesar led his armies into Rome, conquering that place in victory and becoming its Emperor. His actions provided a fateful lesson in the separation of civilian from military authority. Unfortunately, some notable future military leaders would fail to heed this important warning. Caesar also authored one of the greatest works of literature in the ancient world in his classic *Commentaries*. The calendar month of August was dedicated in tribute to his son, Caesar Augustus. Marcus Aurelius' *Meditations* philosophical reflections was perhaps the earliest rendition of the popular phrase, loosely translated from the Latin, "It is what it is."

Through the efforts of the Emperor Constantine, Rome converted to Christianity, forming a powerful Judeo-Christian ethic. Mohammed came too, thereby creating Islam, the third and newest of Western Civilization's three religions. Militarily, Islam would challenge the West and spread almost all the way across the territorial expanse of the European continent by the Moorish conquest of Spain. Although its spread was ultimately repelled and pushed back, much of its influence and culture remains. But then there was darkness, for many centuries.

***

Middle Passage

What we refer to as parliamentary government owed its origin to the *Magna Carta*, the "great list" of the peoples' grievances with a demand

41

for redress, brought to the British throne, circa 1216. This was followed by the Renaissance, born in Florence, Italy in the 1400s and representing an intellectual and cultural flowering of the arts, literature, philosophy and the sciences. One of the most important tenets of the Renaissance was the belief in human progress and the betterment of society.

The *Protestant Reformation* of 1517 was largely the credit of one man, Martin Luther, the German priest and professor of theology, with an assist from another, Henry VIII, the English King. It shattered the unity of the Roman Catholic Church, the most powerful institution in medieval Europe, convulsing Europe and provoking bloody wars.

Martin Luther had begun to seriously question certain unspiritual practices of the Roman Catholic Church. Highest among them was the selling of indulgences in the form of cash payments to the church to make amends for past sins and otherwise ensure expeditious journey through purgatory to heaven's gates. Martin Luther rejected, in essence, the Roman Catholic practice of monopolizing the concept of salvation by conditioning it upon satisfactory material giving. In so doing, he popularized what would become a familiar phrase: "Salvation. They make it unattainable." Moreover, Martin Luther did not believe that priests were necessary to interpret scriptures. Rather, and importantly, he envisioned an educated populace capable of improving its own lot in life.

King Henry VIII's problem was more one of politics than theology. Priding himself on his devotion to Roman Catholicism, Henry VIII had published his *Defense of the Seven Sacraments*, which berated Martin Luther for arguing in favor of only two sacraments, baptism and communion. Rome responded by rewarding Henry VIII with a new title, "Defender of the Faith."

However, worried about the inability of his wife to produce a male heir to ensure the perpetuation of the Tudor line, he asked Pope Clement VII to annul his marriage. When the Pope refused, Henry VIII formally repudiated the Pope, severed all ties with Rome, divorced his queen and remarried. Declaring himself to be God's regent over England, Henry VIII confiscated monastic lands, opening the way for a series of Protestant reformers which followed.

In 1620 the Mayflower Compact was the first known democratic calling in colonial North America. Blown off its intended course, the *Mayflower* landed near Cape Cod, Massachusetts at a place they named Plymouth. Fearing for their collective survival in an unknown and presumably hostile environment, the passengers on board made a solemn agreement. The decisions of the majority would bind them all to obey, an essential precaution in a colony with uncertain legal status.

Back in Europe, in 1688 the English Bill of Rights provided a written statement on the concept of human rights. The following year, John Locke's *Two Treatises on Government* spoke to the nature of society and the right of revolution. In France, Baron de Montesquieu authored *The Spirit of the Laws* in 1748, speaking of liberty and separation of powers. In 1782, Jean-Jacques Rousseau's *The Social Contract* delineated the rights and obligation of citizens.

This was the period known as the Enlightenment, also called the Age of Reason. The era unleashed a tidal wave of new learning that helped promote the notion that human beings, through use of their reason, could solve society's problems.

In reaction to more secular, rationalized thinking characterizing the Enlightenment, the Great Awakening renewed emphasis on vital religious faith. In particular, the movement emphasized personal choice, as opposed to state mandates about worship, in matters of religious faith. Both movements spilled over to the American colonies, influencing such important historical figures as Benjamin Franklin and Thomas Jefferson, leading proponents of Enlightenment thinking in America.

***

The American Contribution

Thomas Paine had called for Americans "to begin the world all over again." [54]

And so, while in 1776 Western Civilization was not exactly new to the idea of democratic principles and democracy in general, Thomas Jefferson's Declaration of Independence was the first articulation of the concept of "certain inalienable Rights." This comprised one half of the Social Compact of the United States of America.

However, the grand American experiment in democracy, of which Europe was so skeptical, was nearly doomed to failure from the start.

Enacted in 1781, the first constitution was essentially a failed experiment in democracy. It had permitted each state to retain its own "sovereignty, freedom and independence, and every power, jurisdiction and right" not expressly delegated, requiring unanimous consent to pass laws. There was no effective president, no executive agencies, no judiciary, no tax base and no military. America's first constitution was too weak for an effective government.

Replacing the old constitution with the present US Constitution in 1789, the founding fathers thus formed the second half of the Social Compact, comprising the concept of federalism. Authored by James Madison, it largely mirrored the work of John Adams, whose previous effort had produced the Constitution of the Commonwealth of Massachusetts. In contrast to the old, the new constitution provided for a strong, central federal government, by majority rule, with the power to tax, raise an army, and provide the basis for sustained economic growth (i.e.: a national bank). Loosely worded authority was also provided to do everything "necessary and proper" to accomplish these goals. It was an attempt to establish federal supremacy over the rights of the individual states, conditioned only on the evolving central idea: "Let the ends be legitimate."

Some, like Thomas Jefferson, warned that the new federal framework infringed unacceptably on the rights of the individual states and their citizens to self pursuit and betterment. As a result, the Bill of Rights was added as a package in 1791. Comprising the first 10 amendments to the US Constitution, the Bill of Rights provided a uniquely American statement and list of basic human rights. It cemented the new democracy, since the southern states would not have agreed to adopt the new US Constitution without its passage.

At the time the American federal system of government was created, at issue was the concept of public virtue. Would citizens subordinate their own self-interests to advance the greater good or common cause of the entire community? In George Washington's day, leaders who believed that citizens would not abuse public privileges for private advantage were a radical minority in the Western world.

Yet in implementing the new US Constitution, the founding fathers had not, for example, prepared their plan of government with political parties in mind. Associating political factions with the British form of government, they hoped that the "better sort of citizens" that we had in

America would rise above popular self-interest. They would debate key issues and reach a common consensus on how best to legislate for the nation's future. Indeed, John Adams, later our nation's 2nd President, had "insisted that where European diplomacy was secret, bellicose and riddled with intrigue, American policy would be open, peaceful, and honest." [55] The goal, after all, was to form "a more perfect union."

***

The Seven Great American Presidents

Of the forty-four men who have served as President of the United States as of the date of publication, what binds the seven great American Presidents together is that each in his own right championed progress and reform for the common benefit of the ordinary citizen. Each, in his own way, put the interests of the collective nation above his own self-interests, any individual group or particular interest. The elevation of man and the advancement of Western Civilization have continued.

In order, the seven great American Presidents are George Washington (1789-1796), Thomas Jefferson (1800-1808), Andrew Jackson (1828-1836), Abraham Lincoln (1860-1865), Theodore Roosevelt (1901-1908), Franklin D. Roosevelt (1932-1945) and Harry S. Truman (1945-1952).

Four of the seven pre-dated, while the last three post-dated, the late 19th century Industrial Revolution. This forms a familiar mid-point of reference. While it is true that we haven't had a great American President now in more than 50 years, some say there *could* have been an eighth great American President. His life, however, was cut short before he would have his time. Others say Ronald Reagan (1980-1988) is the eighth. Our current President, Barack Obama, is not yet considered to be eligible. But yes, we are probably overdue, historically, for another great American President.

***

The First Four Great American Presidents.

George Washington is the only one of the seven great American Presidents who has earned the title, "Father of our Country." Upon his death came this further accolade: "first in war, first in peace, and first in the hearts of his countrymen." [56] The introduction does not overstate the significance.

45

When analyzing the impact of George Washington, it is inescapable but to dwell in the realm of "firsts." During the Revolutionary War, the fledgling new nation chose Washington unanimously to command all of the military forces, which consisted of the army (infantry and militia) only. Washington earned the title of lieutenant-general, which would not be bestowed again on an American military man for more than 80 years. Upon the conclusion of the war, and after a somewhat brief return to the life of a Virginia planter, it was Washington's support which was indispensable to the enactment of the US Constitution.

What made Washington's contributions so significant was his awareness that his decisions in the new federal government framework involved matters of first impression. Accordingly, those decisions were extremely important not only for their correctness but also for the *precedent* they would set for future leaders. Under the new tri-partite system of government and in its executive branch, Washington could rely upon no historical frame of reference, as the subject was without parallel. For example, even the basic matter of what to call the head of the new executive branch was without precedent. So many titles were tried on for size; from "King" to "Chief" to "Mr." Finally, it was Washington, who settled upon the simple title of "President."

Next was the important matter of setting up and organizing the executive branch. President Washington considered the efficient organization of the command structure of the continental army. This had served him extremely well and by all accounts was a major factor in surviving the British onslaught and then finally defeating them at Yorktown. So he felt it only natural to apply and adapt that command structure to the executive branch of the new government, thereby creating the first civil cabinet. President Washington further strongly endorsed the centralizing policies of the Federalists, becoming its first leader. He further endorsed the brain trust of Alexander Hamilton, his former military subordinate, in implementing important systems of finance and banking.

While the US Constitution was silent on the issue of the number of four year terms a president could serve (there was no stated limit), President Washington wished to serve but for a single term. However, he was reluctantly persuaded to serve a second term to cement the new government in place and forestall subsequent intriguers, who all knew would plot and scheme to become president. Washington, of course, was seen as being above that.

But following his second term as the nation's chief executive, Washington *voluntarily* stepped down, believing that eight years was enough for any man to serve in an executive capacity. This precedent was honored strictly by every future chief executive for almost 150 years until 1940. Due to exceptional circumstances then (a Great Depression at home and a raging World War II in Europe), it was felt that circumstances were serious enough for F.D.R. to break with Washington's tradition and serve a third presidential term. Shortly after F.D.R.'s death, however, Congress passed, and the states ratified, an amendment to the US Constitution, formally adopting the two term limit exemplified by Washington. The 22nd amendment eliminated the future possibility of expanding presidential powers to a status of dictatorship in the mold of a Hitler, Mussolini or Stalin.

In his Farewell Address, President Washington presciently issued two warnings to future Americans. The first warning was to avoid permanent alliances "with any portion of the foreign world," as the "primary interests" of America and Europe were fundamentally different. This warning would in later times form the basis of America's "isolationist" policy of neutrality in foreign affairs. In 1916, then-President Woodrow Wilson relied on Washington's first warning, achieving election to a second presidential term, on the basis that "he kept us out of war" (World War I). The US continued to follow this policy into the early part of World War II, prior to the Japanese attack at Pearl Harbor, Hawaii in 1941. To any remaining doubters, that incident made clear that America's great oceans could no longer serve as natural buffers against foreign aggression for all time.

The second warning, far less publicized, was for America to avoid "the baneful effects of the spirit of party," or the partisan divisions of politics. Remarkably, it appears that our founding fathers envisioned neither partisanship nor a party system. But President Washington noted that "This spirit, unfortunately, is inseparable from our nature, having its root in the strongest passions of the human mind." The President continued, "but, in those (governments) of the popular form it ... is truly their worst enemy." It certainly appears as if the petty and incessant partisan bickering of early 21st century America can well attest.

Lastly, Washington drafted his will alone, without any "professional character" being "consulted." Mindful of the evil institution of human slavery which was practiced in his home state of Virginia, his will called for the manumission or freedom of all his slaves upon his own death, or his wife's death. His will also called for the ongoing material provision of those newly freed who were in need, and that the clause respecting slaves "be religiously fulfilled without evasion, neglect or delay." Second, Washington divided his estate, which consisted primarily of speculative land west of the Alleghenies in the Ohio Valley, into 25 equal shares. By doing so, he avoided a legacy among his heirs over which to fight and so that there would be no Washington family fortune created for posterity. [57]

***

Thomas Jefferson, the second of the seven great American Presidents, was the winner of America's first "contested" election of 1800. The heretofore mentioned author of the Declaration of Independence, Jefferson was the founder of the new Democratic-Republican Party (the "Republican" part of the label was later dropped, until resurrected by Lincoln in 1860, leaving Jefferson's Party with its familiar name, the "Democrats").

The party's main goal was to reverse the centralizing policies of the Federalists and provide greater freedoms for the states and respect for the rights of citizens in their own individual pursuits. The Bill of Rights would become the primary protection of citizens from the centralizing policies of the Federalists. According to Jefferson, in 1800 a new Revolution was necessary, "as real a revolution in the principles of our government as that of 1776 was in its form." [58] Indeed, much of his first term was devoted to fighting off the effects of the defeated Federalist Party and his frustration with it having "retired" to the judiciary to continue the fight.

Jefferson listed among the "essential principles" of government

> the support of the state governments in all their rights, as the most competent administrations for our domestic concerns and the surest bulwarks against anti-republican tendencies.

Suggesting "a shift of emphasis in the direction of states' rights, without specifying just what these were," Jefferson listed another principle:

> the preservation of the general government in its whole constitutional vigor, as the sheet anchor of our peace at home and safety abroad.

Jefferson also spoke somewhat more specifically of the distributions of functions within the federal structure. He felt that small government was best suited for ordinary problems, while larger government was better suited to handle problems of greater magnitude:

> To the united nation belong our external & mutual relations: to each state severally the care of our persons, our property, our reputation, & religious freedom. This wise distribution, if carefully preserved, will prove, I trust from example, that while smaller governments are better adapted to the ordinary objects of society, larger confederations more effectually secure independence and the preservation of republican government. [59]

Though seemingly plagued with controversy and some degree of paradox, Jefferson's policies would serve to return the country to the principles of republican simplicity, economy and wisdom. Additionally, his policies directed an extremely popular movement toward limited, frugal, debt free government. This would leave the people free to regulate their own pursuits of industry and improvement, absent any pretense about hereditary titles or privileges in the manner of the British. In fact, some of Jefferson's ideas might sound like those coming more from a classic, modern day conservative Republican or Libertarian. At the time, however, his views were considered to be on the cutting edge of "enlightened liberalism." Such is the problem with the use of labels.

The prior administration of John Adams had felt it necessary for the fledgling new nation to avoid war with France. Consequently, the controversial Jay's Treaty in effect created a British commercial alliance especially in the conduct of foreign trade. Through further passage of the Alien and Sedition Acts (akin to today's version, the Patriot Act), jail terms and fines (meant for sympathizers who were partial to France) were set for those who advocated disobedience to federal law or who wrote, printed or spoke "false, scandalous and malicious" statements against the US government. It was the first example of laws curtailing 1st amendment freedom of speech where there existed a stated threat to national security. The laws were extremely controversial, enforcement proceedings contentious.

In response, Jefferson authored what became known as the Virginia and Kentucky Resolves (1798). These resolves championed the rights of the minority to dissent, arguing that error (the tyranny of the majority) was best tolerated, only when reason was left free to combat it. The resulting consequences helped to frame the issues in the election of 1800 and spilled well into Jefferson's first presidential term. Jefferson's backing of these objections to federal law effectively anticipated constitutional theories that "states' rights" southerners would use after 1830 and specifically at the time of the Civil War in 1861.

President Jefferson preferred a "strict interpretation" of the US Constitution, reminding Congress that the Alien and Sedition Acts gave the government powers not mentioned. Under the 10th Amendment these powers were expressly reserved to the states. It was the first attempt to question whether states could disregard or "nullify" a federal law with which they did not agree. But similar laws would be used by President Lincoln during the Civil War and by President Bush "43" following "9/11" to address matters of national security.

Foremost among Jefferson's presidential accomplishments was the 1803 Louisiana Purchase, which effectively doubled the size of and destined the new nation for physical greatness. Interestingly, however, critics claimed that the authority of the government and specifically his executive branch to make the purchase was nowhere stated in the enumerated rights of the US Constitution. In contrast to his position on limited government prior to his administration, President Jefferson's response could be succinctly paraphrased here as "Where does it say that I can't?"

Finally, on his tombstone Jefferson would compose his own epitaph: author of the Declaration of Independence and the statute of Virginia for religious freedom and founder of the University of Virginia. The latter may be the finest accomplishment on a list of many superlatives, for it formed the basis of the American democratic tradition which separated church and state, seemingly still as radical today as it was then. His presidency was conspicuously left out.

***

The third of the seven great American Presidents was the colorful and entertaining Andrew Jackson, the President of the Common Man. He was a Tennessee southerner and self made man, wildly popular in the South, the "bridge" from Washington and the nation's founding to Lincoln and the Civil War. Known as "Old Hickory" for his mental fortitude, Democrat Andrew Jackson would boast that as President, he was the *only, direct* representative elected by *all* the people. No other elected representative could make that claim, elected as they were to represent merely their local constituents. Jackson alone, therefore, had the interests of *all* the people in mind.

Upon his 1828 election, Andrew Jackson introduced America to a system of rotating federal office workers, what became known as the "spoils system." Intended as a means to implement reform in federal worker productivity, the policy sought to root out incompetence, political cronies and inefficient hangers on from the previous administration. Contrary to the views of his predecessor, Jackson believed in keeping things fresh. No special expertise was therefore required to hold federal employment. Ordinary people (like Jackson himself) could learn. The "People's President," Jackson stressed the common peoples' virtue, intelligence and capacity for self-government.

Turning the office of the President into a powerful legislative force, Jackson made American government more "user friendly" to more of its citizens, especially the common, ordinary citizen. Empowering the states to eliminate voice voting, residency requirements, property and tax paying qualifications for voting and office holding, more ordinary citizens could project a voice in their government.

Moreover, as a check on the power of Congress, President Jackson strengthened the office of the presidency by utilizing his veto authority as no president had done before. Under the previous administration, the executive had been viewed as a subordinate branch or puppet at the heel of Congress. Not so under President Jackson. Significantly, by making strategic use of the presidential veto power, Jackson assured the required stature of equality as between the executive with its legislative sister.

President Jackson's parties at the White House were said to be legendary. Overtaken by common men, of no particular distinction, they drank the beer to excess, ripped down the curtains and broke up the furniture. The White House staff was aghast, having been used to the much more formal, staid celebration of his predecessor. The mayhem and destruction brought to his attention, Jackson was said to have responded: "Leave them alone. This is their house. These are my people."

Andrew Jackson's "people" were the people of the South, whose passions had been inflamed over the enactment of a large federal tariff by his predecessor. Revenue from the tariff provided support for an extraordinary federal program of economic and scientific development. The program included construction of public roads, bridges and canals, exploration of the country's virgin territories, a national university and the first mandatory public education for the nation's youth. It even included such far fetched programs as astronomical observatories, "lighthouses of the skies" as they were known. All were financed by the Tariff of Abominations, placed squarely on the South through its prized crop, cotton.

President Jackson opposed both the federal programs and the tariff for two reasons. First, they flew in the face of traditional Jeffersonian principles of limited self government, states' rights and strict interpretation of the US Constitution. Moreover, Southerners feared that any further expansion of federal authority might set a negative precedent for interference with their prized institution of slavery. There was even the threat of secession from the Union from such prominent leaders as John C. Calhoun of South Carolina. Lastly, the federal programs were seen as a "corrupt" payback among the privileged well-to-do dating back to the election of the previous administration.

Andrew Jackson was sympathetic to the views of his people of the South whose position was still in the nation's minority. But a true measure of his greatness was his subordination of that interest to the larger goal of preserving and perpetuating the federal Union.

In the nation's capital at an 1830 celebration of the birthday of Thomas Jefferson, several Southern political leaders had given toasts advocating secession. Jackson then stood and gave his own memorable toast, which would be the last of the evening. His toast shocked and stunned his Southern critics, denouncing and rebuking them in powerful fashion: "Our Federal Union," Jackson said in measured tones, "*It must be preserved*" and would be preserved, "*Tariff or no Tariff.*" One of Jackson's aides noted that all the Hotspurs who had attended the dinner "*know that Old Hickory means what he says.*" [60]

Not many days later, a Congressman from South Carolina came to the White House to pay his respects as he was returning to his home state. Jackson received him with great courtesy, as was his wont. After a brief conversation the Congressman asked the president if he had anything he wanted him to convey to his friends in South Carolina.

"No, I believe not," came the immediate reply. But then the President remembered his toast and quickly amended his remark. "Yes, I have. Please give my compliments to my friends in your State, and say to them, that if a single drop of blood shall be shed there in opposition to the laws of the United States, I will hang the first man I can lay my hand on engaged in such treasonable conduct, upon the first tree I can reach.

The Congressman's eyes almost popped out of his head. He got out of the room as fast as possible. [61]

The Union had been preserved. Importantly, at the same time, the Tariff, while not eliminated, was significantly reduced, and in rather quiet fashion. Equal opportunity would continue to be available, for the white man at least, but remain abundant only for so long as emphasis on an agrarian economy and land for western migration held out.

***

Neither luck nor any particular good fortune would grace the arrival of Abraham Lincoln, the fourth of the seven great American Presidents and arguably the greatest. A self-educated man from Illinois, there is obviously insufficient room in this book to honor the contributions of one man to an uncommonly rare kind of leadership. His persevering hand would see to the preservation of the federal Union, the abolition of slavery, and laying the remaining ground work for the Industrial Revolution that would propel America into the 20th century.

How dear is the price of fame? Why do some stop at nothing to achieve it, yet it eludes them consistently? Why do others pay fame little regard, yet it finds them, becomes cemented into our culture and so endures?

It is interesting to understand Lincoln from his own perspective, given his aspiration for public service. "Understanding the spirit of our institutions is to aim at the *elevation* of men. I am opposed to whatever tends to degrade them." [62] And with respect to the Civil War, Lincoln saw it not just as a conflict in arms but rather, a "people's contest."

> On the side of the Union, it is a struggle for maintaining in the world that form and substance of government whose leading object is to elevate the condition of men ... to afford all an unfettered start, and a fair chance, in the race of life. [63]

Lincoln felt that a black man was entitled to that same fair chance in the race of life as his white counterpart. He kept regular office hours at the White House, long hours where he felt obliged to meet as many of the people who had elected and come to see him, for one reason or another. Usually, they had come seeking an appointment for cronies or "a friend of a friend" to the myriad of political patronage positions incumbent to his powers in the office of the president.

Imagine the requests made upon Lincoln, during this extraordinary time of conflict during the Great Rebellion among the States. But Lincoln patiently and tirelessly met all comers, although given the times, he could promise but little. Lincoln responded frankly, formulating what became a standard reply to the pressures of political patronage, characteristic of his ability to use the English language so effectively like few others in his position:

> 'Two others, both good men, have applied for the same office before. I have made no pledge; but if the matter falls into my hands, I shall, when the time comes, try to do right, in view of all the lights then before me.' Still another gained assurance that his application would receive 'that consideration which is due to impartiality, fairness and friendship.' [64]

In colonial times, it was said that the need for unity among the colonies to obtain independence from Great Britain had been more important on balance than the desire to extend civil rights to the black man. Besides, most believed that slavery would die a slow, natural death on its own, but for the invention of the cotton gin circa 1793 by Eli Whitney, a Connecticut Yankee, who had come south to work as a tutor.

There had also been a series of federal legislative compromises over the next almost 60 years designed to avert a catastrophe. The last of those compromises, in 1850, had repealed the Missouri Compromise, which had in part prohibited slavery entirely from the northern territories of Jefferson's Louisiana Purchase. The North had considered the Missouri Compromise line to be a "sacred compact" which was to be permanent, not temporary. It mattered not that California's admission to the Union as a free state had tipped the sectional balance of states to 16-15 in favor of the North.

The compromise had been sold to Northern Congressman on the basis that cotton did not grow in those territories and so slavery could never spread to those areas. But Lincoln knew better. Cotton grew just fine in Missouri, which was adjacent to his own state of Illinois, and just to Missouri's west was the territory of Kansas. The Missouri Compromise had prohibited slavery from the Kansas territory, but the Compromise of 1850 had changed all that.

By 1860, the political landscape had also changed drastically since the time of Andrew Jackson. Lincoln had taken up the cause on a seemingly innocuous political platform of reform, which advocated "no further extension of slavery into the western territories" which had yet to become states. He made that pledge the cornerstone of the new movement of the new political party, the name which caught on evoking memories of America's first fight for freedom in 1776: Republican.

For the South, a Republican victory in the presidential election would put an end to the political control of its own destiny. From 1789 to 1860, two-thirds of the time Southerners (all slaveholders) had been president of the United States. No Northern president had ever won re-election. Moreover, Southern justices had been a majority on the US Supreme Court since 1791. Lincoln's election would mark an irreversible turning away from this Southern ascendancy.

But in the election of 1860 the South had split into divided political camps, each putting up its own man for president. Lincoln's name was not even on the ballot in 10 southern states. However, the split among his political opposition enabled Lincoln to win the election with less than 40% of the popular vote. But in an ominous sign, Lincoln had received exactly 0 electoral votes from the 15 southern slave states.[65] On the basis of the so-called states' rights argument (individual states being supreme over federal authority based on the US Constitution's 10th amendment), these states believed, in essence, that they had the right to nullify the results of an election which they did not win. Consequently, they agreed to leave the Union and form their own country, the Confederate State of America.

So it was no mystery between the presidential election in November 1860 and Lincoln's inauguration in February 1861 that 7 Southern states would secede from the Union. After the attack on Fort Sumter, South Carolina a few months later, 4 more states would secede, bringing the total to 11. Additionally, 4 "border" slave states would remain precariously loyal to the Union during the course of the war.

Northerners could scarcely deny the right of revolution, they too being heirs of 1776. But Lincoln stressed that revolution was never a legal right, but at most, a moral right for a morally justifiable cause. Unlike 1776, the motto, according to Lincoln, was not liberty, but slavery. Accordingly, the South's revolution was more akin simply to a wicked exercise of physical power.

The South believed that Lincoln's election was akin to a death knell, so *dependent* was the Southern economy on slavery. Either slavery grows or it dies, so the Southerners believed, and despite what Lincoln had said, Lincoln wanted to kill it.

But it was Frederick F. Dent, a Missouri slaveholder, and the father of General Grant's wife, who perhaps put it best:

> Good Heavens! If old Jackson had been in the White House, this never would have happened. He would have hanged a score or two of them, and the country would have been at peace. I knew we would have trouble when I voted for a man north of Mason and Dixon's line. [66]

But it was now apparent that the issue could not be solved by political means. A rebel plot in 1861 to assassinate Lincoln in Baltimore *before* his inauguration on the train ride from Illinois to Washington, DC was foiled. Disguised in a sleeper car and without guard, Lincoln rode through the station the night before he was scheduled to come through. The would-be assassins were left scratching their heads, when the train Lincoln was *supposed* to be on came through the station the next day, empty. The issue would finally of necessity have to be submitted to the battlefield. And, as the expression goes, the war came.

Lincoln's handling of the whole calamitous affair was a masterful stroke for the ages. First, he promised the South that there would be no war at all, unless the South brought on the war by firing the first shot. When the South brought on the bloodshed by firing on Fort Sumter, a federal fort which the government was attempting to re-provision, the North was prompted to take up arms to "defend" the Union.

Lincoln could not however, ignore the mounting casualties on both sides over time, realizing that the cause must somehow be *greater*. Artfully, he was able to shift the focus from simply the defense of the Union to the larger goal of "Equality and Union." With a stroke of his pen he issued his Emancipation Proclamation, freeing the slaves but only in those states still in rebellion as of January 1, 1863. Importantly, that left out the border slave states, as a reward to them for their loyalty.

The Battle of Vicksburg (Mississippi) through military siege and the Battle of Gettysburg (Pennsylvania) followed later that summer, both concluding during the same fateful "4th of July weekend." In the latter, almost 60,000 lives were lost in just three days. Some months later, Lincoln traveled to the battlefield at Gettysburg and delivered but a simple 272 word speech.

In that speech, Lincoln concluded:

> It is rather for us to be here, dedicated to the great task remaining before us–that from these honored dead we take *increased* devotion to that cause for which they gave the last full measure of devotion–that we here highly resolve that these dead shall not have died in vain, that this nation under God shall have a new birth of freedom, and that government of the people, by the people, for the people shall not perish from the earth.
>
> *– Gettysburg Address* (excerpted from), November 19, 1863.

Sticking to the master plan through his commanding Generals, U.S. Grant and William T. Sherman, Lincoln would prosecute a harsh, unforgiving "total war." This was designed to demonstrate to the Confederacy the resolve of the North to preserve the Union intact by defeating the South decisively in battle on its own turf. Lincoln would insist through Gen. Grant on simple terms of "unconditional surrender" and submission to the sovereignty of the federal government.

Sherman's subsequent telegraph of the fall of Atlanta, which would later inspire Margaret Mitchell's epoch, *Gone With the Wind*, electrified the North. In large result, Lincoln won an unlikely victory in his 1864 re-election to a second presidential term. A curious Europe looked on, impressed that a democratic election could take place even during civil war.

Following the election, in March 1865, Lincoln addressed the people in thanks, looking to the war's end:

> Both parties deprecated war; but one of them would make war rather than let the nation survive; and others would accept war rather than let it perish. And the war came.
>
> Each looked for an easier triumph, and a result less fundamental and astounding. Both read the same Bible, and pray to the same God; and each invokes His aid against the other. *It may seem strange that any men should dare ask a just God's assistance in wringing their bread from the sweat of other men's faces; but let us judge not that we will be not judged.* (emphasis mine)
>
> With malice toward none; with charity for all; with firmness in the right, as God gives us to see the right, let us strive on to finish the work we are in, to bind up the nation's wounds; to care for him who shall have borne the battle, and for his widow, and his orphan–to do all which may achieve and cherish a just, and a lasting peace, among ourselves, and with all nations. [67]

Many ordinary Americans are unaware that the full text of both of these great speeches, the Gettysburg Address as well as Lincoln's Second Inaugural Address, are etched in stone on the inner walls of the Lincoln Memorial located in our nation's capital.

And note the italicized language above from Lincoln's Second Inaugural Address: *Let us Judge not that we will not be judged.* Lincoln was, of course, commenting on the peculiar institution of Southern slavery. But he stopped well short of passing judgment.

It is important enough to be considered the second lesson of US History, authority for which Lincoln footnoted to the Holy Bible. [68] It is a significant lesson, since it was learned as a result of a Civil War which saw the greatest number of casualties suffered than in all other wars in which the nation has been involved *combined,* to the present day.

To set in motion his plan for the "return to Union," or Reconstruction as it is more commonly known, Lincoln sat in the company of his commanding Generals, Grant and Sherman, and Admiral Porter representing Navy. This famous meeting was held on the boat named the *River Queen,* which served as Lincoln's floating headquarters on the James River, to frame the parameters of a peace doctrine.

In stark contrast to the harsh way the war had been prosecuted, President Lincoln would set forth extremely *lenient* and compassionate terms of peace to the people of the South. All Southern soldiers had to do was simply lay down their weapons, and promise never to take up arms against the US government ever again. In exchange, the soldiers would be paroled and promised that their civilian lives would not be interfered with by the federal government.

Lincoln proposed such lenient terms to ensure, and cement, the idea of Union, to put plows back into the hands of Southern men instead of weapons, and to promote and facilitate the healing process. His terms would also eliminate the possibility of a longer, protracted period of guerilla warfare (today we are more comfortable calling it "terrorism"), which many in the North had feared should the South refuse to surrender.

In the days preceding his death, President Lincoln had been having a recurring dream that was getting the better of him. The dream was of his assassination. Abraham Lincoln would not live long enough to enjoy the fruits of Robert E. Lee's surrender to U.S. Grant at Appomattox and the resulting Union victory. Just five days following Appomattox, he was assassinated by a Southern sympathizer. Called home, Abraham Lincoln's favor and success, such as he enjoys today, was not achieved until someone had first put a bullet in his head, and then not assured until long after his death. Such is the price of fame—sometimes.

Even worse for the nation, Lincoln's untimely death removed from the picture perhaps the South's surest friend in the federal government. This meant that his lenient plan of Reconstruction would have to be implemented by others whose sympathies toward the South would not match Lincoln's. The historical period of Reconstruction, spanning a period of 12 tumultuous years, from 1865 to 1877, would be tumultuous. For generations thereafter, the idea of Union would be seen by Southerners as nothing more than a futile attempt to put Humpty Dumpty back together again.

Chapter 4
Lenses, Filters and Walls

Something there is that doesn't love a wall,
That sends the frozen-ground-swell under it,
And spills the upper boulders in the sun,
And makes gaps even two can pass abreast.
...
No one has seen them made or heard them made,
But at spring mending-time we find them there.
I let my neighbor know beyond the hill;
And on a day we meet to walk the line
And set the wall between us once again.
We keep the wall between us as we go.
To each the boulders that have fallen to each.
...
One on a side. It comes to little more:
There where it is we do not need the wall:
He is all pine and I am apple orchard.
My apple trees will never get across
And eat the cones under his pines, I tell him.
He only says, "Good fences make good neighbors."
Spring is the mischief in me, and I wonder
If I could put a notion in his head:
"Why do they make good neighbors? Isn't it
Where there are cows?
But here there are no cows.
Before I built a wall I'd ask to know
What I was walling in or walling out,
And to whom I was like to give offence.
Something there is that doesn't love a wall,
That wants it down."
...

- from the poem, *Mending Wall,*
by Robert Frost (1914)

***

61

Before we should get to the "second half" of US History, we should permit ourselves to entertain a diversion into how we see things, what we are seeing, and who, in particular, has the keys to the video room.

The person who "looks at the world through rose colored glasses" describes someone who is filled with optimism, sees the positive in everything, to a fault. That someone cannot be deterred from the mission of turning an abstract idea into a reality, sometimes against all odds.

Have we ever paused to consider how we see things? Our eyes are nothing more than lenses, so the eye doctor says. Thanks to the retina and the optic nerve, they allow us to see things. We call this vision. Filters help us see certain things and exclude certain other things. Walls provide the mechanism to permit some to see all things on their side of the wall, and to deny those on the other side from seeing anything at all. Fences are a sort of wall.

Lenses, filters and walls each influence the way we see things. Why do we have them? The ordinary citizen's understanding of reality flows through a prism that reflects all sorts of things other than reality, self-interest being among them. Muckraking author Upton Sinclair [69] once said that "It is impossible to make a man understand something if his livelihood depends on not understanding it."

***

The 9-year-old, third grade vintage, relates a familiar story. She goes to school one morning on a day just like every other day. But on this morning something is different. Looking up at the blackboard, all she sees is a blur. She can swear that the prior day the writing on the board had been crystal clear. Her uncle had warned that if she sat too close to the television set, the day would come when she would need eyeglasses. But she never supposed the day was to arrive so soon. Of course, her mom dutifully brought her right to the eye doctor, and she instantly became a "four eyes." But despite the negative connotations, the glasses work like magic. Alternating back and forth between glasses and no glasses, she marvels at the scientific miracle those glasses represent in her little world.

Of course, there are all sorts of lenses out there. A camera aficionado can easily relate about some of the common lenses. There's the 35mm lens, the wide-angle lens, the telephoto "zoom" lens, each with its own unique optical properties that materially change the view. Growing ever more popular today, there's the phenomenon of 3D glasses. How can something which looks so mundane or completely ordinary without look so interesting in three dimensional view?

Next there are filters. Sunglasses filter out the harmful, ultraviolet rays of the sun, at the same time reducing glare and improving clarity. Some eyeglasses are photo sensitive, their filtering power changing automatically and in proportion to the strength of light. Some eyeglasses do not have corrective properties at all, containing simply "non-glare" properties. Polarizing filters change the light just a little bit, and intensify it, helping the photographer to see more clearly.

Television channels are a filter of certain media content. The technology of the 1960s included only a handful of channels. The VHF band consisted of channels 2 (CBS network), 4 (NBC network), 5 (Metromedia, later Fox network), 7 (ABC network), 9 (WOR, the old flagship that carried baseball's NY Mets' games), 11 (WPIX, which carried the NY Yankees) and 13 (PBS network). Additionally, the UHF band included just one station, Channel 47 (*quarenta y siete, Newark, New Jersey*), the only *Spanish* broadcast.

Televisions back then were of the analog variety, requiring the viewer to manually "change" the channel dial by hand. Grandma's house fascinated with cutting edge television, which had evolved to the new, *wired* "remote control." The long wire running precariously from the set to the remote control caused a repeated parental reminder to "be careful not to trip on the wire." This technology portended the shift from analog to digital and from wired to wireless remote technology. At this point in the technology evolution, however, one was still able to watch only what was "programmed." What about what *you* wanted to watch? Or the familiar question of "What's on tonight?" evoking the familiar response: "Nothing."

Over the years, the handful of TV stations was augmented by the phenomenon of "cable TV" which had more channels and advertised fewer commercials. Today, with the advance of the internet, fiber optic and broadband delivery, an impressive supply of website channels projects a diverse content which continues to expand the viewer's horizon. Live, streaming web feeds are gradually taking the place of the familiar television networks. Yet still, they are only filters.

Google, the internet search engine, is perhaps the ultimate filter to date. Ask Google a question, and one gets an answer either in words, images, videos or maps, as the inquirer may specify. Narrow the search terms, for example, by date or phrase, to further expand, narrow and thereby "filter" the search result. Certain nations like communist China and the religious theocracy of Iran perform some pre-filtering (what we call "censorship" in the free world) for the viewer. And while in our country some censorship must invariably occur, the 1st amendment right to free speech serves as the people's constitutional protection against unlawful infringement of this right. Permit someone to have done the search for you already, and you have Wikipedia, the online encyclopedia phenomenon.

Corporations have achieved perhaps the ultimate in media dominance, expertly filtering what we see *and don't* see to suit their own agenda. It is important to point out that this influences the reality of ordinary citizens. Corporate media giants like CNN, on the left, and Rupert Murdoch's Fox News, the "fair and balanced" viewpoint on the right, are but prime examples. Oil companies may advertise an attention to the environment. Pharmaceutical companies, in turn, may advertise an attention to safety detail and quality of life advances. Financial services firms tout the "fact" that the average returns of their managed investments typically well exceed historical norms over time. But does the ordinary citizen ever stop to consider what these major industries may *not* be saying about their prized, revenue generating products?

Dust, pollen, air and oil: all of these are types of filters. The earliest Marlboro, Camel and Lucky Strike brands of cigarettes were unfiltered. This is filtering in the literal, physical sense. In the case of cigarettes, filters change the flavor (as in menthol) and lessen the effects of nicotine and the concentration of harmful smoke and tar breathed into the human lung.

Alcohol and certain illicit drugs, such as marijuana, distort perception and thus filter our sensory experiences. The same can be said for certain mind altering drugs like LSD, whose chemical properties change orientation to time and space from that which is familiar and ordered. The regulation of drugs such as alcohol by the government, restricting consumption to those ages 18 and older, then 21, or an outright ban in certain bygone eras, constitutes a filtering mechanism. Limitations as to quantity mean yet another filter, as our drinking and driving laws remind us. Drinking to excess, however, has also at times been said to constitute a kind of "truth serum" for whatever aspect of verbal communication may follow.

There is a seemingly limitless variety of potential filters. For example, different food spices alter the taste of the foods we eat, often disguising certain unpleasant taste sensations, while amplifying others. Many historians write about history, not in the familiar limiting form of "US History" or the "History of Western Civilization." Rather, they have written through the lens of cod, the fish and food source, and oil, the petroleum product and fossil fuel.

One writer of particular skill has reasoned that wars have been fought, revolutions ignited, national diets based, economies depended, and the actual settlement of North America driven, all by cod. It is said that cod was the reason that European settlers set sail across the Atlantic for the New World, as well as the only reason they could. [70]

In the case of oil, Grant was literally chasing Lee across the state of Virginia to Appomattox in 1865, when a fellow named Rockefeller was signing a lease on the nation's first oil field on a farm in Pennsylvania. Oil had originally been planned as a commodity which would replace candle light with lanterns. But with Thomas Edison's discovery of the light bulb, the future for oil seemed to be dead, that is, until the invention of the internal combustion engine. Shortly thereafter, the automobile assured oil's place as the preferred fuel source to ignite the Industrial Revolution.

During World War I, at the behest of an undersecretary named Churchill, the British converted its naval fleet from coal to oil ahead of the Germans, tipping the balance of power, and the war's outcome, in Britain's favor. As a result of actions at Versailles, the treaty to shape the post-war peace, the British created the Iraq mandate. This administrative arrangement facilitated the transportation of a stable supply of oil from the Middle East to Western Europe. In World War II, Japan's attack on Pearl Harbor was motivated primarily by the need for a secure supply of oil that could be secured in the Dutch East Indies, if only America were out of the picture. Tremors from these fateful events still reverberate today on a world scale as seen through our military ventures into Iraq and Afghanistan, with the control of oil supplies very much front and center. [71]

In the case of natural science, when discussing man's early attempts to arrange the natural sciences into classifications, Thomas Jefferson felt that

> Every mode of class must be liable (to imperfection), because the plan of creation is inscrutable to our limited faculties. Nature has not arranged her productions on a single and direct line. They branch at every step, and in every direction, and he who attempts to reduce them into departments, is left to do it by the lines of his own fancy.

Resisting the temptation to innovate in the settled nomenclature of nature's productions, at least in terms of the natural sciences, greater service would be rendered

> by holding fast to the system on which we had all once agreed, and by asserting into that such new genera, orders, or even classes, as new discoveries should call for. [72]

Religion is but a filter, its many iterations and fractures over the course of the centuries serving only to demonstrate the different pathways to the one supreme being. The books of the Bible's Old Testament, as well as the Gospels of the New Testament, are filters of a kind. At certain key times, groups of influential and powerful men have gathered and agreed to include some books, yet exclude others. A reasonable observation would seem to include the question of what human motives were at stake, other than the belief in God. For example, some of the writings of the Quran, Islam's holy book, include passages about Mary, the Blessed Mother, who Muslims also revere. Yet, for some reason, these passages were passed over by the organizers of the Bible and consequently omitted.

In the realm of politics, specifically our Republican and Democratic Parties, and even the Independent status in its various forms, are but limiting ideological mechanisms. And, so there it is. The two great institutions of American civilian life, which define and shape us, yet continue to evolve, are at the same time both empowering and limiting.

In the end, filters possess two very important characteristics. First, as the preceding dialogue attempts to demonstrate, the process of classification through use of various filtering mechanisms is seemingly an exercise in possibilities which are without limit. Secondly, at the same time, filters do limit.

***

The discussion to this point contemplates filters in the objective sense, that is, in a way that is not subject to the viewer's interpretation. For example, if one were shown a picture of a stop sign, there can be no doubt that, as a rule of the road, the red octagon means only one thing.

But it gets tricky when the filter becomes *subjective*. This distinction is well illustrated through a traditional exercise. First, flash an image to a group and quickly remove the image from sight. Then, ask each participant, individually, to describe what in particular was seen. Note that the image does not change. But the same image from a different view—as seen from a subjective individual perspective—often generates a vastly different interpretation. As is often said, beauty *is* in the eye of the beholder. [73]

Of course, the human mind is a filter too, and a very powerful one at that. Our perceptions are shaped in the first instance not only by each of our own families, but also by our culture, learning, individual beliefs and experiences. If beauty is in the eye of the beholder, then it is also true that we are but a product of our environment and in large part see what we want to see.

Previous discussion included Alexander Hamilton's sentiments on "happiness." But how, on the other hand, did Thomas Jefferson view "liberty and the pursuit of happiness?" The answer is as powerful as it is interesting, and yes, ties into our discussion of lenses and filters. As with a majority of Jefferson's ideas, his differences of opinion with Hamilton were centered on a philosophical basis.

For the individual, according to Jefferson, the essence of the pursuit of happiness commenced with the removal of all forms of arbitrary, artificial or hereditary distinctions, influences or preconceived ideas. The desire was to attain full, unencumbered intellectual and religious freedom of the mind, unconstrained by previous efforts to set authoritative delineation using lenses and filters. Absent these external influences and thus empowered, the mind would exist in a completely and intellectually free state: to master its environment and attain its *natural* potentialities. [74] Central was the belief in the improvability of the human mind and the limitless progress of human knowledge. [75]

On the collective side, Jefferson felt that the happiest society was one where inequalities of condition were not great. [76] Then-President Jefferson asked what else was needed for the happiness and prosperity of its people:

> a wise and frugal government, which shall restrain men from injuring one another, shall leave them otherwise free to regulate their own pursuits of industry and improvement, and shall not take from the mouth of labor the bread it has earned. This is the sum of good government, and this is necessary to close the circle of our felicities. [77]

Jefferson believed that the status of aristocracy, based as it was not on merit but inherited privilege, made it doubtful that this class would exercise its public obligation for human progress on its existing foundation. Consequently, his ideas sought to restore "the natural order of freedom to give talent and virtue, which were scattered through all ranks of society, a chance to rise." Jefferson described his purposes in terms of "natural philosophy." [78] Throughout his life, he never ceased to believe that men (white men, that is) by right were free in their minds and persons and that human society should guide its steps by the light of reason. [79]

It can be fairly assumed that the first major obstacle to the freedom of the mind that he perceived was primarily in the sphere of religion and morality and, specifically, the doctrine of supernatural revelation. Consequently, events which could not be scientifically proven were to be rejected, Jefferson believing that "No hypothesis ought to be maintained if a single phenomenon stands in direct opposition to it." Jefferson learned to apply to the Bible and theology the same tests as to secular history and scientific hypotheses, reasoning as follows:

> When I was young I was fond of the speculations which seemed to promise some insight into that hidden country, but observing at length that they left me in the same ignorance in which they had found me, I have for very many years ceased to read or think concerning them, and have reposed my head on that pillow of ignorance which a benevolent Creator has made so soft for us, knowing how much we should be forced to use it. [80]

Thus, Jefferson's only attack on religion was if it assumed a political character, or because it limited the freedom of the mind, upon which the progress of the human species toward happiness depended. [81] This helped to explain his well known authorship of the Virginia statute for religious freedom. This statute served as the basis of the right to free religious expression and the separation of religion (church) from government (state) as embodied subsequently by the 1st amendment to the federal US constitution.

Jefferson even went so far as to complete a favorite pet project, controversial today as it was then. He cut out from the Holy Bible's New Testament all references to miracles, revelation and the slanted opinions of men, which were written later, and in some cases much later. Left were only the words and teachings of Jesus Christ, Jefferson finding them to be "the purest system of morals ever before preached to man." He was fully convinced that the "priests" (Protestant as well as Catholic) had "adulterated and sophisticated" the teachings of Jesus for their own selfish purposes. [82]

After he was able to rid himself of these confounding issues, the next main problem was finding adequate moral sanction elsewhere [83], subjecting his pursuit of happiness only to two significant exceptions. First, he found "moral sanction in the monitor within every human breast," and second, he found them "in the laws of nature." [84] He looked first to the writings of classic antiquity, mainly the Greek classics, for a body of ethics. [85] But he settled on the basic idea that a special moral sense was to be found within an individual's own breast in the conscience, as truly a part of man's nature as his sense of sight or hearing, his arm or his leg. [86] Jefferson thus concluded that "The great principles of right and wrong are legible to every reader; to pursue them requires not the aid of many counselors." [87]

But "for ideals of human relationships and universal benevolence, Jefferson looked higher than" both the Greek and Roman classicists. He perceived in the ethics of Jesus Christ fullness and sublimity on a plane never attained by a classic moralist. [88] In sum, to one of the most notable champions of freedom and enlightenment in recorded history [89], happiness was the aim of life, and virtue was its foundation. [90]

Returning to the more mundane concept of Hamilton's financial plan, Jefferson strenuously objected. He was at the head of a class of citizens whose prosperity was derived from a farming economy. From that vantage point, the plan proposed to create an *artificial* class of wealth with certain inherent privileges to certain of its benefactors, which were not the privileges of all citizens. As such, it clashed with and violated Jefferson's ideals, which were in direct conflict.

Specifically, in Jefferson's opinion, Hamilton's

> system flowed from principles adverse to liberty, and was calculated to
> undermine and demolish the republic, by creating an influence of his
> department (i.e.: Treasury, within the executive branch) over members of
> the legislature (i.e.: Congress). [91]

As Hamilton well knew, the "influence" to which Jefferson was referring, and which Hamilton's banking system created, was inherently susceptible to corruption, according to the laws of human nature. In permitting some to hold for life, some hereditary, an influence by patronage or corruption over the popular legislative branch, the free election of the people would be reduced to a minimum. The government would consequently be narrowed into fewer hands and approximated to a hereditary form. [92]

Economically, according to Jefferson, Hamilton's plan meant the need for a paradigm shift to restore simple republican principles. In this context, a traditional, "real" economy had to be restored, where a bushel of wheat was worth whatever a bushel of wheat was worth at the particular time it was brought to market. This was opposed to a contrived, artificial, futures trading economy of corrupt Wall Street money speculators that Hamilton's banking system created, attracted and nurtured. Once unleashed, the ominous, dark side of human nature was unfortunately showcased in full display.

George Washington, the president, was faced with quite a dilemma. The new constitution was not intended to embody a particular economic theory. The difficulty was in weighing the advice of his cabinet members, which was at odds. On the one side was the recommended financial plan of his Secretary of the Treasury, Alexander Hamilton, and on the other the objection of his Secretary of State, Thomas Jefferson.

In the end, Washington endorsed Hamilton's financial plan based on a balancing of interests. On the one hand, the plan would do the greatest amount of good for the greatest number of people (on the "happiness" scale!). This overrode the collateral damage, on the other hand, which the plan would invariably cause to the system and some people, however small it would likely be portrayed. Yes, in the end it was a numbers game.

As early as July 4, 1792, in the time period immediately preceding Washington's re-election to a second Presidential term, a proponent of Thomas Jefferson published a provocative article. A set of rules were set forth " 'for changing a limited republican government into an unlimited hereditary one,' the most important of these being to increase the national debt and establish a bank." [93] However, by the time he had his turn as chief executive, and with the popular support to do as he wished, Jefferson performed an interesting about-face. Although he viewed the national bank as both an unnecessary and corruptive influence, he chose to extend its charter, on the evolving theory, simply, that "the ends be legitimate."

The stage had thus been set, and would be intensified later by the material progress of the Industrial Revolution, for the US to become the greatest and most wealthy goods-producing machine in the world. Well, one where wars would no longer be fought, at least internally, over God. This was the positive aspect. On the negative side, the stage had also been set for an insidious contest among ordinary citizens to accumulate the trappings of material wealth, as a symbol of success and status for other ordinary citizens. Further, when intermingled with the principles of Jefferson's separation of church and state, the new standard of worship for American society would not be God, but rather, money.

It certainly turned out to be a wise decision—for empire. But reducing the Almighty to secondary status would not be without continuing moral consequences. For a nation which prides its foundation on Christian principles, was it the *right* decision? [94] If as it is argued by many that America has lost its way, is the self-interest component which has become so pronounced the primary culprit? Is the ordinary citizen "happy" that noble virtues like compassion and mercy yield to organized corruption which expresses the moral sickness of a greedy society? [95]

***

And finally, there are walls—an abundance of them in various applications to the daily lives of ordinary citizens. And so by no means can this ode to walls be exhaustive, nor is it meant to be. But the following discussion attempts to analyze the primary design properties pertaining to walls.

When it comes to walls, whether appreciated or not, principles of behavioral cause and effect, remarkably similar in each instance, are at work according to the laws of human nature. For example, how do people react when they are ostensibly protected by a wall? When they are on the outside looking in? Or when there is no wall at all either for protection, to block an unwanted view or merely to just lean on? The corresponding human behavior in relation to walls, therefore, becomes somewhat predictable, if not exactly physical science.

A good beginning point revisits Robert Frost's poem, *Mending Wall*, excerpts from which lead this chapter discussion. Notable for the popular line *"Good fences make good neighbors,"* it is rather the following lines which stand out: *"Before I built a wall I'd ask to know/ What I was walling in or walling out,/ And to whom I was like to give offence./ Something there is that doesn't love a wall,/ That wants it down."*

The physical walls are the easy ones. We can see them. In fact, some can't be missed. The most famous, perhaps, is the Great Wall of China. It is so large a structure that space-based myth frequently bills it as the only man-made object visible from space. However, it isn't generally visible from space. And it certainly isn't visible from the moon. [96]

Courses on early colonial US History do not cover China in any way. The rationale is that US History is categorized as part of *Western* Civilization, while China encompasses *Eastern* Civilization. Certainly, China had the necessary means, together with early Western European settlers, to participate in the American colonial era. But it did not. The question is: Why not?

At the time, Chinese civilization had its own distinct culture and tradition. It had religion. It had science and architecture. It had wealth. In short, China was self-sufficient, having everything it needed to flourish and prosper, at standards which were the envy even of the Western world.

China then had to make a key decision. Should it export its civilization? Or should it close ranks and build a wall to protect it from the outside, and simply enjoy the fruits internally? China, of course, chose the latter. When the morning alarm clock rang, China peeked out from under the covers and could readily observe the unsavory contest between Western European powers for American colonial conquest. It then simply hit the "snooze" button, rolled over and went back to sleep.

But over the centuries, absent change, innovation and resulting progress, and dependent only on familiar traditions from within which had come success, Chinese civilization leveled off and eventually began a gradual descent. Finally, China fell behind its western counterparts, its dependency justifying the need to protect the territory gained, that is, to keep the wall in position.

At other times, in other civilizations, dependency would also justify the conquest yet to be made. Recognizing this, and with its culture and civilization vulnerable to outside forces and consequently at risk of survival, China has shifted presently to catch up mode. Quickly, in fact, from a historical perspective, China has returned over the last several decades to the status of a formidable, if not yet fully dominant, power on the world stage.

In Eastern Europe, the Berlin Wall was constructed by the communists of the former Soviet Union (USSR) in 1961 during the height of the Cold War, literally to wall in its people from fleeing to the free West. The twelve-foot concrete wall extended for a hundred miles, surrounding West Berlin. It included electrified fences and guard posts, and stood as a stark symbol of the decades-old Cold War between the US and USSR.

The two politically opposed superpowers continually wrestled for dominance, projecting spheres of influence but stopping just short of actual warfare. The rationale for the wall was to control the local economy of the then-East German state and the satellite states of the Soviet bloc. The Iron Curtain, so named by Great Britain's Winston Churchill, was the USSR's solution for creating a protective Russian buffer against future attacks from the direction of Western Europe. Two such attacks were at the hands of Germany in the 20th century following an earlier one by France in the 19th century.

Today, the construction of a new wall is in progress, although, curiously, it is not being called a wall. In the Middle East, along the West Bank of the Jordan River, the state of Israel is currently building what has been labeled a "security fence." When completed, it is argued that this fence will serve to protect Israeli citizens from future terrorist incursions from its hostile neighbors.

It is highly controversial, however, as its route is said to encompass large swaths of land which run deep into the West Bank, and which far exceed any previously delineated or recognized boundaries. But some seemingly credible reports indicate that since construction of the fence began, the number of terrorist attacks has declined by more than 90%. Moreover, the number of Israelis murdered and wounded has decreased by more than 70% and 85%, respectively, after erection of the fence. [97]

Here in the US, many people in the desert Southwest favor the construction of a large, physical wall, a forbidding structure which would span some 800 miles. The objective is to keep out illegal immigrants from infiltrating the US border with Mexico, our impoverished neighbor to the south. Seen as a promised land, America has never before

73

considered such a drastic measure, at an economic cost which most concede would be astronomical, at a time when government resources are already stretched thin. Many others feel that resources might be more productively utilized to build roads, bridges, desalination plants, solar farms and other infrastructure components for economic growth.

Some walls are not physical. Rather, they are psychological—and can be more troubling. The human vice of *fear* is most definitely a psychological wall, used by those in a position of authority to assure conformity to a desired behavior. *Envy* is also a very powerful psychological wall, as is *arrogance*. The rich look down upon the poor with arrogance; the poor, in turn, look up on the rich with envy. Within his analysis of labor-ownership strife during the early days of industrialization, Theodore Roosevelt made an astute observation. Finding only a compressed, negative metaphor for an exhausted self and the social forces he sought to mediate, T.R. remarked: "Envy and arrogance are the two opposite sides of the same black crystal." [98]

In this realm, the wall in the form of a so-called "glass ceiling" for women and minorities is also evident. Presently, in fact, of the companies that comprise the Fortune 500, the number being run by women is only 15. [99] While the phrase is merely metaphorical, those who find themselves bumping their heads on it find it very real indeed. It is most often used to describe the sexist (and racist) attitudes which many feel, either accurately or not, in the workplace.

The word "ceiling" implies that there is a limit to how far someone can climb, in a discussion of ascending the corporate ladder of success. It implies further that men, typically, are deeply entrenched in the upper echelons of power, and women and minorities, try as they might, find it nearly impossible to break through. And the idea that it is "glass" means that, while it is very real, it is transparent and not obvious to the casual observer.

The metaphor continues with the British rock band, Pink Floyd, through the phenomenon of a signature work, entitled *The Wall*. Released in 1979, it is the story of a boy who is oppressed by his overprotective mother, and tormented at school by tyrannical, abusive teachers, culminating with the verse, *"We don't need no education./ We don't need no thought control./ No dark sarcasm in the classroom./ ... Hey! Teachers! Leave them kids alone!/ All in all it's just another brick in the wall./ All in all you're just another brick in the wall."*

74

The concept of a wall's protective benefits is explored in tantalizing detail in the 1992 classic movie, *A Few Good Men*. Jack Nicholson plays the villain's role of Col. Jessup, a US Marine officer. He is called to the witness stand by the defense in a military court martial prosecution of two Marines charged with the untimely death of Pr. Willy Santiago, a fellow Marine under Jessup's command. Tom Cruise plays Lt. Kaffee, the defense attorney, who masterfully cross-examines Jessup, baiting him to unwittingly admit to giving the fateful "Code Red" order. This order had set in motion the mechanism for Santiago's death, in which the following classic dialogue takes place:

Col. Jessep: You want answers?

Lt. Kaffee: I think I'm entitled.

Col. Jessep: You want answers?

Lt. Kaffee: I want the truth!

Col. Jessep: You can't handle the truth!

(*pauses*)

Col. Jessep: Son, we live in a world that has *walls*, and those walls have to be guarded by men with guns. Who's gonna do it? You? You, Lt. Weinburg? I have a greater responsibility than you could possibly fathom. You weep for Santiago, and you curse the Marines. You have that luxury. You have the luxury of not knowing what I know. That Santiago's death, while tragic, probably saved lives. And my existence, while grotesque and incomprehensible to you, saves lives. You don't want the truth because deep down in places you don't talk about at parties, you *want* me on that wall, you *need* me on that wall. We use words like honor, code, loyalty. We use these words as the backbone of a life spent defending something. You use them as a punch line. I have neither the time nor the inclination to explain myself to a man who rises and sleeps under the blanket of the very freedom that I provide, and then questions the manner in which I provide it. I would rather you just said thank you, and went on your way. Otherwise, I suggest you pick up a weapon, and stand a post. Either way, I don't give a damn what you think you are entitled to.

Lt. Kaffee: Did you order the Code Red?

Col. Jessep: I did the job I...

Lt. Kaffee: Did you order the Code Red?

Col. Jessep: You're Goddamn right I did!

At the end, the two accused Marines are found Not Guilty on the serious charges of murder and conspiracy to commit murder. But, importantly, they are found Guilty on the charge of conduct unbecoming a US Marine. They are sentenced to time already served and a dishonorable discharge from the Marines. After all, they had executed an order, which was morally flawed.

They shared this insightful, closing exchange:

Pr. Downey: What did that mean? Hal? What did that mean? Col. Jessep said he ordered the Code Red. What did we do wrong?

Corp. Dawson: It's not that simple.

Pr. Downey: We did nothing wrong!

Corp. Dawson: Yeah, we did. We're supposed to fight for people who can't fight for themselves. We were supposed to fight for Willy (Santiago).

***

If the Great Wall had its benefits, in the end it nearly proved to be China's undoing. Similarly, the antitrust exemption which the sport of baseball enjoys may yet prove to be the wall which ultimately causes the demise of America's national pastime. The controversial federal antitrust exemption dates back to 1903, granting baseball the right and *legal* protection to conduct its operations in the form of a monopoly. That is, competition to form a rival baseball league or product is prohibited under the law. The status of a legal monopoly is perhaps the strongest, most efficient kind of wall.

With such a seemingly insurmountable competitive economic advantage, the ordinary citizen might reasonably conclude that the baseball picture is altogether positive and rosy. Well, maybe once rosy. But that is not, in fact, the case anymore. Rather, here is the pattern which evolves over the course of time. It is both familiar and predictable.

Everything starts off well and with the best of intentions. Fast paced, highly entertaining games are the norm, most played in 2 hour or less, all during the daylight. A typical family of four obtains cheap entertainment, including game tickets, a program, a hat, hot dogs, soda, pretzels and a beer. So cheap, in fact, that a ballplayer must have a second job in the offseason to compensate for his meager salary. It is a boy's game, a simple, beautiful game. A tradition is born: baseball, hot dogs and apple pie (and Chevrolet, if you believe the old TV commercial) become part of American folklore. With the full faith and credit of the US government behind it, Major League Baseball (MLB) achieves the pinnacle of success, perhaps justifiably so.

But then, it begins to get complicated. As popularity increases, so do costs and salaries, as a player's right to work where and for whom he chooses is protected. Innovation, however, does not keep pace.

For example, there is neither league regulation nor control of individual player salaries. As a consequence, the payrolls of the 3 highest teams on an active 25 man MLB roster are typically about 450% higher on average than the payrolls of the 3 lowest teams. [100]

Accordingly, MLB has come to be dominated by so-called large market teams like the New York Yankees, dubbed the Evil Empire by its northern rival, the Boston Red Sox, also itself a large market team. Moreover, the totaled salaries of just the 3 highest paid players on the New York Yankees exceed the payrolls of as many as 12 *teams* at the bottom of the team payroll scale. [101] Each team is essentially completely at will to catch what it can, eat what it catches and keep the excess. There does not exist a meaningful sharing of the bounty to "level" the playing field.

A weak, some say nonexistent, central management structure, permits the interests of the large market teams (the rich) to go unchecked. As a result, the small market teams (the poor) have little realistic chance to compete successfully for a world championship. The MLB commissioner has doubled as one of the team owners from 1998 to 2005, when he finally sold his interest in the team both to remove an unnecessary distraction as well as a disturbing conflict of interest. Today, he is seen by many as nothing more than a puppet of the large market teams to protect their "revenue base."

As the general economy continues to unravel, the owners of the large market teams further close ranks to protect their dwindling profits. The heck with the small market teams. This is how capitalism works, these large market owners say. The argument, of course, fits one of the classic rules of human nature: an expectation of reasonable men acting reasonably in their own best interest. At the same time, the weak small market links are neglected and left to fend for themselves. They become weaker still.

Furthermore, teams have the freedom to schedule their games whenever they want, seemingly without restriction, in their own exclusive discretion. With the advent of artificial mass lighting, it is not uncommon on a typical summer night to have a full schedule, consisting only of night games. Not one game is typically played during the day any more, especially during the week, even when kids are out of school on summer vacation. Consequently, despite the fact that there are some 30 teams, there are also countless hours of dead time, when no games are played.

Huge opportunities to stream the product live 24/7 not only to the sport's fan base but future prospects are squandered. To accommodate the nation's west coast viewers, World Series' games, the sport's crown jewel otherwise known as the Fall Classic, begin so late on the east coast that an ordinary citizen is lucky to catch but the first couple of innings.

Marketing is also a patchwork proposition at best. Whatever marketing exists is haphazard, by each of the teams individually. Some teams do little or no marketing at all. The hands of these budget conscious, small market teams are tied by economics, and they are doing all they can simply to survive. They can't afford to make but a single financial mistake in overpaying a player; if they do, they are set back literally for years. And so they are major league teams in name only. In reality, they are suffering, bleeding cash, and their players serving merely as an extended farm system to serve their large market counterparts.

Unfortunately, it gets worse. Each of the two leagues, the National and the American, has evolved to a state where each has its own, different set of rules.

In the National League, for example, the pitcher bats when his turn comes up in the lineup. In the American League, however, there is a unique rule which gives teams the option of replacing the pitcher's batting turn by a so-called designated hitter (DH). Enacted to boost scoring and offensive excitement, and thereby extend the careers of some of the game's older but popular players who, theoretically, could still hit but no longer play the field adequately, the DH rule is well intentioned. But the rule completely changes the strategies that some say helped make the game beautiful. And while the DH rule was designed to be but an experimental, "temporary" arrangement, it has now been in place without interruption since 1973. In the World Series, the rule is in effect only when the American League team is the game's host.

Meanwhile, as the predictable human vice of greed slowly seeps into and overtakes the mindset of the large market owners, the wall is both raised and electrified. The large market owners effectively deploy the barrier of *fear* that change would bring to effectively control the conduct of their small market "brethren" and preserve a failing status quo. With the large market teams firmly in control of the economics picture, the curious MLB culture stifles change, innovation and progress which might actually bring improvement to the quality of the product, and shifts into lockdown mode.

With a legal wall of monopoly protection, the MLB culture has no incentive to innovate, absent competition. All that matters is that profits must be protected, and *are* protected, by the wall. Owners, specifically the large market neighborhood bullies, fight seemingly to the death to keep that wall in place in the name of baseball's "rich tradition." With their artificially created *dependence* on the wall increasing, they have become complacent, lethargic, lazy.

On the other hand, the small market owners act as if they are in a form of suspended animation. They, too, have become *dependent*. However, it is dependence of a different kind. Their dependence is not on the wall but rather exclusively on the generosity of the large market teams for their continued survival. Perhaps they have just become accustomed to the reality of being continually beaten down by their larger market "brethren" to the status of permanent subservience.

Meanwhile, the grand old game is neglected. Nero fiddles while Rome burns, as the expression goes. Whereas games *used to be* played briskly, it has become virtually the routine to see regulation 9 inning games endure for 3 or 4 hours, some even longer. The pace of the game has become excruciatingly slow, the delay time between individual pitches inordinate. Games contain no rhythm, no flow. Increasingly, it is insufferable to watch baseball on TV. The product is simply not watchable.

Invariably, so it seems, someone has a "problem" with a pitch. The batter thinks a called strike was "outside," the pitcher thinks a ball called "high" was a strike; the umpire becomes perturbed with the body language of both pitcher and batter. Adding to the frustration, umpires neither call the strike zone properly nor insist on moving the game along. At times, they make themselves out to be a bigger spectacle than the game. This violates the umpire's cardinal rule.

The use of readily available technology—to help get the calls right, improve the game's quality and move it along—is summarily rejected. For example, innovations such as instant replay and team challenges, which generate interest and are endorsed by fans in all the other major sports, remain but an illusion in MLB. TV increasingly displays a mechanized strike zone alongside the live action in real time, exposing just how often the umpires miss the calls.

The fallibility of the umpires measured up against state of the art technology makes them look like blind squirrels. Although these blown calls can at times be traced directly to change a game's outcome, MLB simply doesn't seem to notice—or care.

MLB fails to recognize that it is but an entertainment product on television, where the real revenue is generated. Rather, it plods along with its head in the sand like TV doesn't even exist, or is a necessary but inconvenient annoyance. Marching to its own tune, oblivious to outside circumstances, MLB says its popularity has never been greater. But the reality is: baseball simply doesn't "get it."

But the news is not apparently all bad. Players no longer have to take a second job in the offseason, for they have, in fact, become millionaires in their own right. Their salaries have reached levels which most find to be unconscionable. The interests of the players are protected by a MLB's players' union to such an extent that the crisis of illegal performance enhancing drugs, the steroid era, has largely gone unchecked. Players are protected, owners are similarly protected. But in this setting there is no central casting, no team bus, essentially there are 25 separate cab rides to the ballpark. But who is looking out for *baseball*, that is, the integrity of the game?

The cumulative effect is that the beauty of the game is diminished. The end result is a slow, painful decline. While there remains some local or regional interest, mainly in some of the large market cities, the game has essentially become irrelevant for the rest of the nation. In truth, this phenomenon has been ongoing for decades. The extent of MLB's decline is such that the idea of baseball as the national pastime exists today in name only. Ultimately, from want of attention, the patient dies a slow death by a thousand small cuts. These are the warning signs.

Is it not interesting to compare MLB's stubbornly individualistic approach to America during the time of the Articles of Confederation? Yet baseball's situation may even be worse, since only the large market teams carry veto rights. While the founding fathers presciently replaced the old Articles on the basis of commitment to a collective identity, MLB continues to teeter, having allowed itself to be bypassed by other forms of entertainment. Despite its earlier dominant market position and legally protected status, and absent the adoption of some basic remedial measures, MLB is in trouble.

It is worthwhile to contrast the path of baseball with that of the National Football League (NFL). Recalling the fierce competition and rivalry to sign players from the old NFL/AFL wars of the 1960s, the first thing the ordinary citizen must appreciate is that the NFL does not have a federal antitrust exemption. There is no corresponding legal wall of protection. However, and by all reasonable measures, the NFL has surged ahead and runs circles around MLB, riding high on a wave of popularity.

This begs the question: How is football different? In its early years football flirted with MLB's individualistic approach. However, in more recent decades the NFL leadership has wisely taken a turn, retaining individual franchise identity but operating instead through a collective framework. Note that the NFL does not appear to have the same structural problems as MLB and is consequently thriving. Perhaps this is more than mere coincidence.

Following the merger of the NFL/AFL into one league, the NFL formula for success has its origins in the collective idea that a chain is only as strong as its weakest link. Noting that there was plenty of money to be made by *all* the respective franchises, the television contract revenue is shared equally by each team. The NFL quickly recognized that it is but a collective, made for television, entertainment product. It has molded the game accordingly.

All games fit neatly into 3.5 hour time segments, perfect for a scheduling format televised by the major TV networks operating in concert. The networks also spread out the timing sequence of the games as directed by the central league offices. On any given Sunday there is NFL football which is broadcast live on prime time, network television for almost 12 straight hours. Then there are the phenomena of Sunday Night and Monday Night football too, widely popular by all accounts, with a few Thursday night and other "special" (Thanksgiving) games thrown into the mix for maximum effect. As the popular pre-game programming song of Hank Williams Jr. asks, *Are you ready for some football?*

Certain technologies (for example, the use of instant replay) have not been rejected. Rather, they have been embraced by way of experimentation. These technologies are innovative and are designed to enhance the quality of the product. What works is kept and expanded upon, what doesn't is discarded.

During the offseason a progressive rules committee tweaks the rules from year to year, improving the game continuously, working with one single set of rules. An ordinary citizen who is old enough may remember plays being sent in to the game by a rotation of substituting tight ends on each successive play. Today that arrangement is no longer necessary. The helmets of both the quarterbacks, offensive and defensive, are wired for audio with the coaches and coordinators on the sidelines, to facilitate the play-calling process.

As a result of all these innovations and incremental improvements, massive television media contracts with *all* the major national broadcasting networks have resulted, transforming the NFL into a financial juggernaut. The revenue numbers are truly staggering. Individual teams generate even more revenue by selling "officially licensed" equipment, clothing and memorabilia, all under the NFL umbrella.

Moreover, the league sets uniform standards to regulate the equally important matter of revenue sharing. A central feature of the NFL is a hard salary cap for players, which limits each team's payroll expense, without exception, from exceeding the designated cap in a given year. Importantly, the salary cap also requires NFL teams to spend at least a stated *minimum* amount on team payroll, thereby setting *both* a ceiling and a floor.

In this way, the playing field is truly level. At the beginning of the season, each of the NFL's teams with few exceptions has a reasonable prospect of competing for a league championship. The notion that either team can win "on any given Sunday" is evidence of football's resulting popularity and ever growing prosperity. The league calls it "parity," a stated goal, which generates broad fan interest and excitement.

The Super Bowl, the showcase championship game, is even played at a neutral, typically warm weather site. Both the half time show and even paid sponsorship TV commercials have become media events in their own right. The success of the group collectively, including the strength of the small market teams, is evident, as both the revenue stream and resulting popularity continue to grow.

Even the NFL's college player scouting combines and draft have been transformed into much hyped media events, spread over several days, which some fans have elevated more to cult status.

In short, the NFL seems to capitalize on just about every available, legitimate marketing opportunity to creatively grow its brand on a national scale. A few regular season games are now even scheduled in Europe, as the game ponders the logistical difficulties but enticing possibilities of expansion to the international arena.

The sum and substance is that few sports fans could argue that football has overtaken baseball as the national pastime, in fact, if not in official title. The determinative measure is the customers casting their vote every season at the cash register.

The NFL's collective approach and selfless visionary ideals are bolstered by its commitment to strengthen its smaller franchises and weaker links, treating them as equals with the large market franchises and at the latter's *voluntary* expense. The arrangement is the brainchild of ownership families with character and smarts. They have old, familiar names—like Mara in New York and Rooney in Pittsburgh.

Is it not evident that this commitment to individualism only through a larger collective identity closely mimics the political condition in the US following the enactment of the US Constitution? Through a series of compromises, the rights and power of even the smallest market teams is assured in the democratic league scheme. The resulting economic success of the NFL is the envy of the nation, as the success of the US continues to be the envy of the world.

***

How does it all turn out? Is there yet time to save baseball from itself before it's too late?

The following story serves as a constructive illustration. Some old friends, a husband and wife team, shared an interesting experience. Their 13-year-old daughter had invited over a girlfriend for a sleepover at their home. As the evening progressed, the two girls could be heard in the adjoining room. They continued to talk late into the evening, cackling away like hens as they prepared for bed. A concerned "mom" entered the bedroom, her voice soothing yet at once taking on more of an authoritative tone: "Now girls! I want the light out by 1:30 (a.m.)." Then, after a brief pause, "and I want you to be sleeping by 2:00 (a.m.)."

The girls kept it up nonetheless and did not, in fact, retire (according to mom, who had, of course, been tuned in, listening for the silence), till about 2:30 a.m. But this was of little consequence, as neither the girls nor mom were at all displeased with what had become an acceptable compromise.

How fortunate were these girls to be the product of a stable childhood, with a fair, but firm, reassuring mother to handle the affairs of the umpire? A selfless role model was looking out for their own best interests, and nothing else. These girls were well on their way to becoming valuable contributing members of adult society and tomorrow's leaders in their own time. And like these girls, the thought occurred: "What baseball *needs* is a mother."

Chapter 5
Distinguishing the Wheat from the Chaff

Another lie and lie the love
Hangin' on, with a push and shove
Possession is the motivation
that is hangin' up the God-damn nation
Looks like we always end up in a rut (everybody now!)
Tryin' to make it real–compared to what?
...

The President, he's got his war
Folks don't know just what it's for
Nobody gives us rhyme or reason
Have one doubt, they call it treason
We're chicken-feathers, all without one gut ...
Tryin' to make it real–compared to what? (Sock it to me, now)

Church on Sunday, sleep and nod
to duck the wrath of God
Preacher's fillin' us with fright
They all tryin' to teach us what they think is right
They really got to be some kind of nuts (I can't use it!)
Tryin' to make it real–compared to what?

- from the song, *Compared To What?*,
by Eugene McDaniels (1969)
Live performance by Les McCann (piano)
& Eddie Harris (saxophone)
available on the *Swiss Movement* collection

***

One of the more challenging and less talked about difficulties of human existence involves distinguishing what is real from that which only appears to be real. Some use the old farmer's cliché of separating the wheat from the chaff. Perhaps it is easier on a farm. In real life, for example, when the vices of greed and pride are presented or appear as virtue, it's not so easy. Beneath every truth and appearance there seemingly lies a measure of paradoxical opposite. Although confounding at times, that which has one guessing keeps life interesting.

Consider the plight of a house packer who toils for the large moving company. His labor is not complete at the end of the day until the homeowner supplies a customary tip. This is neither solicited, nor discouraged.

One such job brings the packing crew into New York City, midtown Manhattan, specifically Park Avenue, which is very much the high rent district. The customer is an old couple, a medical doctor and his wife. The office that assigns the various crews has been forewarned that the wife is very particular in how she wants her things packed. So the office assigns its best crew, to which the neatest packer is assigned as the kitchen guy. The kitchen guy also has the ability to engage the customers in gentle conversation and thereby relax and disarm them. He relates the story.

The crew never did get to see the husband, but the wife was all she was advertised to be, and then some. Physically, she was petite, her posture frail and hunched forward, her eyeglasses sporting impressively thick lenses. She hovered over the crew and seemingly everything they did. As with some of the more lucrative jobs, that is, where the customer had the money, the staff would come in ahead of time to pre-measure wooden crates to protect some of the more expensive items from breakage. The crates would be built off site and then brought in on packing day.

The dining room chandelier was typically one of the most fragile items. And the fixture in this apartment contained more tiny glass crystal ornaments than the kitchen guy had ever seen together in one place. The wife's hovering reached its climax when the moment of truth arrived, the point where the fixture was about to be removed. Its formidable weight was to be transferred gingerly from the ceiling to the four packers, perched precariously below.

If all went well, and in this instance the packers had their fingers crossed, the fixture would be placed gently into the crate, then secured and cushioned for shipment. As the packers contemplated the successful transfer of weight, the wife blared out with an uncanny instinct for timing: "Do you boys know how expensive that chandelier is?" A collective sigh of relief was exhaled when the delicate prize was secured safely, without incident.

The kitchen guy was attending college at the time, on summer break. His employer said that customer did not like part-timers packing their prized possessions. So by prior agreement, a story was made up for the customer, about how he had quit college and was doing this packing job on a full-time basis, while lost and trying to find himself.

The story must have struck a chord of sympathy with the old lady on Park Avenue, her encouragement for the kitchen guy's return to school taking on a passion at nearly every turn. When the job was finished, she had tipped the others outside his presence. The kitchen guy was later to learn that she had tipped *each* $20, a princely sum in those days.

When the kitchen guy's turn came, the old lady pulled him aside and told him the others mustn't see what she was doing for him, given his wretched condition and under the circumstances. Smiling, she confided that while the others were receiving only ordinary money, she had a "special" tip for him, a $10 paper bill of the Confederate States of America. She told him that if he were to place the bill in safe keeping, and keep it in excellent condition, in time it would have significantly more value than what the others had been given. The kitchen guy remembered looking at the bill, then at her, not knowing whether to laugh or cry. But he maintained his composure, thanked her profusely and made his way back to the truck, where the others were waiting to begin the long ride back to home base.

When the crew compared tips, as they invariably did, and heard the kitchen guy's sad story, they howled with laughter, a scene that was for awhile uncontrollable. For the kitchen guy it was unbearable. Of course, he was humiliated. He felt he had been had. While the others were to spend their tip money on beer, the kitchen guy could simply await the day when his tip was to attain value. The kitchen guy was distraught. How cheap could this old goat of a rich doctor's wife be, and how gullible the kitchen guy, that she would pass a Confederate bill off as a thing of value? And to a native New Yorker, no less?

Anger turned quickly to rage, as is the wont of youth. After withstanding the scorn and ridicule of his colleagues, immediately upon returning home, the kitchen guy was alone. Stomping over to the kitchen trash can, he systematically ripped up the bill into a million pieces and deposited the contents therein. Somehow, the exercise released negative energy and made him feel better. He also hoped to forget the episode entirely, which he did.

Fast forward about 30 years. One day, the kitchen guy (who was by then no longer a kitchen guy) was watching that TV show where people bring in their junk to be appraised by experts in the various fields, to determine whether the junk had value, or was just junk. It was innocent enough. But then a woman on the show brought in a paper bill of the Confederate States of America. Though it was more or less worthless in the decades following the Civil War, due to its age, fine condition, and relative rarity, the bill was now worth—somewhere in the *thousands*.

It wasn't until this point that the memory of that old Park Avenue couple was jogged. But unfortunately, not all the story had returned, at least momentarily. The old lady came back, in vivid detail. Somewhere in this house now there was a certain Confederate bill that *could* be worth thousands. But where was it hiding?

The former kitchen guy possessed a small, modest collection of old US coins and a few slips of paper money. He leaped out of the chair, went to the safe box and reviewed the contents. Inexplicably, the Confederate bill was not there. This was not possible. He was *sure* he had such a prize. He continued searching, but still he couldn't put his fingers on it. Where was that little devil?

And then, like a bolt of lightning, the rest of the story came back, including the part about ripping up the bill into a million pieces. Surely, that part was only a dream. His mind was playing tricks on him. After all these years, the bill must still be hiding somewhere. The day of just compensation for packing that old lady's kitchen and safeguarding the care of her chandelier had finally arrived. At last check, the bill is still in hiding, though in truth he still looks for it on occasion whenever he pulls out the collection, just to make sure that it's not there and had simply been misplaced, after all.

***

Separating the wheat from the chaff is a tricky science, not as easy as it may sound. Dad's occupation was an insurance broker. He had done quite well for himself, having raised five children with a traditional, stay at home mom. Dad was a great speaker, not so great at changing a light bulb or a chandelier.

Here's a good example. One day he said, "If you don't remember me for anything else, remember me for this: The best thing a father can give his children—is his mother's time." Now, obviously that statement had a self-interest component, and was ripe for attack on many sociological levels, but the essence of the point was well taken, and remains.

Another day found dad pontificating about the various traps and pitfalls which one must encounter on the way up the corporate ladder of success. As a good friend likes to say, "Remember, the toes you're stepping on today could be attached to the ass you're kissing tomorrow."

Anyway, dad was starting to sound a bit frustrated. He continued with notable passion: "You know, when you get to the top, there's only two things, basically, which you'll find there: cream and human excrement (actually, he used a different word that began with "sh" and ends with "it"). They *both* float to the top. And, as incredible as it may seem to you now, it's exceedingly difficult sometimes to tell the difference between the two!"

What on earth was dad talking about? But today it seems he had been right. Despite his celebrated struggle with floating objects, one of dad's strengths was that he always seemed to judge the character of people extremely well. This greatly aided his career as a salesman, he who lived in a professional world not necessarily of "what was," but rather, "what do you want it to be?" In other words, dad's world was about image making or creative marketing.

For example, US History paints the mid-20th century American Western man as being basic in his needs, fiercely independent, individualistic and self-sustaining, without the need for (government) assistance. The image was of John Wayne, the cowboy, and the Madison Avenue marketing creation of the "Marlboro Man." Moreover, some historians, lusting for a more perfect, utopian society, compared the Kennedy years (President John F. Kennedy, 1960-1963) to Camelot, the fairy tale image suggesting that everything was perfect. In reality, however, most textbooks are in agreement in their assessment that the Kennedy years were, by title, "Something Short of Camelot."

Still others believe they are the sole torch bearers, the reality on which the hope of enlightened progress depends. Consider the example of an old friend and high school classmate, who was required to discharge certain military obligations before continuing with and completing his professional education. This had delayed his graduation from an Ivy League law school by about 7 years.

One of the tables at his wedding reception was filled with his Ivy League classmates. The pre-meal salads were consumed in complete silence, which was most unusual. The only non-Ivy League graduate at the table rose and introduced himself, trying to break the ice and get the festivities rolling. Except that when he had finished, they all simply looked back down to their salad bowls, with neither a hint of interest nor emotion. The non-Ivy Leaguer took the bait with the line, "So, do you people have names, or what?" Thankfully, however, his wife came to the rescue, yanking him back into his seat.

The curse, as was learned later, was the simple sin of not having attended an Ivy League law school, as they had. Such an individual was not worth the expenditure of even an iota of their energy. They were the best and the brightest. They were tomorrow's leaders. Their conduct toward the non-Ivy Leaguer made it perfectly clear that he was not. Despite a 7-year head start on their careers—which is not insignificant in terms of experience—there was wheat, and there was chaff. And that was going to be the way it was.

There are yet other people who walk the walk, talk the talk, and actually sound quite real and legitimate, except that they are fake through and through. The pathological liar is the most egregious example. They live in a nebulous world, their brain short curcuited from the ability to separate fact from fiction. What sets them apart is one would swear they were telling the truth, even when it became certain that they were not. There is no intention to deceive, but the message is clearly disconnected.

Distinguishing what is real from what is merely a facsimile was boiled down to its essence by Bill Parcells, the successful, former NFL head coach with two Super Bowl rings to his credit. One after another, many of his former players have marveled at his uncanny ability to press all the right buttons in a unique timing sequence to motivate each individually to achieve his maximum potential.

Coach Parcells lamented players who made excuses for poor or unacceptable performance. Those players typically attempted to rationalize their particular team's slow start (for example, an 0-3 record out of the gate) with a proviso that the team really was "good" and would turn it around. Coach Parcells would have none of it, however, formulating his standard response: "You are what your record is."

For anyone who has played team sports, it is apparent that such a statement is unassailable. Rarely in life does reality tend to be that black and white.

***

A concrete example of dad's metaphor in action came to America by way of the 1991 Senate confirmation hearings of Clarence Thomas for the position of Associate Justice of the US Supreme Court. Thomas had been nominated for appointment by President Bush "41" to succeed the celebrated Hon. Thurgood Marshall, holder of the so-called "black, liberal seat."

Previously, it had been understood during the Marshall era that the black seat was to be liberal, as Marshall had come to define that seat. This meant a "pro choice" position on the abortion issue. It was expected that Thomas would continue the role of Mr. Justice Marshall seamlessly. Like Marshall, Thomas was black. But unlike Marshall, Thomas was a conservative, who, for example, maintained a contrary "pro life" position. This was bound to create a problem of sorts.

The Bush/"41" nomination of Clarence Thomas sought to upset that balance, with conservatives mobilizing in an attempt to overturn the controversial 5-4 majority decision in the 1973 US Supreme Court case of Roe vs. Wade. The landmark decision had legalized abortion in certain circumstances. And so the significance of a potential successful confirmation of black, conservative Clarence Thomas for Thurgood Marshall's liberal black seat could not well be minimized. The only certainty about the issue of abortion is that Americans remain hopelessly conflicted, with passions on both sides running deep and always seemingly on edge.

At Thomas' US Senate confirmation hearing, things got strange. A witness was put forth to testify in such a fashion as to discredit Thomas and thereby attempt to dissuade the Senate from voting in Thomas' favor. The witness, Anita Hill, was an attractive, educated black woman, who had initially been hired by Thomas in connection with his first federal job appointment. Ms. Hill also worked under Thomas later at the Equal Employment Opportunity Commission (EEOC), where Thomas had headed up that agency as appointed by President Reagan. [102]

91

Disregarding the fact that the allegations supposedly occurred some 10 years earlier, but had not been reported previously, Hill's testimony proved to be a bombshell. She testified in graphic detail how over the course of their years together, Thomas had engaged in a systematic pattern of sexual abuse, harassment and discrimination. Should they choose to find her testimony credible, members of the US Senate had ample justification to turn Thomas' nomination aside. For her part, Anita Hill was articulate, pleasant and sounded very believable. In short, she *seemed* highly credible, and that spelled trouble for Thomas' pending confirmation.

In what was to be his own defense, Clarence Thomas also took the stand, meeting Anita Hill's testimony head on, flatly denying her allegations as an utter fabrication. Thomas compared the motive behind Hill's attack to what was, in his view, the oldest blunt trick in the book: to accuse him of a crime of sexual misconduct. She set out to destroy a black man, in what was still white America. Typically, the misconduct was alleged against a white woman.

Some may recall the classic 1960 novel, *To Kill a Mockingbird*, which took place in a setting of early 1930s rural, white Alabama, at a time when legal segregation of the races was still the law of the land. As the story went, young Atticus Finch, the small town Southern lawyer, played by Gregory Peck in the movie, defended the accused black man. During the course of the trial it was proven beyond question that the attacker was not Finch's helpless client, but rather, the accuser's own father in a crime of incest. Despite the facts, Finch's client was, of course, convicted by the jury, which ultimately led to his lynching before the law could impose sentencing.

What made the allegation even *stronger* in the case of Clarence Thomas, however, was that the accuser in this case, namely Anita Hill, was attractive, believable and black. Thomas testified admirably that his behind-the-scenes adversaries had impressively raised the stakes in his case to the level of "an invitation to a high-tech lynching." His covert opposition had well planned and carefully orchestrated its attack to discredit his testimony, reject his nomination and ultimately destroy his character. It was described as a complete media circus, magnified hysterically by the blossoming power of the internet and the cable news networks.

And so, day after day the battle raged on during the confirmation hearings, broadcast via live TV into the living rooms of ordinary citizens, who watched in fascination. The public was mesmerized, one day by Thomas, the next day Hill, then Thomas again in a final rebuttal. And it seemed all but impossible to tell who was telling the truth. Perhaps we'll never know for sure, the only certainty being that such is the way of the political process. In the end, Clarence Thomas was confirmed by the US Senate by a narrow margin of 52-48 and has been a member of the Supreme Court ever since. Anita Hill landed a secure, fulltime professorship in academia, where she is still employed. And Roe vs. Wade remains the law of the land. We'll touch upon Clarence Thomas again later. [103]

Some characters are, in fact, wheat as opposed to chaff, but were perhaps the subject of poor timing, or the whim of the then-prevailing popular opinion. For example, there is former US Senator Barry Goldwater, R-AZ, the architect of the present day conservative movement for individual initiative and responsibility, a strong, national defense and small, frugal, debt-free government. Goldwater's ideas created a movement which inspired southern white Democrats, the so-called "solid South" dating back to the pre-Civil War era, to leave their party and join the Republican Party. They remain there firmly today. It was the second (of only two) major social and political transformation of the 20th century.

In the presidential election of 1964 Goldwater had been defeated in a landslide. But Ronald Reagan would be elected a mere 16 years later, in 1980, on virtually the identical Goldwater political platform. And as the Congressional mid-term election setbacks of Mr. Reagan in 1982, Bill Clinton in 1994, and President Barack Obama in 2010 further demonstrate, even popular, successful leaders are apt, in certain instances, to be the subject of particularly poor timing.

The balance of this chapter is dedicated to the memory of two great American heroes who featured indomitable will and supreme self-confidence. Andrew Jackson was the iconic champion of the common man, a highly distinguished military general in his own right and, later, two term president. And William T. Sherman was the brilliantly successful military general of Civil War fame.

Each has a well earned reputation, strictly on merit. Neither is without controversy. Their stories contain at least a modicum of reality on the wheat vs. chaff litmus test scale.

***

The colorful Andrew Jackson was the epitome of a self made man. His father had died before Jackson was born, in the year 1767. When he was still very young, Jackson's mother left him and his older brother to care for the Revolutionary War soldiers, who had been wounded in action and were convalescing. As a result, Jackson had grown up as an orphan on his own.

During the Revolutionary War, a British soldier arrogantly demanded that the young boy get down on his knees and clean the soldier's boots, immediately. At the time, Jackson was but age 13 and quite impressionable. When he refused to obey the order on grounds that he was a prisoner of war, the soldier lashed out at him with his sword. Jackson ducked and partially deflected the blow with his left hand, blunting its full force. The resulting deep gash left a permanent indentation on Jackson's skull and fingers. The episode served as a reminder for the rest of his life of his extreme contempt for all things British. [104]

Later, at age 39, already having achieved the military rank of General, Jackson had gotten into a scrap with a local braggart on the frontier of western Tennessee. It seemed incredible that the slightest misunderstanding over the "merest word play" should lead to tragedy. However, each demanding "satisfaction" from the other, the two agreed to a duel. Jackson's adversary was a man of local prominence, who was also known to be one of the best shots in Tennessee. For his part, Jackson knew that neither his aim nor speed at the draw of a pistol was any match.

Understanding this, together with his second, he devised a plan. The two calculated that the only way he could survive the duel, and win, was to let his adversary draw first and hope that the wound inflicted upon him would not be fatal. Amazingly, the plan worked. His adversary's quick shot had shattered two of Jackson's ribs and buried in his chest, but it had missed his heart. Whereupon, Jackson calmly raised his left arm and clenched it against his throbbing chest, took aim with his own pistol, and fired.

The bullet struck his adversary in the chest, passed clean through his body, leaving a gaping hole from which he bled to death.

The bullet in Jackson's own chest could not be removed, because it was lodged so close to Jackson's heart. The wound never healed properly. His discomfort was considerable. For many years thereafter, Jackson suffered intense physical pain, on account of a gunfight to restore his reputation. "I should have hit him," Jackson said at the time, "if he had shot me through the brain." [105]

What set Jackson apart was his willpower, which was *not* ordinary, nothing normal or even natural. It was superhuman, almost demonic, sheer total, concentrated determination to win and thus achieve his goals, at whatever cost. Consequently, as the preceding story illustrates, Jackson was capable of extraordinary feats of courage, daring and perseverance in the face of incredible odds. Nothing less than victory was acceptable. Defeat was unthinkable. This fierce exercise of will, supported by supreme self-confidence and a healthy measure of talent, shaped his considerable triumphs.

Andrew Jackson's most distinguishing physical feature was his bright, deep, blue eyes, which could shower sparks when passion seized him. Anyone could tell his mood by watching his eyes; and when they started to blaze it was a signal to get out of the way *quickly*. But they could also register tenderness and sympathy, especially around children, when they generated a warmth and kindness that was most appealing.

As a military man, his singular determination was instrumental to rid what is today the Southeastern section of the US of peoples arguably hostile to a growing America. First, resistance from the native American Indians to democratic government had been finally overcome. And second, Jackson's military undertakings eliminated once and for all both Spain and Great Britain as foreign influences, in the name of military protection from outside threats. It was the sheer determination of Andrew Jackson alone, it has been said, which was largely responsible for the present shape of our Southeastern border. As some have noted, imagine how differently the final borders of the US might look today, had Jackson's energies been expended toward our northern, rather than southern, boundaries.

His success as a military general for achieving victory against long odds was also legendary, in particular during the Battle of New Orleans, which occurred during the War of 1812. During this famous battle, Gen. Jackson had drawn together a seemingly rag tag collection of disjointed poor Southern whites, black slaves, Indians, local Creole and Cajun mixes, and even illegal shipping pirates. All had nothing much in common, other than the unifying goal to defend their city from foreign occupation.

An impressively large naval flotilla had been sent by Great Britain, the most powerful military nation on earth, to capture the city of New Orleans. The British goal was to control navigation of the Mississippi River and thereby send the upstart Americans a clear message of military superiority. Jackson's "forces" were outnumbered in military strength by a factor of almost 3 to 1, and a good number of his men had received only limited, if any, prior training.

The British invasion of New Orleans had begun a month earlier, but the climactic four-day battle was waged in early January 1815. During the battle, Jackson's forces fought valiantly, not only defending but also counter-attacking, startling the British into retreat and, ultimately, defeat. At the conclusion of this decisive battle, the British had lost more than just a battle, and Jackson's reputation as an American Hero had been immortalized. [106]

Andrew Jackson had succeeded well beyond the modest expectations of many an expert. The British threat had been eliminated from New Orleans and the US assured exclusive navigation of the mighty Mississippi. Unable or unwilling to curb Indian incursions into the border states, Spain subsequently ceded to the US the Florida territory, which was admitted to statehood in 1815. And by the controversial Indian Removal Act of 1830, those native Indian tribes which chose not to submit lawfully to the various state governments within the federal authority were removed forcibly to western locations. Although a Trail of Tears ensued, leaving many of the displaced Indians dead along their path to relocation west of the Mississippi, there remained a promise of continued autonomy and perpetuation of their culture.

Projecting his success into the political sphere, Jackson ran for the nation's highest office in the election of 1824. Although he had a decisive advantage in both the popular and electoral votes cast, the total was insufficient for victory by any one of the four candidates. In that case, the US Constitution provided that the election was to be decided by the House of Representatives, where each state would have a single vote, not bound to the results of the general election.

Essentially, Jackson claimed that his adversary, John Quincy Adams, had cut a back room deal with US Rep. Henry Clay, KY. The story went that if Clay could orchestrate the presidency to Adams, JQA would, in turn, appoint Clay as Secretary of State. Thereafter, Adams would repay Clay's political cronies by implementing a massive federal spending program to implement Clay's "American System." When the vote was tallied in the House of Representatives, Clay's state of Kentucky, which had gone to Jackson in the general election, cast its sole in behalf of JQA. The presidency was claimed by JQA in what Jackson referred to as a "Corrupt Bargain."

Jackson pressed the corruption theme all through what would become a tumultuous and contentious JQA presidency. He positioned himself as a corruption fighter and reformer for the next presidential election of 1828, in which this time Jackson defeated JQA handily. Jackson's ascendancy to the presidency ushered in America's first era of reform. He himself called it "reform, retrenchment and economy," by which he attempted to end an era of corruption and restore the country and the government to virtue and honesty. [107]

But the victory would not come without a considerable price. Jackson had shielded Rachel, his wife of many years, from the usual campaign vitriol. But in preparation for the trip to her husband's presidential inauguration, which was to be held in the nation's capital, she had visited her hairdressers' shop. Mistakenly, a frail and emotionally weak Rachel picked up and read a piece of particularly vindictive campaign literature, which was pointed at her. She suffered a breakdown, and quickly succumbed.

Delivering her eulogy at The Hermitage, the family's Tennessee plantation, Jackson uttered some chilling words, calmly, firmly and in such deep silence that they were heard distinctly by everyone in the room:

"Friends and neighbors," he began, "I thank you for the honor you have done to the sainted one whose remains now repose in yonder grave. She is now in the bliss of heaven, and I know that she can suffer here no more on earth. That is enough for my consolation; my loss is her gain. But I am left without her to encounter the trials of life alone." Jackson paused at that point as though meditating on what he had just said. "I am now President of the United States," he continued after the pause, "and in a short time must take my way to the metropolis of my country; and if it had been God's will, I would have been grateful for the privilege of taking her to my post of honor and seating her by my side; but Providence knew what was best for her. For myself, I bow to God's will, and go alone to the place of new and arduous duties, and I shall not go without friends to reward, and I pray God that I may not be allowed to have enemies to punish." His eyes kindled a little as he spoke these words. "I can forgive all that have wronged me, but will have fervently to pray that I may have grace to enable me to forget or forgive any enemy who has ever maligned that blessed one who is now safe from all suffering and sorrow, whom they tried to put to shame for my sake!" With that Jackson ended his short eulogy, but everyone in the room was deeply moved by what he had said. "We can never forget it," said one. [108]

As a widower for its duration, Jackson assumed and executed the office of the presidency, but he did not forget. Jackson never forgot. Picking up where Thomas Jefferson had left off, he had articulated the fundamental doctrine of Jacksonian Democracy long before his presidency:

The obligation of the government to grant no privilege that aids one class over another, to act as honest broker between classes, and to protect the weak and defenseless against the abuses of the rich and powerful. [109]

Much of this language appeared in his message accompanying his veto and ultimate demise of the national bank re-charter bill in 1832. Facing re-election to a second term, he had been warned by his advisers that the bank issue was too hot, too risky, that any action as to the national bank's continued existence should come after the election.

Disregarding the warning, however, President Jackson instead chose to make the bank re-charter the central issue of the election of 1832. During the course of events, citing an example of the corruption that had been commonplace to the era, he had uncovered a damaging letter, written by a Congressman to the bank president. The letter openly lamented that the Congressman's bank "retainer" had been exhausted and should thereby be replenished at once. Jefferson's earlier warning of an "influence" by the money interest over the legislature had come home to roost, in plain view.

Consequently, President Jackson figured that the people would have a clear choice: they could either vote for him, or they could vote for the bank and the corruption it had come to represent. What made the challenge even more enticing was his opponent in the election, Henry Clay, who supported the bank. As he had put it to Martin Van Buren, the "Little Magician," as his loyal colleague from the state of New York was called:

> 'The bank, Mr. Van Buren, is trying to kill me, *but I will kill it.*' He said this very quietly, without any passion or tone of rage. Nor was it a boast. Just a simple statement of fact. [110]

A fierce battle against the challenge of an openly corrupt Congress ensued. Congress reacted predictably to Jackson's planned maneuvers, denying key Jackson appointments to the positions of Secretary of State (Martin Van Buren) as well as Secretary of the Treasury (Roger Taney). Congress' stated grounds were that these men were "unfit" to hold office. Never to be deterred, President Jackson upped the ante. During the 1832 election campaign, he proposed to make Van Buren his new Vice President and Taney the new Chief Justice of the US Supreme Court, if he were to win the election. The people would have another clear choice, as between his judgments, against those of Congress.

Of course, the people sustained him, as they always did. President Jackson was re-elected by a popular vote of 55%-42% and an overwhelming majority in the electoral college. Thereafter, as promised, he effectively killed the national bank, first by authorizing that federal deposits should be re-routed elsewhere. Henceforth, the deposits would be directed to a group of smaller, state "pet" banks, so as to end the national bank's monopolistic practices and promote fair competition. In a coy move, he did this while Congress was not in session. When Congress returned, it publicly censured him for acting without its cooperation. Later, however, Jackson having been sustained by the people, and the wisdom of the move becoming certain, Congress had no choice but to rescind the censure and thank him.

President Jackson left office in 1836, after serving two hugely successful and popular presidential terms. Yet, he continued to have a considerable influence on the national political scene through the decade of the 1840s.

Of course, the present account is not intended to be exhaustive, which would be all but impossible in this limited space. But an early biographer had interestingly summed up Andrew Jackson in this way:

> Columbus had sailed; Raleigh and the Puritans had planted; Franklin had lived; Washington fought; Jefferson written; fifty years of democratic government had passed; free schools, a free press, a voluntary church had done what they could to instruct the people; the population of the country had been quadrupled and its resources increased ten fold; and the result of all was, that the people of the United States had arrived at the capacity of honoring Andrew Jackson before all other living men. [111]

The accolades continued. "He is a much abler man than I thought him," commented one US Senator from Pennsylvania, "one of those naturally great minds which seem ordinary, except when the fitting emergency arises." [112]

It has been said that no American ever had so powerful an impact on the minds and spirit of his contemporaries as did Andrew Jackson. As late as the election of 1844, Andrew Jackson was instrumental in the election of President James Polk, a fellow Tennessean, claiming supreme satisfaction in having defeated Henry Clay now for a third time (1824, 1832 and 1844). In fact, no other man ever dominated an age spanning so many decades. "No one, not Washington, Jefferson, or Franklin, ever held the American people in such near-total submission."

Remarkably, as a testament to the devotion and confidence of the people—if not madness, some continued to vote for him in numbers for President of the United States nearly fifteen years after his death. As the nation stumbled toward the crisis of Civil War, these votes desperately sought to summon him from his grave to rescue once again his beloved country. [113]

And, lastly, in Andrew Jackson's own words:

> When I review the arduous administration through which I have passed, the formidable opposition I have met to its very close, by the combined talents, wealth, and power of the whole aristocracy of the Union, aided as they were, by the money monopoly, US Bank, with its power of corruption, with which we had to contend, the result must not only be pleasing to me, but to every patriot. It shows the virtue and power of the sovereign people, and that all must bow to public opinion. It was the sovereign people that nobly sustained me against this formidable power, and enabled me to terminate my administration so satisfactory to the great body of the democracy of our Country. [114]

* * *

Finally, in the case of William T. Sherman, a somewhat different story of a real American hero presents itself, although his nature was indeed eerily similar to that of Andrew Jackson. The letter "T" in his name stood for Tecumseh, the Shawnee Indian chief of legendary fame, for whom the baby's father had taken a fancy. He had been given the name of Tecumseh Sherman upon his birth in Ohio in 1814, where he spent his youth. His mother, an ardent Catholic, had wanted for him to be baptized. But the fortunes of his father, who had reached the level of the Ohio Supreme Court, went downhill as a result of one of the many nuances of the national bank. As a result, his father had gone into debt and died, causing the breakup of his family.

Young Tecumseh Sherman ("Cump" for short), a flaming redhead, was taken in by the family of friends, but never formally adopted. Treated as an equal in the family, religion was the first thing attended to, the children being taught by a Dominican priest. When it was brought to the priest's attention that Cump had never been baptized, someone ran down the block to ask his mother if he might be baptized by the priest. His mother consenting, Cump was taken into the parlor, where the priest asked the boy's name. Told it was Tecumseh, the priest pointed out that a scriptural or saint's name had to be used in the ceremony. Since it happened to be St. William's Day, Tecumseh was baptized William. From that day forward, although he was not a Catholic, the 15-year-old became William T. Sherman. [115]

Sherman attended West Point, graduating in 1840, and remained in the military service until 1852, although he did not see action in the recently concluded Mexican-American War. Like that of numerous other West Point graduates, he muddled through good times and bad, seeking the means to support a growing family. He spent some time as a surveyor, lawyer (for which it was said he had more common sense than ability) and banker; although he stated that he had regretted leaving the army.

When hostilities began that marked the launch of the Civil War, Sherman was the superintendent of the Louisiana Seminary of Learning, known better today as the Louisiana State University. It was said that Sherman had more friends on the Southern side, perhaps, than any other military leader from either side. But Sherman objected to Louisiana's secession, causing him to leave the South and return to St. Louis, where he had spent some time earlier. [116]

Six months into the Civil War, as a Union officer, Sherman had estimated that it would take some 200,000 troops to defend the Western borders (understood to be Ohio, Kentucky and Indiana) from rebel infiltration. At the time, few understood either the scale or the magnitude of the growing conflict. Consequently, questioning where these men were to come from, his superiors placed him on temporary leave, on the report that he was "crazy, insane and mad." [117]

After the war, it would be scary to learn just how accurate Sherman's own estimate of required troop strength had proven to be, the others having grossly underestimated the figures.

Sherman considered himself to be "as a second self" to his trusted colleague, Gen. U.S. Grant. [118] Their relationship was said to be legendary and a decisive factor in the North's victory. When asked later to confirm the rumor of Grant's tendency to abuse alcohol, Sherman remarked: "Grant stood by me when I was crazy, and I stood by him when he was drunk." The level of Sherman's friendship with and loyalty to Grant was also quite rare and special.

During the early days of the Civil War, it was Sherman who had literally begged a despondent Grant not to quit, after Grant had been repeatedly passed over for promotion. [119] In the siege of Fort Donelson, in what would portend future movements, Grant recorded the following observation of his colleague:

> During the siege General Sherman had been sent to Smithland, at the mouth of the Cumberland River, to forward reinforcements and supplies to me. At that time he was my senior in rank and there was no authority of law to assign a junior to command a senior of the same grade. But every boat that came up with supplies or reinforcements brought a note of encouragement from Sherman, asking me to call upon him for any assistance he could render and saying that if he could be of service at the front I might send for him and he would waive rank. [120]

William T. Sherman was selfless. He possessed a singularity of purpose, a will of steel, a discipline for planning, preparation and execution, leaving no stone unturned. These were the rare personality traits which he shared with the likes of Andrew Jackson.

In the campaign toward the election of 1864, Lincoln's campaign was teetering, his determination and perseverance notwithstanding.

His opponent was former Gen. McClellan, who Lincoln had fired for perfecting procrastination and an unwillingness to engage in battle to an art form. McClellan had returned to Washington to run for president essentially on the platform that the war was a failure, there had been enough bloodshed and the South should be let go. [121]

But Gen. Sherman's successful siege and the eventual fall of Atlanta ("Atlanta was ours and fairly won") re-energized the North and catapulted the president to an upset re-election victory.

From there, Sherman's passionate yet logical argument convinced both Lincoln and Grant that it was necessary for the North to *demonstrate* decisively to the Confederacy its military superiority. Gen. Sherman proposed the execution of a military maneuver through the very heart of the Confederacy, laying out a plan to slice it in half and hasten the war's conclusion. While the plan was fraught with both risk and peril, the overwhelming benefits, if successful, could not be underestimated.

Sherman's plan called for his army to be authorized to leave Atlanta, cut its own supply *and* communication lines, and live instead off the hostile, native lands in foraging his army from Atlanta to Savannah. This was the architecture of the famous March to the Sea: a 300 mile long, 60 mile wide path of destruction and infamy, a full 200 miles of railroad track destroyed. Sherman's army, 70,000 men strong, would leave a path of utter destruction and a physical scar on the landscape, the reminders of which would endure for generations to follow. All was executed successfully, on foot, in just over 30 days.

But it did not always appear that it was going to end up that way. During the march, the local Southern newspapers that Sherman and his men would read along the way foretold how his men were scared, starving and desperate, against what was the eventual reality. The truth is that neither side would know for sure the result of the venture, until upon their arrival Sherman's men gave the pre-determined signal to the Union ships waiting offshore of Savannah's coast. Only then were both the scope and magnitude of the success known to both sides. The reward? Sherman dedicated the capture of Savannah as an 1864 "Christmas present" to President Lincoln and the Union.

From there, Gen. Sherman's army turned north, feinting movements on both Charleston, South Carolina to the east and Augusta, Georgia to the west. He marched his army right through the center of those two locations, intending all along to unleash its full fury on the state capital at Columbia, South Carolina. It was at this official home location that the cradle of the confederacy would receive its repayment in kind from Sherman's Union army. After orchestrating the systematic, physical destruction of Columbia, including all official documents, his army continued northward.

As the army crossed over into North Carolina, the destruction would cease, on orders from President Lincoln, who wanted to provide the South with an inducement to surrender. Further, Sherman remembered "Mr. Lincoln's repeated expression that he wanted the rebel soldiers not only defeated, but 'back at their homes, engaged in their civil pursuits.'" [122] Finally, Sherman's army came to rest along the Raleigh-Durham line, up against the army of the Confederate Gen. Joe Johnston. Sherman would receive in that location the terrible news to the cause of peace, that is, the assassination of President Lincoln.

At that moment Sherman commanded what was then understood to be the most powerful army ever assembled on earth. But in another extreme test of will, he had to demonstrate the utmost in restraint of his men in breaking the news to them. Sherman reminisced later and was "gratified that there was no single act of retaliation" by his men. He feared that all he had to do was look at his men the wrong way, "that one single word by me would have laid the city in ashes, and turned its whole population houseless upon the country, if not worse." [123]

Gen. Sherman retired from the army in 1884, showing persistent, personal disdain both for politics and ambition. Famously, he refused to be considered a candidate for president, although his choice could be seen as somewhat obvious after Grant's two terms had run their course. The episode culminated in word sent from the Republican Convention that his name was the only one which could be agreed upon.

Without changing his expression, this colorful, yet controversial, American hero drafted his reply: "I will not accept if nominated and will not serve if elected." He tossed the note to the messenger for delivery and "went on with the conversation … as if the Presidency was to him nothing." [124]

On his deathbed, the place where we all must go, Sherman had requested to his daughter, Mille, that these words should be put on his tombstone: "Put 'Faithful and honorable; faithful and honorable!' " [125] Unveiled in 1903, his bronze, equestrian statue, like its granite base figure, is gilded, and follows Lady Liberty. It presently decorates the Fifth Avenue entrance to Central Park, New York City. [126]

Chapter 6
Equal Access to the American Economic Opportunity Structure

Some folks are born made to wave the flag
Ooh, they're red, white and blue
And when the band plays 'Hail to the Chief'
Oo, they point the cannon at you, Lord.

It ain't me, it ain't me
I ain't no Senator's son
It ain't me, it ain't me
I ain't no fortunate one, no

Some folks are born silver spoon in hand
Lord, don't they help themselves, oh
But when the tax men come to the door
Lord, the house look a like a rummage sale, yes
...
Yeah, some folks inherit star spangled eyes
Ooh, they send you down to war
But when you ask them how much do you give?
Ooh, they only answer "more, more, more"

It ain't me, it ain't me
I ain't no millionaire's son
It ain't me, it ain't me
I'm no fortunate one

- from the song, *Fortunate Son,*
by Credence Clearwater Revival (1969)

***

I ain't no Senator's son either, unfortunately. Is it any wonder that we seem to know very little of the sons and daughters of our US Senators? Or of other historically noteworthy citizens? Perhaps this is because, typically, born with the silver spoon, as the song goes, the house looks like a rummage sale. That is to say, they don't amount to much. Call it human nature.

107

But a few notable exceptions come to mind in our own lifetime. Roger Goodell, the current and only 3rd commissioner in NFL history, is one. Mr. Goodell has picked up where his predecessor left off, growing rather nicely into the job he landed in 2006, leading the NFL to new heights of prosperity. He is the son of Charles Goodell, the late US Senator, R-NY, appointed to his seat by Gov. Nelson Rockefeller to fill the vacancy upon the assassination of US Sen. Robert F. Kennedy, D-NY in 1968. Did the connection assist the commissioner in obtaining his first NFL position, an administrative internship in the league offices in 1982? Did it assist him in being named commissioner? It certainly couldn't hurt.

Another is Al Gore, the former two term Vice President to Pres. Bill Clinton and the winner of the consolation prize in the hotly, and legally, contested presidential election of 2000. Gore's father had been a US Senator from Tennessee, as was Mr. Gore at one time. Before beginning his years of public service, however, Mr. Gore served time in Vietnam in 1969, having enlisted in the army. He reasoned that he did not want someone with fewer options than he to go in his place. A 1969 graduate of Harvard University, he would become one of only about a dozen of the 1,115 members of his class who went to Vietnam.

Since the election of 2000, Mr. Gore has been involved mostly in environmental causes, founding and serving as the current chair of the Alliance for Climate Protection. He has also been on a campaign to educate citizens about global warming via a comprehensive slide show that, by his own estimate, he has given more than a thousand times. The slide show is the subject of the 2006 documentary film, *An Inconvenient Truth*, winner of an Academy Award in 2007. He was also the subject of a joint award with the Intergovernmental Panel on Climate Change of the Nobel Peace Prize, also in 2007. He has championed the idea of stewardship of the environment as a moral issue, more than anything else.

Yet another is President George H.W. Bush "41" who was the son of US Sen. Prescott Bush, R-CT, a Wall Street banker. That makes Prescott a pretty distinguished fellow. He was the father of one president, the grandfather of another president (George W. Bush "43") and the grandfather of the Governor of Florida, Jeb Bush, who many believe is also presidential material.

And although he was not the *son* of a US Senator, Gen. Sherman had friends in high places looking out for him, too, among the politicians

108

in Washington, D.C. His *brother*, John, was a political mover and US Senator from Ohio during the General's time. Subsequently, John Sherman would become a future Secretary of State and the primary sponsor of major federal anti-monopoly legislation, which dates back to the 1890s.

Two of our 44 US Presidents were the sons of presidents: John Quincy Adams was the son of John Adams, and the aforementioned Bush "43" the son of Bush/"41." As distinguished was the career of each son of a president, the question for the ordinary citizen remains: Would either have had the remote chance to become President of the United States if his respective father weren't?

Put another way, who holds the keys to the video room? Who among us commands access to the American economic opportunity structure? An ordinary citizen who dismisses these questions would be well served to consider the following proposition. Understanding this complicated dynamic may provide the essential force in identifying what is necessary to preserve the American Dream. The stakes cannot be fairly understated.

***

The inquisitive mind may peer across to the green grass on the other side of the fence and wonder why the neighbor next door works at the job he has. Why would the neighbor suffer the angst of running his own business? Consider the individual who chooses to run a solo law practice. Surely there would be days when even the simplest task seemed impossible to complete without the expenditure of Herculean effort.

The job interview process is a subject all its own. A young, inexperienced job applicant may receive this typical feedback: "You're well dressed. You present well. You appear to have *exactly* what we're looking for, *except* you don't have enough experience." Then, perhaps 5 years later, the feedback changes notably to "You appear to have exactly what we're looking for, except you have *too much* experience."

The older, experienced professional who is held in great respect by the community might tell the aspirant to "Just keep doing what you're doing, and one day your break will come. Someone had told me the same thing when I myself was younger, and that's exactly what happened." But, sometimes, many times, the break never does come.

Meanwhile, the individual is convinced he has worked for a series of incompetent idiots as bosses. His spouse may rightfully ask him, "Let me get this straight: They're the idiots, yet *you* work for *them*." He accepts the advice in good nature and endeavors to figure it out. This neutral observation helps him to break the *barrier* of fear, that he knew how to end up in hell in a hand basket all by himself, without anyone's help in particular. Failure he could deal with. That was the day he decided to just up and quit and start his own business from scratch.

Of course, there is much more to it than that, but every movement requires a spark.

***

Those who attend school "straight through" complete their first, formal phase of education by the time of their mid-20s. Like most students who have had the privilege of higher education, they are wise to consider it a cherished blessing and conduct themselves accordingly. But for many, a second, informal phase of education and personal development begins, sometime after the 40th birthday, although this is by no means a magic date.

Typically, they are indebted for this to their parents, who undoubtedly pushed education as the primary means to sustain one through the economic uncertainties and vicissitudes of life's trials and tribulations. A wise parent will say that "An education is something no one can take away from you. If you have an education, you can always find work." Sure, one needs money to buy the fish to eat, or, to rely precariously on the generosity of the particular fisherman. But if one learns how to fish, reliance upon someone else for sustenance will be unnecessary. An education teaches the individual how to fish. It is simple, irrefutable logic. And it makes good, common sense.

But what if the individual didn't like what he had studied to become? What if he was too young, immature or naïve to know any better? What if he was doing it because people like his trusted parents said he'd be good at it, even if they *happened* to be right? What if he was doing it strictly for the money? What if he was doing it because it's what he *thought* he'd want to spend his life doing, except he later changed his mind? Finally, what if he had persevered with great discipline and resolve to land that "dream" job, landed that job and performed it successfully for many more years, discovering that there came a point where he didn't enjoy doing it anymore?

Unfortunately, most parents are ill-prepared to help answer these questions.

Where exactly is it written that the individual has to do what it is he does for the rest of his life? A typical and not unreasonable parental response might go something like this: "What else *could* you do? The law is what you *know*." The inference is clear. There is nothing else the individual is trained to do, so therefore, that is what must be done.

And there it is. The devil you know is preferable to the devil you don't know. It is Plato's *Allegory of the Cave* all over again. Human nature is such that we seek a comfort level. Once achieved, we find it is exceedingly difficult to break out of that zone. It is the pull and tug of the lure of change vs. the security and comfort of the status quo. Call it fear of the unknown. Call it thinking inside the box vs. thinking outside the box. Whatever one chooses to call it, the idea of change evokes a fear response, a fear of the unknown. This is a natural feeling. This is human nature. Typically, the great majority of humans seek to play it safe, to be risk averse. To choose change over the status quo, then, one supposes that things have to be really pretty awful to finally break through that barrier.

Our society has an expectation of what people are supposed to do with their lives. If one graduates from law school, one is expected to be a lawyer. If one is trained as an architect, one should work as an architect. An old friend went to law school and never cared for it. She cared for the day-to-day practice of law even less. After practicing law for about six years, she stopped and never looked back.

The various reactions of ordinary people to her not practicing law are not without a humorous component. Once, while she was the project manager on a house she had designed, the kitchen installer told her he felt it was "such a waste" that she no longer practiced law. She responded, "No it's not. You know what would be a waste? To do something I dislike for the rest of my life, just because I went to school for it for three years in my 20s." She has joined the ranks of people who have turned away from their "professional" training and chosen to mold their lives in a less conventional manner. In fact, and not surprisingly, only 50% or thereabouts of law school graduates actually engage in the practice of law.

In life there are no dress rehearsals. When an individual reflects on his earlier years, he can be amazed at how much he thought he knew, measured against how little in reality he actually did know. Some say it is the difference between being book smart vs. experience smart. It's knowing that the lessons learned as a kid on the playground in grade school may be more relevant and important than the high-minded intellectual concepts studied later in professional school. It's also the difference between knowing when to talk, and knowing when to shut up and listen. Others say it's the difference between amassing knowledge and gaining wisdom. In all respects, anyway, it is for others to measure.

This second informal phase of education and personal development on the path to lifelong learning involves a shift—from "*what* is the law"—to "*why* is it the law." How many times are the familiar words uttered: "If only I knew *then* what I know *now*." The truth is there is always more to learn. If the individual didn't know what he *now* thinks he knows, and there is always more to learn, then perhaps he would be unable to make this connection.

Whether it's about politics, religion or even the local Little League program, it makes good sense and is prudent to question the motives of the leaders involved. What do *they* have to gain, or lose, should a particular policy which is being put forth prevail? Or whether the institution permits discussion of any changes to its arranged order? In dealing with human nature, doesn't it seem that self-interest is typically the proponent's top priority? Even (especially) if it does not appear to be presented that way? And is the delivery of the proposal true and unbiased, as Jeffersonian simplicity would demand, or are the familiar forces of physical and psychological manipulation hard at work?

Membership in the US Congress provides an illuminating example. A typical grade schooler may justifiably believe that the 535 individuals who comprise the US Congress (435 from the House of Representatives and 100 from the Senate) stand on a higher intellectual plane. They are seen as idealists who maintain character and integrity first and foremost. These lawmakers subordinate their own self-interests, bestowing favor instead upon policies for the benefit of the masses. After all, this is the oath they have taken to public service. They are distinguished citizens, people who are esteemed, respected and admired for all they have accomplished and stand for. And as for those in the Senate, the more reserved, deliberative body, it is all the more so.

A typical grade schooler may continue to think this way for many years, until learning Abraham Lincoln's views. Many ordinary citizens are unaware that Lincoln was a member of the House of Representatives in 1846, where he served a brief, two year term, some 15 years before he was elected president. The grade schooler would be much pleased to learn that Lincoln shared at the outset the same speculations and musings about the character and motivations of the men who filled the seats of Congress, and who he was about to meet, encounter and interact with.

But when he had occupied his own seat, then-Congressman Lincoln's views changed. He quickly became disappointed, finding members by and large to be "men of mediocre ability and only local reputation." [127] This was a huge letdown for Lincoln. The thought also strikes the grown up grade schooler with a dull thud. It provokes another sobering question: If that was the makeup of Congress *then*, could it possibly be any different *now*?

How did these men get there? To the US Congress, that is. Then and now, were they simply born into status, wealth, aristocratic and hereditary privilege? Were they handed the opportunity as a matter of expectation and routine that, to some, would be treated otherwise with a great deal more care and circumspection? Some use the interesting term "crony capitalism" to describe this phenomenon as it is applied in the world of business. But it applies to the world of politics as well.

Lincoln was a self-taught intellectual pioneer of the Western back country. The benefit of his non-traditional education was that there were no pre-ordained topics that he had to be or become familiar with, no books he *had* to read. As a student of human nature, Lincoln's learning was also a lifelong process.

Intellectually, the idea of lifelong learning is like using the TV remote (with a DVR, of course). The reader of the printed word gets to jump back and forth, to and fro between "channels" or topics, and can pause, stay as long as he wants or move on at his own pace and pleasure. If the reader likes what he's reading, he can stay with it, easily discover where more material can be located, and delve into greater detail. He can concentrate on one subject, or, as some do, read multiple things at the same time.

Although no "paper degree" is conferred by and through this exercise, the state of happiness and contentment reached is extremely rewarding. It's all a gigantic debt of gratitude owed to extremely wise parents.

***

A kid growing up in Brooklyn in the 1960s would often hear complaints about "the Puerto Ricans," who, it was said, had it made (as did other Latinos) because they had "everything handed to them." Of course, human nature does not seem to permit an individual ever to see himself as the recipient of a handout, no matter how blatant.

A first-generation Italian American child, in the World War II years, learned Italian in the home as a first, native language. But the child was forced at sufferance to learn English in order to attend American public schools. There were no two ways about it. The child's grandfathers, in fact, could tell a similar story. Many had quit school well before high school graduation, on account of the "American kids" who mocked them mercilessly for their foreign accents. A human being may naturally feel that since he was compelled to learn English by threat of expulsion from school before his education even commenced, that Latinos should have the same fate. It is known as "misery loves company," another trait of our curious human nature that many learn through experience from an early age.

However, largely on the back of the prior immigrant's own quiet assimilation, the Latinos, on the other hand, are felt to have an unjust benefit. An enlightened change in the law to "bi-lingual education" is seen as anything but enlightened. Through this program, Latinos have the benefit of taking Spanish, their own primary language learned in the home, and can bring that language with them to school. The school, at taxpayer expense, has bi-lingual teachers in place, in turn, to help these Latinos with the difficult task of migrating over to English. This is the law, but for some reason the idea of migration to English, if communicated, is not fairly understood.

White men from the south (of Europe, that is) stand accused of breeding a race of human beings decidedly inferior to those from Europe's western and northern sections. Still, they're not completely in tune with the plight of Latinos, African Americans, Asians, the so-called "people of color." Or women, for that matter.

By way of example, one day an African American student relates a simple demographic fact. But his delivery is monotone. So at first it is simply dismissed by a teacher who is busy, with a full, hectic schedule for the day ahead, and with a lot on his mind. Receiving no acknowledgment, the student repeats the demographic for a second and then a third time, becoming more passionate with each successive delivery. Finally, he senses that his teacher has snapped out of his daze and is finally listening, his emotion finally getting through. This is another trait of human nature: If one is passionate about what he's doing, deliver the message with conviction. People will notice the conviction, if not the message.

"Why is it," the student begins again, "that a black person has to be wildly successful, beat seemingly insurmountable odds, fly like superman, to become that nationally popular one-in-a-million rapper or hip hop artist, before he is able to afford what is to most white people the common luxury to reside in an affluent southern California neighborhood like Beverly Hills? While, for example, his white neighbor on one side *only* has to be a dentist—his white neighbor on the other side *just* an insurance salesman?" The issue framed from this perspective causes the teacher to take the time to reflect and think it through. The student has a point.

After all, the history of rock and roll music, defined in the textbook as "the bastard mulatto child of a heterogeneous American culture, combining black rhythm and blues with white country music," offers a case in point. Originally written and recorded by black artists, the music is accepted only after sexually explicit recordings are re-written and re-recorded, by white performers, and then sold to white youth. Only thereafter does it become mainstream.

And if those are the odds for the plight of the ordinary black man, then just where does the "lower" class of white men (the ones who are not WASPs) slot in? Many white people today resent the fact that blacks receive at least a perceived, unfair advantage through the mechanism of affirmative action. This controversial program gives a hiring preference based on race, ethnicity or gender over the application of a similarly situated white male citizen. Many white men, especially on the lower rungs, believe that, perhaps, it is time to reverse or undo affirmative action, that *enough* has been done, that blacks, anyway, have effectively "caught up."

This question is presented to a professional colleague whose ethnicity is a mix of African American and Asian. He answers without hesitation: "Hell no! The black man is not even close to catching up." He proceeds to relate a metaphor which is not soon forgotten. A white man and a black man each line up to compete in a hundred yard dash. The white man is fit and all trained up, with state of the art running gear. By contrast, the black man has a pair of lead shackles locked around his bare ankles. The gun goes off. The race starts. The white man zips along smartly, sporting a huge smile. When he gets to about ten yards from the finish line, someone in the crowd has the decency to call for the black man's shackles finally to be removed. The crowd waits impatiently, wondering why the black man hasn't caught up in an instant. He must just be lazy, they conclude.

It is argued that whites typically lack empathy for their black brethren, taking for granted things that do not come as naturally or predictably for blacks. For example, a white colleague is known to speak rather casually about having inherited his father's successful printing business. Although it is largely due to his efforts that the business has taken off to the next level, he tends to speak as if such businesses commonly grow on trees. After all, it's *just* a printing business, right? Or it's just a GM dealership; it's just an accounting firm, and so on.

Working people are also rather nonchalant about the financial cost and economic drain of social programs for their dispossessed co-workers. Programs such as workers' compensation to protect the injured and unemployment insurance benefits to protect those who have been the subject of layoffs are routinely criticized. Even successful, self-employed entrepreneurs tend to complain about the social costs of subsidizing the failed business ventures of others in a brutal, survival of the fittest, take no prisoners mentality.

Of course, the situation changes when the working man loses his own job. Then, as the saying goes, it's not a recession, it's a *depression*. Suppose, for example, the self-employed entrepreneur happens to be a GM dealer, whose father ran the business proudly before he did. For years, the entrepreneur's wishes are basic. He wants the "government" simply to get—and stay—off his back and out of his life.

Until, that is, the music stops playing, GM declares bankruptcy on account of decades of incompetent management, and the entrepreneur is finally left without a chair. All of a sudden, the attitude changes, fundamentally. Then the government *must* step in, naturally, to help *him* in *his* time of dire need.

Lastly, there is amusement in considering the story of a woman who says she has no idea how she is going to pay for her child's college education. She is therefore going to vote "Democrat" in the next election, as one of the ordinary people to whom the party has strong appeal. The next interaction with this woman reveals, however, how her politics have undergone a complete transformation. Now she is preaching how the Republicans *must* win the next election. She confides that she has been the grateful recipient of a generous bequest from her parents, which is to cover the child's education in full. And all of a sudden, everything changes.

***

It seems that change is in the air today. For their part, blacks have traditionally been part of the Democratic Party base since the 1930s. But today, can a black man really dare to become a Republican? It is a provocative question and perhaps best explored once again through the example of the Hon. Clarence Thomas, Associate Justice of the US Supreme Court.

At the time of Thomas' confirmation hearings, the main problem for Democrats was that Clarence Thomas did not fit into the stereotypical definition of a "Republican." Barry Goldwater's conservative movement had attracted to the Republican Party a certain type of citizen. That citizen generally was affluent, white, male and old, and also from the South, and who also advocated the preservation of the status quo.

On the other hand, the Democratic Party attracted many types of ordinary citizens. This included blacks and other people of color, the poor, the young, the elderly on fixed incomes and also some well-educated whites with "liberal" and socially tolerant yet fiscally conservative beliefs. They were pro-choice and generally in favor of affirmative action. The Hon. Thurgood Marshall, Thomas' predecessor, matched that general characterization reasonably well.

However, Clarence Thomas' individual views, unorthodox as they *seemed*, threatened to turn the established order on its head. For example, on social issues like abortion he was pro-life, and on civil rights issues he stood curiously opposed to affirmative action. He advocated personal responsibility, individual initiative and not government help, but self help. These were generally the views of a Republican, not someone from Thomas' ethnicity or background. ———

Additionally, having received his college degree from Holy Cross (where just 6 of the 550 members of his all-male class of 1968 were black), Thomas had been an early product of affirmative action in his own right in achieving a place at Yale Law School. He received no financial break at Yale, however, still making payments on his student loans over the next two decades, including the time he joined the US Supreme Court. [128] His advocacy of so-called "conservative" views, then, was unconventional. His own people called him an ingrate, his thinking nothing less than blasphemy.

A journey through US History from a civil rights perspective revealed, however, that the views of Clarence Thomas were based on a seemingly intelligent, powerful argument. For Thomas, it had all started with the white man's agreement to exclude the black man from the Declaration of Independence, and the adoption of the US Constitution, and the Bill of Rights, which followed. Slavery was the law of the land, at least in the South.

Consequently, every Southern state had enacted a "slave code," so called, that defined the slave owner's power and the slave's status as the white man's "property," and designed to control the slave's life. Of course, the slave code had been written and enacted by the same Southern white elite group, who had authored the Bill of Rights. Thus, the slave code could be viewed, correctly, as the Bill of Rights, only upside down! [129]

With the abolition of slavery, the slave code was replaced by so-called "black codes." Although free, blacks became the subject of the legalized segregation of the races, "separate but equal" facilities, so the US Supreme Court decided in 1896. [130] Legalized segregation was meant to demonstrate once and for all the superiority of whites over blacks as evidenced by a system of control of one race over the other. Incredibly, even the simple act of a black man whistling at a white woman, walking down a public street, was deemed illegal in the South in this context.

By the early 1950s, however, it was factually determined that for every $150.00 spent at the "white schools," only $50.00 was spent at their counterpart "black schools." And so, after a stormy, 50+ year existence, the US Supreme Court finally overruled legalized segregation in 1954, deciding unanimously that "When it comes to opportunities in education, separate but equal is inherently unequal." [131] The ruling was hailed as a "Second Emancipation Proclamation."

Ten years later, the 1964 Civil Rights Act prohibited discrimination in public places and with regard to public accommodations. The familiar signs which had read "colored waiting area" and such were to come down. Meanwhile, the Voting Rights Act of 1965 greatly increased black suffrage, especially in Southern states, where that right had been systematically restricted in the decades following Reconstruction. The vision of Abraham Lincoln's Emancipation Proclamation was thus nearly fulfilled, almost 100 years later, culminating in the progression to the system of affirmative action in the present day.

Affirmative action is a US government program, which provides advantages for minorities and women who were seen to have traditionally been discriminated against. The aim is to create a more egalitarian or equal society through preferential access to education, employment and social betterment. The rationale, as typically stated, is to redress past discrimination against minority groups through measures to improve their economic and educational opportunities. In other words, it is a catch up plan. Many whites, however, call it "reverse discrimination."

The views of Clarence Thomas are squarely at odds with the concept of affirmative action, and the liberal "consensus" on race, for three substantive reasons.

First, as the argument goes, since the applicant's seat, typically, was not "earned," fair and square, the recipient receives what is the equivalent of a free handout. Consequently, the applicant has been robbed of his or her individual initiative and is ill-prepared to tackle the rigors, for example, of a medical school program. In this situation, the recipient of the "benefit" is left with no alternative but to drop out, his or her self-worth demeaned in the process. For the recipient's class (in this case, blacks) the exercise thereby perpetuates not only a cycle of failure but also ensures the continued subservience to and dependence upon its white counterpart. In short, a system which creates a sense of entitlement is also but a trap which leaves a trail of victims in its wake. [132]

119

Second, according to Thomas, based as it is on factors which include race, ethnicity and gender, affirmative action unfairly discriminates against similarly disadvantaged whites. These whites are also arguably of limited means and opportunities. Specifically, affirmative action violates the constitutional provision that citizens may not be denied the right to equal protection of the laws, under the 14th amendment. Moreover, since the Constitution is *supposed* to be color blind, a fairer, more neutral "test" would be based not on race, ethnicity and/or gender, but rather, on poverty. In short, in order to pass constitutional scrutiny, the test to be applied must be race neutral and based solely on *need*.

Lastly, the subjects of the particular affirmative action program who manage to succeed are then *expected* by the program's architects to think in a certain way. "How could a black man be truly free," Thomas asserted, "if he felt obliged to act in a certain way? And, how was that any different from being forced to live under segregation?" [133]

Thomas categorizes the program's architects with the pejorative label of "The Man:" a mostly white Anglo-Saxon protestant elite power base that has controlled the nation's institutions, since the landing of The *Mayflower*. So long as the successful recipients of affirmative action toe the company line, everything is fine. But should there be a step out of line, for example, by expressing an independence of thought which is the unique hallmark of liberty, natural law and higher education, there is trouble. Like the water moccasin from Thomas' rural Georgia homeland, "The Man" rears up his ugly head to strike him down. According to Thomas, the water moccasin is the most dangerous of snakes, more so than the rattle snake, because it strikes a deadly blow, silently and without warning.

Thomas' argument puts things into better perspective. A black man/ product of affirmative action is *supposed* to be pro-choice on the abortion issue in the great liberal tradition espoused by "The Man." Instead, when the black man advances a pro-life position, an Anita Hill is systematically resurrected from his past, and then transformed into a monster to destroy him. All for refusing to bow to the supposedly superior wisdom of white "liberals" who continue to think they know what is best for the black man. Since Thomas did not "know his place" and refused to ingest the liberal Kool-Aid, he has to be put down. This, if true, is indeed sobering.

120

Thomas admits under affirmative action that perhaps a few minorities and woman will be successful and thereby swap places with some similarly situated whites. Now, on the totem pole of success, the black man figures to swap 4th and 5th places with the lower class white man. However, the program of affirmative action shares only one *guarantee* in common with the slave code and black codes before it: "The Man" will retain his #1 position on top of the pyramid, where he has been for centuries, and where he figures always to remain.

***

Persuasive, cogent and compelling arguments challenge the ordinary citizen to grapple with these thorny issues. The stakes are high: obtaining better, more equal, access to the American economic opportunity structure, or, as more commonly known, the American Dream.

Factually, the unemployment rate may be hovering between 7% to 8% of all Americans, but 20% of American teenagers, and 50% of American black teenagers. In such times, the ordinary citizen may feel an urge to reflect. At the end of the Civil War, blacks were so impoverished, so illiterate, and for the most part so lacking in skills that freedom meant little more to them than the ability to leave the place to which they had been bound by slavery. The post-war records are replete with tales of blacks who took to the roads and retraced their paths back to the plantations from which they had been sold, in search of the families they had lost. Surely there were blacks who were so battered by the system of slavery that they became sexually promiscuous or irresponsible parents, and apparently remain so, today. [134]

An ordinary citizen may be urged to reflect further. There are a multitude of decent Americans, who not only are unmoved by the fact that 40% of black children are living in poverty, but use that fact to buttress their own convictions about black inferiority. Is it reasonable for an ordinary citizen to consider that blacks should constitute 49% of America's prison population? Is it reasonable for an ordinary citizen to ignore persistent disparities between black and white health, income, wealth, educational attainment, and employment? [135]

The argument of Clarence Thomas aside, is it also reasonable for an ordinary citizen to consider that a significant number of decent Americans regularly assert enormous efforts to destroy affirmative action?

Is there empathy for the fact that the fragile affirmative action program was enacted in the 1960s and 1970s to compensate for deep injuries sustained over 350 years of legally sanctioned subordination? Some label the campaign to do away with affirmative action as "brilliant rhetorical propaganda." But Cory A. Booker, the black mayor of Newark, NJ calls on the ordinary citizen to consider the economic reality that, in fact, "Yale is cheaper than jail."

One scholar has warned that his

> recurring nightmare in recent years has been that there will be such a significant separation of the black upper and middle classes from poor blacks that when America declares total victory over anti-black racism, substantial numbers of well-off blacks and members of other minorities will be complicit in the deceit. We will then have a society much like that found in Brazil. We could tell ourselves that we have a 'racial democracy' here, and overlook the fact that the only thing the blacks at the bottom have in abundance is misery, made permanent by their virtually complete lack of access to the national opportunity structure. We will have put the finishing touches on our national scapegoat; an untouchable, impoverished caste of permanent mudsills, filling a role not at all unlike the one John Smith had in mind for Native Americans almost four centuries ago. [136]

When it comes to civil rights, history does suggest a sort of rather dim view of prior times. But what about the present? Put another way, how will *our* contribution be judged by future generations? Today, the 400 richest Americans possess more wealth than the bottom half (150 million) combined. [137] Does this sobering statistic uphold the basic ideal of social justice which is this nation's moral foundation?

While we will contemplate "tomorrow" in the final chapter, for now, it is understood that if America stands for one thing, more than any other, it is the following. America provides the ordinary citizen with the opportunity to make something of himself. The ordinary citizen may accomplish this by exerting his God-given abilities to engage in struggles for decency, discharging the responsibility to hold up his own end of the challenge. [138] In the end, Judgment Day may demand nothing less.

***

One final story smartly facilitates this chapter's conclusion. An older colleague, a master in the ways of local politics, observed that for the ordinary citizen "the resume typically is *there*, all that's *needed* to happen is one of two things: first, simply to be in the right place at the right time, when a good opportunity presents itself, or, someone who is in an influential position to take a special interest in his career."

When the onion is peeled back, what is the relevant take away message?

The thought turns to a tale of two citizens, who were created equal, more or less. The setting is toward the end of the first decade of the 21st century A.D., in a part of the empire that is old, decaying and has been so for more than 50 years. These citizens have much in common. These citizens have little in common. Their journey down the same and separate paths is symptomatic of the larger issues. Perhaps you may have run into them.

Each citizen is educated, trained in the familiar liberal doctrine which declares scorn to accept a privilege which is not the right of every citizen. Each has attained professional degree and status, with many years of life experience. Each is now in mid-life, with active plans to leave this rusty, old palace and move to a place they call the Sun Belt, where it is warmer, cheaper to live, simpler, and perhaps more pleasant.

One citizen is more of a public figure, the announcement of whose surprise departure was a matter for the local newspapers recently. "Respected State Judge Declines Re-appointment to 2nd Seven-Year Term and Elects to Retire and Move South," the headline read. Portrayed it was as a genuine loss to the local community, which he served honorably for many years.

The article highlighted this citizen's career. Before the judgeship he had been the county prosecutor, participating in some high profile cases as the top county-level law enforcement officer, and before that municipal prosecutor. It was said that his service will be missed. The article concluded with a quote from the citizen judge, melancholy in tone, that he feels he's where "he's supposed to be," that with his life's experiences there's still a lot of things to do, and "he'll figure it out." One wonders, with all that's going for him, however, and still very much in his prime, why he would choose to retire and move away.

The article fails to mention that the earlier appointment of this citizen judge to municipal prosecutor was fresh out of law school, with no legal experience. He was from a fine, local family, it was said. That appointment led to other similar local appointments, which, although the pay of each was rather pedestrian, he handled uneventfully for almost twenty years.

The article also fails to mention that his competence, together with partisan work on the political campaign of a successful candidate for governor, landed him the more prestigious and lucrative appointment to county prosecutor. This was a significant promotion, which set the stage for the further promotion to judgeship.

How significant was the promotion? Upon his retirement presently, the citizen judge is in line to receive a lucrative annual state pension, with full medical insurance benefits, for life. Should he live only to his actuarial life expectancy of 22 additional years, the citizen judge will "figure it out" with future retirement benefits of approximately $2.3 million dollars, at the expense of the ordinary taxpayer.

In fairness to the citizen who became a fine judge, his story is not altogether unique in these parts of the empire. Unfortunately, there is a multitude of stories, some far more egregious. Consider, for example, the account of the recently retired local building inspector, in a similar stage of life. His retirement benefits package is understood to be roughly equal to, if not greater than, that of his public employee colleague, the citizen judge. The *local building inspector* is in line to receive a state pension in excess of $100,000.00 per year, for life.

This brings us back to the story of the other citizen, who is much more of a private figure, and who guards his personal business. Little is known of his fine and proud family, the less the better. There is no announcement of his departure, not that anyone would care to know, for it is not newsworthy. He has built a successful career largely by doing the right thing in small, private law practice for close to three decades.

Starting his own business essentially from scratch almost two decades ago, with no rabbi looking out for him, he has been his own boss. Voluntarily, he trades off his anonymity against full autonomy in the workplace, which has its own benefits, and counts for something. He is of the rare breed that still makes house calls. His business is strictly word of mouth referrals. More recently, in his spare time he began also to teach history at the public university. It makes him feel more alive, like he is making a meaningful impact in building kids.

Early in his career he had declined an invitation, put forth by the political party in a one party town, to run for office. Ever since, he has successfully avoided the ethical minefield of political service. He is independent through and through. About 10 or so years into his career, he was told politely that he lacked sufficient if not the requisite experience as a basis for appointment to serve as local municipal prosecutor. He served voluntarily on the local zoning board for 15 distinguished years, retiring as its chairperson. But apparently, he is not attractive like the citizen judge. And so the political appointment game has gone, even in his own "home" town of 20-something years.

Presently, this private citizen is waging a mighty personal battle, as are many, with the high cost of living, and the intense pressures of running a small business in a wrecked economy. On top of that, he has been able to save but few precious dollars towards his own golden years. If he stayed, he would have to try to figure out a way not only to pay for his own retirement, but also the retirement of the citizen judge and the building inspector, as well. For the truth of the matter is that under the law these latter public obligations must be honored, before his obligation to himself.

He is as if on the high seas, in a rowboat without a paddle, no one directing the ship, and ill-prepared to continue to direct the ship himself. The truth also is that his state is bankrupt, both economically and politically, if not morally, and it is one mountain simply too tall for one ordinary citizen to climb. So he, too, chooses to leave.

Perhaps, someday, the citizen who became judge and the citizen who chose to remain private will become Sun Belt neighbors. They will have many common experiences to share, much to talk about, for sure. They would probably enjoy being neighbors. They could reminisce. They could intellectualize. Maybe, they would agree among friends to dispense with the formality of the traditional white picket fence that would otherwise neatly separate their respective homes.

Each sees the hope if not the promise of a better life, the next chapter, if you will, in the geographical wonderment of the Sun Belt, still within the physical confines and protection of the American umbrella. Perhaps you did not have the opportunity to recognize them in their earlier carnation. But surely, you will have the opportunity to see them there, in the Sun Belt, where each will live out the remainder of his days, and attempt to fulfill his remaining dreams, equal, more or less.

Chapter 7
A Few of My Favorite Things: US History (Part 2)

Ain't getting old, ain't getting younger though
Just getting used to the lay of the land
I ain't tongue-tied, just don't got nothin' to say
I'm proud to be livin' in the USA

Ready to go, willin' to stay and pay
USA, USA
So my sweet love can dance another free day
USA, USA

In history we painted pictures grim
The devil knows we might feel that way again
The big wind blows, so the tall grass bends
But for you don't push too hard my friend

- from the song, Hawks & Doves,
by Neil Young (1980)
available on the *Hawks & Doves* collection

***

The first "half" of US History concluded, most historians would agree, at the point when Reconstruction "ended" in 1877. This coincided with the removal of federal troops from the South, finally, by mutual agreement.

In truth, the US was "ready" for the Industrial Revolution long before it actually arrived, but divisiveness on the slavery question held back progress. Compromise after compromise had put off resolution of the most basic of civil rights issues, until it could be put off no longer. When the Civil War ended, and the states were reconstructed, the US could return to the matter of industrial progress and prowess at the turn of the 20th century.

Some say the birth of the Industrial Revolution was a precipitous event, transitioning America from a promised land into a crusader state, to capture and protect the wealth of foreign markets for its own citizens. [139] In this way America was said to mimic every great empire which had come—and gone—before.

***

The Industrial Revolution was the great free for all, US government "guided" by principles of Social Darwinism. Basically, it was a game of survival of the fittest, most adaptable, Darwin's theory of evolution as applied to society. Those individuals who had figured out how to amass great personal wealth were viewed as being in the best position to make leadership decisions for the good of the masses.

Government's role was either to support these individuals and their industries or avoid meddlesome interference (laissez-faire acceptance of supply and demand theory). Industrial ventures operated through large, capital massing business organizations, called "trusts." But the relationship of these trusts to their government was to test severely the lawmaker's role as the impartial umpire in the people's pursuit of happiness.

The so-called titans of capitalism were bolstered by the collective success of the nation occasioned by explosive economic growth brought on by the Industrial Revolution. The early Social Darwinists featured names like Rockefeller in the business of oil, Morgan in banking, Carnegie in steel, and Vanderbilt in railroads. They were firm believers in a free, unregulated market promoted by competition, with a new consumer class, a thriving force in the industrial economy. With the incentive to reap great profits, these titans consolidated operations into large mega-corporations, streamlined the various systems of production, eliminated redundancies and maximized efficiencies. While consolidation permitted them to control their industries, a primary goal was still to give the customer the best product at the lowest price.

It is perhaps helpful to think of the process of "making" an Industrial Revolution as similar to baking a wedding cake. There were several key ingredients. Among them were natural resources, such as oil, copper, land and water; a capital supply serving as "fertilizer." Government support was in the form of protective tariffs for the new, fledgling American industries, the birth of the modern corporation, low interest loans and adherence to the monetary gold standard. Entrepreneurs took risks, mastered the art of vertical integration, business re-organization, and buying low and selling high. Technological developments, such as electricity, steel, glass and the internal combustion engine, permitted innovations in rail transit, and the invention of the telephone and canned food.

128

A work force/consumer class was fueled mostly by an abundant flow of previously uneducated and unskilled laborers comprised mainly of a seismic inflow of new immigrants. They had migrated to the cities in search of opportunities, filling the abundance of new industrial jobs.

For sure, there were many positives to consider. In the span of a mere generation, the US became the #1 industrial power in the world, during which time a modern industrial economy emerged. Skyscrapers were constructed, soon began to overtake the urban landscape, and our modern, industrial, steel and glass cities were born. Immigrants comprised a new economic unit, a powerhouse called the "middle" class, a new term for the era. With rising income, industrial workers doubled as what became known as *consumers*. Their collective purchasing power permitted them to achieve a raised standard of material existence previously unknown. It also kept the economy humming.

While the titans of industry were champions of competition, ironically, their goal was to eliminate competition. Specifically, they sought to accomplish this by creating and then maintaining a hierarchy with themselves at the top. Many had arrived there through superior intellect or other legitimate means. But some used questionable or even illegal business practices. Bribes, kickbacks and other monopolistic trade practices were all utilized to destroy competitors.

The times were seen in negative terms as the Gilded Age, with great wealth flashed to the masses but accessible only to a precious few. Those precious few were sometimes referred to not so nicely as robber barons. Style points in both politics and culture triumphed over substance. [140] Consider the image of sunglasses attached to a bright, smiling face.

But, Andrew Carnegie, for one, articulated a call for these wealthy business titans of industry to return their wealth to society, which illustrates Lesson 3 (of 4) of US History. The king of steel strongly believed that the rich man had not the option, but rather a corresponding *duty*, to voluntarily return his wealth to society from whence it came.

Carnegie's *Gospel of Wealth* writings set forth a model of how the wealthy man should conduct his life. First, the capitalist's primary goal was to make money. But he should then live only modestly, so as to bring no undue attention to himself.

Then, since the rich man had figured out how to achieve great wealth in the first place, he alone should choose how to spend that wealth. Whether on charity, society, science, or any other worthy cause, in his sole discretion, he should accomplish all this *before* he dies.

According to Carnegie, it would be a curse for a rich man to die with money in the bank, and which the government could then get its hands on by mechanisms such as the inheritance tax. In the end, if all went according to plan, the rich man who made it would, in turn, give it all away freely, the government involved neither while making the money, nor spending it in the end.

And Carnegie acted. As part of his considerable financial legacy, Carnegie donated substantial sums for a pension relief fund to the families of killed and injured workers, based on merit, and not given indiscriminately. Additionally, he made bequests to build 67 libraries forming the backbone of the venerable New York City public library system and some 1,689 public libraries in the US during his lifetime. The program was expanded to include church organs. Lastly, he made a gift to establish the International Court at the Hague, in support of a world court of arbitration, where international disputes could be resolved without resort to war. [141]

As the so-called "Apostle of Peace," Carnegie has been quoted as saying: "We have abolished the duel. Let it be our race that truly takes the first step to abolish international dueling." And Carnegie (remember, the year was 1910, *before* the World Wars) had also stated:

> The whole matter is so simple … Germany, Great Britain and the US coming together (somewhat covertly) to form a joint police force to maintain peace is all that is needed. [142]

But the impact of the Industrial Revolution on American society was not all positive. Neither were the results all pretty, nor without a heavy price. Consider that the process generated a sink full of dirty dishes. The growth of corporations and trusts raised immense amounts of targeted capital but, importantly, decreased social responsibility. Materialism was pronounced over all other values. Natural resources were exploited, despoiling the land, to increase profits. Wealth and industry, over production, people and politics, became overly concentrated. This, in turn, led to corrupt political machines led by party bosses, the overcrowding of cities, the straining of resources and services. It also necessitated the combination of diverse cultural groups which were unfamiliar with American city life or each other.

Moreover, American industrial workers faced deteriorating labor conditions. Women, children and the unskilled immigrant factory worker were exploited, suffering work conditions which could perhaps best be described as unsafe, inhumane and produced substandard products. Hours were excessive, on a daily and weekly basis. Wages failed to keep pace with the cost of living. Still, the abundant supply of cheap, new, unskilled immigrant workers greatly exceeded the supply of new factory jobs in the nation's big industrial cities.

Workers also faced strong opposition not only from their employers but also the courts. Government policy and judicial decisions fiercely protected not the industrial worker but the entrepreneurial spirit of American businessmen to lead by way of innovation. Sweatshop working conditions and stagnant wages stimulated a movement toward the formation of labor unions. However, attempts at unionization led to violent confrontations between big business *and* government in tandem against the interests of labor.

One thing was clear: America was making more products than it could consume. This factor, added to the free-for-all, further stimulated unstable economic cycles of boom and bust that produced unrest on farms. Due to increasing productivity, farmers faced declining prices for their crops, as well as a diminution of their land, with laws and government interested in protecting neither. Land foreclosures skyrocketed.

This instability spawned a first of its kind political movement, a populist wing of the Democratic Party traced to the protection of the nation's agrarian and common man labor interests. Dramatized by William Jennings Bryan, "The Great Commoner," "on the wings of a single great speech about a cross of gold," [143] it rose briefly to political prominence but ultimately failed and was swept away by 1896. [144]

In cities, living conditions degenerated into tenement slums filled with crime and poverty, racism and nativism. Advances in transportation, specifically the railroad, *exacerbated* segregated living arrangements for an increasingly diverse cultural society. And the entire process, given the magnitude and swiftness of the forces of change, fueled a painless escape to drugs.

The ultimate result and impact, it has been said, was a society in chaos, seeking reform. This was the state of affairs as the American industrial machine rolled into the 20th century.

***

The Last Three Great American Presidents.

Many are in agreement that the stage had been set quite naturally for Theodore Roosevelt, the fifth of the seven great American Presidents and the last from the Republican Party. T.R. succeeded to the presidency in 1901 on the assassination of Pres. William McKinley by a Polish immigrant, at a time when immigration was so prevalent that 1 in 5 Americans were immigrants. While McKinley represented the maintenance of the old guard status quo, T.R. represented very much a new order. He was the successful architect of a reform agenda in what otherwise became known as the Progressive Era, stretching from 1900 to 1917. Many of his ideas have carried through with great relevance and insight to the present.

The Progressive struggle was really nothing more than an umbrella label for a wide range of economic, political, social and moral reforms. These reforms were undertaken to confront the diverse problems plaguing American society and the strong impact the movement had on US development. But there was still a reluctance to come to terms with the America's cultural and ethnic diversity. However, the process of identifying the problem had begun. By way of metaphor, the American social garden had been weeded and tidied up, not replanted, producing bitter fruit for some but benefit for many. For blacks, unfortunately, it meant the continuation of discriminatory treatment, a relic left over from the pre-Civil War South that the nation was not yet prepared to address.

For women, the results were, however, generally good. A survey of some of the notorious women from US History would necessarily include the likes of Pocahontas (whose 1614 marriage to John Rolfe implied a political alliance of sorts), Abigail Adams (venerable First Lady, who reminded her husband, John, to "remember the Ladies ... and be more generous to them than your ancestors"), Elizabeth Cady Stanton (Seneca Falls Convention of 1848, an early suffrage movement), Harriet Beecher Stowe (author, *Uncle Tom's Cabin: or, Life among the Lowly*, 1852, to whom Lincoln referred on meeting as "the little woman who wrote the book that made this great war") and Ida Tarbell (muckraking journalist, John D. Rockefeller's "Lady Friend," whose articles for *McClure's* magazine would be expanded to a book, *The History of Standard Oil*, 1904, largely credited with the demise of that entity). Finally, Susan B. Anthony's campaign for full suffrage in 1920 produced the crowning event, the ratification of the 19th amendment to the US Constitution, providing women the right to vote, in 1921.

Later, women would raise the bar for American society by the likes of Eleanor Roosevelt (spouse of President Franklin D. Roosevelt, expanding the role of First Lady in a drastically new direction from 1932), Frances Perkins [145] (first female appointed to the US cabinet, Secretary of Labor, 1933), Margaret Mitchell (author, *Gone with the Wind*, 1936, heralded as the Great American Novel), Jacqueline Kennedy Onassis (spouse of J.F.K., thrust into the spotlight in 1960 as the wife of "Camelot"), Sandra Day O'Connor (first female Justice of the US Supreme Court, 1981) Madeline Albright (first female Secretary of State under Pres. Bill Clinton, 1997), and finally US Rep. Nancy Pelosi, D-CA (first female Speaker of the US House of Representatives, 2007). The list is indeed impressive and continues to expand.

At a time when 1% of families possessed 7/8 of all wealth, the reform agenda of T.R.'s Republican Party called for efficient government run by competent, able people with a need for expanded government action. The ground-breaking work of Ida Tarbell, progressive journalist, provided the impetus to take on and ultimately succeed in breaking up the gargantuan oil monopoly, Rockefeller's Standard Oil.

Utilizing a previously toothless, obscure federal law, the 1891 Sherman Anti-Trust Act, T.R.'s administration rejected the previous Republican policy of laissez-faire and passive, limited government. Henceforth, and for the very first time, the government would *reject* the principles of Social Darwinism and recognize labor (i.e.: the ordinary citizen) as a necessary ingredient, if not equal partner, in its struggle with entrenched businesses (i.e.: ranging from finance to railroads to steel to coal mines). It was then labeled as the "triumph of conservatism."

T.R.'s program of reform exemplified an *activist* government to combat the various ills plaguing society as a result of the Industrial Revolution. At a time when statistics showed that black lynchings in the South were then being carried out at a rate of approximately one every four days, T.R. had articulated his signature "Square Deal" message in the following passage:

> I fought beside the colored troops at Santiago (Cuba, during the Spanish American War), and I hold that if a man is good enough to be put up and shot at then he is good enough—for me to do what I can to get him a square deal. [146]

Some of the noteworthy legislative achievements included the enactment of workers' compensation, child labor and compulsory education laws, as well as laws to ameliorate excessively long shifts and unsafe work conditions. In short, T.R. used his presidency to make laws to protect people "on the make" as opposed to those "already made," in the attempt at "making an Old Party Progressive." [147] It was in line with what he identified as the Jackson-Lincoln view of the presidency: to act when it is your duty to act as the steward of the people, unless explicitly forbidden by the US Constitution. [148]

With respect to foreign policy, T.R. popularized the phrase "Speak softly and carry a big stick" in what became known as Big Stick diplomacy. His successors, William Taft (R) and Woodrow Wilson (D), utilized their own particular brands, Dollar Diplomacy and Missionary Diplomacy, the latter in an attempt to "make the world safe for democracy."

T.R. felt that it was the "white man's burden," a sense of duty carried on by the Anglo-Saxons, to elevate mankind via the two great ideas of civil liberty and "spiritualized" Christianity. As "keeper of the light," the goal was to civilize the "lesser" peoples and bring democracy to the "darker corners of the earth," both literally and figuratively. He did this by viewing our oceans no longer as protective barriers permitting isolation, as Washington had envisioned. From now on, they would be considered as "stepping stones" to expansion of lucrative foreign markets overseas for trade and other strategic, national security initiatives.

T.R.'s foreign policy strategy was twofold, and as such set the blueprint for combating a recurring future nightmare he had envisioned: a two ocean naval war. First, as a student of history T.R. well knew that what stood behind every great power was a great navy. However, in the decades following the Civil War, the US Navy had been essentially disbanded. Consequently, T.R. embarked upon a controversial endeavor to re-build the navy, almost from scratch, to world class standards.

At the same time, T.R. determined that the project to complete construction of the Panama Canal, in which France had most recently failed, had to be successfully completed by the US. Only then would our westward destiny, West and East merging in a new global strategy, be fulfilled. "In the century that is opening," T.R. proclaimed, "the commerce and the command of the Pacific will be factors in the world's history." [149]

As a result, the US became actively involved in places like the Philippines, Guam, Samoa, as well as the annexation of Hawaii. Obtaining funding appropriation from a wary Congress to construct a new naval base at Pearl Harbor, the US could both protect Pacific interests and enforce the "Open Door" policy with China. Under this policy, the US proclaimed that the lucrative Chinese market would no longer be the exclusive province of Japan but would henceforth be open to free trade with the US and all European nations. [150] The Great Wall was, in fact, coming down. In exchange, the US would provide important military protection to China stemming any further European, Russian or Japanese aggression. "Our chief usefulness to humanity," T.R. preached, "rests on our combining power with high purpose." [151]

At the same time, T.R. disagreed with Carnegie's world court of arbitration to resolve international disputes without resort to war. Armament and war were sometimes necessary to check those nations that did not have the same values or standards for civilization:

> The nation that pledged to arbitrate its differences would end up dishonored and impotent, like the man who, when his wife was assaulted by a ruffian, took the ruffian to court instead of attacking him on the spot. [152]

Lastly, while American hearts had been warmed to the tiny island nation of Japan, that "warlike little power," to check Russian menacing into the Philippines, T.R. worried secretly about Japan's growing strength. The stark fact was that it then took a full 90 days to sail an American warship from the Atlantic around the Cape of Good Horn in Africa to the Pacific theatre.

Knowing full well that trouble with Japan would loom some day, T.R. orchestrated a massive military exercise, which had not been accomplish by *any* of the major European powers to date. In what was seen as a logistical nightmare, T.R. arranged for the US Navy to sail around the world, in a feat that would take one full year to accomplish. Initially intending to transport the fleet to San Francisco only, T.R. then expanded the mission to include the Far East, New Zealand, Japan, Suez, Egypt, the Mediterranean and Gibraltar. Two weeks prior to the end of T.R.'s presidency in February 1909, the mission concluded in Hampton Rhodes, Virginia.

The Great White Fleet venture had succeeded well beyond the expectations of many on two important levels. First, the venture facilitated US military transport between the oceans/continents. Second, as a show of force to Japan, it bought precious time, until the Panama Canal was completed. [153]

***

World War I put an abrupt end to the Progressive Era. While the US had a civil war of its own in the 19th century, for its part, the continent of Europe had *two* civil wars in the 20th century. More commonly known as World War I and World War II, respectively, perhaps it would be best to remember them simply as the First European Civil War and the Second European Civil War. [154]

World War I was known as the Great War, since conventional wisdom held out that it was to be the last major war. It was fought primarily between Great Britain and Germany, the predominant powers, for colonial supremacy, as defined by control of the world's major shipping lanes. The Great War consumed the lives of an estimated 13 million people. Exacerbating Anglo-German relations above everything else was the phenomenon of naval superiority. It thus became a race between these rival industrial (and imperial) powers. [155] For the US, the First European Civil War began in 1917, and was prosecuted on *both* sides, strictly with American oil supplies.

Ultimately, the war turned on two decisive factors. First, a then obscure First Lord of the Admiralty named Winston Churchill made an astute recommendation, which was approved. The British Royal Navy fleet, especially the battleships, would be swiftly and aggressively converted from steam power to the internal combustion engine. The conversion from coal to oil, ahead of the Germans, permitted significant gains by way of greater speed, efficiency and maneuverability of the fleet. In hindsight, it revolutionized naval strategy. [156] The second factor was the US entering the war on the side of Great Britain.

But the conversion of the British Royal Navy fleet was not without inherent risk. Having vanquished Germany, thereby securing continued dominance of the world economic order, Great Britain needed to obtain a secure supply of oil, one commodity it did not command in abundance. And so, it was not the war itself, but rather the peace that ended this war in 1919, which unlocks one of the mysteries concerning the future. We will place the Treaty of Versailles into sharper focus and context in our final chapter.

For now, suffice to say that Congress rejected President Woodrow Wilson's pleas warning against a return to isolationism, following US involvement in the First European Civil War. The US was not yet politically ready to take on the role of global superpower.

After the victory, the US simply went home, to a place familiar but where the voices of progressive government were either drowned out or dying off. The coordinated, central planning effort so vital to produce a successful industrial war machine does not typically translate to the peacetime domestic theatre, and this occasion was no exception. It was as if the patient, so long confined to a strict, involuntary diet, was finally released without condition. In its place was substituted a compensatory menu of domestic caloric self-indulgence on a massive scale. Some would call it a binge.

***

History does not look kindly upon the era of the "Roaring 20s," and perhaps for good reason. The continuous Republican administrations of Presidents Harding, Coolidge and Hoover (1920-1932) can perhaps best be summed up in the context of the following inquiry: What happens when leaders entrusted with public interest reform cease doing so and are driven instead by selfishness and their pursuit of personal gratification? This period is correctly identified as the *climax* of total cooperation between big business survival of the fittest and laissez-faire government in partnership. It is not meant as a compliment.

A period of unprecedented material prosperity, especially for private business interests, culminated during the 1928 presidential campaign. Then candidate Herbert Hoover had stated that "We in America today are nearer to the final triumph over poverty than ever before in the history of any land" and "given a chance to go forward with the policies of the last eight years, we shall soon with the help of God be in sight of the day when poverty will be banished from this nation." Stock prices were reaching what had looked like a permanently high plateau. [157]

Upon Mr. Hoover's election it was being said that national leadership could not be in safer or more expert hands. Respected economists noted that for the first time in the nation's history "we have a President who, by technical training, engineering achievement, cabinet experience, and grasp of economic fundamentals, is qualified for business leadership." For his part, President Hoover in his March 1929 inaugural address stated that "I have no fears for the future of our country. It is bright with hope." [158]

No one, perhaps, was better suited to anticipate catastrophe than President Hoover. Following a successful entrepreneurial career with an engineering background in the private sector, he served for almost eight years in the cabinet position of Secretary of Commerce before ascending to the presidency. This provided him with a unique opportunity to observe the workings and influence the policies of the American business system. But seeing all problems from the viewpoint of business, the federal government which he now headed "had mistaken the class interest (of business) for the national interest. The result was both class and national disaster." [159]

In late October 1929, a matter of just a few months following President Hoover's inauguration, the stock market crashed, ushering in the greatest economic downturn in US History. The Great Depression lasted a full, painful 10 years, and together with the differing government responses, transformed the American political and economic landscape.

President Hoover served merely as a spectator of events, as the number of those unemployed and the unemployment rate spiraled upward during his term from 3 million (3.1%) in 1929, to 4 million (8.7%) in 1930, to 8 million (15.9%) in 1931, to 12.5 million (23.6%) in 1932. Industrial productivity contracted by 50%, while investment shrank by a staggering 98%. When asked whether he felt the capacity for human suffering to be without limit, a banker reportedly replied, "I think so."

138

Invoking moral justification, many conservatives regarded federal aid to idle workers as spelling the end of the republic. [160]

Consistent with these sentiments, President Hoover reminded the ordinary citizen of what had become the basic philosophy of the Republican Party: The Great Depression was nothing more than a "temporary slump in a fundamentally strong economy" and that government intervention to combat its baneful effects was both "unnecessary and unwise." Stubbornly, he refused to act. Vilified over the years for his failure to act, perhaps rightly so, President Hoover believed that relief should come from the private sector, not the government.

As a result, a capitalist system which denied work or relief to the unemployed millions was increasingly called into critical doubt. [161] Rugged individualism seemed dead. Both real estate and farm commodity prices had collapsed. Banks effectively ceased to operate. While the heart of industry was only beating faintly [162], the private sector offered nothing. It had failed. The 1932 election would provide a last chance for politics. [163]

***

The stage had also been set quite naturally for the introduction of Franklin D. Roosevelt as the sixth of our seven great American Presidents. F.D.R. is by his 1932 election the first great president of the Democratic Party's modern era. As far as plaudits are concerned, it has been said that Franklin D. Roosevelt left an enduring print on American life as the Commander-In-Chief, not only of the Armed Forces, but of his generation as well. One recent biographer has stated that "He lifted himself from his wheelchair to lift this nation from its knees." [164] The metaphor is not understated. But why?

Private boarding school pedigreed and Harvard educated, F.D.R. took the oath of office with the simple confession that he did not have ready answers to solve the problems of the Great Depression. But unlike his predecessor, he vowed that he would at least try to do "something" rather than nothing. In short, he would improvise, experiment, see how the experiment worked. And if it didn't work, he would try something else in an approach that put practical realities ahead of any particular political ideology. [165]

The social experiment would become famous in US History as the "New Deal." Its base would consist of a new middle ground. To the left were the welfare states of Western Europe and extreme totalitarian communism in Asia. To the right were Hoover's rugged individualism, a survival of the fittest, unregulated (failed) approach, and fascism to its extreme in Germany and Italy. The Great Depression was a great unifying experience for all Americans, where rich and poor, black and white, experienced it together. Both were wiped out simultaneously, finding themselves on the same bread lines. Both sought warmth by the same smoky, trash bin fires and shelter in public common areas. Consider that there was no place else to turn, except to each other.

From the failure of the private sector's old order and out of its ashes, F.D.R.'s New Deal represented nothing less than the creation of a new order. It represented a fundamental transformation of epic social and political proportions. On a societal level, rather than continuing the previous failed policy of championing big business or staying out of its way, from now on the government was to position itself as guarantor of the social well-being of its citizens. Henceforth, the government was to be the very *agent* of reform, committed to an active role of economic betterment on behalf of its citizens. By the New Deal, constitutional dedication of federal power to the general welfare, or the social safety net as it is better known, was born. Thus began a new phase of national history, saving capitalism from itself. [166]

Both the faltering agrarian interest and the sputtering industrial machine had seized and, like a mechanical pump, required priming for action once again. Central was the idea of restoring the mass purchasing power of the ordinary citizen, who provided the best and most efficient means, in fact the only realistic means, to jump start the economy. Spending in numbers would boost demand, facilitating economic recovery and expansion. At the time, it was an untested, somewhat radical economic policy. But it worked. A spirit of collective action and planned cooperation supplanted that of individualism and cutthroat competition. [167]

In the "First 100 Days" F.D.R.'s New Deal brought emergent relief in various forms. The first priority was the nation's banks, which had ceased to operate entirely. Of utmost importance was to get them propped up and running again.

Toward that end, F.D.R. declared an immediate banking "holiday," then persuaded their re-opening with the inception of federal guarantees to insure individual deposits (FDIC). Deposits quickly began to exceed withdrawals. The acute panic was at an end. [168]

A fiscal conservative, like Hoover, F.D.R. was reluctant to permit deficit spending but would make an exception here, "if we had to." Nevertheless, an economy bill was quickly passed to reorganize and reduce veterans' pensions and reduce federal salaries, including those of Congress. "Too often in recent history," the new president warned, "liberal governments have been wrecked on rocks of loose fiscal policy." [169] To fight deflation, the gold standard was suspended. It was said that citing inflation as an objection to increased government spending and expansive monetary policy in time of emergency was like warning an emaciated patient of the dangers of excessive corpulence. [170]

The next priority was assistance for the long neglected farmer. New Dealers implemented price supports and mortgage debt relief for agriculture, including subsidies and surplus purchases (AAA). A plan to regulate industrial production (NIRA) sought to raises wages and prices and stimulate demand. The federal government pumped money into public jobs' creating programs to advance such desirable social objectives as public works (WPA), national resource preservation, conservation and soil control in the Midwest (CCC) and national planning for a complete river watershed, including regional infrastructure development, public power generation and rural electrification (TVA). [171]

Through use of his famous "fireside chats" over the radio airwaves, F.D.R. explained his programs to ordinary Americans in plain, simple terms, telling the people to have "confidence" and "courage." He warned ordinary citizens that unless they rejected the human vice of fear, they would never be able to pull out of their malaise. Instead, he urged them to embrace its opposite: hope. His confidence in his own determination to defeat the disease of polio, and rise out of his wheelchair with the aid of heavy metal braces, inspired the ordinary citizen. Ultimately, F.D.R.'s consistent message of encouragement began to take hold on the American psyche.

In the longer term, F.D.R.'s New Deal[172] signature twin legislative triumphs of historic importance included the 1935 National Labor Relations Act (NLRA) and Social Security Act (SSA). NLRA delivered the right of every worker to join a union of his or her own choosing and the corresponding obligation of employers to bargain collectively with that union in good faith. SSA, in turn, required the states to set up welfare funds from which money would be disbursed to the elderly, poor, unemployed, unmarried mothers with dependent children, and the disabled. By this law the federal government also effectively encouraged the individual states to adopt unemployment insurance plans. SSA was labeled a triumph of social legislation.

Gradually, the sharpest edges and cruelest effects of capitalism were softened. The beast of capitalism was tamed, made more humane. The New Deal created in the mind of the ordinary citizen an expectation of an expanded sense of entitlement and support from the government to *all* its citizens, *especially in time of need*, rating as Lesson 4 (of 4) of US History. The new relationship cemented the social contract between the federal government and its citizens.

Although the New Deal did not solve the Great Depression, government efforts blunted its worst effect and helped restore the faith of the ordinary citizen in capitalism and democracy. Despite some uncertainties, both survived the economic carnage. But the structure of the unregulated capitalist system which had existed under the old order was modified to be sure. Modest, sensible regulation under the new order safeguarded against an otherwise harmful concentration of economic power which benefited only the privileged few. This was in the class interest of the nation.

Of equal importance, the New Deal facilitated a political transformation of historical proportions. African Americans and other similarly situated poor whites shifted away from the Republican Party of Abraham Lincoln and Theodore Roosevelt, where they had been long-standing, loyal supporters dating back to the Civil War. En masse, they migrated over to the Democratic Party of F.D.R. The inclusion of blacks "struck vitally at the conception of a party" which had also "respected the peculiar claims of the white South" since Jefferson's time. The switch was occasioned by the realization that the Republican Party had done "nothing" to protect their interests or advance their cause or repay their earlier support. [173]

In foreign policy, F.D.R. guided America through the uncharted waters of World War II, the Second European Civil War, begun in 1939, and the atrocities of Hitler's Nazi Germany. He implored ordinary Americans to cherish and hold onto the four freedoms: freedom of speech, freedom of worship, freedom from fear, and freedom from want. In 1940, shortly before the Japanese attack on Pearl Harbor, F.D.R. announced the controversial "lend lease" policy, promising to help the British and Russians through the lease of American military equipment. He assessed the situation, using a metaphor to which ordinary Americans could well relate:

> Suppose my neighbor's home catches fire, and I have a length of garden hose four or five hundred feet away. If he can take my garden hose and connect it up with his hydrant, I may help him put out his fire. [174]

F.D.R. depicted the US as the "Arsenal of Democracy," although the "Grand Alliance" between the US, Great Britain, France and the communist USSR (Russia) existed only to defeat Nazi Germany. Additionally, F.D.R. and Churchill announced the Atlantic Charter, a set of noble principles confirming US-American-Anglo ideological solidarity. Like Lincoln, F.D.R. moved only gradually in wartime, frustrating some, by skillfully maneuvering public opinion behind his targeted position, before acting on a consensus.

***

In the election of 1944 to what would be his 4th (and most observers knew his final) term in office, F.D.R. on recommendation of his party chose Harry Truman to be his presidential running mate. It was a surprise to most. An ordinary farmer with no formal education and a common man in all respects, Harry Truman did, however, possess gifts of plain speaking and good, common sense judgment.

A voracious reader of history and biography in particular, Truman was a consummate student of human nature. Largely through the course of self-education, of significance, he had also risen up from his common upbringing to become one of Missouri's two US Senators. Now in his second six-year term with that deliberative legislative body, Truman had made many loyal friends among the rank and file members of the US Senate.

Given the critical nature of the international situation, with World War II still raging, F.D.R. wanted a successor who was honest above all things. If that person did not know all he needed to know, he could learn. And, significantly, Harry Truman was the only individual considered who felt unworthy of the position and actively shied away from it. By contrast, each of the other candidates, while respectable and impressive in their own rights, more or less fell all over themselves attempting to obtain the elusive prize. The significance of this sort of behavior had not been lost on F.D.R., although the backgrounds of the two men could not have been in starker contrast.

It was said that Harry Truman followed "the second most controversial president in a century, who was, when living, perhaps also the most popular in our history." Outside the US, "the world ... had just gone through greater disruptive change than at any time during the life of our nation." His task, "reminiscent of that in the first chapter of Genesis," would be formidable: "to help the free world emerge from chaos without blowing the whole world apart in the process." [175]

In speaking of his old boss (F.D.R.) and concluding with his new one (Truman), former Secretary of State Dean Acheson had said,

> He could charm an individual or a nation. But he condescended. Many reveled in apparent admission to an inner circle. I did not ... To me it was patronizing and humiliating.
> ...
> This, of course, was a small part of the man and the impression he made. The essence of that was force. He exuded a relish of power and command. His responses seemed too quick; his reasons too facile for considered judgment; one could not tell what lay beneath them. He remained a formidable man, a leader who won admiration and respect. In others he inspired far more, affection and devotion. *For me, that was reserved for a man of whom at the time I had never heard of, his successor.* [176] *(emphasis mine)*

Harry S. Truman, "the captain with the mighty heart," Dean Acheson had called him, is the seventh and last of the great American Presidents. Acheson continued his praise of Truman, providing some unique insight into the man and human nature at the same time:

> The 'little touch of Harry,' which kept us all going, came from an inexhaustible supply of vitality and good spirits. He could, and did, outwork us all, with no need for papers predigested into one-page pellets of pablum. One 'little touch of Harry' appeared in a motto framed on his desk—'The buck stops here.' When things went wrong, he took the blame; when things went right, he followed his hero, 'Marse Robert,' General Robert E. Lee, by giving one of his lieutenants the credit. None

of his aides had a trouble in his public or private life that the President was not quick to know and quick to ease.

These are qualities of a leader who builds esprit de corps. He expected, and received, the loyalty he gave. As only those close to him knew, Harry S. Truman was two men. One was the public figure—peppery, sometimes belligerent, often didactic, the 'give-'em-hell' Harry. The other was the patient, modest, considerate, and appreciative boss, helpful and understanding in all official matters, affectionate and sympathetic in any private worry or sorrow. This was the 'Mr. President' we knew and loved.

Today no one can come to the Presidency of the United States really qualified for it. But he can do his best to become so. Mr. Truman was always doing his level best. He aspired to the epitaph reputed to be on an Arizona tombstone ___ 'Here lies Bill Jones. He done his damnedest.' His judgment developed with the exercise of it. At first it was inclined to be hasty as though pushed out by the pressure of responsibility, and— perhaps so—by concern that deliberateness might seem indecisive. But he learned fast and soon would ask, 'How long have we got to work this out?' He would take what time was available for study and then decide. General Marshall had called this capacity the rarest gift given to man and often said that President Truman had it to a high degree.
...
The capacity for decision, however, does not produce, of itself, wise decisions. For that a President needs a better eye and more intuition and coordination than the best hitters in the major leagues. If his score is not far better than theirs, he will be rated a failure. But the metaphor is inadequate; it leaves out the necessary creativity. A President is not merely coping with the deliveries of others. He is called upon to influence and move to some degree his own country and the world around it to a purpose that he envisions. [177]

On his first day as the new president following F.D.R.'s death Harry S. Truman knew little detail of the problems he would have to immediately confront. He himself had said that

There have been few men in all history the equal of the man into whose shoes I am stepping. I pray God I can measure up to the task. [178]

His statement was no exaggeration. For example, when he took office in April 1945, Truman knew absolutely *nothing* of the US government's Manhattan Project to develop an atomic bomb. The secrecy surrounding its development was so strict that, even as Vice President, Truman was kept completely in the dark. But all that would change. Like Lincoln and F.D.R. before him, President Truman would have his own first 100 whirlwind days to contend with. First, there would be a crash course of self-education on "the bomb." Second, he alone would also have to make the fateful decision to use it, twice, on the cities of Hiroshima, then Nagasaki, Japan in August 1945.

At the conclusion of the Second European Civil War, Europe was, in a word, destroyed, as was Japan. An estimated 60 million lives, including the lives of some 20 million Russians, and 6 million Jews, were lost. The peoples of those regions were war weary, cold, hungry, beaten down. At the end, only two countries in the conflict, the US and the USSR, were left standing. Neither was from Europe.

Central questions posed tremendous domestic controversy amid concerns over the future. In the present, how could a failing Western Europe be fed, clothed and warmed as early as the coming winter? Consistent with that end, how in the nearer term could Western Europe be spared and saved ultimately from the threat of communist USSR infiltration or military overrun from the east? And in the intermediate to longer term, how best could the once mortal enemies and now vanquished empires of Nazi Germany and Imperial Japan be secured and integrated into the "free world" economic mainstream and Western sphere of influence? [179]

Under President Truman's watchful eye, a number of critical, foreign policy initiatives would significantly shape the second half of the 20th century, to the present day. First, President Truman implemented F.D.R.'s vision for a United Nations (UN) world body, which would succeed where the prior League of Nations had failed following World War I. The UN combined the *five* strongest world powers, US, UK (Great Britain), France, USSR and China into a *permanent*, security council membership arrangement. *Unanimity* among these members would be required to undertake military action. The intent was to discourage and thereby drastically reduce, if not eliminate, the potential for a rogue state like Nazi Germany to menace the world again in the future.

A second important foreign policy initiative included what was labeled NSC-68, better known generally as the containment policy. This foreign policy document cogently analyzed how US power should actively meet, match and, preferably, outmatch the looming communist threat posed by the USSR. The idea was not simply to react but rather to continually build strength in collaboration with willing allies, blend with high purpose and persevere with steady, patient resolve. [180]

During the Cold War which followed, the Truman Doctrine was a practical example, providing US economic aid for Turkey and Greece, countries that requested US aid in support of democracy. The controversial Marshall Plan was another. In a gesture of great liberality, America provided Europe with the fruit of its own farms and factories, from which Europe would first be fed and then re-built. [181] The alternative, Europe's fall to communism, was unthinkable. The Korean War, a UN sponsored military action, was seen as Japan's Marshall Plan to jump start its post-war industrial economy.

NATO, the North Atlantic Treaty Organization, offered another example. Through a system of military alliance, a communist attack on one member nation would be considered an attack on all. This was effectively designed to give the USSR pause before instigating military action in any sphere against what would be a unified reprisal. Finally, the new nation of Israel, on its declared sovereignty in 1948, was immediately recognized by President Truman and the US government in a symbolic transfer of the torch of Western Civilization from Great Britain to the US.

Back at home, President Truman's "Fair Deal" domestic program continued the principles of F.D.R.'s New Deal agenda, including the extension of F.D.R.'s GI Bill of Rights. Under this program, as with World War II veterans before, returning Korean War veterans in the early 1950s received certain government incentives regarding citizenship, education, housing, seed money for business. By this public policy enactment, whole groups of then immigrants were able to obtain housing, education, jobs and provide a better future for their families, while assimilating seamlessly into American society. It was a win, win proposition for American society.

Additionally, Truman significantly increased the level of benefits under SSA, expanding the retirement portions, and extended coverage to more than 10 million people, including agricultural workers. Importantly, no new financing system accompanied this expansion, a consequence of twin beliefs. First, it was believed that sustained economic growth could underwrite the cost of domestic programs; second, that politically divisive adjustments, if necessary, could be addressed at a later time.

But Truman had reflected in writing to his mother in autumn 1945: "Everybody wants something at the expense of everybody else and nobody thinks much of the other fellow." [182] This would prove to be prophetic to future generations of leadership.

***

Who could have been the eighth great American President? Many believe it was Robert F. Kennedy. In June 1968 California voters had given candidate Robert Kennedy a narrow victory in their Democratic Presidential Primary, a victory that may have propelled him to the White House. During his victory speech and in a festive, frenzied atmosphere, he thanked his supporters for what was truly a people's victory: "We are a great country, an unselfish country, and a compassionate country. I intend to make that my basis for running." [183] Shortly after leaving the stage, however, a tragedy unfolded, set in motion by a bullet discharged from the handgun of a fanatically deranged, Palestinian assassin. [184]

The brief presidential administration of John F. Kennedy (J.F.K.) (1960-1963) had succeeded that of Dwight Eisenhower, the US military General and former commander of Allied Forces during World War II. At the conclusion of his two terms President Eisenhower's 1960 Farewell Address warned Americans about possible future problems. In particular, he pointed out the "military-industrial complex," a new term in the lexicon of the ordinary citizen. This complex, an alliance between government and business, had the potential to threaten the democratic process in the country. [185]

John F. Kennedy, the new President, was undeterred. His 1961 inaugural address touched upon the torch of leadership being "passed to a new generation of Americans." But following J.F.K.'s own assassination in Dallas, Texas in November 1963, that lofty aspiration had been seemingly changed forever.

Passionate investigations to determine *who* had killed J.F.K. in turn later evolved to *why* he may have been killed. Many difficult questions remained. Moreover, his ambitious civil rights agenda languished in Congress. And he left a "hopelessly divided legacy" on the direction of a still nascent American military incursion into Vietnam. [186]

As J.F.K.'s younger brother, Robert Kennedy was an over-achiever. He was neither a natural athlete, nor student, had no natural gift for popularity. "What he had was a set of handicaps and a fantastic determination to overcome them." Robert Kennedy was an underdog with "persisting sympathy for other underdogs." [187]

He had always faithfully subordinated himself to his brother's interests, the coordinator and focal point of J.F.K.'s 1960 election campaign.

Robert Kennedy despaired in the personal tragedy of his brother's violent death. His was the nation's tragedy, and it lowered him to great depths. However, in helping him to face down his despair and on the suggestion of his brother's young widow, Jacqueline, Robert Kennedy would turn to study the ancient Greek poets. In reality, he could have received this advice from Thomas Jefferson, as well. Among these was Aeschylus, who would become his favorite, and the poem was one he could recite easily from memory:

> He who learns must suffer.
> And even in our sleep
> Pain which cannot forget
> Falls drop by drop upon the heart
> Until, in our own despair, against our will
> Comes Wisdom—through the awful grace of God.

Meanwhile, two unheralded African Americans were also forging a lasting impression on the national conscience. Although neither possessed a formal link to Robert Kennedy, each proceeded down parallel paths, a spiritual brotherhood of human decency opposing racism, poverty and war. [188]

The first was a young Baptist minister, reared in Atlanta, Georgia with a doctorate degree in theology. Dr. Martin Luther King, Jr. advocated civil disobedience, but in a different way. He preached *nonviolent*, direct action guided by the Christian ideal of love and not through racial hatred. Jailed in Birmingham, Alabama for such protests in 1963, King wrote that his people had been told to "Wait!" for constitutional (and God-given) rights, for nearly 350 years. This *wait* had almost always meant *never*. His people were no longer willing to wait patiently for equal rights, that the "Time is now."

The phenomenon of sit-ins and the 1963 civil rights march on Washington, D.C. would follow. "The arc of the moral universe is long," Dr. King liked to say, "but it bends toward justice." [189] His powerful "I have a dream" speech would become famously embedded into American culture.

Later, in 1968 Dr. King gave another speech in Memphis, Tennessee which would become famous. His words were these:

> Like anybody, I would like to live a long life. Longevity has its place. But I'm not concerned about that now. I just want to do God's will. And He's allowed me to go up to the mountain. And I've looked over. And I've seen the Promised Land. I may not get there with you. But I want you to know tonight, that we, as a people, will get to the promised land! [190]

Following the speech on the very next day, Dr. King would face his own mortality at the hands of an assassin's bullet.

The second was a man from Louisville, Kentucky who, like his father before him, had been named in tribute to a white Kentucky abolitionist. In 1964, on the day after winning the heavyweight boxing championship of the world, Cassius Clay rebelled against the Southern status quo like the abolitionist from an earlier time. Clay renounced both his "slave" name and the Christian faith that had given him that slave name, changing his name to Muhammad Ali and his religion to Islam. In further refusing induction into military service in the highly controversial Vietnam War as a conscientious objector, Ali, too, was jailed, focusing public attention on his actions, as well.

When it came to Vietnam, Ali expressed words that would become infamous: "I ain't got no quarrel with them Vietcong. They never called me nigger." It was true, the Vietnamese rice farmer had never called Ali "nigger." Some, though, happened to be communist, and America was at war with these communists in Vietnam. Rather, Ali's quarrel was with an American government that gave lip service to the idea of equal rights but practiced and was perpetuating de facto discrimination and racism at home.

Meanwhile, President Lyndon Johnson, J.F.K.'s successor, escalated the Vietnam War exponentially through the mid-1960s, motivated in part by fear of a soft on communism label. [191] As time went on, resources once slated for the domestic war on poverty were increasingly squeezed, diverted to prosecuting the military war effort. It was becoming apparent by 1967 that the Vietnam War was swallowing up the Great Society, making the president's domestic achievements a fading memory. [192] The war had grown terribly divisive, due in no small measure to the administration's deception of the public as to the war's scope, magnitude and stated goals.

With Dr. King and Ali hitting their full stride, Robert Kennedy gradually emerged from his despair. He became US Senator from New York, a changed man finding his own voice. Re-evaluating America's involvement in Vietnam, in early 1968 he would become the first politician of national stature to publicly break with the Johnson administration on the prosecution of the war. [193] At the time, he had said that there was plenty of blame to go around for how the country had landed in the predicament that it was in. He himself had been involved as the Attorney General and member of J.F.K.'s inner policy circle. [194] But he was prepared to accept his share of the responsibility, which he admitted was more than a little.

On an official visit to South Africa, still under the insidious grip of legalized segregation, Robert Kennedy talked first of the long American struggle for racial justice, rejecting the notion that precise US solutions could "be dictated or transplanted to others." Let know one be discouraged, he said, by

> the belief there is nothing one man or one woman can do against the enormous array of the world's ills—against misery and ignorance, injustice and violence. ... Few will have the greatness to bend history itself; but each of us can work to change a small portion of events, and in the total of all those acts will be written the history of this generation.

> It is from numberless diverse acts of courage and belief that human history is shaped. Each time a man stands up for an ideal, or acts to improve the lot of others, or strikes out against injustice, he sends a tiny ripple of hope, and crossing each other from a million different centres of energy and daring those ripples build a current which can sweep down the mightiest walls of oppression and resistance. [195]

Back at home, Robert Kennedy led a bold, anti-poverty initiative designed to stem the seemingly irreversible decline of the nation's cities into decaying slums. It featured a partnership, aligning local citizens and private enterprise with government. He did not believe in welfare or government handouts to people, nor that the federal government could do all things for all people. Rather, he focused on support for a critical element—"the full and dominant participation by the local residents," empowering the downtrodden to take control of their own destiny. The experiment was an innovative application of the idea of community action—to build from the ground up—not from the top down.

It was a success, elevating the predominantly poor and black people of Brooklyn's Bedford Stuyvesant, a blighted New York City neighborhood. Kennedy felt this experiment could serve as a model for other similarly situated US urban areas in decline. "Government belongs," he said, "where evil needs an adversary and there are people in distress who cannot save themselves." [196] His faith in the belief that America could do better provided yet another example of the effects of a changed persona.

A man of deep faith and moral courage, Robert Kennedy was the kind of leader who had the potential to change the course of American history. [197] He could see through the eyes of the poor, the dispossessed. People of all colors and denominations—minorities and the young—came to trust him, believe in him, have faith in him. He had a "fantastic ability to communicate hope to some pretty rejected people." [198] He would speak for these people in a way they could not speak for themselves.

Robert Kennedy was on to something. [199] He had a "deep, almost mystical" bond with the "Other America." [200] They saw who he was, and so they were for him. Throughout history, a leader with these qualities was exceedingly rare.

***

A few further highlights are of note. Then-General Eisenhower had observed the Autobahn in Nazi Germany during the World War II years. He marveled at its utility in efficient movement of both troops and military equipment. Upon returning to the US, President Eisenhower would become the architect of our national interstate highway system (NSIHA) in the 1950s. Based on the German model, it would be most useful in the US, as well. This massive public works undertaking was a national investment in infrastructure which was to pay multiple dividends. And it would also be most useful for the mass movement of citizens, in the event of a nuclear strike on the US from the outside.

In 1978 President Jimmy Carter was understood to be the architect of a peace treaty between Israel and Egypt, eternal military rivals. The peace treaty was negotiated in secret over a period of 13 days and signed at the presidential retreat in Maryland, and is otherwise known as the Camp David Accords. The importance of this triumph cannot be understated, as all three wars from Israel's declaration of statehood (1956, 1967 and 1973) to that point in time were against Egypt. The largest military and economic power in the Middle East region would now be taken off the table as a formidable military threat and become Israel's stated partner in peace.

***

Many others claim Ronald Reagan, who served from 1980-1988, to be in the category of our eight great American President. Consequently, Mr. Reagan's reach for presidential greatness must be examined.

First, President Reagan persuaded Americans to rethink old attitudes about government as provider. [201] He reminded the ordinary citizen that he "used to be a Democrat" and had stood behind F.D.R. and his popular New Deal agenda (at the time, in fact, he stood demonstrably left of F.D.R.). American liberalism was at or near high tide under President Lyndon Johnson's declaration of a "war on poverty" in the 1960s. During the 1964 presidential election against ultra-conservative US Senator Barry Goldwater, R-AZ [202], President Johnson's campaign had challenged ordinary Americans to build a "Great Society" that eliminated the troubles of the poor. Hadn't Goldwater been trounced in a landslide?

But in a break with 1960s New Deal liberals, Mr. Reagan tacked to the right. He believed that social welfare programs expanded the government's role into the lives of the ordinary citizen to levels which were simply unacceptable. Mr. Reagan felt that these government programs that expanded the New Deal, from education to retirement to health care in the name of "entitlements," were essentially free giveaways. As such, they threatened unconstitutional intrusion into citizens' private affairs and posed a threat to individual initiative and responsibility.

Mr. Reagan's plain, homey style and conservative agenda were extremely effective in reminding the ordinary citizen that the term "Democrat" had since become synonymous with the phrase "tax and spend liberal." Additionally, Mr. Reagan felt that the government was not the solution. Rather, "the government was the problem." In addition to unifying his own party, Mr. Reagan attracted disaffected "Kennedy Democrats" in impressive fashion to broaden his governing coalition.

Moreover, President Reagan's policies were widely acknowledged to be largely responsible for the end of the Cold War (although the fall of the Berlin Wall in 1989 in partitioned East Germany and the collapse of communism in the former USSR in 1991 occurred after his presidency had ended). Who among us, old enough to remember, can forget President Reagan's passionate speech in June 1987 at the gates of the Berlin Wall?:

> Today I say: As long as the gate is closed, as long as this scar of a wall is permitted to stand, it is not the German question alone that remains open, but the question of freedom for all mankind. Yet I do not come here to lament. For I find in Berlin a message of hope, even in the shadow of this wall, a message of triumph.
>
> …
>
> there stands before the entire world one great and inescapable conclusion: Freedom leads to prosperity. Freedom replaces the ancient hatreds among the nations with comity and peace. Freedom is the victor.
>
> …
>
> We welcome change and openness; for we believe that freedom and security go together, that the advance of human liberty can only strengthen the cause of world peace.
>
> …
>
> General Secretary Gorbachev, if you seek peace, if you seek prosperity for the Soviet Union and Eastern Europe, if you seek liberalization: Come here to this gate! Mr. Gorbachev, open this gate! Mr. Gorbachev, tear down this wall! [203]

Lastly, President Reagan began to reverse the troubling stigma that his own Republican Party had stood against the movement in favor of black civil rights. In at least the two or three decades leading up to Mr. Reagan's presidential term, the Republican Party had earned a troubling, but well founded, reputation. Stated demonstrably to be pro civil rights in the open, the Republican Party was suspected of doing everything in its power behind closed doors to inhibit the civil rights progress of blacks. After all, it was argued, Barry Goldwater, the main architect of the conservative movement, had as a US Senator cast his vote *against* the Civil Rights Act of 1964.

The suspicion received a label, the "Southern Strategy," which was widely enshrined by liberal Democrats in the media. Republicans would campaign in the South using "regional code words," demonstrating that the White House would not be working to enforce civil rights laws, while appearing publicly to endorse them. [204]

In the 1980 presidential campaign, then-candidate Reagan had stated, "We must not allow the noble concept of equal opportunity to be distorted into federal guidelines or quotas which require race, ethnicity, or sex—rather than ability and qualifications—to be the principal factor in hiring or education." [205] He would stand opposed to affirmative action, while at the same time championing the rights of people of color to equal protection of the laws. The two were not deemed mutually exclusive.

Accordingly, the "Southern Strategy" stigma of the Republican Party would begin to change under the Reagan administration. At the same time, President Reagan still maintained that he felt "no higher duty than to defend the civil rights of all Americans." [206] At the same time, the lines between conservative and liberal labeling were beginning to blur once again.

Then there was the controversy about making the birthday of Dr. Martin Luther King Jr. into an official federal holiday. For almost 15 years, the bill languished in the US Congress, which finally passed it in 1983. President Reagan signed the bill a month later, making him the first president to sign a bill commemorating an African American with a national holiday. At a King observance the year after the holiday officially was celebrated in 1986, President Reagan denounced racial bigotry and discrimination, effectively wrapping himself in King's mantle, while continuing to speak out against racial discrimination. [207]

***

If it is premature, or remains yet a subject of debate, whether Ronald Reagan can be considered our eighth great American President, it would, of course, be neither fair nor appropriate to attempt to include President Barack Obama in the present discussion. His body of work is largely undetermined, remains yet to be seen and can be judged best only in hindsight. But early results show promise.

In the election of 2008, then-candidate Obama had offered to replace a long and wide shadow of fear cast over the landscape with an audacity of hope. [208] It hearkened back to F.D.R. Following Mr. Obama's election victory, the theme for the 2009 inauguration was "A New Birth of Freedom," in honor of the bicentennial of Abraham Lincoln's birth.

During his first term, President Obama showed that his administration was not afraid to "think big" in trying to set a forward, progressive course for future generations. Major legislative reforms included a breakthrough on affordable health care as well as new, tougher financial regulations for Wall Street. Additionally, significant increases in automobile fleet mileage standards [209] (with initiatives on alternative, renewable and cleaner, more efficient use of energy), coupled with ending one war (Iraq) and a definitive end date for the other (Afghanistan), signal a promising new national direction.

Following President Obama's narrow but convincing 2012 re-election, his major second term priorities are entwined with multiple thorny issues. Among these are comprehensive immigration reform, further national energy initiatives to combat the effects of global warming [210] and the stabilization of the nation's long term financial health through equitable reformation of the tax code to counter wealth disparity.

***

A parting thought on the world in which we live may help to understand America's present "direction."

The central political, social, economic and cultural fact of the second half of the 20th century is the gradual shift of people, and power, from the older industrial states of the Northeast and Upper Midwest to the South and Western rim. Since 1964, all elected presidents are from there, with the exception of our current President Obama (Illinois). In 1958, baseball's Brooklyn Dodgers of Ebbets Field left for Los Angeles, while the New York Giants of the old Polo Grounds followed them out to San Francisco. In 1960 California passed New York as the most populous state. Long gone are the days when *all* the NFL games were scheduled to start on Sunday at 1:00 p.m., eastern standard time.

For the South, it's about cheap land, wages and prices, less government bureaucracy, regulation and the proliferation of the phenomenon of air conditioning. The invention of an electrical system which simultaneously cools, dehumidifies and cleanses the air which we humans must breathe has signaled a change of mindset from the "long hot summer" to the "Sunbelt." Names like Disney World and places like Florida seem to make people smile.

For the West, it's about the prudent management of scarce water resources in what is referred to as a "hydraulic society." It's also about the task of attempting to move around without the benefit of any major public mass transit systems, to which anyone who has experienced a Los Angeles "freeway" traffic jam can well attest. Despite what many claim are its superior benefits, life in the West, then, suffers from a "twin dependency" on both the automobile as well as diverted water.

In both cases, it's also about the deep suspicion and mistrust of both New York money and Washington, D.C. politics, and a further reliance on federal defense spending to bolster local economies in the shadow of the military-industrial complex.

Chapter 8
Needs vs. Wants

When I was young, it seemed that life was so wonderful,
a miracle, it was beautiful, magical
And all the birds in the trees, well they'd be singing so happily,
joyfully, playfully watching me
But then they sent me away to teach me how to be sensible, logical,
responsible, practical,
And then they showed me a world where I could be so dependable,
clinical, intellectual, cynical

There are times when all the world's asleep,
The questions run too deep
for such a simple man
Won't you please, please tell me what we've learned
I know it sounds absurd
but please tell me who I am

I said now watch what you say, they'll be calling you a radical,
a liberal, fanatical, criminal
Won't you sign up your name, we'd like to feel you're
acceptable, respectable, presentable, a vegetable

- from the song, *The Logical Song*,
by Supertramp (1979)
available on the *Breakfast in America* collection

***

In February 2008 an ordinary citizen penned a letter to the Hon. Jon S. Corzine, then-Governor of the state of New Jersey. The former CEO of Goldman Sachs, the venerable investment bank, Gov. Corzine was in his first term, having correctly identified as a candidate the pressing economic problems of the day and promising reform. Some say he bought the office with his own money, or Wall Street money, that is. So it was going to be interesting to watch the candidate's reforms purport to unfold.

In any event, the letter contained some personal thoughts, addressing a severe budgetary crisis affecting New Jersey, in which many other states found themselves similarly a situated. The aim was to pinpoint the problem through use of historical context, and then propose some basic remedies.

The original draft has been edited for style purposes, while the substance remains unchanged. An excerpt is re-printed here:

February 14, 2008

Hon. Jon S. Corzine, Governor

State of New Jersey

Re: State of New Jersey's Budget Crisis: Analysis and Proposals

    Addressing the Needs of the Citizens

Dear Governor Corzine:

It is with the interest of a deeply concerned Citizen that an ordinary citizen addresses You at this time as our Governor and chief executive of the state of New Jersey.

You have informed the Citizens of serious financial issues in the state that are "clear and present," that "We must take action, some kind of action." The problem is the state's mounting debt service, currently at $32 billion, and the state's inability to manage that debt, a financial crisis, if you will.

You are now apparently about half way through an ambitious itinerary of conducting Town Hall meetings across the state. You have proposed a controversial Plan to revamp state finances and to fund significant infrastructure improvement projects out 75 years into the future, by raising the tax burden on the Citizens. Specifically, Your Plan significantly raises the user fees on the state's revenue generating toll roads and borrows against the projected revenues on a long-term basis.

You have assured the Citizens that You "do not consider your plan to be a *fait accompli*" but that at present You "don't see better alternatives." You say that "if there are better alternatives, You want to hear about them," that You "are listening and legislators are listening."

You are hearing that the most frequently asked question has been: Why not slash state spending? Many other concerned Citizens apparently remain unconvinced as to the merits and wisdom of Your Plan. In an ordinary household, "If you're on a budget, you don't spend more; you figure out ways to cut back."

You have responded in principle that "We have to raise revenues to meet our contractual obligations." You say that "pension and health benefits are the state's largest and fastest-growing expense," despite some concessions from unionized state workers. You say that "most of the tidal wave of expenses that will rock the state budget in coming years is locked in by past legislation or contracts and cannot be disturbed." [211]

And it is not lost on the Citizens that much of the "past legislation and contracts" was "locked in" by public servants who have been public servants for years. Many have served continuously even for decades, and so remain as public servants presently. All are now apparently scrambling in a combined effort to find innovative ways to pay for these ever-expanding state programs.

It is also apparent that the policies of past legislators and executives to permit and then cause these ever-expanding state programs to be "locked in" were perhaps imprudent and misguided. Given its limited resources, the Citizens assume the government never had, nor contemplated having, adequate resources to honor the tidal wave of pension and health benefits. The Citizens further assume that the system is prone to abuse and corruption. Moreover, it is equally apparent, and unfortunate, that the stated oath of public service in promoting the Public Good was at all times in direct conflict with individual self-interest. Election and reelection efforts, the purchase of votes and offices, maintaining only their own individual interests: all strike the Citizens as being odious and in violation of the oath of public service.

In such a sorry state of affairs as the Citizens find themselves, it is beneficial to attempt to seek Wisdom and guidance in the examples of our founding fathers and subsequent leaders who sought to emulate the spirit of the founding fathers. You would do well to consider doing likewise.

The first such individual is Benjamin Franklin, the Enlightenment thinker—the Grandfather of our Country, an exalted title, but one which is well-earned and deserved. From the earliest days of the republic, Ben Franklin had warned of the inherent danger of ambition and greed, when combined, having the human tendency to turn posts of honour into places of profit.

During the tumultuous days leading to the enactment of our present US Constitution in 1789, Franklin discussed the merits of limiting the perks of elected lawmakers within the laws of human nature:

> Sir, there are two Passions which have a powerful influence in the Affairs of Men. These are *Ambition* and *Avarice*; the Love of Power and the Love of Money. Separately, each of these has great Force in prompting Men to Action; but when united in View of the same Object, they have in many Minds the most violent Effects. Place before the Eyes of such Men a Post of *Honour*, that shall at the same time be a Place of *Profit*, and they will move Heaven and Earth to obtain it. The vast Number of such Places it is that renders the British Government so tempestuous. The Struggles for them are the true Source of all those Factions which are perpetually dividing the Nation, distracting its Councils, hurrying it sometimes into fruitless and mischievous Wars, and often compelling a Submission to dishonourable Terms of Peace.

He turned to the type of men which such personal incentives would attract:

> And of what kind are the men that will strive for this profitable Preeminence, thro' all the Bustle of Cabal, the Heat of Contention, the infinite mutual Abuse of Parties, tearing to Pieces the best of Characters? It will not be the wise and moderate, the Lovers of Peace and good Order, the men fittest for the Trust. It will be the Bold and the Violent, the men of strong Passions and indefatigable Activity in their selfish Pursuits. These will thrust themselves into your Government, and be your Rulers. And these, too, will be mistaken in the expected Happiness of their Situation; for their vanquish'd competitors, of the same Spirit, and from the same Motives, will perpetually be endeavoring to distress their Administration, thwart their Measures, and render them odious to the People.

Those personal gains would be smeared into the fabric of our bedrock institutions, where they would leave an impressionable and lasting stain. And before long, extensions would be sought, leading to a tipping point pitting the governing against the governed:

> Besides these Evils, Sir, tho' we may set out in the Beginning with Moderate Salaries, we shall find, that such will not be of long Continuance. Reasons will never be wanting for propos'd Augmentations; and there will always be a Party for giving more to the Rulers, that the Rulers may be able in Return to give more to them. Hence, as all History informs us, there has been in every State and Kingdom a constant kind of Warfare between the Governing and the Governed; the one striving to obtain more for its Support, and the other to pay less. And this has alone occasion'd great

Convulsions, actual civil Wars, ending either in dethroning the Princes or enslaving the People. Generally, indeed, the Ruling Power carries its Point, and we see the Revenues of Princes constantly increasing, and we see that they are never satisfied, but always in want of more. The more the People are discontented with the Oppression of Taxes, the greater Need the Prince has of Money to distribute among his Partisans, and pay the Troops that are to suppress all Resistance, and enable him to plunder at Pleasure. There is scarce a King in a hundred, who would not, if he could, follow the Example of Pharaoh,—get first all the People's Money, then all their Lands, and then make them and their Children Servants for ever. It will be said, that we do not propose to establish Kings. I know it. But there is a natural Inclination in Mankind to kingly Government. It sometimes relieves them from Aristocratic Domination. They had rather have one Tyrant than 500. It gives more of the appearance of Equality among Citizens; and that they like. I am apprehensive, therefore,—perhaps too apprehensive,—that the Government of these States may in future times end up in Monarchy. But this Catastrophe, I think, may be long delay'd, if in our propos'd System we do not sow the Seeds of Contention, Faction, and Tumult, by making our Posts of Honour Places of Profit. If we do, I fear, that, tho' we employ at first a Number and not a single Person, the Number will in time be set aside; it will only nourish the Foetus of a King (as the honorouble Gentleman from Virg' very aptly express'd it), and a King will the sooner be set over us. [212]

Mr. Franklin then considered the concept of Property rights. He reminded the Citizens that these (like pension benefits) are Our creation, that for a seat at the table of the American Dream, what We have conferred as a Right, We also have the Power to take away:

All Property, indeed, except the Savage's temporary Cabin, his Bow, his Matchcoat, and other little Acquisitions, absolutely necessary for his Subsistence, seems to me to be the Creature of public Convention. Hence, the Public has the Right of Regulating Descents, and all other Conveyances of Property, and even of limiting the Quantity and the Uses of it. All the Property that is necessary to a Man, for the Conservation of the Individual and the Propagation of the Species, is his natural Right, which none can justly deprive him of: But all Property superfluous to such purposes is the Property of the Publick, who, by their Laws, have created it, and who may therefore by other Laws dispose of it, whenever the Welfare of the Publick shall demand such Disposition. He that does not like civil Society on these Terms, let him retire and live among Savages. He can have no right to the benefits of Society, who will not pay his Club towards the Support of it. [213]

Additionally, Mr. Franklin warned the Citizens, generally, that "No revenue is sufficient without economy:"

Indeed, some among us are not so much griev'd for the present state of our affairs as apprehensive for the future. The growth of luxury alarms them, and they think we are, from that alone, on the high road to ruin. They observe that no revenue is sufficient without economy, and that the most plentiful income of a whole people from natural productions of their country may be dissipated in vain and needless expenses, and poverty be introduc'd in the place of affluence. This may be possible; it however rarely happens, for there seems to be in every nation a greater proportion of industry and frugality which tend to enrich, than idleness

163

and prodigality, which occasions poverty, so that upon the whole there is a continual accumulation. ...

... He that puts a seed into the earth is recompens'd perhaps by receiving twenty out of it; and he who draws a fish out of our waters draws up a piece of silver. Let us (and there is no doubt but we shall) be attentive to these, and then the power of rivals, with all their restraining and prohibiting acts, cannot hurt us. We are the sons of the earth and seas, and like *Anteus*, if in wrestling with Hercules we now and then receive a fall, the touch of our parents will communicate to us fresh strength and ability to renew the contest. *Be quiet and thankful.* [214]

Andrew Jackson represents another great American whose inspiration may guide the Citizens through troubled times. Instinctively, Jackson understood the perils of a legislative establishment paradise, unchecked. [215] Jacksonian Democracy ushered in America's first age of reform. Previously, the Era of Good Feeling had been marked by a rare absence of partisan conflict, yet a period of widespread corruption had infiltrated many American institutions. Mr. Jackson saw that period not as the Era of Good Feeling but rather as the Era of Corruption. And no institution was perhaps more corrupt than the Bank of the United States (BUS), the nation's sole, legally sanctioned central banking institution, a banking monopoly. Its director was the subject of political appointment, not answerable to the electorate. Many Congressmen were on open retainer and as such more than eager and willing to do its bidding.

Mr. Jackson, however, saw the danger inherent in this set up, arguing that not only was the BUS corrupt but so was all of Congress for supporting it. Appealing over the head of Congress directly to the Citizens, Mr. Jackson sought to "kill" the BUS. Not surprisingly, Congress fought bitterly to oppose the death of the BUS, going so far as publicly censure of the president for his actions on the road to its demise. Against the strong advice of his advisors, Mr. Jackson even chose to make the issue of whether to re-charter the BUS the central issue of his 1832 re-election effort. He gave the Citizens a clear choice, challenging them to vote either for him or the BUS. Of course, the Citizens sustained President Jackson, the BUS suffering its demise in the name of necessary reform.

Similarly, Mr. Jackson had inherited from his predecessor a federal government which was bloated with debt and excessive spending. The culprit was also stated to be "past legislation." Embarking on a disciplined approach involving personal management and oversight over all the public expenditures, Mr. Jackson employed a systematic policy of "reform, economy and retrenchment." In the process, he managed to virtually eliminate the entire public debt and returned the nation to surplus. No wonder the bankers hated him.

Critical to his success, Mr. Jackson enacted a popular system of rotation in office. Unproductive federal office-holders were systematically removed, as necessary, and replaced with fresh, though inexperienced replacements. Singular in purpose, Mr. Jackson constantly reminded the Citizens that experience was overrated and that even ordinary, common Citizens could learn. Further, lifetime or long-tenured office-holding often led to inefficiency and even corruption. The fresh, new blood of the ordinary Citizen was required to bring strength, grounded, common sense qualities and the ability to renew the contest.

In May 1829, shortly after Mr. Jackson was inaugurated as the 7th President of the United States, he elaborated thus:

> There has been a great noise made about removals—This is to be brought before Congress with the causes—with the propriety of passing a law vacating all offices periodically–then the good can be sustained. & the bad,—left out with murmurs—How every man who has been in office a few years, believes he has a life estate in it, a vested right, & if it has been held 20 years or upwards, not only a vested right, but that it ought to descend to his children, and if no children then the next of kin—This is not the principles of our government. It is rotation in office that will perpetuate our liberty. [216]

President Jackson further elaborated:

> Office is considered as a species of property, and government rather as a means of promoting individual interests than as an instrument created solely for the service of the people. Corruption in some and in others a perversion of correct feelings and principles divert government from its legislative ends and make it an engine for the support of the few at the expense of the many. The duties of all public officers are, or at least admit of being made, so plain and simple that men of intelligence may readily qualify themselves for their performance; and I cannot but believe that more is lost by the long continuance of men in office than is generally to be gained by their experience. I submit, therefore, to your consideration when the efficiency of the Government would not be promoted and official industry and integrity better secured by a great extension of the law which limits appointments to four years.
>
> In a country where offices are created solely for the benefit of the people no one man has any more intrinsic right to official station than another. Offices were not established to give support to particular men at the public expense. No individual wrong is, therefore, done by removal, since neither appointment to nor continuance in office is matter of right.... It is the people, and they alone, who have a right to complain when a bad officer is substituted for a good one. He who is removed has the same means of obtaining a living that are enjoyed by the millions who never held office. The proposed limitation would destroy the idea of property now so generally connected with official station, and although individual distress

165

may be sometimes produced, it would, by promoting that rotation which constitutes a leading principle in the republican creed, give healthful action to the system. [217]

Harry S. Truman, the 33rd President of the United States, is the third great leader who is able to guide and inspire the Citizens. Mr. Truman's stewardship in support of the Allied war effort and at home thereafter in its return to peace, earns him a place of eternal gratitude in the conscience of the nation. Mr. Truman presented valid criticism of the executive figures in the years prior to the nation's Civil War as failing in leadership: "That was one of the very worst periods in our history, the twenty years before Lincoln was elected, before the Civil War," he had said. Mr. Truman continued:

> There's always a lot of talk about how we have to fear the man on horseback, have to be afraid of the … of a strong man, but so far, if I read my American history right, it isn't the strong men that have caused us most of the trouble, it's the ones who were weak. It's the ones who just sat on their asses and twiddled their thumbs when they were President. [218]

Mr. Truman was critical of what he termed the *Five Weak Presidents* (Tyler, Polk, Fillmore, Pierce and Buchanan). He lamented that they seemed to feel that if they just kept quiet and didn't rock the boat, the differences between the slave states and free states and the opponents and proponents of slavery would just disappear. Mr. Truman was sure that would not be the case:

> That's right, and that's the one thing that won't ever happen, not in a million years. That's the *meaning* of government. If you're in it, you've got to govern. Otherwise, you're in the wrong business. … The five of them coming one right after the other made the Civil War inevitable. [219]

Using these great American Patriots for guidance and authority facilitates the following analysis to identify and solve the mounting state budget crisis. It is respectfully offered with sincere apology for lack of command of all pertinent facts and details, as You may possess, uniquely situated as the chief executive. It also occurs that the fallibility of judgment is real, exists in no small measure and is likely increasing with the passage of time.

We are apparently in a peculiar, yet not unique, predicament in our evolutionary history. We appear to be in the throes of a very real, if not officially recognized, economic state of emergency. The Citizens have current financial obligations, for which there is not sufficient present revenue to honor, and for which debt is accruing. The situation is exacerbated by a mountain of prior debt, which it appears, the Citizens will never realistically be able to honor. The Citizens may be near the occasion of an actual civil War, which can only end either in dethroning the Princes or enslaving the People. While the revenue may be increasing, the Prince remains unsatisfied but in want of more. The more the People are discontented with the Oppression of Taxes, the greater Need the Prince has of Money to distribute among his Partisans. The end result anticipates the potential that they are made Children Servants forever.

You are to be commended for articulating the emergent nature of the present state of financial crisis, in manner as to command the immediate attention of the Citizens and a presumed call to action. However, Your Plan, essentially to continue to increase the revenue through further tax augmentation to meet growing "commitments," is inherently flawed. A recommendation to further "lock in" or institutionalize the repayment of the debt burden over ensuing generations, absent a rigid examination of monetary details, is inherently flawed. Discussion which examines the premises on which a great majority of the debt was amassed, continues to be amassed, and whether it should yet continue, unabated, is necessary. For these reasons, Your Plan must be rejected.

What does the ordinary citizen really need? An excellent place to begin analysis is on the expense side, that is, how the Prince is prioritizing the expenditure of the People's money. Common sense dictates that those items which relate to what the People "need" must first be identified as the so-called necessities of life. These must be distinguished from the things which the People merely "want," relating rather to a whole host of discretionary items, or simply greed. In a capitalist economy that often expresses itself in terms of excess, the distinction cannot be underestimated.

In the category of "needs," much of the conduct of Mr. Franklin's early life evidences the truth that the only thing we need is the mere subsistence of bread and water. Over the ensuing centuries, We as a self-proclaimed, "enlightened" People have continually and consistently expanded on what We presume to be our needs. Concepts incorporating more scientific theories about diet (other necessary subsistence in addition to bread and water), standards of "adequate" housing, "equal opportunities" in education, and "good," meaning high-paying, jobs are identified.

In the more recent decades of the late 20th century, prior Princes and legislatures have presumed to add to the basic list of needs certain

167

guaranteed "benefits" atop the salaries of public sector jobs. Although contractually promised, and subject to protection under our laws, it is doubtful these benefits were ever the subject of valid actuarial accounting practices. Surely, secure retirement payments in the form of lifetime pensions, unconscionable annual expenditures in too many cases, as well as free, unlimited access to health care and related services, are *not* on the Citizen's list of needs. But, hence, the Prince calls for more revenue anyway.

When it comes to analysis of "need," the People are guided by the example of Franklin D. Roosevelt, our 32nd President. In the throes of the Great Depression, F.D.R. left the People with the enduring legacy: a primary obligation of the government is to provide help to its Citizens, *especially in their time of need.* During that time, need meant food, government bread delivered to hungry people waiting desperately on long lines. The government subsidized clothing, housing and sponsored programs designed to put the People back to work. The "New Deal" experiment was designed to confront an ongoing emergency.

In the category of "wants," all the People must do to distinguish needs from wants is watch just a bit of television in prime time. In less than an hour, it is apparent that 99% of what talented Madison Avenue marketing professionals advertise involves a wish list, for which the ordinary citizen falls easily. Just how badly do the People need another prescription, marketed by the powerful pharmaceutical industry, to alleviate the phenomenon of "restless leg syndrome?"

Mr. Franklin's warning with respect to the potential adverse consequences of Debt is chilling. Debt is an ugly but sometimes necessary evil. If permitted to grow unchecked to the point where it cannot realistically expect to be repaid, Debt robs the People of the ability to act independently. Debt thus poses perhaps the greatest danger to threaten Our fundamental liberty.

It is understood that many individuals and business interests on both sides claim affiliation with powerful and politically connected lobbies and/or labor unions. Neither addresses the needs of the People. Should these guaranteed "benefits" which have been "locked in" by prior legislatures and executives be permitted to continue? This question suggests the obvious response.

But before the People should draw premature conclusions, the analysis first requires that the substance of the guaranteed state pension "benefit" be identified. Interestingly, the state pension "benefit" formula is neither familiar nor simple. Moreover, it is not well-publicized and in many respects appears to be shrouded in great *secrecy*, as if a sacred cow which cannot be disturbed. What is abundantly clear, however, is that the guaranteed defined "benefit" is currently being funded with the People's borrowed tax dollars.

Nevertheless, the guaranteed for life annual pension formula is understood to take the average of the worker's annual salary from the three highest years of the prior five years, then multiply that number by the sum of the total number of years of service as a percentage–times two.

Let's illustrate with a real life example. A state worker holds one of many low paying municipal jobs ($15,000.00 per year, plus full medical benefits), like that of part-time local school board attorney, for 22 years. Over time, the worker or friends on his behalf make the required financial contributions to one or the other political party. These political contributions pay off with a plum appointment to a drastically higher paying job in the twilight years of the worker's government service career, like a state court judgeship (paying about $175,000.00 annually to start, plus full medical benefits). Although the appointment term is for 7 years, the worker "retires" 3 years later, or at 25 years of total service.

In this example, the state worker's annual pension benefit equates to $87,500.00 per year, for life (the calculation is .25 x 2 = .50 or 50% of $175,000.00). That comes out to almost $7,300.00 per month, for *not* working, all at taxpayer expense. [220] Moreover, the 25 years of service used in the example is a magic number. At 25 years, the worker also receives comprehensive medical benefits, also for life. It is noteworthy that no worker contribution whatsoever is required, either during the employment period or after retirement, in what is referred to as a "defined benefit" plan.

This arrangement is like thousands of people across the state literally paying to rig the lottery for success, and then winning the lottery, all simultaneously. Incomprehensible? No, sadly it is quite true, an artificial contrivance of the state legislature, akin to a rope around the neck of the ordinary citizen.

169

Unfortunately, as if the situation weren't reprehensible enough, the real life example doesn't end there. The now retired state worker then leaves for another (i.e.: cheaper) state, retaining the opportunity to throw around all that corrupt pension money funded with borrowed taxpayer dollars. The end result is that the home state is saddled with noxious payments. The home state is also deprived of any further derivative economic benefit whatsoever. Quite simply, it is a corrupt drain, favoring a relatively privileged few, plowing the state of New Jersey and other states into the ground.

The guarantee of state pension and health "benefits" began, perhaps, with the best of intentions. The salaries of public school teachers and municipal workers were so low that there would at least be a small perk to lure and keep them in such pursuits.

But over the years politicians and "prior legislatures" added higher salaried positions to the state pension system. Executive appointments, legislators and their "aides," judges, prosecutors, their staffs, law enforcement personnel, a volume of administrative agency and board members, sports agency bureaucrats and other "official" positions were added. That appeared to efficiently cover the gamut of the governing class, a disproportionate number of who, as political appointees, were not subject to the will of the electorate. Incredibly, the system even had room to include *lobbyists* with six figure incomes on the state payroll. In the meantime, what provision did "prior legislatures" make at the time for corresponding revenue increases to balance the state's books? And before these contracts were said to be "locked in?"

The abuse of the state retirement system is rampant and insidious. In other instances of routine administration, each of the state's hundreds of municipalities fiercely resists consolidation of services into more productive central administration. Rather, each municipality insists upon its own hand picked soldiers at the various intra-department levels in defense of the *stated* concept of "home rule." The *real* motive may be to secure as many individuals as possible into the bloated, state retirement system. Moreover, it is not uncommon for local government "officials" in routine positions to find creative ways to "stack" the system to obtain six figure lifetime annual retirement "benefits packages."

Securing such a position in the state pension system is akin to an individual in a small boat hooking the big fish. But given the spirit of partisan politics, the scenario of proliferating political appointments repeats itself like a broken record. When the party which has been turned out objects to these developments, the party in favor responds that it is just making up for past wrongs. The cycle continues and expands unabated as the worm turns. In the end, will not the meaty flesh of the big fish be reduced to a carcass of bones, as in Ernest Hemingway's 1952 classic, *The Old Man and the Sea*?

Power, politics and lobbying are the rule of political patronage. Jobs, even those which involve great public trust, become the subject of political campaign. Unfortunately, the oath of conducting the People's business is diverted to merely securing those self-serving "benefits." All along, the human vice of greed firmly grounds these "benefits" into principles to die for. As a result, the expense side mushrooms out of control into a monstrous boondoggle of a cash drain with no end in sight. In this system, everybody is a winner, except the ordinary citizen and the taxpaying pubic, oppressed with the burden of carrying these growing benefit "commitments" through ever increasing taxes.

True, the retirement "benefit" is a Property Right, as presently constituted. But common sense suggests that it is *not* a "need." It grossly exceeds that which exists for individual workers in the private sector. Moreover, it is tarnished with the insidious and blatant influences of inherent abuse and corruption.

The claimed retirement "benefit right" for the large and ever increasing state "pool" of individual workers is anathema and can no longer be afforded nor tolerated. You *must* eliminate these inherent abuses and corruption. When You were elected, You took an oath to do so. It is now time to deliver on the promise.

Remember and be sustained by Your oath and duty to all the Citizens of the great state of New Jersey. Remember that the Citizens cannot live under the false burden of honoring debts which violate the public trust. Remember, too, that all who claim the benefit and their political supporters will oppose You, because they are entrenched in the system, from which they derive significant material advantage. While, perhaps, some retirement subsistence is still warranted, what is not needed, it is apparent, is a continued minting of free money and a giveaway of the keys to Fort Knox.

Having identified the problems, it is time to turn to some proposed specific solutions. An extreme situation calls for a leader to be called to extreme action, as may be necessary. If that be the case, as Mr. Truman would suggest, it is time for You to lead. If we are in an emergency, then why not make it official, and then act? Accordingly, it is suggested that after conferring with the leaders of the other two branches of the state government, You use the power of the office of the chief executive to declare an "official" but temporary state of emergency. This will permit You to invoke temporary emergency powers to address the financial crisis at hand and avert financial disaster.

Your first order of business must be to call an emergency bargaining session with the state public union under the provisions of the collective bargaining agreement. You must carefully explain in partnership with the union that given the financial emergency the options are limited. The union can either continue to be a legislative partner by agreeing to be a part of the solution to make some necessary concessions on the conferred retirement "benefit." Alternatively, the union can simply choose to sit back and watch, as You utilize emergency powers to freeze all future retirement payments.

This can be done, presumably, on a potential host of sound legal principles. [221] Or perhaps, some new or novel contract defense can be successfully argued and which the flexibility of the law will permit. In the final analysis, what seems clear is that freedom of contract must give way to *correct* legislative abuses in disregard of the public interest. [222]

There is precedent for this action. Facing record historical unemployment and large, "locked in" expenditures, how was F.D.R. able to free up sufficient money to implement his New Deal agenda? At the time, F.D.R. sought to put the government's house in order: to balance the federal budget before undertaking emergency relief. In F.D.R.'s eyes, the two biggest culprits were government salaries and bloated veterans' benefits. His plan called for cutting all government workers' salaries, including his own, by at least 15% to bring them into line with the reduced cost of living since the Great Depression had begun. At the same time, his plan called for scaling back the elaborate array of entitlements enacted for veterans since World War I—which were consuming a quarter of the federal budget. [223]

After fierce debate, the US Congress passed the bill, many Republicans crossing the aisle to support the president. "I am for giving the President whatever he wants in the way of power," spoke US Senator Arthur Capper, R-KS. "This is an emergency situation." US Representative Mary Norton, D-NJ, only the 6th woman in Congress and the first from an eastern state, fittingly, was reported to say that

> This is not a Democratic bill and it is not a Republican bill. It is a bill to maintain the credit of the United States, and I shall support it. [224]

However the action is couched in legal terminology, the mechanism of systematic reform to redefine a reasonable retirement benefit will have been set in consequential motion. At the same time, the union's basic right to collective bargaining will have been legally preserved.

How can all this be fairly accomplished? The federal Social Security system provides an excellent illustration. SSA has set a *maximum* available benefit, which is *capped*, regardless of the worker's total contributions. Why not adopt this system's basic principle? The sum of $25,000.00 per individual per year is suggested (an amount approximately equal to 2x the current annual federal expenditure under SSA). But the final figure should be left to the actuaries and bean counters. It must be flexible enough to permit an increase or decrease on a sliding scale, depending upon the number of eligible workers who must be accounted for. Lastly, the amount of payroll contributions necessary per individual to implement and sustain the proposed action and honor the existing debt service must similarly be re-set.

The issue of the health insurance benefit should be handled similarly. But the stated goal must be to provide affordable, universal minimum levels of health care and a family doctor to every Citizen, not just the state workforce. Toward that end, You are in a unique position to use the economies of scale of a class whose numbers are in the hundreds of thousands to reduce the costs of the present system. At the same time, workers must be obligated to make reasonable contributions in partnership with the state for their health benefits, as is done in the private sector. Finally, You can facilitate an environment in which access to state health insurance is open to all Citizens and businesses who may choose to pay for it.

Some excellent suggestions are highlighted in Bill Bradley's book, *The New American Story* (2007) and will not be repeated here, but they are worth an intensive look. Rather than an adversarial process, the legislature should work with both the state union and private insurers in partnership to implement these initiatives. But one thing is abundantly clear, and which should control the conversation. Money cannot be spent, which simply doesn't exist.

The litmus test of Your administration will be shaped by how You will choose to respond to these important issues as our chief executive. If the issues are truly emergent, and if it is truly about correcting the long-standing financial problems on a structural basis, then You will take the difficult but important steps in the public interest. You must *act* against the vested interests of the powerfully entrenched, as outlined herein. Don't worry about the Citizens. They can handle the truth. You will have the courage and wisdom to understand that if the issues are framed and explained to the Citizens properly and carefully, then the Citizens will sustain You.

In so doing, and for Your considerable and noble efforts, You will receive the just and proper reward of being able to dwell both happily and honorably among the People. In essence, what previous Princes and legislatures gaveth, the present leadership *must* taketh away. True, it will not be easy. The road ahead will contain bumps, twists and peril. But, as Ben Franklin has said, individuals who do not like civil Society on these Terms, let them retire and live among Savages.

On the other hand, if the issue for You is simply about maintaining status among the aristocracy, in the name of being our chief executive; or if it is simply about re-election; or achieving a higher elected office somewhere else and sometime later on down the road; or mollifying the many well-entrenched legislators and political animals who are long-standing in office and receive such benefit from an abusive and corrupt system that they helped to create and so must be turned out, then … God continue to help us all. In that case, unfortunately, reform will have to await a future leader. But make no mistake; reform is coming once again to state government. One can feel it in the air.

These sentiments are provided with gentle humility, out of deep concern and conviction as a moral, law abiding ordinary Citizen and further conviction that true leaders must and will rise up in times of great adversity to serve civil society in *its* time of need.

I remain,

Respectfully, your humble, obedient servant,

/s/ author

***

Looking back on that letter now, one observation is immediately apparent. Mr. Franklin had recognized that all we really need for bare subsistence are the basics of bread and water. However, when it comes to human nature, it was amazing to him how many poor souls, given the simple *choice* of bread (needed) or beer (discretionary), in fact, had chosen beer!

As a footnote, Gov. Corzine's office did respond at the time, sending a standard thank you letter for expressing interest with regard to the issues plaguing New Jersey. The form letter went on to direct any ideas to the governor's website, where they were to be shared with others. In many ways, this response was even more ill-conceived than having received no response at all.

In the end, saying that his hands were hopelessly tied by the actions of prior legislatures, Gov. Corzine admitted defeat by abdicating his responsibility to the People and his oath. His administration effectively did nothing, failed to act, leaving the state in considerably worse economic condition than it had been upon his election. Not surprisingly, in November 2009 Gov. Corzine, a Democrat, was, in fact, turned out in his bid for re-election to a second term, in a jurisdiction whose demographic voter base is overwhelmingly Democratic. The ramifications on a national level are understood and cannot be understated.

Upon final reflection, what does it mean to be a "demagogue" in action? The dictionary defines the term as one who obtains power by means of impassioned appeals to the emotions of the common people, but is unprincipled and thus does not follow through, when given the trust. It then occurred that this, in effect, was the actual, real life story of Jon Corzine.

Never to be deterred, however, the patient's condition remaining acute, the cause unfulfilled, in June 2010 the ordinary citizen addressed the letter again, this time to the triumphant, new, conservative Republican governor. With the usual atmosphere of hope and promise of a new administration very much apparent, the following additional suggestion was offered to the Hon. Chris Christie, New Jersey's new chief executive:

> ... And it is against this backdrop that I humbly suggest you would do well to consider T.R., what he stood for during his own public service and the civil war he waged, unsuccessfully, at the Republican National Convention of 1912.

175

While a discussion of the Republican National Convention of 1912 will have to wait a later chapter, for now, suffice to say that Gov. Christie formally has responded neither to the letter nor suggestions. [225] However, in stark contrast to his predecessor, he did act.

First, Gov. Christie continued his predecessor's unfortunate practice of failing to make the legally required annual lump sum state government contribution to the pension system, essentially ignoring this important public financial obligation. Perhaps there was little choice, given the dire straits of the state's economy and its financial picture.

Second, in June 2011 New Jersey became just the 3rd and most recent state to enact a law which strips away collective bargaining rights from its 500,000 member public employee union. The bill legislates pension and health care changes that are typically bargained for, requiring public workers currently in the system to pay a higher percentage of their salary into the pension fund. For new state employees, the bill is also understood to change the structure of the pension system entirely, designed to more closely resemble retirement benefits in the private sector economy. In this arrangement, workers contribute a percentage of their income (typically between 3% and 6%) to individual retirement accounts with a small matching "defined state contribution"—and a greater percentage of premium-sharing for health care.

During the debate on the bills, it was reflected that both retirement systems, pensions and health care, are underfunded by a combined $110 billion. Gov. Christie said the overhaul is the key to *slowing* property tax hikes in the state. He also said the bipartisan compromise would become a national model for addressing rising costs. [226] This, of course, remains to be seen.

Upon closer scrutiny, however, there appear to be at least a couple of unsettling aspects to Gov. Christie's approach.

First, the union-stripping bill fails to meaningfully address the core economic problem for existing retirees as well as active current employees under the old system. For example, what was not stated by the bill's proponents is that the corrupt system of six figure guaranteed annual retirement benefits remains firmly in place for the tidal wave of existing and newly minted retirees. Further, it is understood that those active employees currently enrolled in the old system are "grandfathered," their existing benefits formula remaining firmly in place under the old system.

This means that the newly enacted legislation continues to protect these existing beneficiaries of the status quo, requiring nothing by way of concessions from this extremely large numerical group. Moreover, the old system of corruption "locked in" by "prior legislatures" is now being fully subsidized by this new round of legislation which shifts the economic burden directly onto the backs of an entirely new class of younger workers. If so, unfortunately, the bill figures both to perpetuate and exacerbate the failing status quo for a period of perhaps another 50 years, maybe even longer. Of course, the whole legislative scheme continues to be underwritten by state taxpayers.

Secondly, and even more troubling, the Republican facade of a smaller, "cuts only" government approach seemingly provides an example of exposing a component of an underlying, unstated agenda. That is, Republicans simply want to do away with a union's right to collective bargaining, one of the twin cornerstones of F.D.R.'s New Deal which has been the friend of the middle class for more than 75 years. It is an alarming idea, and one which is a cause for major concern on the part of ordinary citizens. Through the idea of bargaining collectively, a union is able to obtain benefits for its workers which an individual worker would simply be unable to obtain for himself. It's what unions do. It's why they exist.

An ordinary citizen need look back no further than to see that life was not very pretty for the individual worker prior to collective bargaining. And it's why a majority of ordinary citizens prefer a world which contains unions as opposed to one which does not. With collective bargaining removed under the equation, also removed presumably under the new law is the state's corresponding obligation to act and bargain reasonably and in good faith.

In addition, while popular rights may have asserted themselves on the federal union shop floor, statistics show that wealth disparity between rich and poor has increased—as union membership has decreased. And so it may come as little surprise to some that income inequality has worsened at a time when union membership has fallen to levels not seen since the 1920s.

Unions are a positive force for American society. They have been largely responsible for important initiatives that perhaps the ordinary citizen sometimes may take for granted. Progressive reforms which unions have consistently advocated include safe working conditions, increasing the minimum wage (known also as the "living wage"), a limitation on hours, the elimination of sweatshops, employer paid health care in case of accident or injury, and profit sharing. They also exist as a *necessary* reminder to an increasingly hostile management structure which otherwise would have little problem keeping for itself all the profits of labor's sweat.

Unions want pension and health benefits to continue to be negotiated as part of the collective bargaining process, not legislated to them unilaterally. A majority of Americans seem to agree. The other two states which have presently enacted public union-stripping legislation (Wisconsin and Ohio) both have a Republican governor as well as a Republican controlled legislature. New Jersey is the first state to enact such legislation, however, where its legislature is controlled by Democrats, who have said that the governor had agreed to as yet unspecified "other" Republican concessions as part of the deal. [227] These concessions, however, also remain to be seen.

In Wisconsin, at the time the public union contract had come up for renewal, during the collective bargaining negotiations the union conceded *every* major issue to the state legislature. So there really wasn't anything to negotiate, right? Wrong. The Republican governor and state legislature went ahead and passed union-stripping legislation anyway. In a first ever e-mail to the entire membership from its national union president, Randi Weingarten, President of the American Federation of Teachers (AFT), said that "these efforts have been unmasked as shrewd power grabs intended to eviscerate workers' voice and other democratic rights." The ramifications of these actions are left to play out over time.

New Jersey's combined retirement system deficit of $110 billion must be viewed as a symptom of state legislature that is crying out for help. Yet the proponents of union-stripping bills would have the ordinary citizen believe that the blame lies squarely with the public unions and the collective bargaining process. Therefore, it is argued, the unions must be eliminated and the legislatures freed up to act on their own.

But it is somewhat unfair to cast blame on the unions for obtaining for their membership what they are able to negotiate in good faith.

As far as the ordinary citizen is concerned, legislatures have acted voluntarily in meeting union demands. Legislatures were not facing a loaded gun when they agreed to confer retirement benefits which they could never have hoped to honor. Legislatures acted in *partnership* with public unions to create what began as a well-intentioned system but which has fallen to systemic abuse and corruption. It may seem curious, then, that a legislature would omit *itself* from the blame game, target collective bargaining instead as the evil to be eliminated, while at the same time pass a bill that fails to achieve a frontal attack on the core economic problem.

What is the moral of the developing story? Other than presenting what appears to be a clear, defining issue between the political parties, perhaps it is only this. Legislatures are increasingly seeking to abdicate responsibility for their own inept conduct, looking elsewhere for a ready scapegoat. The instance of blaming it all on the union and the collective bargaining process is but one example. It is but another lesson of human nature: Blame someone else for your own problems, problems which you created all by yourself. After all, lawmakers are just imperfect human beings too. But who will they blame going forward now that their public union partners are being effectively shoved out of the way?

In the end, it would be a surprise to learn that the core problem may be neither the public union, nor its right to bargain collectively for its membership. The public union may only be a *symptom* of the larger problem. In New Jersey, we have seen one governor (Democrat Corzine) cave in to while the other (Republican Christie) eliminated the public union. Absent the union, the state legislature now arguably has one less distraction to divert it from the public duty. The core problem, however, that is, the unconscionable benefits conferred by "prior legislatures," was addressed by *neither* of the most recent legislatures. But absent the union to blame, the state legislature will now be left with no alternative but to look in the mirror to view the consequences of the bills it passes.

But other pressures remain. History is replete with examples, from the US Congress down to the local school board, of legislative bodies influenced by private interests, special interests and other potentially corruptive forces. This discussion leads at least this ordinary citizen to conclude that perhaps it is not unions which need to be unduly targeted, reformed or even eliminated. Perhaps, instead, we need to take a fresh look at the mechanics of the constitutional framework involving our *legislative* process. The goal would be to facilitate productivity and efficiency in the making of laws to serve the public interest.

A republic is nothing more by definition than a nation of laws enacted by elected representatives to which its citizens choose to voluntarily submit. That is the essence of democracy. While the US Constitution is understood to be a flexible, organic document, it would be unfair to enliken it to Gumby. Within our "republican" scheme, the primary, big money, self-interest components of American democracy include the financial interests of capitalism, political parties, large corporations, labor unions, lobby groups, political action committees, etc. Importantly, each has evolved only *after* the US Constitution was enacted in 1789.

Together these self-interest components share at least two things in common. First, they are inanimate. They do not think for themselves, nor do they have consciences. Second, they are essentially faceless, anonymous entities. Who are they, really? And who controls them? Yet each is but a contrivance of imperfect human beings and exerts its own particular "influence" over our law-making bodies in a dynamic exchange to stay at least one step ahead of the laws. In the case of corporations, cynics are quick to point out that the primary role of lawmakers is no more than to insulate them from having to comply with the laws. It may only be perception, but perception is reality. It doesn't have to be this way.

Consequently, the rules of the game should be revisited to assist lawmakers with their inherently difficult role of impartial umpire in a level playing field society. The effect of natural corruption by self-interest must be checked. In a capitalist economy that often expresses itself in terms of excess, lawmakers must be *buffered* from these pressures within sensible constraints. Public office must no longer be tolerated as a self-possessed, material prize. How this can be accomplished will be discussed in our final chapter.

Given the complexity of today's industrialized, global society, an understanding of *how* and *why* laws are made—or not made—is not always apparent. As the line between needs and wants loses definition, we have come to see that the greater good is overwhelmed by an identifiable self-interest component. Perhaps what the People truly need—and all they need—is the *will* to contain it.

Chapter 9
The Need for Change ...

Q: *Are you optimistic 'bout the way things are going?*
A: *No, I never ever think of it at all.*

Q: *Don't you ever worry*
      When you see what's going down?
A: *No, I try to mind my business,*
      That is, no business at all.

Q: *When it's time to function as a feeling human being*
      Will your Bachelor of Arts help you get by?
A: *I hope to study further, a few more years or so.*
      I also hope to keep a steady high.

Q: *Will you try to change things,*
      Use the power that you have,
      The power of a million new ideas?
A: *What is this power you speak of*
      And the need for things to change?
      I always thought that everything was fine.

- from the song, *Dialogue–Part One*,
by Chicago (1972)
available on the *Chicago V* collection

***

"Had I been present at the creation," remarked a king centuries ago when Spain sat atop Western Civilization, "I would have given some useful hints for the better ordering of the universe." [228] Its existence far from perfect, such is the dreamer's passion to change the world.

Can one imagine a world *without* change? John Wooden, the legendary UCLA men's basketball coach, once observed that "Failure is not fatal, but failure to change might be." [229] He understood that today's setback becomes tomorrow's victory with but a few key changes. How can the ordinary citizen benefit from the application of this valuable lesson?

***

Consider the implications in the context of the Great Recession of 2008. Innovative thinkers on Wall Street created new financial instruments, private mortgage backed securities, which the ordinary citizen was told somehow fell outside the scope of federal regulation. Through these financial derivatives, the phenomenon of sub-prime residential mortgage lending was born and proliferated.

The impact of these derivatives was exaggerated by another new financial investment vehicle. The hedge fund used leveraged, long, short and derivative positions with the goal of generating high returns on a short term horizon. Unlike mutual funds, hedge funds were for the most part unregulated, it was said, because they catered to "sophisticated investors."

The problem was compounded when federal regulators were found asleep at the switch. The forces of Wall Street capitalism had finally figured a way to circumvent the protections which F.D.R.'s New Deal administration had painstakingly put in place. Central circuits, designed not only to counteract and consequently help pull us out of the Great Depression but also to ensure that it would never be able to occur again, were simply bypassed. The ordinary citizen could trace the direct line from Wall Street money to lawmaker to federal regulator. Its consequences could well be predicted.

In simple terms, the discipline of regulating financial companies had undergone a significant change over the past several decades. A phenomenon which was politically bipartisan in nature, the culture permitted a gradual yet alarming relaxation of the safeguards from F.D.R.'s New Deal. Seemingly, it had become the policy of the federal government that all citizens should be entitled to "own" a home, whether they could afford one, or not.

The phenomenon culminated with the policy of the Bush "43" administration letting the financial industry do pretty much what it wanted. Wall Street had finally infiltrated the old boat's protective coating. When the bubble burst, the US was thrust into, and we are told now emerging from, the Great Recession of 2008. Statistically, it was the worst economic contraction since the time of the Great Depression of the 1930s. [230]

The Congress with President Obama's strong backing passed what we are advised is the most sweeping financial regulatory reforms since the

Great Depression. [231] While well-intentioned, does anyone doubt the profit-induced mindset of Wall Street to creatively devise *new* ways to bypass Federal legislation again? Does anyone also doubt the human element—that federal regulators will one day again be asleep at the switch—when the time comes for decisive action?

It is said that time is the greatest innovator. Last time, it took about 75 years for Wall Street to circumvent the Feds, a tribute in and of itself to the staying power of the New Deal. This time, surely it is again not a question of *if*, but *when*. Is new regulation layered upon old good enough? Where profit is concerned, Wall Street has also proven to be very patient in biding its time. If new solutions are not entertained, then new evils can be expected. [232] Does a day of reckoning with even greater upheaval await?

While the 2008 government bail out may have averted another Great Depression, what motivation will provide the impetus to reverse wealth disparity this time around? [233] Is it to occur simply by osmosis? Aren't those in positions of authority presently the very same people who were in charge before the crisis? What is *their* incentive to change? Is it reasonable to expect different results when the same methods are used?

***

Main Street is still hurting—in a big way—its businesses, or those that remain standing, largely depressed. Belts are squeezed perilously to the breaking point. The nation's banks are not lending in abundance, although they appear to have an abundance of money to lend. Demand is simply lacking. Unemployment also is and remains high, inordinately high by historical standards, stubbornly around 8% of the available work force in 2011. [234] Among certain groups, African Americans and the young in particular, the unemployment figures are significantly worse.

The federal government's solution was, in simplistic terms, to bail out and prop up the banks, insurance companies and the auto industry. Many rationales were articulated. It was said that these large institutions had become "too big to fail," that if they failed, collectively, the economic fallout from refusing to act to "save" them would have produced a devastating ripple effect. The Federal Reserve's chairman, Ben Bernanke, had stated with great authority that a financial bailout would produce less pain than allowing natural market forces otherwise to work. His expertise had been founded on the causes of the Great Depression.

Mr. Bernanke is a very smart man, the bipartisan respect that he enjoyed during the crisis a testament to the wisdom of his policies. Mr. Bernanke also seemed to have a gift of plain speak, such that he related and communicated well with ordinary citizens. Consequently, Mr. Bernanke had earned the trust of ordinary citizens, who acquiesced to his policies, which do *seem* to be working, even as a new chairman has taken his place. Some progress is apparent but remains excruciatingly slow, especially for the millions of ordinary citizens who continue to be unemployed. [235]

But while ordinary citizens may have rightfully given Mr. Bernanke a pass, presently, they remain angry. They are also extremely frustrated. The federal government has bushels of money for Wall Street, the large banks, insurance companies and the auto industry, to name but a few, while Main Street is left to fend for itself. The results and the present economic malaise are apparent. Frustration and anger are rooted in the reality that the rules of the game are not seen as being particularly fair, or the playing field level. Government sanctioned wealth disparity is at the essence of the Occupy Wall Street protest movement festering in major US cities.

Raw emotion is heightened by the fact that financial gain from success is *privatized*, while loss from failure is *socialized*. That is, if Wall Street takes a financial risk which succeeds, Wall Street doles out the reward to individuals privately. On the other hand, if Wall Street's gamble should fail, the loss is spread out socially among the masses. As a consequence, it is said that there is no accountability on Wall Street. It is also of little consequence that the risk taken is seemingly reckless, great enough, in fact, to bring down the entire national economy.

Since ordinary citizens must live within their means, and cannot spend what they do not have, their frustration and anger are further magnified. If the money is not there, they must reduce spending and consequently bring income or revenue back into balance. Ordinary citizens wonder, if these are the rules of the road, then why do they not also apply equally to their state and federal governments which are awash in a sea of financial debt and borrowing?

Moreover, a great majority of ordinary citizens on Main Street are absolutely convinced that there are some on Wall Street and other high places, perhaps but a precious few, who are swimming in a river of wealth. Through the forces of our system of capitalism, they have mastered the rules of the game, manipulating them both within and outside the bounds of the law where necessary to secure their place at the top. The consequences are an acute concentration of wealth in their hands and control of American society. They are the power behind capitalism.

The disparity in wealth in present day America is presently as great as at any time since the start of the carbon-based Industrial Revolution, more than a century ago. Over successive generations, these wealthy few have continued to devise new, creative ways to use their financial resources discreetly, subtly, even covertly. They exert a degree of influence over lawmakers and politicians to maintain their powerful, yet artificial, status. To quote Yogi Berra, it seems like Hamilton vs. Jefferson, "déjà vu, all over again."

These wealthy few are strong swimmers, controlling the flow of capital spending upon which the American economic structure is based. They control banking, including interest rates, money flow, equity and bond prices, debt service and derivative financial investment vehicles. They control taxation policies in their various forms, including income, property and estate taxes. They control insurance and financial services companies. They control spending on political candidates and campaigns and thus have a direct effect on the outcome of democratic elections. They control the media, what ordinary Americans see and *don't* see on television stations like Fox News and CNN. They control energy use and energy "policy" and are virtually the invisible force behind a lack of a concerted national energy policy.

Since these wealthy swimmers control elected representatives, they also control the political appointment process. This includes judicial and law enforcement appointees. They also set the agenda and control both the enactment and enforcement of laws relating to all the institutions of daily life that the ordinary citizen more or less takes for granted. Their reach extending to the laws of inheritance, they can even control human behavior from beyond the grave. Using the concept of leverage, they are able to stop swimming entirely while others do the work for them. They enjoy an unprecedented feast. Afterwards, their bellies full, they can settle in for a nice, long nap on the couch.

The masses of the unknown, who comprise the vital base from which the strength of the nation derives, complete this picture. Newcomers especially are no less energetic, industrious or talented. Attracted to the table by a promise of reward for an honest day's work, they learn the hard way that a feast has previously been served and all that remain are crumbs. Their opportunities effectively foreclosed, newcomers are unlikely to achieve a comparable level of success or prosperity by a reasonable measure.

Meanwhile, the precious few further claim the validation of their actions by the blessings of a divine providence. With God on their side, the anointment process is now complete. They promote skillfully a popular myth that their material position guarantees civic virtue. But their wealth, cemented into the status quo, is only flashed to the masses. They build monuments to themselves, pejoratively labeled "McMansions," in a second Gilded Age that echoes Mark Twain's familiar refrain from the Industrial Revolution era.

In short, the precious few control the myriad of rules and regulations designed to ensure a level playing field for all citizens. But they obstruct and subvert the machinery of democracy to thwart the popular will— prohibiting the kind of change which a healthy society needs but would be their undoing. In a final blow, they accuse others of lacking personal responsibility, of being lazy. Right wing politicians and media operatives are their primary paid spokesmen. Those who would challenge their world view are dismissed as un-American, non-Christian, or both.

We have contemplated the catalyst for germination of the seed of economic discontent which breeds social unrest. The result confounds and oppresses the ordinary citizen to the point of near madness. Understanding this, the ordinary citizen must take a step back. The first order of business is to identify and then acknowledge the legitimate forces which permit the necessary mechanism of change to occur. Let's explore this further.

***

The need for change is directly related to the corresponding obligation to protect the status quo, or as it has been couched in political terms, the need to preserve internal political stability. In one corner are the have nots, who, since they "have not," seek to bring about change to improve their plight. And in the other corner are the haves, who, since they already "have," see no valid reason for change and thus strive simply to maintain a state of order, control and the existing status quo.

Throw in the "fear" factor, played astutely by politicians over the generations to maintain the status quo from which their economic power base derives, and the situation can become acute. A line in the sand is drawn, both sides dig in and are said to be driven by "ideology." The arguments of each become polarized, intractable, though highly volatile. The political atmosphere becomes downright toxic. Is it really any more complicated than that?

By definition, change is nothing more than a subtle yet sufficient deviation from the existing order, a difference from what was observed before. Preserving the benefits of the status quo, balanced against the need for change, even change which is incremental, as opposed to radical, presents one intricate dilemma. The reasons for change are sometimes no different than those identified in long bygone eras.

In the Revolutionary War fervor, Thomas Jefferson had stated that "The tree of liberty must be refreshed from time to time with the blood of patriots & tyrants. It is its natural manure." [236] Jefferson believed that constitutions ought to be changed frequently to keep up with the will of the moment, that "no society can make a perpetual constitution, or even a perpetual law. The earth belongs to the living generation." Moreover, Jefferson felt that every constitution and every law, naturally, should expire within approximately 20 years. [237]

Later, however, after his presidential term concluded, a more circumspect Thomas Jefferson had refined his views of change with an eloquence that stands the test of time:

> I am not an advocate for frequent changes in laws and Constitutions. But laws must and institutions must go hand in hand with the progress of the human mind. As that becomes more developed, more enlightened as new discoveries are made, new truths discovered and manners and opinions change, with the change of circumstances, institutions must advance also to keep pace with the times. We might as well require a man to wear the coat which fitted him when a boy as civilized society to remain ever under the regimen of their barbarous ancestors. [238]

Previously, we saw that it was Thomas Jefferson, who objected to Hamilton's banking system as flowing from principles adverse to liberty.

This was accomplished by creating an "influence" of the Treasury over members of Congress, inherently susceptible to corruption, and tending to narrow the government into fewer hands and approximate it to a hereditary form. And it was Andrew Jackson, who swore an oath as an obligation of the government to grant no privilege that aids one class over another. He vowed to act as honest broker between classes, and to protect the weak and defenseless against the abuses of the rich and powerful.

But it was Theodore Roosevelt, who keyed in on the essence of the Jefferson/Jackson lineage, as part of a concept known as *noblesse oblige*. According to this concept, citizens of wealth, power and privilege were balanced by public responsibilities to help those who lack such privilege or are less fortunate. [239] T.R. had been raised in New York City, in a family where the occupation of his Dutch father was listed as an "altruist," or a "selfless" individual. An altruist had sufficient means, such that he found ways to give away his money for a living.

For his own part, T.R. had an interesting insight into the pursuit of happiness:

> But for unflagging interest and enjoyment, a household of children, if things go reasonably well, certainly makes all other forms of success and achievement lose their importance by comparison. It may be true that he travels farthest who travels alone; but the goal thus reached is not worth reaching. And as for a life deliberately devoted to pleasure as an end – why, the greatest happiness is the happiness that comes as a by-product of striving to do what must be done, even though sorrow is met in the doing. [240]

Although T.R. had come from wealth, there had always been "foreign" elements in him. He had an independent streak, which had never shown much respect for wealth. This streak manifested itself in disturbing differences of will, rather than mere quirks of character, that belied something vaguely traitorous about him. "I find I can work best with those people in whom the money sense is not too highly developed," he had said. He mistrusted the tendencies of the wealthy to form tight, self-protective social cliques, which, in business, spilled over to combinations in restraint of trade. The tighter each grouping, the more obsessed it became with its own cohesion, and the more resentful of outside monitoring. [241]

As a member of what he called the "governing class" of practical politicians, T.R. frankly admitted that he was engaged in a "campaign against privilege" that was "fundamentally an ethical movement."

He targeted stock gamblers "making large sales of what men do not possess," writers who "act as the representatives of predatory wealth" and "men of wealth, who find in the purchased politician the most efficient instrument of corruption." He reserved his strongest warnings for these multimillionaires. [242]

T.R.'s early 20th century policies sought to make ordinary citizens aware of the most ominous of the great fundamental questions before us. The great issue was to reform the "unnatural alliance of politics and corporations" to enthrone privilege. In this manner, he broadened the scope of the offensive conduct to be regulated. [243]

His policies flatly rejected the idea of "too big to fail." What was required was control and regulation in clear and unmistakable terms, drawing the line neither on class nor size, but the *conduct* and illegal business practices of business monopolies. It did not matter that the business was large or small, the individual rich or poor, or a factory owner vs. a union leader. The distinction was to be sharply drawn in *moral* judgment between those that do well vs. those that do ill. [244]

T.R. understood that capitalists, as a product of human nature, desired free competition. But they desired it only insofar as free competition was necessary to wipe out their competitors. The means employed were often all too questionable. In the most "successful" situations, capitalists created business monopolies. The scope and conduct of the entities they controlled were often in restraint of trade and, consequently, not always in the best interests of the public at large. This, in particular, was where active government oversight and regulation were necessary:

> These new conditions make it necessary to shackle cunning as in the past we have shackled force. The vast individual and corporate fortunes, the vast combinations of capital, which have marked the development of our industrial system, create new conditions, and necessitate a change from the old attitude of the State and Nation toward the rules regulating the acquisition and untrammeled business use of property. [245]

Likewise, T.R. recognized another anomaly which had developed, a crass inequality in the bargaining relation between the employer and the individual employee standing alone. The great business organizations, which employed tens of thousands, could easily dispense with any single worker.

But what was the recourse of that worker? He could not dispense with his job. His wife and children would starve, if he did not have one. The worker's value, his labor, was a perishable commodity. The labor of today, if not sold today, was lost forever. But the labor was also part of a living, breathing human being. Those who gave earnest thought to the matter saw that the labor problem was not only an economic, but also a moral, a human problem.

Individually, the worker was impotent to negotiate a wage contract with the great companies; they could make fair terms only by uniting into unions to bargain collectively. Individual workers were thus *forced* to cooperate to secure their basic human rights, *compelled* to unite in unions of their industry or trade. These unions "were bound to grow in size, in strength, and in power for good and evil as the industries in which the men were employed grew larger and larger." [246]

T.R. continued:

> A democracy can be such in fact only if there is some rough approximation in similarity in stature among the men composing it. One of us can deal in our private lives with the grocer or the butcher or the carpenter or the chicken raiser, or if we are the carpenter or butcher or farmer, we can deal with our customers, because /we are all of about the same size/. Therefore a simple and poor society can exist as a democracy on a basis of sheer individualism. But a rich and complex industrial society cannot so exist; for some individuals, and especially those *artificial* individuals called corporations, become so very big that the ordinary individual is utterly dwarfed beside them, and cannot deal with them on terms of equality. It therefore becomes necessary for these ordinary individuals to combine in their turn, first in order to act in their collective capacity through that biggest of all combinations called the Government, and second, to act, also in their own self-defense, through private combinations, such as farmers' associations and trade unions. (*emphasis mine*) [247]

A willingness to do equal and exact justice to all citizens did not, according to T.R., "imply a failure to recognize the enormous economic, political and moral possibilities of the trade union." T.R. concluded his discussion of the topic thus:

> Just as democratic government cannot be condemned because of errors and even crimes committed by men democratically elected, so trade-unionism must not be condemned because of errors or crimes of occasional trade-union leaders. The problem lies deeper. While we must repress all illegalities and discourage all immoralities, whether of labor organizations or of corporations, we must recognize the fact that to-day the organization of labor into trade unions and federations is necessary, is beneficent, and is one of the greatest possible agencies in the attainment of a true industrial, as well as a true political, democracy in the United States. [248]

Not surprisingly, a balancing act was necessary, a weighing and mature contemplation of competing interests. On the one hand, the individual risk-taker took full advantage of the civil law of contracts and America's global military strength to protect and preserve his capital investment and vast profit potential. On the other hand, consequently, that same risk-taker had the resulting obligation to permit the law to change to a sufficient degree to protect and improve the fundamental human welfare of the workers who made those profits possible.

After completing two presidential terms featuring an agenda of activist, progressive reform along these lines, T.R. declined to run for a third term in the election of 1908. He was maintaining the tradition of George Washington. Instead, he threw his overwhelming popular support behind his then-Vice President and hand picked successor, William Howard Taft.

T.R. saw Mr. Taft as an able administrator under T.R.'s leadership and an extension of himself. Essentially, it was understood that Mr. Taft would consolidate and expand T.R.'s activist, progressive agenda with all the necessary machinery of government already in place and smartly operating.

Unfortunately, it didn't turn out that way. Upon his election President Taft's approach was basically laissez-faire. Although he did continue vigorous prosecution of anti-trust violations by the large combinations, President Taft was better suited as an administrator who took his cues from strong leadership. Absent that leadership, however, he was proving to be an inept chief executive. He lacked confidence, was overweight, he mired in self-pity, complaining about just about everything including the workload, appearing to find solace only in unlimited time on the golf course. [249]

In fact, President Taft had botched T.R.'s progressive agenda and was now the nation's top reactionary. The effect was akin to a political about-face. Systematically, President Taft began to roll back T.R.'s progressive reforms in a bow to the Republican Party's affluent, conservative base. What was worse, the Congressional midterm elections of 1910 amounted to a rejection of everything Mr. Taft had stood for so far. To be progressive in 1910 was to belong to America's middle class. T.R.'s alarm was palpable.

***

As the calendar turned to 1912 and T.R. contemplated a return to political life, a political transformation was taking place within him. He would begin to argue for wider recognition of the spiritual qualities inherent in all materialistic pursuits, from science to business to politics. [250]

The roots of this transformation can be traced to several sources. The first dates back to T.R.'s presidency, specifically the delivery of a *Special Message to Congress* in January 1908. It argued for automatic compensation for job-related (industrial) accidents and federal scrutiny of corporate boardroom operations. It campaigned "against privilege, part of the campaign to make the great class of property holders realize that property has its duties no less than its rights." It also campaigned against "predatory wealth—of the wealth accumulated on a giant scale by all forms of iniquity." It was to be a war "against successful dishonesty."

The issue T.R. raised in this message, perhaps more than any other utterance in his career, convinced Wall Street that "Theodore the Sudden" was a dangerous man. [251]

But T.R. scoffed at this criticism, stating that it was "fundamentally an ethical movement:"

> The opponents of the measures we champion single out now one, and now another measure for especial attack, and speak as if the movement in which we are engaged was purely economic. It has a large economic side, but it is fundamentally an ethical movement. It is not a movement to be completed in one year, or two or three years; it is a movement which must be persevered in until the spirit which lies behind it sinks deep into the heart and the conscience of the whole people. [252]

Followed quickly on its heels was the publication of Herbert Croly's *The Promise of American Life*, which had become the bible of the new social movement. The book argued the need for a strong central government (Hamiltonian), calling for a war on indiscriminate individualism (Jefferson) and unearned privilege (Jacksonian). And it also called for T.R. as the only leader in America capable of encompassing both aims. [253]

Then, in August 1910 T.R. made a case during a speech which would become famous for what he had called "New Nationalism." Some labeled it "Communistic," "Socialistic" and "Anarchistic" in various quarters, while others hailed it "the greatest oration ever given on American soil." [254]

In his New Nationalism speech, T.R. reflected that there had been "two great crises in our country's history: first, when it was formed, and then, again, when it was perpetuated … ." The third great crisis was upon us, the struggle "to achieve in large measure equality of opportunity."

In every wise struggle for human betterment one of the main objects, and often the only object, has been to achieve in large measure equality of opportunity. In the struggle for this great end, nations rise from barbarism to civilization, and through it people press forward from one stage of enlightenment to the next. One of the chief factors in progress is the destruction of special privilege. The essence of any struggle for healthy liberty has always been, and must always be, to take from some one man or class of men the right to enjoy power, or wealth, or position, or immunity, which has not been earned by service to his or their fellows. …

At many stages in the advance of humanity, this conflict between the men who possess more than they have earned and the men who have earned more than they possess is the central condition of progress. In our day it appears as the struggle of freeman to gain and hold the right of self-government as against the special interests, who twist the methods of free government into machinery for defeating the popular will. At every stage, and under all circumstances, the essence of the struggle is to equalize opportunity, destroy privilege, and give to the life and citizenship of every individual the highest possible value both to himself and to the commonwealth. That is nothing new.

He could envision these socially desirable results:

Practical equality of opportunity for all citizens, when we achieve it, will have two great results. First, every man will have a fair chance to make of himself all that lies in him; to reach the highest point to which his capacities, unassisted by special privilege of his own and unhampered by the special privilege of others, can carry him, and to get for himself and his family substantially what he has earned. Second, equality of opportunity means that the commonwealth will get from every citizen the highest service of which he is capable. No man who carries the burden of the special privileges of another can give to the commonwealth that service to which it is fairly entitled.

I stand for the square deal. But when I say I am for the square deal, I mean not merely that I stand for fair play under the present rules of the game, *but that I stand for having those rules changed* so as to work for a more substantial equality of opportunity and of reward for equally good service. (emphasis mine) [255]

T.R. insisted that only a powerful federal government could regulate the economy and guarantee social justice. His central tenet was government protection of property rights, the traditional approach. But he elevated human welfare, the second critical component, to a *higher* priority. T.R. understood that the success of any presidential administration must be measured by this and would be impossible otherwise.

In addition to the reforms previously noted, the federal government should be used to protect the laboring men, women and children from exploitation. T.R. supported graduated income and inheritance taxes, a social security system, a national health service, a federal securities

193

commission and the direct election of US senators. The platform also supported the democratic principles of initiative, referendum and recall as means for the people to exert more direct control over government. In short, it was a platform which inspired much of the social agenda of the future New Deal a generation later. [256]

> The man who wrongly holds that every human right is secondary to his profit must now give way to the advocate of human welfare, who rightly maintains that every man holds his property subject to the general right of the community to regulate its use to whatever degree the public welfare may require it.

New Nationalism also went further, admitting "the right to regulate the terms and conditions of labor, which is the chief element of wealth, directly in the interest of the common good." Importantly, it also called for the prohibition of corporate funds directly or indirectly for political purposes, the strict regulation of political lobbyists. It was "still more necessary that such laws should be thoroughly enforced."

> No man can be a good citizen unless he has a wage more than sufficient to cover the bare cost of living, and hours of labor short enough so after his day's work is done he will have time and energy to bear his share in the management of the community, to help in carrying the general load.

And there was this final touch:

> One of the fundamental necessities in a representative government such as ours is to make certain that the men to whom the people delegate their power shall serve the people by whom they are elected, and not the special interests.

***

But the heart of T.R.'s political transformation occurred some months after his New Nationalsim speech. In December 1910 he chose to publish an extraordinary essay, entitled *The Search for Truth in a Reverent Spirit*. It was, for him, almost a religious confession.

To measure the progress of social advances and the elusive search for truth, rigid materialistic standards in science that reject the imaginative or metaphysical were simply too regressive. Reason, as in evolutionary science, and the accompanying blunt physical force of materialistic pursuits, was alone insufficient.

He had seen that rigid theories, or dogmas, no matter how provable they seemed in the marketplace at a given time, were typically swept away by the currents of historical change. In other words, today's "law" might be tomorrow's superstition, and vice versa.

Important factors such as, for example, the human emotion of love, and common sense, were not sufficiently accounted for. Similarly, there could be no advancement of knowledge absent the part of wisdom to accept the teachings of experience, and practice humility in the process. For the first essential required the willingness of men to say 'We do not know."

Moreover, where experience had plainly proven that the intellect had reasoned incorrectly, true wisdom required that the teachings of experience be accepted. In such case reason must be humbled—just under like conditions experience would require theology to be humble.

T.R. felt that any steady scientific or social advance would have to give way to "bolder, more self-reliant spirits ... men whose unfettered freedom of soul and intellect yields complete fealty only to the great cause of truth, and will not be hindered by any outside control on the search to attain it."

He was saying that wider recognition must be given to faith, the spiritual qualities inherent in "the narrowness of a shut-in materialism." This would permit the opening up of a new theory that the principle of group development in human beings was as instinctive and organic as that in biological evolution. The embrace of *both* faith *and* reason was necessary for a person of "conscience" in searching for truth, as something entirely practical, yet divine.

Faith and reason were seen as coefficients, not opposites, in the quest for progress. Superior wisdom understood "that outside the purely physical lies the psychic, and that the realm of religion stands outside even the purely psychic."

Those who professed faith while allowing materialism to persuade them were not having philosophy both ways. On the contrary, they were "in a position of impregnable strength," rightly holding that religion itself was evolutionary and had to adapt as it progressed.

> To them Christianity, the greatest of the religious creations which humanity has seen, rests upon what Christ himself teaches: for, ... the performance of duty is faith in action , faith in its highest expression, for duty gives no other reason, and need give no other reason, for its existence than 'its own incorruptible disinterestedness.'

T.R. summed up his argument concerning duty and the notion of an ethical obligation:

> Surely we must all recognize the search for truth as an imperative duty; and we ought all of us likewise to recognize that this search for truth should be carried on not only fearlessly, but also with reverence, with humility of spirit, and with full recognition of our own limitations both of the mind and the soul. ... To those who deny the ethical obligation implied in such a faith we who acknowledge the obligation are aliens; and we are brothers to all those who do acknowledge it, whatever their creed or system of philosophy.

All the books he had consulted concerned *progress* from one state of held beliefs to another over the course of history. All tried in vain to deny, and had accepted, that faith (belief) was as transformative a force as reason (materialism), as well as a necessary catalyst. After a lifetime of rejecting spiritual speculation, in favor of the body electric and the physics of (military) power, T.R. conceded the vitality of faith—not necessarily Bible-thumping, but at least the compulsive "ethical obligation" that distinguished the unselfish citizen from the mere hoarder of gold. [257]

* * *

If nothing else, T.R. was now sure that whatever he did with the rest of his life would have to have moral purpose.

Alarmed by President Taft's passiveness and political about-face, T.R.was compelled to renew the contest, seeking the Republican Party nomination for the presidency once again in the election of 1912. He won the last five voter primaries, including Mr. Taft's home state of Ohio, but found, as is typically the case, that it was nearly impossible to wrest the nomination from an incumbent president. At the nominating convention in Chicago, the Republican Party waged a vicious, internal civil war battle pitting President Taft, the conservative, whose powerful base championed the status quo, against T.R., the upstart, whose base favored the continuation of progressive change.

T.R. concluded his convention speech in an attempt to sway the delegates with the following language:

> Assuredly the fight will go on whether we win or lose. What happens to me is not of the slightest consequence; I am to be used, as in a doubtful battle any man is used, to his hurt or not, so long as he is useful and then cast aside or left to die. ... We fight in honorable fashion for the good of mankind; fearless for the future; unheeding of our individual fates; with unflinching hearts and undimmed eyes; we stand at Armageddon, and we battle for the Lord.

Never before had T.R. used such evangelical language, or dared to present himself as a holy warrior. It was also said that never before

196

had he heard such cheering. Intended or not, he invested progressivism with a divine aura. [258]

But obtaining the Republican Party's nomination was not to be, coming as no surprise when President Taft's conservative base carried the day to beat back the progressive tide. The Republican Party that T.R. knew had lost the liberal conscience of Abraham Lincoln's party. And everyone knew that the Republican National Committee had decided to field a losing candidate (Mr. Taft) in November (1912), rather than gamble on one (T.R.) who would "radicalize" its "traditional" platform. [259]

In turn, T.R. precipitously bolted from the Republican National Convention and the Republican Party to form the new Progressive Party or "Bull Moose" Party. The decision was occasioned by what T.R. saw as his compelling sense of duty, his conscience and his station. Progressive would now contain a capital "P."

***

Many times, over the years, T.R. had compared the machinery of politics to the workings of a kaleidoscope. At times brilliant colors and harmonious patterns could be seen, sometimes carefully shaken into shape, sometimes forming of their own accord. At the slightest hitch, however, brilliance and harmony could fall into jagged disarray, leaving the viewer with clashing colors, shapes and shafts of impenetrable black. [260]

T.R. knew that his third party candidacy was a long shot and that he would not likely win. But he saw it as his duty. "My public career will end next election day," T.R. had told a visitor in the days preceding his new party's own nominating convention. [261]

He asked his wife to say what she thought of his situation. A house guest related that "She was quite radiant with trust and affection, as she expressed her faith that the path through honor to defeat was the one to take." [262]

197

T.R.'s transformational embrace of faith caused critics to suggest at the Progressive National Convention in August 1912 that Progressivism was a religion. He nurtured the theme that he was engaged in Holy Work.

Familiar church hymns rang through the course of the proceedings, which were also held in Chicago, as the delegates sang and chanted, surging the religiosity in the hall to the point of delirium.

Onward Christian soldiers, marching as to war,
With the cross of Jesus going on before.

In his acceptance speech for the party nomination, entitled *A Confession of Faith*, he repeated what he had stated earlier at the Republican National Convention, to a tumultuous response: "I say in closing what in that speech I said in closing: We stand at Armageddon, and we battle for the Lord." A *New York Times* reporter wrote that "It was not a convention at all. It was an assemblage of religious enthusiasts."

The mocking prophecy of Eliju Root, US Senator, R-NY, and formerly T.R.'s Secretary of War and then Secretary of State, appeared to have been fulfilled: "He aims at a leadership far in the future, as a sort of Moses and Messiah for a vast progressive tide of a rising humanity."

Jane Addams, a proponent of women's suffrage, said that "I have been fighting for progressive principles for thirty years. This is the biggest day in my life." The convention committed the Progressive Party to a vast program of social, economic and environmental reform. T.R. had made the Progressive issue a "moral" issue, entitled to use a superlative when he called the program "much the most important public document promulgated in this country since the death of Abraham Lincoln." The Progressive motto was to be "Pass prosperity around." [263]

In his vision of a moral society, ethically based, T.R. posed that the

Material progress and prosperity of a nation are desirable chiefly so long as they lead to the moral and material welfare of all good citizens. Just in proportion as the average man and woman are honest, capable of sound judgment and high ideals, active in public affairs,—but, first of all, sound in their home, and the father and mother of healthy children whom they bring up well,—just so far, and not farther, we may count on civilization a success.

The soldier, or ordinary citizen, had to have the right stuff in him. He had to have "the fighting edge, the right character. The most important elements in any man's career must be the sum of those qualities which, in the aggregate, we speak of as character."

> We must have the right kind of character—character that makes a man, first of all, a good man in the home, a good father, and a good husband—that makes a man a good neighbor. You must have that, and, then, in addition, you must have the (right) kind of law and the (right) kind of administration of the law which will give to those qualities in the private citizen the best possible chance for development. [264]

It came as no surprise that the platform of the Progressive Party of 1912 amounted to a re-drafting of T.R.'s New Nationalism program. It would not be matched again for initiative and specificity in detail until the platform of the Democratic Party in 1964.

***

But if superior wisdom accepts that reason lies on one side, and faith on the other side of the purely psychic, then it is appropriate that the psychic receive some noteworthy mention.

A twenty-six-year-old unemployed recluse named John Schrank lived above a New York City saloon which had employed him once. This was before T.R., then police commissioner, had gone on a Sunday-closing crusade. Schrank had been unable to get a job.

Shortly after President McKinley had been assassinated in 1901, elevating T.R. to the presidency, Schrank had a dream. His shabby surroundings were transformed into a funeral parlor full of flowers. An open coffin lie before him. President McKinley sat up in it and pointed to a dark corner of the room. Peering out, Schrank made out the figure of a man dressed as a monk. Under the cowl Schrank recognized the bespectacled features of T.R.

"This is my murderer," McKinley said. "Avenge my death." Schrank awoke from his nightmare and checked his watch. It was 1:30 A.M. He went back to sleep. The appeal would not be renewed for another eleven years.

In September 1912 Schrank sat writing poetry in his two-dollar-a-week apartment in downtown Manhattan. It was the anniversary of the McKinley assassination.

When night draws near
And you hear a knock
And a voice should whisper
Your time is up. ...

As he doodled, he felt the ghost of the dead president lay a hand on his shoulder. It did not stop his pen.

Refuse to answer
As long as you can
Then face it and be a man.

Later, it was revealed that the appeal of McKinley's ghost had been renewed at the same hour of the same night of the week as the earlier episode. [265]

Back in the real world, on October 14, 1912 T.R. was scheduled to give an important speech on Progressivism in Milwaukee. On the way to the hall he took his customary right-hand seat in his roofless, seven-seat automobile. His escorts fanned out to take their seats. Acknowledging the crowd, T.R. stood up to bow. At that moment, no more than seven feet away, Schrank fired.

The bullet lay embedded against T.R.'s fourth right rib, four inches from the sternum. Heading straight toward the heart, its upward and inward trajectory had to pass through T.R.'s dense overcoat into his suit jacket pocket, then through a hundred glazed pages of his bi-folded speech into his vest pocket, which contained a steel-reinforced spectacle case three layers thick, and on through two webs of suspender belt, shirt fabric, and undershirt flannel, before eventually coming into contact with skin and bone. Even so, the force had been enough to crack the rib. T.R.'s personal doctor pointed out that the spectacle case had deflected the bullet upward. Had it gone through the arch of the aorta or auricles of the heart, his patient would not have lived 60 seconds.

A witness to the shooting marveled at the freak coordination of all these impediments. Had Schrank's slug penetrated the pleura, T.R. would have bled to death internally in a matter of minutes. "There was no other place on his body so thoroughly armored as the spot where the bullet struck." [266] As if by some miracle, T.R. survived the attempt, and actually recovered quickly.

At times Schrank claimed he was penniless. Other times, he claimed he had inherited Manhattan real estate from his father, a Bavarian immigrant. Whatever his finances, he had enough cash to purchase a gun and pursue T.R. for two weeks through the Deep South and on across the Midwest—intending but failing to shoot him in at least five cities before Milwaukee. "I intended to kill Theodore Roosevelt, the third termer. I did not want to kill the candidate of the Progressive Party."

Schrank later claimed that he was neither insane nor a socialist. T.R. was inclined to agree. "I very gravely question if he has a more unsound mind than Eugene Debs (the Socialist Party candidate for the presidency)." [267]

T.R. delivered a final speech in Chicago in the days before the general election. Occasionally he attempted to raise his right arm, then winced and dropped it.

> Friends, perhaps once in a generation, perhaps not so often, there comes a chance for a people of a country to play their part wisely and fearlessly in some great battle of the age-long warfare for human rights. The doctrines we preach reach back to the Golden Rule and the Sermon on the Mount. They reached back to the commandments delivered at Sinai. All that we are doing is to apply those doctrines in the shape necessary to make them available for meeting the living issue of our own day. [268]

The end result might have been a nation of individuals, cooperating intelligently instead of competing recklessly, with the requisite character to understand duty—a democratic society that could reach new heights in both moral and material progress.

* * *

In the ensuing national general election, T.R., now the political third party outsider on the Republican left, actually outpolled the incumbent president on the Republican right. But it was to be little consolation. The Republican Party vote was thereby split. The election was thrown to the candidate who commanded the center, former president of Princeton University and Gov. of New Jersey, Woodrow Wilson, a Democrat. [269] Progressivism was to take on the newly developing image of the Democratic Party.

Chapter 10
... or The Obligation to Protect the Status Quo

My child arrived just the other day
He came to the world in the usual way
But there were planes to catch and bills to pay
He learned to walk while I was away
And he was talkin' 'fore I knew it, and as he grew
He'd say "I'm gonna be like you dad
You know I'm gonna be like you"

And the cat's in the cradle and the silver spoon
Little boy blue and the man on the moon
"When you comin' home dad?"
"I don't know when, but we'll get together then son
You know we'll have a good time then"
...
I've long since retired, my son's moved away
I called him up just the other day
I said, "I'd like to see you if you don't mind"
He said, "I'd love to, dad, if I could find the time
You see my new job's a hassle and the kids have the flu
But it's sure nice talking to you, dad
It's been sure nice talking to you"

And as I hung up the phone it occurred to me
He'd grown up just like me
My boy was just like me

- from the song, *Cat's in the Cradle*,
by Harry Chapin (1974)
available on the *Verities & Balderdash* collection

***

That's the way presidential politics has gone, all the way back to the time of Mr. Taft in 1912. Interesting to emphasize the Republican Party's preference to field a *losing* candidate, rather than gamble on one who would "radicalize" its "traditional" platform. Better to lose the election, regroup and use the lawful mechanisms available in our democracy to obstruct and wait it out until next time. The position has what should be by now a familiar ring—Republicans followed the very same formula in the 2012 election. It isn't the first example of reasonable people acting reasonably in their own best interest, only the latest.

The election of 1912 is a case study in how seemingly impossible the task of upsetting the status quo. The unpopular conservative, President Taft, merely tolerated the futile contest, viewing the Progressive insurgency as a challenge to "the principles of the party … the retention of conservative government and conservative institutions." [270] Mr. Taft knew he was unlikely to win, either.

A few more vintage 1912 conservative point tidbits are of interest. At the time, many conservatives, both Republican and Democrat, opposed the woman's right to vote. The argument was that extension of the suffrage would lead to the breakup of the American home.

T.R.'s rebuttal was enlightening. On the contrary, he believed it would "tend toward an increase in the sense of co-partnership between man and woman" and make each think more of the rights of the other. "People say to me, 'Men are different from women.' Yes, but I have never met any differences so great as the differences between some men and other men." [271]

Similarly, 1912 marked the first use of a phrase that would re-enter the American political vocabulary in criticism to the policies of Republican Party conservatism nearly 70 years later under the Reagan administration. T.R. had remarked at a campaign speech that "The Republican proposal is only to give prosperity to (wealthy industrialists) and then to let it trickle down." [272]

In the ensuing century, there can be no mistaking that the Republican Party has remained firmly within the control of an entrenched, affluent, conservative, some say reactionary base, squarely in support of the status quo. This is both sweeping as it is powerful.

***

The ordinary citizen who talks with five people who call themselves a "conservative" will surely receive five different definitions of that political term. For many, the idea is of small, frugal, debt-free government with the freedom to enjoy individual pursuits without the interference of government. That's what Jefferson had in mind. It is the kind of conservatism that Republicans have been preaching, but have been remiss in their practice, for at least the past 40 years. The more recent variety would also add a healthy dose of militarism.

So, what is a conservative? According to Wikipedia, conservatism is defined as

> A political and social philosophy that promotes the maintenance of traditional institutions and supports, at the most, minimal and gradual change in society. Some conservatives seek to preserve things as they are, emphasizing stability and continuity, while others oppose modernism and seek a return to the way things were.

A more moderate definition was pronounced upon seasoned reflection late in life by the legendary Coke Stevenson, the 20th century self-made rancher, beloved as "Mr. Texas" back home. He put it this way:

> A conservative—he's one who holds things together. He shouldn't fight all progressive movements, but he should be the balance wheel to hold the movement to where it won't get out of hand. [273]

Proponents point out that conservatism supports the larger, desirable idea of a common culture or identity, who we are as a people. Hard earned and built with the blood and sweat of prior generations, that culture must continue to evolve deliberately, upon consensus. It must not be casually discarded. In its simplest sense, it's an argument of order and control over chaos. The point certainly has great validity.

Consequently, perhaps, whenever it perceives an opening, the Republican Party has attempted to take measures designed to grind the wheels of progress and change to a halt, preserving the status quo or even rolling it back. Of course, the same argument in reverse can be made against its main targets: T.R.'s activist Progressivism; F.D.R.'s New Deal; Lyndon Johnson's Great Society and the civil rights movement of the 1960s; affirmative action and a woman's right to choose, among others. The administration of President Obama and the progressive agenda he advocates also lie directly within its targeted scope.

T.R., however, identified what he referred to as the "true conservative:"

> The true friend of property, the true conservative, is he who insists that property shall be the servant and not the master of the commonwealth; who insists that the creature of man's making shall be the servant and not the master of the man who made it. The citizens of the United States must effectively control the mighty commercial forces which they have called into being.
>
> There can be no effective control of corporations while their political activity remains.
>
> ...

We must have complete and effective publicity (disclosure) of corporate affairs, so that the people may know beyond peradventure whether the corporations obey the law and whether their management entitles them to the confidence of the public. It is necessary that laws should be passed to prohibit the use of corporate funds directly or indirectly for political purposes; it is still more necessary that such laws should be thoroughly enforced. Corporate expenditures for political purposes, and especially such expenditures by public-service corporations, have supplied one of the principal sources of corruption on our political affairs. [274]

Despite the flowery prose, and with the best intentions, unfortunately it never seems to work out that way. Neither is it conservatism as that term is generally understood today.

***

History provides numerous examples of the conservative hold on the Republican Party in action. Following immediately on the heels of the progressive, Woodrow Wilson, the consecutive 1920s presidential administrations of Harding/Coolidge/Hoover featured nothing more than individual fits of pure self-indulgence. "A chicken in every pot" was the familiar catchphrase during the period. [275]

But any doubt that reform was basically dead and buried was dispelled by an incident which occurred during this time. President Harding's then-Secretary of the Interior, Albert Fall, had been accused of selling off public lands to private interests and pocketing the money. Following World War I, national security interests had dictated that valuable energy resources contained within these lands should be entrusted to federal reserve. In the spring of 1922 President Harding defended his Interior Secretary, saying that "This isn't the first time that this rumor has come to me." The president continued: "But if Albert Fall isn't an honest man, I'm not fit to be President of the United States." [276]

President Harding died in the spring of 1924, and was succeeded by his Vice President, Calvin Coolidge. In 1931, while Herbert Hoover was President, Fall was convicted and imprisoned for the felony of accepting bribes while in office, the first cabinet member to earn that distinction in what would be known as the infamous Teapot Dome Scandal.

At the time, there was no difference for Republicans and Democrats on their thoughts of communism. But there would be a difference in action. F.D.R., the Democrat, took the helm of leadership in 1933 at the height of the Great Depression. He noted that the Republicans, by rejecting the obligations toward social justice, encouraged social and economic unrest which bred communism. Democrats, on the other hand, struck communism at its roots, by tackling the causes of unrest. "The most serious threat to our institutions," F.D.R. continued,

> comes from those who refuse to face the need for change. Liberalism becomes the protection for the far-sighted conservative. ... 'Reform if you would preserve.' I am that kind of conservative because I am that kind of liberal. [277]

But following 20 years of activist, Democratic presidents F.D.R. and Truman, it was said that the country needed more of a "dirt smoother" than an "earth shaker." That "hidden hand leadership" environment was provided by the 1950s Republican administration of Dwight D. Eisenhower. Two separate examples are relevant for our purposes, one at home and the other in the field of foreign policy.

On the domestic front, the US Supreme Court had just published its celebrated decision in 1954 overruling separate but equal educational facilities and ordering the desegregation of the nation's public schools. Perhaps one of the most significant decisions of the 20th century was rendered unanimously, 9-0 in favor. President Eisenhower was reluctant, however, to throw his support behind the ruling and embrace the landmark change. The decision was a "mistake" and "not a great moral issue." The president continued: "I don't believe you can change the hearts of men with laws or decision."

The burgeoning civil rights movement, however, had other ideas. [278] The still relatively new phenomenon of television aided the cause of human rights. Stark images of police water canons and German Shepherd dogs, pointed at blacks, many who were young children, were broadcast into the living rooms of rural and suburban white America. The troubling images gave a face to racism, a concept that for many white Americans was still an abstraction. These images soon *forced* Mr. Eisenhower to take desperately needed action.

On the world stage, another precipitous event would present itself only a couple of years later. In 1956 in the tiny Asian nation of Vietnam, the military forces of communist leader, Ho Chi Minh, had finally vanquished France, its colonial occupier, in a stunning rebuke of America's loyal World War II ally. It was another round in the Cold War pitting the "free world" (US/UK/France) vs. communism (USSR). French/Vietnamese peace talks in Geneva lead to the idea of elections unifying the "free" south with its communist northern counterpart under Minh's control.

Backed by the US, however, the south refused, although the US had said it did not want to send troops to perpetuate colonization and the white man's exploitation of Asia. Vietnam was said to be a "small corner of a bigger picture," where the status quo must be preserved. Otherwise, if South Vietnam fell to communism, then communism would spread like dominoes, finally coming home to American shores. San Diego would be next. Better to confront the problem half way around the world in Indochina than be forced to confront it at home.

But a top expert had advised that absent a dominant local will backing foreign involvement in Vietnam's internal affairs, America's substitution into the war in France's place would be ill-conceived. [279]

Despite that warning, the US was fully committed in Vietnam by the end of President Eisenhower's term in 1960, exemplifying an evolving Cold War policy. US support of a corrupt, tyrannical dictator like the one in South Vietnam, so long as he was *our* dictator, was understood to be more desirable than the potential fall of another "domino" to communism.

The president's decision would set in motion a precipitous chain of events that would mire the US in a 20 year quagmire. On a human scale, some 60,000 American soldiers and many more Vietnamese soldiers and civilians would perish. While Vietnam's quest for self-determination would ultimately succeed, the divisions of the Vietnam era would continue to strain American life during the remainder of the 20th century.

The examples continue. At the Republican National Convention of 1964, Nelson D. Rockefeller [280], then-governor of New York, had put forth a series of five amendments to counter the conservative Goldwater plank. Favored by moderate and liberal Republicans, Rockefeller "represented virtually everything that antagonized social conservatives." As one historian had put it, he "accelerated the rebellion" from what was then still a nascent "new right" movement under Goldwater. [281]

Rockefeller was given five minutes to speak in support of his amendments. While he stood firmly at the podium insisting on his right to speak, right wing delegates booed and heckled him for a full 15 minutes. The episode came to an inglorious conclusion with the conservatives successfully booing Rockefeller off the convention stage, before anointing Goldwater.

Following the tumultuous, activist years of the Kennedy/Johnson administrations, the nation had hoped for a softer landing. But the late 1960s/early '70s Republican administrations of Richard M. Nixon and his successor, Gerald R. Ford seemed to be anything but that.

At home, the Southern Strategy was evolving during this time period to *secretly* impede civil rights progress for African Americans and people of color. For these groups a perpetuation of discriminatory practices would continue to be a bitter pill to swallow.

And in the foreign arena, Mr. Nixon continued his predecessors' failing policy in the continued prosecution of the Vietnam War. Mr. Nixon had been elected in 1968, promising to end the Vietnam War. But some say Mr. Nixon extended the war just to ensure his 1972 re-election, although it would be neither the first time, nor the last, such a charge had been made in presidential politics. "Guns and butter," it was also said, were the perfect recipe to keep a capitalist, industrial economy humming.

The war appeared to be winding down through 1969. But the president then made a fateful decision to escalate the war by ordering the secret, night time bombing of the Ho Chi Minh Trail in neighboring Cambodia and Laos, two countries that were not involved in the war.

Across the country, campuses erupted in protests in what *Time Magazine* had called "a nation-wide student strike." Then, in a 1970 incident on the campus of Kent State University the Ohio Army National Guard fired on unarmed, student protesters, killing 4 and injuring 9 others. The Kent State massacre, so called, would be a lasting testament to the president's call to execute the will of the "silent majority."

Mounting public disapproval coincided with increasing domestic civil unrest, notably in the nation's poor, urban areas, inhabited mostly by people of color. The Nixon administration countered with a government crackdown, conceived to control and check a perceived national security threat. The stated intent was ostensibly to maintain and ensure domestic order, tranquility and the rule of law by stifling criticism of administration policies and dissent. The war on drugs was born, effectively replacing the outdated war on poverty. [282]

Yet every rule is said to have an exception. And if the hundred year famine has any, it would be here. In acknowledgment of the environmental movement, Congress passed the National Environmental Policy Act (NEPA) in 1970. That law required the preparation of environmental impact statements for all federally funded highways, dams, pipelines and power plants. In 1973 Congress created the Environmental Protection Agency (1973) to set and enforce pollution standards, as well as the Clean Air and Clear Water Acts.

And Mr. Nixon's visit to communist China in 1972, together with corresponding détente with the Soviets, exposed the rift between those two countries. It further exposed the myth that communism was a movement to take over the world.

Following the Reagan administration in which he had served as Vice President, the late 1980s/early '90s Republican administration of President George H.W. Bush "41" produced this once familiar rhetoric. He was the spokesperson for a Republican Party which sought judges "who will interpret the law, not look to change the law."

Still smarting over the US Supreme Court's decision to legalize abortion in certain instances, it was a not so subtle hint from deep within his conservative base to stamp out what was described as "judicial activism." The legislature was supposed to make the laws under our constitution, *not* the court. The president did have a valid point. In a time when the US Congress seems more and more prone to abdicate its responsibility to make laws, the rationale for having a judicially conservative court seems to be even more compelling.

But in a twist of irony, perhaps, President Bush "41" conservative judicial appointees would be instrumental in taking the idea of judicial activism to a new extreme. In "creatively" deciding the election of 2000 by judicial decree, the US Supreme Court elevated the president's son, George W. Bush "43" to the presidency.

The Republican Party's theme to preserve the status quo and roll back progressive initiatives has continued, seemingly unabated. Almost since its inception in 1973, the principle of a woman's "right to choose" has been the source of constant attack by the Republican Party's conservative base. The principles of affirmative action have been the subject of similar attack.

Who can forget the key moment during the 1996 presidential debates when US Senator, Robert Dole, R-KS, the Republican candidate, smiled, reminiscing about the good old days. We needed "a bridge to the past," Mr. Dole yearned in nostalgic fashion. His opponent, the incumbent president, Democrat Bill Clinton, was quick to pick up on this. What we need, Mr. Clinton said, is not a bridge to the past, but a "bridge to the future." But in the last 100 years the Republican Party has consistently sought a bridge to the past.

And the Bush "43" administration expended whatever political capital it thought it possessed in an attempt to "privatize" Social Security. Proponents said that individual citizens could more efficiently manage their benefits and maximize their return on investment than "the government." But in view of the Great Recession of 2008, an ordinary citizen can only wonder what further economic disaster would have been befallen the nation, had that particular "initiative" succeeded.

What the Bush "43" administration did accomplish effectively was the preservation of big oil and the protection of US oil and natural gas supplies atop both the national and global carbon-based energy pyramid. Of course, this was accomplished through the prosecution of two wars in Afghanistan and Iraq that lead directly to the rich oil fields of the Middle East. Neither was funded on present tax dollars.

The significance of the ordinary citizen's relatively high living standards and continuing way of life occasioned by the uninterrupted flow of oil cannot be understated. But not one domestic policy *initiative* seems to have been successfully concluded during the administration of President Bush "43," other than a dangerous de-regulation of businesses which brought the nation to the precipice of another great depression.

And most recently, although it does not occupy the White House presently, the present day Republican Party is seeking to thwart the policy initiatives of President Obama's administration seemingly at every turn. [283] Its predictable call is to "repeal and replace" or "de-fund and delay" the nation's new affordable health care law, before any of its main provisions become effective; reduce Medicare/Medicaid to a series of individual "block grants" to states [284]; eliminate unions and restrict access to the voting booth. [285]

The Republican Party is also seemingly against a coordinated national energy policy, although the initiatives of so-called "cap and trade" originally came from the mouths of Republicans. [286]

The Republican Party also appears to favor immigration reform, so long as reform begins with "securing" our borders. Of course, even the ordinary citizen has probably figured out by now that "securing" in all likelihood means "closing" our borders and deporting all illegal aliens. And "repeal and replace" in all likelihood just means "repeal." The "replace" part appears to be merely a subterfuge for policies which have not as yet been identified and are not presently known to exist.

***

The cry for less government involvement in the lives of ordinary citizens remains provocative and headline-grabbing, however. As it ebbs and flows along the pendulum of US History, it's as if "the government" is the source of our economic, social and political problems. Somehow, the source of our frustration can never be "us," which is again noted to be a particularly self-serving characteristic of human nature. Reminiscent of the famous line from the song, *Gloria: In Excelsis Deo*, rock and roll Hall of Famer, Patti Smith, sings that *Jesus died for somebody's sins, but not mine.*

We all consider ourselves to be without fault, looking first to a source other than ourselves, upon which to blame our problems. Ordinary citizens need only to be reminded of the role of the lawyer in their lives, as exemplifying this fact of life.

People spend years, decades in some instance, screwing up their lives. Then, they hire a lawyer, and expect that their considerable problems will be resolved in a matter of a couple of weeks. When that timeline fails, as it must, people necessarily blame their lawyers. Shakespeare's rueful, mocking line from the play, *Henry VI*, often expresses the ordinary person's frustration with the tradition and complexity of law: *"The first thing we do, let's kill all the lawyers."* Human nature is such that we look for scapegoats.

***

The attraction to the idea of "rugged individualism" is even more interesting in view of the framework of the US Constitution. True, individualism was still prized within the continuing experiment in democracy, but importantly, only within a solemn commitment to a *collective* social identity first and foremost.

Let's highlight some examples in the real world. An ordinary citizen who "fills up" at a choice of any number of independent, competitive gas stations today will typically not appreciate that at one time there was only a single gas station, Standard Oil. One man named Rockefeller owned and controlled this oil monopoly, using his power and wealth to control the systems of government to keep himself on top. After all, these are only the forces of capitalism and human nature at work here. And it should be noted that nearly everyone benefitted from the system, which ran quite efficiently at relatively low cost to the customer.

But as no individual or private interest had done previously, T.R. used the mechanism of our collective federal government to break up the Standard Oil monopoly under the Sherman Anti-Trust Act. In the aftermath, several smaller, competing, "sister" companies were created, effectuating the law's intent to reclaim the proper balance between lawful competitors.

What the ordinary citizen knows, simply, as the "telephone" presents a similar case. An ordinary citizen who chooses today from among any number of independent, competitive home or wireless carrier service plans will not, perhaps, appreciate that it was not always that way. In the 1960s and 1970s there were no wireless home phones, nor were there cell phones. Consequently, there was no texting. Can one imagine life without texting? Both the You Tube and Facebook internet sites were understandably out of the equation then, too.

The standard for the mass of citizens was what is known today as the "land line," wire and all, which was monopolized by just one company, AT&T. The telephone monopoly of "Ma Bell" controlled not only "local" service within a particular customer's locality but also "long distance" service, which included everywhere else. As such, AT&T's gigantic footprint was as pervasive as it was familiar to the ordinary citizen.

Not surprisingly, college students back in the day typically attended classes, carrying only a textbook and umbrella. An intriguing dynamic also presented itself when came the appointed time to meet someone for lunch on a particular date, and that someone else didn't show up. Today, the reason for the delay or postponement can be ascertained instantaneously. But in the "dinosaur" era, it might (and routinely would) take a couple of weeks to finally figure out "what happened to Johnny." One (or a colleague) had to bump into him, literally, and the word travelled back.

As with the oil monopoly, AT&T, the large, mega-corporation, used its power and wealth to control the systems of government to maintain its monopoly on top of the telecommunications pyramid. But yet, in a repeat of history for the benefit of the ordinary citizen, the mechanism of our collective government was brought to bear to break up Ma Bell, as no individual or private interest had done previously.

In the ensuing settlement with the government, AT&T's local service was split into several smaller, competing "Baby Bells," as they became known (names like Pacific Bell, Bell South, Ameritech and what is presently known as Verizon, the merger of former Baby Bells, Nynex and Bell Atlantic—yes, they're consolidating once again!).

The settlement further called for AT&T to agree to permit competition in the long distance space, and consequently, companies with names like Sprint and MCI were born. Lastly, the settlement called for the divestiture of Bell Labs, AT&T's research and development arm, vital for technological breakthroughs in transistors, wireless communications technology and military advantage. The new, stand-alone company was called Lucent Technologies. While Lucent was later purchased by Alcatel, the French conglomerate (raising concerns regarding the compromise of US national security), the effect of the overall settlement at the time reclaimed the proper balance between businesses in competition.

Lastly is the case of Microsoft and the example of its rise to monopolistic supremacy, which remains a favorite US post-graduate "business school 101" core case study. By the early 1990s (thereby post-dating the "dinosaur" era), the world of personal computers and the intense competition among providers to the public consolidated to a race between Apple and Microsoft.

Apple is listed first in the case study, since Apple had what was, by all accounts, the superior product. Known today as the "windows" operating system (OS), Apple founder and master innovator, Steve Jobs, created an intuitive, "plug and play," user friendly platform that any ordinary citizen could figure out and use. By contrast, Microsoft's Bill Gates at first utilized only the old, arcane and complicated "DOS" language system, which meant basically that one had to have a degree in computer programming to use it. A primitive windows platform followed, which was grossly inferior to Apple's windows OS in all respects.

Meanwhile, Microsoft aligned strategically with IBM, becoming the standard by targeting and thereby owning the corporate business market. Microsoft negotiated OEM (Original Equipment Manufacturer) agreements with IBM and new emerging manufacturers like Dell and Gateway, and many other manufacturers of what were known as "IBM clones." They also bundled in their applications programs like Office (Word, Excel, and PowerPoint), further cementing Windows as the dominant standard.

Apple's business model focused on the education market and "creative" consumers, its computers coming bundled with all of the software. By contrast, Microsoft machines were advertised without the applications for which Microsoft charged monopoly style premium prices. Microsoft's efficiencies and shrewd marketing techniques created what appeared to be a competitive price advantage with Apple. But since Apple refused to lower its prices in the segment where it was dominant, its market share lagged.

It is said that the personal computer and resulting Internet Revolution which followed were as meaningful in impacting the lives of ordinary citizens for the better as was the Industrial Revolution a century prior.

Slowly but surely, Microsoft began to take market share, while developing its own first legitimate window's OS, labeled Windows '95, with a full professional marketing campaign. Microsoft smartly used the Rolling Stones song, *Start Me Up*, as its jingle. It was a huge success.

Apple was warned to lower the price on its superior system but stubbornly resisted. And by the time Apple was ready to listen, it was too late. Microsoft had gained control of approximately 98% of market share. By 1997 Apple was on the verge of bankruptcy.

Since virtually every personal computer used Microsoft's OS, Microsoft thus had achieved monopoly status. Despite industry demands to open its source code, Microsoft refused and closed ranks, thereby eliminating not only competition but also innovation within its own corporate culture. Thereafter, it used its power and influence like the big oil and telephone monopolies of the past to control the systems of government, to maintain its monopoly in the world of personal computing.

But again, in a repeat of history, the mechanism of our collective government was summoned, as no individual or private interest had done previously. The administration of President Bill Clinton, a Democrat, filed a federal lawsuit against Microsoft in restraint of trade, for the benefit of the ordinary citizen. The goal was to break up Microsoft's OS monopoly status.

In a second shrewd move, Bill Gates used his enormous wealth and influence in an effort simply to obstruct and outlast the Clinton (Democratic) administration. The hope was that the succeeding presidential administration might be more sympathetic, meaning more Republican.

The highly contested presidential election of 2000, which ushered in the Republican administration of George W. Bush "43" would be fortuitous for big business in general and Bill Gates in particular. Microsoft argued that the disclosure of the source code to its operating system software would jeopardize national security, in a highly competitive global economy. Microsoft also argued that this presented a novel situation, which had not existed previously in the other cases.

***

Probably dating back to 1896 and President William McKinley, the Republican Party had also earned the reputation for being the party of big business. The reputation was well earned for two reasons. First, the Republican Party supported the gold standard, which better protected the value of the owners' capital investment in the plants and factories where the goods of industry were generated. Second, the Republican Party supported high protective tariffs, which made American products more competitive in relation to foreign producers.

The Republican Party had also been the standard bearer for the ideology of Social Darwinism, a survival of the fittest ideology that applies Darwin's evolutionary theory to society. It also has a long, rich history as the Grand Old Party (hence the term "GOP") dating back to the Civil War era. But it is widely understood that it has given ordinary citizens only a couple of true progressive reformers, Abraham Lincoln and T.R. Some argue that Ronald Reagan, the party's conservative icon, was a third.

But the Reagan Revolution of 1980, so called, was not built on a foundation which stressed the value of a collective identity, as was the case with Lincoln and T.R. Rather, President Reagan's platform stressed individualism and self reliance, that the Great Society and war on poverty entitlement programs were free giveaways, which robbed the ordinary citizen of requisite self-worth. "Government does not empower. Freedom empowers," as the saying went.

Under President Reagan, the US government's essential domestic role was seen to be limited to the maintenance of domestic order and tranquility. Painful domestic spending cuts were implemented in such vital areas as education and social services, which would permit a corresponding reduction in taxes. This would incentivize the private economy (i.e.: big business, some might label special interests) to invest and thus stimulate tremendous economic growth and development. It was classic Social Darwinism theory.

If all went according to plan, the size of the government would be shrunk. Although taxes were cut, the stimulation of economic growth would yield a net increase in federal revenue as the economy grew. Consequently, the national debt would be reduced.

On the other hand, many criticized Mr. Reagan's policies of "supply side" economics (so-called "Reaganomics") as nothing more than re-badged, previously failed, "trickle down" theory. Taking full advantage of favorable government treatment, wealthy private interests would become even wealthier, to be sure. But whereas a rising tide lifts all boats, or so the expression went, would enough crumbs trickle down to satisfy everyone else? Even within the Republican Party, T.R.'s own discrediting remarks aside, Mr. Reagan's policies were also disparaged with the slanderous term "voodoo economics." [287]

In reality, the phenomenon of private enterprise and impressive economic growth could not be questioned. However, the numbers from the aftermath of the Reagan Revolution, considered to be a 12 year period (encompassing Mr. Reagan's two terms and additionally the one term of Mr. Bush/"41"), were something less than a phenomenon. These numbers reflected deficit spending which, in fact, quadrupled the national debt during that time period [288] and placed America on a deficit-spending path that continues to this day.

At the conclusion of the 12 years of the Reagan/Bush/"41" administrations in 1992, it looked as though the bill would have to be paid by future generations of Americans, who had neither a voice nor stake in the Reagan ideology.

This Republican free-spending phenomenon was particularly vexing, in view of Mr. Reagan's pre-election pledge to reduce the size and scope of government in the lives of ordinary citizens. After all, Mr. Reagan had broken with the F.D.R. ideology by the 1960s over excessive government, specifically in the area of entitlements.

But it is important to remember that in his day, F.D.R. was also a fiscal conservative. His long-term vision for Social Security, a signature legislative triumph of social legislation and historic importance, insisted that the scheme be self-funding. The system would be freestanding: a property right, not a civil right, with contributions to be paid jointly by employers and employees.

Further insisting that the Social Security plan be actuarially sound and that no government contribution would be required, F.D.R. had concluded upon the plan's enactment in 1935 that

> It is almost dishonest to build up an accumulated deficit for the Congress of the Unites States to meet in 1980. We can't do that. We can't sell the United States short in 1980 any more than in 1935 (when the plan was enacted). [289]

President Reagan was seemingly fortuitous, however, in one respect. A healthy portion of the capital from the US domestic spending cuts was re-deployed to a massive military build-up. The intent could not have been clearer: to defeat, once and for all, in a life and death struggle that perceived international menace, the Soviet Union, and communism as a worldwide movement.

The state of the USSR's economy was in general grossly misunderstood by President Reagan, President Bush/"41" and nearly all US top military advisers, cold war analysts and foreign policy thinkers at the time. In fact, it was in chaos. But the extent of the chaos was largely unknown, due to the highly secretive nature of Kremlin planning and execution of the Soviet economy. In reality, it just so happened that the Soviet economy was on the brink of collapse. [290] Its attempt to match the US arms build-up led directly to its ultimate downfall.

Even decades later, however, the jury is still out on the question of whether the US economy had been placed on an irreversible path toward bankruptcy, as well.

***

It is time to get back to our story of Microsoft. Bill Gates was, of course, aware of the fact that the Bush name was synonymous more or less with Texas oil and an entrepreneurial leadership role in the oil industry. Mr. Gates was also surely aware that the name of Dick Cheney, the Vice President, was synonymous with large oil and natural gas holdings in his home state of Wyoming. After all, Mr. Cheney had served previously as the CEO of Halliburton, which is, according to its own website, "one of the world's largest providers of products and services to the energy industry."

Like his father, President Bush/"43" campaigned on a platform of reduced government size, spending and economic growth spurred by private capital investment and lower taxes. In reality, however, President Bush/"43" was an aggressive protector of the status quo. Additionally, President Bush/"43" was a proponent of the principles of Social Darwinism to such an extent that his polices were said to put the country up for sale to special interests like at no time previously in US History. [291]

One such example was the creation of a new federal entitlement program, in the form of legislation extending prescription drug benefits to Medicare recipients (i.e.: the elderly). Standing alone, this new entitlement legislation represented the largest increase in federal social welfare spending since President Lyndon Johnson's Great Society of the 1960s.

An ordinary citizen might have suspected, however, that there would be an obvious, major benefit of the legislation. That benefit was the leverage of the federal government to negotiate lower prices from the pharmaceutical industry for drug purchases, due to the collective purchasing power of such a large numerical constituency. But the legislation contained a specific ban on what appears to be such a meaningful and necessary provision. Why? The legislation was written by the drug industry and private insurance companies. [292]

There is a fact perhaps even of greater significance. Remarkably, the free-spending nature of the new Medicare entitlement came without a corresponding source of revenue, balancing tax increase or spending reduction elsewhere in the budget. In other words, like the two wars, this new entitlement program was funded on borrowed dollars. This has been a significant contributing factor to the mood of federal budgetary gloom which has gripped the nation's Beltway.

The free-spending hallmark of the Bush/"43" administration included four main components: the Medicare prescription drug benefit; the prosecution of two wars (in Afghanistan following "9/11" and the 2003 Iraq War); and the Bush/"43" era estate tax cuts on inheritance for even the wealthiest 2% of Americans. Unfortunately, *none* of them included a corresponding source of revenue, balancing tax increase or spending reduction elsewhere in the budget. Collectively, each was simply put on the nation's credit card.

As a consequence, the federal government's annual budget deficits have steepened, and consequently the size of the national debt has also grown like at no time before in US History. By these examples, it is apparent that the Republican Party is or should be *denied* the platform of *limited government.*

At the same time, projected deficits for the next president in the ensuing several fiscal years portended a staggering sea of expanding red ink. Following the election of 2008, these were the grim economic facts faced by the new president, Barack Obama, *before* he had taken the oath of office and proposed to spend even one dime.

And so, to conclude our Microsoft story, it was not even a mild surprise to learn that the big bet of Bill Gates to outlast the Clinton administration paid off handsomely indeed. Predictably, President Bush/"43" was persuaded to agree with Microsoft's claims and dismissed the federal government's suit, leaving private "market" forces to determine the ultimate fate of Microsoft. Whether this decision was or will be a benefit or detriment to the ordinary citizen remains to be seen and is beyond the scope of this work.

Nevertheless, there is a footnote to the story. Microsoft infused a large sum of cash into Apple, thereby averting the latter's bankruptcy, and restored Steve Jobs to his role of master technological innovator. Had that not happened, the world may never have seen iPods, iPads, iPhones or iMacs. The main difference was that Steve Jobs would now, in a sense, work for Bill Gates, as much of Apple's financial success would inure to Microsoft under its large umbrella.

Bill Gates' investment fueled Apple's resurgence to the leading technology company in the world in what has been labeled the greatest corporate comeback story of all time. In the process it has made Bill Gates that much richer.

Is the ordinary citizen better served by this arrangement? It all depends on what role and to what extent, if any, one feels the government should play in the life of the ordinary citizen. The government provides incentives. But sometimes those incentives create disparities and perpetuate inequities. Should the fix be left to private market forces? Or should the government that created the disparities endeavor to remedy them? While contemplating this, the ordinary citizen is reminded that the mission statements of a large US corporation like Microsoft, and that of the US government, are *not* inherently one and the same.

***

In the end, how does the ordinary citizen balance the need for change, against the obligation to protect the status quo?

Conservatives, said T.R., "are taught to believe that change means destruction. They are wrong. ... Life means change; where there is no change, death comes." [293]

> If I could ask but one thing of my fellow countrymen, my request would be that, whenever they go in for reform, they remember the two sides, and that they always exact justice from one side as much as from the other.
> ...
> But we must be ready to face temporary disaster, whether or not brought on by those who will war against us to the knife. Those who oppose reform will do well to remember that ruin in its worst form is inevitable if our national life brings us nothing better than swollen fortunes for the few and the triumph in both politics and business of a sordid and selfish materialism. [294]

But if the law of evolution applied to precious works of art, art being one of the few subjects in which T.R. was not an expert, those fittest to survive typically change little within an environment of change. The masterpieces resist any temptation:

> It is true, as the champions of the extremists say, that there can be no life without change, and that to be afraid of what is different or unfamiliar is to be afraid of life. It is no less true, however, that change may mean death and not life, and retrogression instead of development. [295]

Consider that change is messy. Great achievement is all but impossible absent an individual willing to incur a dangerous level of risk that is unacceptable to most. The first person through or over the wall always gets hurt. This ordinary yet peculiar but necessary citizen gets beaten up, beaten down and absorbs the full brunt of the damaging blows of the entrenched status quo. Taking it square in the teeth, the innovative risk taker on the front line often becomes a regrettable casualty. But the process exposes the powerful force of resistance as but a dying voice.

Where human nature is concerned, perhaps the individual who happens to have things in abundance has a valid point and typically the final say. You can do pretty much whatever you want in your own pursuit of happiness, but just don't try to change *my* status quo.

Do we play it safe and fly under the radar, shining our beacon from under a bush? Do we have any further obligation? Or do we act more aggressively, throw caution to the wind, knowing that the harder we push for change the greater the assurance of our own personal destruction?

Chapter 11
Moral Issues:
When Are They "Secondary?"

Life is bigger
It's bigger than you and you are not me
The lengths that I will go to
The distance in your eyes
Oh no, I've said too much
I set it up

That's me in the corner
That's me in the spotlight
Losing my religion
Trying to keep up with you
And I don't know if I can do it
Oh no, I've said too much
I haven't said enough

I thought that I heard you laughing
I thought that I heard you sing
I think, I thought, I saw you try

Every whisper
Of every waking hour I'm choosing my confessions
Trying to keep an eye on you
Like a hurt lost and blinded fool
Oh no, I've said too much
I set it up
...
But that was just a dream

- from the song, *Losing My Religion*,
by R.E.M. (1991)
available on the *Out of Time* collection

***

Whatever forces may be in play to attempt to change a powerful and hardened status quo are typically compelled to proceed at their own peril. President Eisenhower had resisted the change in the law integrating

223

public schools as not involving a great moral issue. Sometimes, that is the way the issue of change is ultimately portrayed. That is to say, is a *moral* issue at stake, or not?

If so, typically, change may be more likely to occur than not. Otherwise, one may forget about it. But it is important to note that the word should alert an audience that the speaker is advocating change.

In the preceding two chapters the word "moral" or one of its derivative forms was used 10 times. These are the *easy* cases. But what about when the audience is told that the moral issue is *secondary*? What do we do then?

***

An analysis of US history makes one fact abundantly clear: the American democracy does not care to undertake major change or reform, unless and until there is a clear consensus. But the phenomenon of consensus is becoming increasingly rare. Typically a consensus is brought about only by the onset of crisis, only the degree of which is ripe for debate. In the latter category, the ordinary citizen can point grimly to the Civil War, the Great Depression and the two European Civil Wars. Looking back with the benefit of hindsight and reflection, each crisis appeared to relate to a moral issue in one form or another.

When one is in a forward, leadership position, unchallenged and protected by government, simply mucking along, there is no incentive to take risk, to continue to innovate. The sole interest is to consolidate and perpetuate gain—and to revel in the rising stacks. Lost is the idea of what it was that got America and American businesses to the point of leadership in the first place.

When one thinks of morality, one must also think of ethics. And the definition of ethics must include the idea of obedience to the unenforceable. Woodrow Wilson, the highly principled man that he was, once said that "there is a higher law than profit" and that people "should be broader-minded to see what was best for America." [296]

We ordinary citizens have all heard the expression: "I can't do *that* – it's the *principle* of the matter!" If a lawyer who spent a good deal of time in the courtroom had a dime for every time principle had to be defended, he'd be a rich man. Wilson believed that arguing issues in the realm of principle made compromise an (unacceptable) abdication of conscience, ending in a clash of personalities, on account of the assumption that the *challenges* were unprincipled. [297] Nevertheless, he felt, to a fault, that one's principles, once formed, could not be compromised.

But in the political process, compromise is *not* a dirty word. [298] Those guided by strict adherence to ideology become dangerous, when they are unyielding and their majority moves to dominate self-righteously. They do not compromise. The governed only get to march, the music, cadence and beat pre-determined. Rigid minds leave no room for differing viewpoints, which reflect the spectrum of human needs. Yet in certain respects we do need those who demand more than humanity can deliver, aggravating as they can sometimes be.

On the other hand, some are guided simply by political expediency, believing in little or nothing other than the upward mobility of ambition and self-interest. They are confounding, having risen without commitment to any general ideology. Since they function without program, principle or consistency, they, too, are a dangerous lot.

What is required to unite the rigid proponent of ideology with the political expedient who believes in nothing? Between these two extremes lies an area ripe for compromise. Suppose the whole loaf is not available? Does one not accept a slice or two or maybe only just a few crumbs? The democratic system requires that this point be fairly understood. But the compromise of principle often comes at the expense of conscience. Sometimes, particularly when the stakes are greatest, the choice is not pleasant. For these reasons, it is said that the graveyard of politics is littered with principled men. Who does that leave us with?

For some in politics, it is sufficient that "the duty of the opposition is to oppose." The need to suggest alternatives, to curb internal radicalism and irresponsibility, is irrelevant. Truth and reality have little substance in the shadows of political gamesmanship.

Moral issues can certainly confound us. In 2004, Jim McGreevey, then-governor of the state of New Jersey, was forced to resign his office, in disgrace, amidst allegations that he had violated the ethical oath of his office. He was criticized for having appointed as homeland security adviser a man named Golan Cipel, who reportedly lacked experience or other qualifications for the position. In addition, Cipel could not gain security approval from the federal government, as he was Israeli and not a US citizen.

On the day of his resignation, McGreevey proclaimed publicly that he was gay and also said that he had "engaged in an adult consensual (extra-marital) affair with another man." During the course of that relationship, it had been suspected and alleged that the man had improperly gained access to high level homeland security information. The man subsequently left the US and returned to Israel after the affair was revealed, all the while insisting that he wasn't gay and accusing McGreevey of sexually harassing him. McGreevey said the man tried to blackmail him and that he resigned rather than succumb to threats. [299]

In the meantime, it was reported subsequently that Kean University had agreed to hire McGreevey as an adjunct professor to teach, of all things, "ethics, law and leadership." [300] If these were the skeletons in the former governor's closet, some not improperly inquisitive students wanted to know, what skeletons might also be found in any other adjunct professor's closet? It was an excellent question, one which could have neither an expedient nor effective answer. It might come down to a question of ethics.

***

More books have been written about Abraham Lincoln than any of the other US Presidents. [301] One story in particular relates to Lincoln's discussions with the political leaders of the various Southern states, as they contemplated secession, at the brink of the Civil War.

Thomas Jefferson once said of the South's dilemma that the institution of slavery was like holding a tiger by the tail: You can't let go, but you can't very well hold on, either. August St. Clare, the fictional Louisiana master to our friend, Tom, the loyal slave in the 19th century classic novel, *Uncle Tom's Cabin* [302], had presented the Southern intellectual's view towards slavery:

> It comes from the devil, that's the short of it;—and, to my mind, it's a pretty respectable specimen of what he can do in his own line. [303]

We've all heard the expression at one time or another: "Give the devil his due." The fictional St. Clare had been frustrated by a moral conflict. On the one hand was his moral rejection of slavery as an insidiously evil institution. But it stood against the reality that to stand alone as a pariah in its public rejection or to organize a force in the larger cause of its defeat was all but impossible.

226

One summer, St. Clare had invited down his cousin, Miss Ophelia, from the northern state of Vermont to observe firsthand what Lincoln had called the "peculiar institution" of slavery. All the while, Miss Ophelia scolded and admonished him. "Easy for you to preach," St. Clare responded, "for *you* don't have to live with them." It was a reference to the fact that the number of African Americans living in Vermont at the time was on the order of less than 1%. [304]

Harriet Beecher Stowe's book would serve to educate and enlighten Northerners as to the particular horrors of slavery and energize them to fight for its abolition. At the same time, the book provoked widespread anger in the South. She had been roundly criticized by Southerners for writing not a fictitious tale, but one that had absolutely no basis in fact. Critics cited the fact that Stowe had never lived in the South. So how was it that she was able to portray the situation so vividly in her writing, were it not all just a fabrication?

Stowe was reared in Connecticut in a family that was the perfect incubator for her talent. Her father was a prominent New England minister at the head of a family that stressed education and social awareness. She was educated at a girls' school and received a wide ranging education. It was said that social reform was the Beecher family business, producing progressive ministers, educators, writers, and a feminist agitator. Stowe became highly influential in writing, one of the few pursuits available to women at the time.

At age 21 Stowe moved to Ohio, where she became involved in various literary circles and became concerned with social issues of the day. She visited a slavery auction in Kentucky, an experience that profoundly moved her. Married at age 24, Stowe and her husband were committed to abolishing slavery, taking part in the legendary Underground Railroad which temporarily housed fugitive slaves. Through these experiences, she gained firsthand knowledge of the institution of slavery. She felt it her Christian duty to write about the injustice of slavery.

A deeply religious woman, Stowe also engaged in considerable research to write the book. One of her primary methods was through interviews of family, friends and those with direct experience. One of her research subjects was Frederick Douglass, the famous abolitionist and former slave. [305]

Sometime in 1851 it was reported that the Stowe family had been sitting in church listening to an anti-slavery sermon. When the preacher quoted the New Testament phrase, "Inasmuch as ye have done it unto one of the least of these my brethren, ye have done it unto me," Stowe was gripped with a vision that would eventually become a pivotal scene in her still-unwritten book: the death of a slave named Uncle Tom. As soon as church was over, she wrote down all she had imagined of this emotional moment. Stowe was quoted as saying:

> My heart was bursting with the anguish excited by the cruelty and injustice our nation was showing to the slave, and praying God to let me do a little, and to cause my cry for them to be heard. [306]

Then there was Dred Scott, a Missouri slave who sued to gain his freedom. Scott had argued that while he had been the slave of an army surgeon, he had lived in Illinois, a free state, and Wisconsin, a free territory, for 4 years and that his residence on free soil had erased his slave status. His case traveled all the way to the US Supreme Court and was decided 7-2, although all 9 justices issued their own opinions. Chief Justice Roger Taney, the same Taney appointed by President Jackson some 25 years earlier, delivered the majority opinion. [307]

In what many constitutional scholars have asserted was one its worst decisions, the high court made several sweeping rulings. First, the Taney opinion said that Dred Scott had no right to sue in federal court, because neither slaves nor free blacks were US citizens. The Declaration of Independence and the Bill of Rights were *not* intended to apply to African Americans. Moreover, since blacks were considered property and not people, Congress did not have the power to exclude slavery from the territories. This was despite the will of the people who lived in those territories, which may have been to the contrary. Taney ruled that what needed protection was the slaveholder's *property* rights, under the 5th amendment. To rule otherwise would violate the prohibition against the seizure of property without just compensation.

Designed to solve the controversy over slavery once and for all, the Dred Scott decision was a major political miscalculation. In reality, the opinion represented a judicial defense of the most extreme slavery position. Instead of solving the crisis, the decision intensified sectional strife, undercut potential compromise solutions and weakened the moral authority of the judiciary.

***

Enter Abraham Lincoln, who regarded the decision as part of a slave power conspiracy to legalize slavery throughout the US. The ordinary citizen should consider the fact that Abraham Lincoln was *not* particularly popular in his own time. He was the first President from the "West," as such. And he was self-taught; that is, he did not attend one of the Northeastern colleges, attended by the children of families of means and privilege. Lincoln was not physically attractive, either. His tall, clumsy appearance did no justice to his razor sharp mind. He appeared aloof, distracted, as if he weren't paying attention. But when he began to speak, the veil lifted. Popularity, even reverence, did not come until later—*after* an assassin had put a bullet in his head in April 1865.

What could Lincoln have been thinking about upon his inauguration in March 1861? Prior to his election, Lincoln's goal had simply been to preserve the Union. Whether that meant a Union that was to be all free, all slave, part free and part slave did not matter, that anything would be possible with compromise. But since the South was economically *dependent* on slavery, the Southern states were not of a mind to compromise. "Either slavery grows or it dies," they reasoned. And the platform of Lincoln's new Republican Party to ban its further extension to the western territories meant the death of slavery.

Consider an analogy involving "the South, slavery and the feeding tube." When the feeding tube is removed from a patient on life support, in consequence the patient dies. Such was the South's dilemma in the case of slavery: remove it and the economy of the South would also crumble.

Moreover, from the South's perspective dating from the time of Texas statehood in 1845, the idea of the spread of slavery westward flowed quite logically from the concept of Manifest Destiny. Under that concept, the US had a right and special destiny by the power of God to surge westward, stretching clear across the continent from coast (Atlantic) to coast (Pacific).

But was the land grab in the creation of an empire to be for liberty—or slavery? For adherence to the Southern view would compel the ordinary citizen to consider the following:

> Natural rights, of course, are derived from natural law, the author of which is Nature's God. Americans might well have believed that God had staked out North America as their Promised Land, but it was a dangerous claim because it implied a responsibility to obey all of God's *other* laws. [308]

According to the theory of secession, each state, when it had joined the Union, had authorized the national government to act as its agent in the exercise of certain functions of sovereignty. However, each state had never given away its own fundamental sovereignty. Since the agreement or "compact" of the states was not permanent, any state could withdraw from the compact and reassert its individual sovereignty. In practice, the South was bound neither by national laws with which it did not agree, nor the result of an election (in this case, Lincoln's election of 1860) which it did not win. The South was free to secede from the Union and form its own country.

Lincoln was well aware, and Northerners knew, that the South could scarcely be denied the right of revolution. He knew that the secessionists were attempting merely to follow the example of their forefathers in declaring independence from a government which was threatening their civil rights and liberties. Lincoln was also well aware that the South was basing its position on a constitutional argument, whose question had yet to be decided on a political basis.

But Lincoln claimed that secession was unconstitutional, since the voluntary "compact" among the states was intended to be a permanent, binding arrangement. This permanent compact could not be legally broken, absent the unanimous agreement of the states to permit secession.

After the results of the election were known, some held out an olive branch of compromise to the point of exhaustion to keep the Union intact. But Lincoln believed that no appeasement should be entertained regarding the *extension* of slavery, after an election had just been carried on principles fairly stated to the people. To surrender the government to those we have beaten, "is the end of us." Lincoln hoped against hope that "right would make might."

It was then, and only as a last resort, that Lincoln played his final card, the one that bespoke "morality." Unlike 1776, the motto, according to Lincoln, was not liberty, but slavery. Lincoln reasoned that

> the right of revolution, is never a legal right. At most, it is but a moral right, when exercised for a morally justifiable cause. When exercised without such a cause, revolution is no right, but simply a wicked exercise of physical power. [309]

The South was not persuaded. It stuck doggedly to the argument that it was about states' rights over federal under the constitution and the loss of some $4 billion in property rights (that the slave labor purportedly represented). An exasperated Lincoln was compelled to pose the direct question: "How about the *morality* of slavery?"

But the South remained unmoved. As even the casual observer of drug and substance abuse addiction well knows, dependency will play evil tricks on the mind of an otherwise sensible, rationally thinking individual. And so the South's response rang with an air of determined finality: "The moral issue is *secondary*." [310]

Although both sides claimed God to be on *their* side during the ensuing carnage of the Civil War, Lincoln's concern was not so much whether God was on *his* side but, rather, whether he was on *God's* side.

Another story about ethics involves the familiar tale of a man who finds a lost wallet on the sidewalk. Like a majority of ordinary citizens, the man had a good job but had virtually nothing to spare, once all the bills were paid, until the next paycheck.

Picking up the wallet, he put it in his coat and continued on to work, examining its contents as soon as he got there. At around $600 in cash, he stopped counting. His first thought was that he had won a mini lottery. But he quickly dismissed that foolish notion. The man called the owner to tell him to come by to pick it up. The owner spoke gruffly, however, unlike what one might expect from a man whose wallet had just been found.

The owner did come by later that afternoon, turning out to be an older, white man with a permanent scowl. The man handed the owner his wallet, and the owner immediately began counting his money. Audibly irritated, the man said it was all there. The owner stopped counting, grudgingly pulled out a $5 bill and handed it toward the man, who refused to accept it, stating that he hoped the owner would return somebody else's wallet someday. The owner turned on his heel and stalked away without uttering another word.

The man learns two valuable lessons from that experience. The first is as familiar as it is simple: Honesty is what one does when no one is looking. The second is perhaps more important, and more relevant, described as the defining moment in the man's ethical development: A need, however great it might be, does not convert a wrong to a right, or bad to good. The owner's wallet was not his, no matter how much the man needed the money, or how rude the owner happened to be.

The man later became a member of the highest court in the land, the US Supreme Court. The Hon. Mr. Justice Clarence Thomas often had occasion to remind himself in years to come that self-interest isn't a principle—it's just self-interest. [311]

One of Clarence Thomas' heroes, the late Robert Kennedy, had said that it was really a moral issue, the continued prosecution of the Vietnam War, against the increasingly violent street protests of the younger generation calling for its end. The truth is that the US had expended more ordnance on the tiny Asian nation of North Vietnam than *all* the participants in World War II against each other, *combined*. This inspired R.F.K. to pose the following question: "If we bomb every square inch of North Vietnam to rubble, then what exactly have we saved it from?"

Robert Kennedy had been inspired by the message conveyed in *Dante's Inferno*: "The hottest places in hell are reserved for those who, in times of great moral crisis, maintain their neutrality." And so, using an argument inspired by morality, he changed his position on the Vietnam War. Such can be the power of morality to nudge the immovable object.

For his part, Clarence Thomas rejected the idea that "The Man" was to do his thinking for him and that he must just do as he had been told. His thoughts, his dreams, his expectations—were thereby his own. Before he was appointed to the high court, Thomas had agreed to accept an earlier job as assistant secretary for civil rights in the Dept. of Education in the Reagan administration. The decision had been this black man's initial foray into the old school world of the Republican Party, as Thomas had become a Republican to vote for Mr. Reagan. In making the final decision to take the job, Thomas had heeded only the advice of a trusted friend. "It wasn't enough merely to talk about (race): I had a moral obligation to see if I could put some of my ideas into action." [312]

And so, in this spirit, the balance of the chapter will turn to some of the difficult moral imperatives of our time. These include human rights and torture, oil and the environment, and American business systems.

***

Madeline Albright, the first woman Secretary of State in the Clinton administration, the one they call "Madam Secretary," has made a key observation. Americans think two things of themselves: first, they think they're smarter than everyone else; and second, they think that non-

Americans listen to everything we Americans say. Both are untrue. As for the first, the reasons should be rather obvious by now. And as for the second, people are much more interested in what Americans *do* than what we *say*. We've all heard the expression that "talk is cheap," and in this regard it is no different. And so, it is appropriate to return to the subject of human rights.

When is conduct in the name of national security an acceptable "interrogation technique"—and when is it illegal "torture?" The obvious reference is to the insidious practice of "waterboarding." Unfortunately, the Bush/"43" administration is understood to have widely utilized waterboarding in attempt to infiltrate and root out certain insurgencies and terrorist networks. Mr. Bush's administration had argued forcefully that these networks posed an imminent threat to domestic national security, the American way of life. Consequently, the technique was justified on balance and under the circumstances.

To be sure, the idea that the ordinary citizen's 1st amendment guarantee of free speech can be curtailed, at a time when national security is threatened, is well settled. The first such laws, the Alien and Sedition Acts of 1798, were enacted during the presidential administration of John Adams under the threat of war with France. The laws had a twofold purpose. First, they permitted the arrest and deportation of aliens, whose pro-France bias interfered with the president's pro-British policies. Second, they sought to stamp out the voices of sympathy for revolutionary France, which were already here legally, many from the opposition party. It's a fancy way to say that the laws were designed to suppress political opposition.

The arrest under the Alien and Sedition Acts of Benjamin Franklin Bache, grandson of Benjamin Franklin, erupted into a public outcry. The constitutionality of these laws was thus brought into serious question. Public opposition became so great as to be responsible in part for the election of Thomas Jefferson, the leader of the opposition party, to the presidency in 1800. Moreover, once Jefferson took office, he pardoned all those convicted, while Congress restored all fines paid, with interest.

During the Civil War, President Lincoln had also used liberally a legal provision to detain and imprison those citizens who were believed to be pro-Confederacy sympathizers. Had there been no war, the law of unlawful detainer (lawyers call it the suspension of the writ of *habeus corpus*) was without adequate legal justification. During World War

233

II, F.D.R. relied on the same legal justification to inter thousands of innocent, law abiding Japanese American citizens in California and elsewhere. The US Supreme Court upheld F.D.R.'s actions in a decision which remains controversial to this day. [313]

These laws are effectively designed to *prohibit* certain free speech, which is guaranteed in otherwise tranquil settings. But how about the alternative, that is, *compelling* someone to speak against his will?

Those ordinary citizens who are old enough to remember the Vietnam War may also remember the insistent demands of US authorities with regard to the communist North Vietnamese. That is, the communists should be made to adhere to the provisions of the Geneva Conventions, regarding the treatment of prisoners of war. These provisions embody the doctrine of a "just war," defined as one carried out by a competent authority with moral intentions for a cause that is right. They also set forth a set of criteria which are morally necessary, both before a war is declared and while it is being prosecuted. Among the criteria, the use of torture in all its various forms against prisoners of war is strictly forbidden.

Waterboarding is understood to be a form of torture, in which the following technique is utilized. Water is poured over the face of an immobilized captive, causing the individual to experience the sensation of drowning, thereby getting the captive to "talk." The technique was identified more than 100 years ago, during the American "pacification" of the insurgent element of the local Philippine population, which was predominantly Muslim. Witnesses testified consistently to its widespread use by American soldiers, "developed by Spanish priests as a means of instilling reverence for the Holy Ghost:"

> A man is thrown down on his back and three or four men sit on his arms and legs and hold him down and either a gun barrel or a rifle barrel or a carbine barrel or a stick as big as a belaying pin ... is simply thrust into his jaws ... and then water is poured onto his face, down his throat and nose ... until the man gives some sign of giving in or becomes unconscious ... His suffering must be that of a man who is drowning, but who cannot drown. [314]

During the Bush "43" administration, US government officials at various times said they did not believe waterboarding to be a form of torture. To justify its proposed use, however, the administration used the provisions of the Patriot Act and issued classified legal opinions that argued for a narrow definition of torture under US law. The technique was reportedly used by the American military in such places as the US Guantanamo Naval Base [315] (also called Gitmo or GTMO) on the island of Cuba and Abu Ghraib, a sprawling penal compound west of Baghdad in Iraq. [316] But did the administration's interrogation techniques go too far?

Before this question can be fairly answered, we must first travel back to the Philippino waterboarding incident. When he learned of it, and told that one officer accused of water torture had been ordered to stand trial, Theodore Roosevelt, another Republican president in another time, was not satisfied. T.R. directed his Secretary of State to flash a cable to the Major General, commanding US army operations in the Philippines:

> The President desires to know in the fullest and most circumstantial manner all the facts ... for the very reason that the President intends to back up the army in the heartiest fashion in every lawful and legitimate method of doing its work, he also intends to see that the most vigorous care is exercised to detect and prevent any cruelty or brutality, and that men who are guilty thereof are punished. Great as the provocation has been in dealing with foes who habitually resort to treachery, murder and torture against our own men, nothing can justify or will be held to justify the use of torture or inhuman conduct of any kind on the part of the American Army. [317]

Returning to the present, in January 2009 during his first month in office, Mr. Bush's successor, Barack Obama, in one of his first presidential acts issued an executive order banning the use of harsh interrogation techniques, including waterboarding. The order set out to "promote the safe, lawful, and humane treatment of individuals in United States custody." [318] Political opponents of his anti-terror policies were quick to point out that President Obama's vow to keep Americans safe was in conflict with his decision. [319] Mr. Obama justified his action, however, stating simply yet eloquently that American core values and ideals *were* our security.

Most recently, Mr. Bush had intended to set out on a trip to Geneva to give a speech. This prompted several human rights groups, including Amnesty International and the New York-based Center for Constitutional Rights, to ask Swiss prosecutors to open a criminal investigation against Mr. Bush. The inquiry was based on suspicion of war crimes over the admission in Mr. Bush's book that he personally authorized the waterboarding of terrorism suspects. When it was conveyed that "calls to demonstrate were sliding into dangerous terrain" and that protests by left-wing groups could result in violence, Mr. Bush unceremoniously cancelled his trip. [320]

Can we identify a dependency in the American economy today, which is significant enough to result in a determination that an underlying moral issue may be secondary?

In the 2006 award winning documentary film, *An Inconvenient Truth*, Al Gore makes the powerful case that stewardship of the environment is not merely a convenience but, rather, a moral issue. The statistics are sobering. The US comprises less than 5% of the world's population, yet consumes about 25% of the world's energy. Each and every ordinary American citizen uses about 3 gallons of oil per day, twice as much as people in other industrialized nations. America is a throw away society, with dismal recycling rates, producing roughly twice as much garbage as Europe. The political parties seem content to put the idea of economic growth on one side of the spectrum and environmental protection on the other, as if the two are somehow mutually exclusive. All the while, the ordinary citizen is stuck in the middle.

While it may be true that the sun heats the earth, it is also true that carbon heats man. Coal had been the preferred fossil fuel, prior to oil, and its use is widely still prevalent at the nation's large electricity generating power plants. The phenomenon of burning coal in such quantity is the largest component for the production of what we call acid rain. While, in combination with oil, the phenomenon of fossil fuel burning on such a mass scale is what scientists attribute to the concept of global warming.

But the wild card today is most definitely oil. The US consumes approximately 21 million barrels of oil per day, about 65% imported. [321] It is not an exaggeration then to say that US *dependence* on imported oil is a greater threat to national security than any threat from terrorism, real or perceived. Perhaps at no time since the pre-Civil War South's economic dependence on slavery can it again be said that the US reliance on oil is so acute as to constitute a life or death economic dependency. The *need* is so alarming, so encompassing, and so pervasive, that any moral issue that may come up along the way, including human rights and/or the environment, can also be dismissed as secondary. Which begs the question: Once all the terrorists are presumably eliminated, is the US then "free" to heat the planet into oblivion?

Typically, the exploitation of human beings is accompanied by the exploitation of natural resources, without any thought given to sustainability. In this model global warming is and will forever be a fiction, a liberal plot to thwart the legitimate aims of business. Will it remain this way until it is too late and the effects of global warming have become irreversible?

The violence of unregulated capitalism, which is portrayed in too many places in the nation's heartland, produces sacrifice zones, areas that have been destroyed for quarterly profit. The images are of coal mining ventures in West Virginia, offshore oil drilling in the Gulf of Mexico, fracking for natural gas in a multitude of geographical locations. Rich natural resources are extracted, yet the money is not funneled back into the communities that are sitting on top of, or next to those resources. Destruction is not limited to the environment. It includes communities, human beings, families. There appears to be no way to control corporate power. The system has broken down, whether it's Democrat or Republican. We've all become commodities. [322]

During the 2008 presidential debates the candidates exchanged argument with regard to US Middle East foreign policy. Speaking of Pakistan, then-candidate Obama noted the "old 20th century mindset" which basically said that "he may be a dictator, but he's our dictator. And as a consequence, we lost legitimacy … ." [323] That mindset was an unintended consequence of the Cold War. Rather than a head on confrontation with the other global superpower, the US sought merely to *contain* the great evil of the day, Soviet communism. However, if left unchecked, it was understood that communism would probe, infiltrate and exploit any weakness in the "free world" and install an alternative communist model. Mr. Obama said during the campaign that this mindset had to change.

But with the collapse of the USSR in 1991, the US still supports right wing governments, which are not democratically elected, in places such as Saudi Arabia and Bahrain. Only recently has the US turned away from such a government in Egypt after 30 years of dictatorial rule, where the people's quest for self-determination is finally impacting. Moreover, the tiny Arab country of Bahrain is the home base of the US Navy's Fifth Fleet, one of the most important and strategic US Navy bases in the world. From that naval base, two US aircraft carriers confined to the relatively narrow waters of the Persian Gulf patrol shipping lanes, keep a watchful eye on Iran and are involved with the war in Afghanistan.

The base is located just a few miles from the site of the mass protests in Bahrain, where US officials also worry about Bahrain's violent response to pro-democracy demonstrators. [324]

For all his accomplishments, T.R.'s own greatest achievement, in his own estimation, was in the area of conservation. During his administration, he provided the necessary impetus to preserve much of the land which serves as the core of the present day US National Park System. In 1908 T.R. had organized the First National Conservation Conference, which was attended by all state governors, and members of Congress as their schedules would permit. The conference led to the idea of "Conservation as a National Policy" and "National Duty," based on "efficient use of finite resources and scientific management of renewable ones." [325]

The utilitarian "greatest good for the greatest number" policy, which favors business at the expense of nature, and property rather than beauty, was curbed by T.R. in his time. John Muir, the iconic founder of the environmental mainstay known as the Sierra Club, had no patience for this pro business bias, where "The 'greatest number' is too often found to be number one." [326] The "Essential Democracy" of Yellowstone National Park had revealed its lesson, that "government can both serve and conserve, and that future generations had as much right to natural resources as contemporaries."

The long lines at the gas pumps and gasoline rationing dating to the time of the first Arab oil embargo in 1973 wreaked havoc on the US economy at the time. Since then, foreign producers, including OPEC (the Organization of Petroleum Exporting Countries), which possesses 75% of the world's proven oil reserves, have sought to use oil as a political weapon. The reason? It appears to be no more than to advance their own self-interest. After all, as we have seen repeatedly, isn't advancing self-interest but human nature?

In sum, given this legacy, it is remarkable, almost incomprehensible, where the US is in today's day and age: the only industrialized nation without a national energy policy. The challenge, then, as with all tangible commodities and collective problems which have come before, is to respect where we are, and how we got here. At the same time, through responsible, accountable action the US must return oil to its rightful place—from a political weapon—to just another commodity. [327]

***

Of the 40-43% of all energy use which oil provides worldwide, 70% is consumed by transportation. [328] Consequently, the conversation must shift logically to an analysis of American commerce and business systems.

Talented professional marketers continue to convince ordinary citizens that we *need* to drive large, gas guzzling motor vehicles, all the better if manufactured by American companies. But traditionally, these companies have, until very recently perhaps, been uninterested in any societal benefit, other than reaping large profits, perpetuating their own self-interest and the status quo. For example, prior to the Great Recession of 2008, and absent a subsequent government/taxpayer bailout, what was GM's "incentive" to produce dependable, durable, fuel efficient vehicles? Further, what was the "incentive" for Exxon Mobil, America's largest energy company, to promote the development of alternative, clean energy technologies?

Perhaps one of the greatest problems which bridges both domestic and foreign policy issues today is the antiquated thinking of American business systems. Business goals are grounded in an old school profit-centered mentality whose horizon is increasingly short-term. [329] They achieve monopoly status first by being a leader in innovative ideas. Then, with government support and protection behind them, companies like GM and Microsoft stagnate and close ranks around their monopoly status. They impede the free flow of ideas and become lethargic. In short, they become overpaid order takers for their once cutting edge products, which eventually grow stale.

A bunker mentality ensues to consolidate, maintain and perpetuate status. Even after the 2008 crash, management and labor continue to see themselves as adversaries competing with one another. The environment—and the government—are also viewed as unwelcome obstacles. The culmination is a fall from grace. The road map is familiar.

For example, from 1947 to 1977 General Electric (GE), a multinational industrial manufacturing giant, dumped as many as 1.3 million pounds of PCBs, a known carcinogen, into New York's Hudson River. [330] Upon "discovery," GE responded with the old argument that what it was doing was not illegal at the time. Congress, in turn, reacted as an ordinary citizen would expect a responsible legislative body should, enacting laws to assess environmental impact and address pollution issues in a meaningful way. [331] The idea was that corporations, as well as ordinary citizens, had a stake not only in profit but also in social responsibility.

Other major US corporations, however, responded with consequential actions of their own. They complained that American labor was too expensive, environmental laws too strict, to justify continued manufacture in the US. Further, US corporations complained that there was excessive US government "regulation" to compete successfully in a highly competitive global environment.

Beginning in the 1970s, in order to level the playing field with foreign competition, American businesses reacted by exporting American jobs to foreign shores en masse. Heavy manufacturing jobs came first, exported to countries like Mexico and along the Asia Pacific rim which welcomed the industry. Next, more specialized, higher paying technology jobs were exported to countries like Japan, Taiwan, South Korea and India. For their impressive manufacturing capabilities, some have called Japan and more recently South Korea our de facto 51st and 52nd states.

The arguable justification—reduction of operating costs—maximizes short-term corporate profits, while maintaining valuable core market share. But in the countries where the jobs were sent, neither are there adequate laws to protect the environment nor the local worker pool. So what of *their* air and river quality? So what if the wages paid to unskilled, foreign labor are significantly lower and the work hours required exceed levels not seen since the darkest days of the Industrial Revolution? Walmart, the world's largest public corporation—and the largest majority private employer and grocery retailer in the US—provides an excellent but chilling model of just how one company is (mis)shaping the global economy. [332]

Certainly outsourcing is legal—and beneficial. And it hardly breaks new ground. The idea that a country should outsource a particular service or commodity to another country which does the job cheaper and better traces to Scottish economist, Adam Smith, and his iconic book, *The Wealth of Nations*, published in 1776. This is how business efficiencies are created, and imbalances restored.

Outsourcing is but an example where human labor is viewed merely as a line item expense on an income statement. Everything is viewed as a commodity to be leveraged, including human beings. Why is the manufacturing base vital to the health and vitality of American society?

The main economic component, as well as the glue that binds our society together, is a job.

But when a business outsources, it unwittingly constructs a dependency which destroys individual initiative and self worth. Consider this an unintended consequence. Think of the American Indians both before and after the arrival of the white man. We remove the buffalo herds. We remove their livelihood. We make it impossible to sustain themselves. We set up government agencies. The net result is lines of people waiting for basic subsistence. They wait for food, cooking materials and alcohol. It comes down to "greed over human life, and the willingness on the part of people who seek personal enrichment to destroy other human beings. That's a common thread." Perhaps we have forgotten our neighbor—and the golden rule.[333]

What ever happened to Henry Ford's simple but then radical idea to double the wages of his assembly line workers? After all, Ford reasoned correctly, it was the workers who would be buying the cars coming off his assembly line. They couldn't buy the cars without money. Henry Ford, the iconic entrepreneur, seemed to know instinctively that his own success would be fleeting without the *participation* of the middle class. [334] He understood that while leveraging labor was one thing, exploitation was quite another.

Instead, ordinary citizens who are left behind as a result of outsourcing are essentially "kept" at a subsistence level, yet dependent on the power structures that would mean their destruction. Some call it a "Walmart economy." At about 30 hours per week, Walmart wages place their workers below the poverty line. Together with an employment application, a would-be Walmart worker is also provided an application for food stamps. The net result is the government subsidizing the Walton family fortune. Others see outsourcing plainly as a "frightening window into the primacy of (monetary) profit over human dignity and human life." [335]

But there is at times a collective revulsion against a competitive system which competes at the expense of human decency. In an unregulated system, labor is the first casualty in an economic crisis. Profits are preserved by cutting costs. Therefore, the company that works its labor the longest and pays it least gains the greatest competitive advantage. Cutthroat competition makes the unscrupulous employer the leader in its field. [336] The rest unwittingly follow in a race to the bottom. It is somebody else's concern to clean up the mess.

Short-term corporate profits, in turn, permit high level business executives and "managers" to award themselves large bonus payments. Some are in the form of un-expensed stock options buried in the fine print on corporate balance sheets. When corporate by-laws inexplicably fail to require connecting these perks with longer-term accountability and bottom-line performance, the ordinary citizens should recognize this conduct to be nothing short of obscene.

And labor is not exempt from the discussion, taking everything it can get, too, when given the chance. In certain instances, public employees are permitted to bury their perks so deep into the footnotes and fine print of their employment contracts that the public cannot ever possibly know what it is paying for. Meanwhile, the ordinary citizen is left holding the bag, cleaning up the mess and underwriting the bill.

Business organizations—both management and labor unions, and US government leaders—understand that in a competitive global economy America must strive for ever increasing efficiencies. These efficiencies are required to increase productivity, to consolidate services, to squeeze more out of the dollar. By the same token, the ordinary citizen also understands that from a historical perspective, given the choice, private enterprise can and does typically execute programs more efficiently than government bureaucracies. However, history has also taught that at times, private enterprise can be blind or callous to the needs of the ordinary citizen. In those situations, government intervention becomes necessary and vital to protect the welfare of its citizens.

When GE's outgoing CEO retired, the new CEO, Jeff Immelt, said that he knew GE had no *legal* obligation to clean up the Hudson River. But he said GE was going to do it anyway, in a show of good, neighborly, corporate social responsibility. And Mr. Immelt then backed up his words with action. For once, it seemed that the concerns of the local residents had finally triumphed over corporate interests in one of the signature battles of the modern environmental movement.

But the case of Mr. Immelt and GE serves unfortunately as a rare exception, and the clean-up of the Hudson remains in some measure of doubt. As an example of voluntary action, can GE's action be relied upon as a model or precedent to set the course of future corporate behavior?

By these examples, American commerce and business systems would appear to have a *moral* imperative to champion laws which better reflect society's needs and the realities of current times. For if antiquated systems should be permitted to continue unabated, supported only by US military power, then American democracy may be deviating from its core values. It may also be sowing the seeds of its own destruction.

***

We should consider one final phenomenon. By definition and in practice, American capitalism idolizes individual initiative as the holy grail. What seems to have been neglected, however, is the vision of the founding fathers—the idea of individualism within the larger context of commitment to a collective social identity—that we are all in this together. When individualism becomes extreme or indiscriminate, the net result is praise for the head capitalist as leading citizen. But the face of capitalism becomes nothing more than a hero among the hoarders of gold.

A narrow view of individualism features an "I built that without help" mentality, even though very few people build anything without a lot of help. This view is selfish, proud and greedy. When a successful person says "Nobody helped me," what they really seem to be saying is "Don't expect me to do anything for anyone else."

Consider the example of Mitt Romney, the 2012 Republican presidential nominee, who many see as the leading face of capitalism. Mr. Romney said it was the goal of his successful company to buy stakes in undervalued companies and then in his own words "harvest them at a significant profit" years later. As his "venture capitalists" maneuvered to "turn these companies around," significant numbers of jobs were eliminated and outsourced to foreign shores. The social costs were not absorbed by the principals but transferred to the balance sheet of the American taxpayer.

Then, the face makes further use of the US tax code which has been favorably tweaked by the *unnatural alliance* to shelter its spoils from taxation in perpetuity. How does it do this? Some of the undervalued company stakes is placed in Roth IRAs where the later harvest at substantial gain is tax free. Some is placed in Swiss bank accounts, some in places like the Cayman Islands, neither within the reach of American law or taxing authority. Through use of complicated generation skipping trusts, the face avoids gift and estate taxation altogether, as it passes the money down safely and freely through succeeding generations. [337]

During the 2012 presidential election cycle Mr. Romney released his 2011 tax return, which reflected $20 million in "unearned income on investments" with a taxable rate of about 14%. This is a lower effective rate than the ordinary citizen earning a pedestrian salary of $50,000 per year. When asked during the presidential debates whether this was fair, Mr. Romney responded affirmatively. But does the face in fact pay a fair share? Or is it just effectively writing off 47% of ordinary Americans as dependents? [338] Some believe the core of the private sector is comprised of an inner sanctum of 2 or 3 percent, an outer party of servicing corporate managers of 10 or 12 percent, and then the rest of us. [339]

Is there any doubt but that Theodore Roosevelt would have recognized a textbook case in successful dishonesty and undertaken certain and appropriate remedial course? But today the spirit of T.R. no longer commands Republicans. Since at least the time of Ronald Reagan, the face of capitalism has argued that lower taxes on high individual wage earners is "fair" as a driver of additional investment and job creation. Indeed, this was Mr. Romney's stated rationale. But employment statistics fail to support his position over time. [340] The one important factor which these so called pro-business policies do bear out decisively is a growing disparity in wealth between the rich and poor. Society's unrest naturally follows.

Where does this all leave us? Corporations and their operating officers must be properly incentivized to better evaluate risk, and its associated collateral costs, and to take into account longer term considerations. Corporations must further place a greater priority on corporate social responsibility, thereby more productively advancing the interests of American society, not just their own bottom line. The role of government, therefore, must be to promote and support the continuing evolution of

244

our capitalist system, reflecting an evolving culture which is more open, direct and transparent. [341]

But in order to be truly effective, change cannot come from the top down like a pronouncement from up on high. Rather, change must come from the bottom up. It must reflect the support of a dominant grassroots will and purpose. More and more, we are seeing that the great majority of ordinary citizens *want* to get involved with local projects in the communities in which they live.

Recycling of paper, cardboard, plastic and glass products is now mandatory in most communities, as is grass clippings, leaves and brush refuse. Discharged batteries, old paint cans, Styrofoam and electronic devices such as TVs, computer peripherals and toner cartridges are increasingly the subject of community recycling drives. Similarly, water conservation, reclamation and alternative source electricity generation and re-generation projects are also increasing.

We are starting to see other, larger signs of bottom-up systems reconfigurations. Some of these are subtle. But they are being driven by escalating transportation costs, brought about directly by the high cost of and increasing demand for oil as a global commodity.

For example, fresh, high quality foodstuffs produced by locally grown cooperatives are proving to be both cost-effective and more nutritious when compared to the mass-produced frozen and canned food alternative. Similar are the dynamics in heavy industry. A staple product like steel may be more efficiently manufactured here in the US by smaller, local facilities in closer proximity to consumption than in far away places like China. Both examples also stimulate local employment opportunities for both entrepreneurs and blue collar rank and file.

There is another extremely important dynamic at work here as well. As we have seen, the exportation of American labor to cheaper third world countries over time has lead directly to increasing unemployment, a cycle of dependency and the steady erosion of our manufacturing base. Consequently, America has also grown to rely on manufacturers in far away places for many of the basic goods and conveniences of our daily living. Some of these far away places are not viewed as politically stable, nor share our cultural values or respect for human dignity.

Consequently, some say that the exportation of American labor may also pose a significant, unacceptable threat to our national security. And so in the end, sometimes the call for "less government involvement" in the lives of ordinary citizens may also be understood to contemplate a mindset which is self-serving and a horizon which is but short-term.

Among our national priorities, many would include the return of jobs to American shores to re-build the middle class and our manufacturing base. This would necessarily include the reformation of our tax code to restructure and simplify rates and close loopholes so that all, including the wealthiest individuals and corporations, continually pay their fair share. They should also pay forward for the next generation.

Perhaps the ordinary citizen will choose to consider it as merely a reformulation of the old Jesse James rule. When asked why he robbed banks, James said that's where the money was. Where did the banks happen to get their money *from* anyway?

A cultural norm which becomes less of a secret, less of a mystery, permits all citizens to enjoy an improved lot in sharing in the right to equal access to America's considerable economic opportunity structure. And ordinary citizens working together also help to serve as a constant reminder that we are all in this together, in common bond. Once these reform initiatives gain the proper traction and are ultimately achieved on a grander scale, America in a way will have experienced a new level of individual freedom. No longer will ordinary citizens be trapped in a box, facing a dreadful decision on whether to compromise our principles to such an extent that the moral issue is seen to be secondary.

Chapter 12
Tolerance and Inclusion: Are They Merely Words?

I am just a poor boy, though my story's seldom told
I have squandered my resistance for a pocketful of mumbles, such are
promises
All lies and jest, still a man hears what he wants to hear
And disregards the rest.

When I left my home and my family I was no more than a boy
In the company of strangers....
In the quiet of the railway station, runnin' scared
Laying low, seeking out the poorer quarters, where the ragged people
go.
Lookin' for the places, only they would know
...
Now the years are rolling by me, they are rockin' even me
I am older than I once was, and younger than I'll be, that's not unusual
No it isn't strange, after changes upon changes, we are more or less
the same
After changes we are more or less the same ...

- from the song, *The Boxer*,
by Simon & Garfunkel (1968)
available on the *Bridge Over Troubled Water* collection

***

One of America's core values is acceptance of different cultures which then blend into one common cultural identity. *E pluribus unum*, or "one from many," is a uniquely American claim. This core value is based squarely on principles of tolerance and inclusion. Often, however, we see in action the other side of the coin. We *preach* tolerance and inclusion but can't seem to avoid the *practice* of intolerance and exclusion.

It would be worthwhile to take a stroll through history, identifying the more egregious examples of intolerance and exclusion through the victim's eyes. We will set the lens of the ordinary citizen on some thorny subjects—ranging from immigration policy, to religion and race, and finally to recent movements from the "New Right" to the "Tea Party."

Many times, there appears to be little realistic alternative but to cope, as the status quo struggles to keep pace with a changing society.

It is said that the cure for intolerance—is diversity—whether it be a diversity of peoples, opinions, or both. A sprinkle of enlightenment wouldn't do much harm, either. Former President Bill Clinton once made a statement of lasting impression. He said he was getting sick and tired of people who simplified America's problems into a finger pointing rant which went something like this: "It's the blacks. It's the Jews. It's the Puerto Ricans. It's the Catholics. It's the Japs. It's the Russians. It's the Muslims. It's the gays." Mr. Clinton then paused for maximum effect, before completing his thought: "When, actually, that's who we are—it's *us*!"

If we are nothing else, we are a nation of immigrants. And perhaps the greatest contribution of immigrants to the fabric of America lies in the rich, cultural diversity which each and every immigrant population delivers consistently, generation upon generation. How else can we explain "the bastard mulatto child of a heterogeneous American culture, combining black rhythm and blues with white country music?" Of course, by definition we are speaking here of the phenomenon of rock and roll music.

One of the most effective ways to increase diversity, including a healthy diversity of opinion, and thereby to consider even marginal views as a healthy byproduct, is simply to increase the size of the tent. The "All Welcome" sign is a familiar one. But talk is cheap. Can we put it into practice? Perhaps a good place to start is by making a conscious effort at *being* more inclusive, more tolerant, of the way things are.

***

How do we increase the size of the tent? Perhaps, a more practical approach involves merely changing the way the ordinary citizen looks at things. To illustrate this point, consider the following story.

A pair of strangers finds themselves together by chance as first time patients in the waiting room of the psychiatrist's office, where each awaits her private session. Invariably, the two strike up a casual but nervous conversation.

"What are you here for?" one innocently asks the other.

The question, innocent enough, seems to open a floodgate of emotion, and the woman begins to let go. "Oh, I've got a ton of issues. My mother is forever trying to control my life. It's bad enough that she can't even manage her own. My father got tired of trying to help her—he just goes down to the local Knights and drinks his sorrows away. The poor guy. Don't know why he just can't exist without that devil alcohol. On top of that, my husband's really stressed out at work. With the recession, his boss is working him like a dog, and he's accepting as much overtime as he can get. But sometimes I think he loves his job, or should I say the money it brings in, more than he loves me and the kids! Since he's never at home anymore, I have to do all the parenting, cooking, cleaning, caring for our pets, and all the other things that a mother does, while still holding down my *own* job. The kids are no help, either. When they get home from school, all they want to do is play video games or get on that stupid Facebook. And what is this business of text messaging anyway? It's like they're in some kind of trance. I saw from the bill that our daughter had over 2,500 texts last month, and our son wasn't far behind."

The woman paused, and then continued, "My sister's husband has a terrible gambling problem, whether it's the football games, lotto or online. My sister told me she gave him an ultimatum recently: It's either the gambling—or her. My other sister moved down to Texas and became one of those born-again-whatever-you-call-them. She gives all her and her husband's money to some evangelical minister, who I swear is a crook. Religion my butt! What a sucker! And she says the immigration problem down there is terrible. The Mexicans are overrunning everything. If that weren't enough, my other sister just pronounced that she is now openly gay–and summarily dropped her husband like a rock. What a great guy he is, too. I feel so sorry for our niece and nephew."

The woman then provided a short summary of her plight: "I'm going to need a lot of prescriptions for all these people who are screwing up my life."

Just then, the door to the doctor's office opened, and the psychiatrist called the woman in. Well, it was apparent that this woman, who was eager to become the psychiatrist's patient, had whipped herself into quite a frenzy. But she had also succeeded in inciting the anxiety of the other woman, who had been listening intently. And so, the second woman continued to sit there in the waiting room, fixated, trying in vain to read a magazine, watching the wall clock as the second hand ticked along.

She marveled at the spectrum of problems which the other woman was facing, wondering just how the doctor was going to navigate his way through and fix them all.

The woman's session was done soon enough, though, and the door opened once again. Expecting to see her exit with a pad full of prescriptions, the woman who had been waiting was quite surprised to see the other grasping onto but a single slip of paper. "Well, how did it go? Only one prescription?" the woman inquired in understated manner. "I thought you'd have several."

"So did I," the first woman countered. "But the doctor told me I couldn't worry about matters beyond my control. He said I only needed one prescription. The only person who needed to change was *me!*"

The moral of the story? If you want to be somebody else, if you're tired of battling with yourself, then change your mind.

A second story places a 7 or 8 year-old boy in the setting of 1960s Brooklyn. His family had been visiting cousins. The boy and his older brother were close with their cross-town counterparts, a pair in the same age group. It was a time of innocence. His aunt (his father's sister) could usually be found in the kitchen, where he learned that most of the action took place. She was a lot like his father—a lot of intimidating barking—but her bite was pretty much harmless. It was Sunday, family day. His family never ate at home alone on Sunday, alternating weeks at mom's or dad's respective homes.

Neither the boy's aunt nor uncle had attained education past the high school level, but they were salt of the earth people and always good to the kids. Aunt was typically carrying on about one thing or another, while uncle (and Godfather) would try to engage her, trying to get a word in edgewise, usually to no avail. That particular day had been no different. Yet, even a young boy could identify the pattern: Every "but" which uncle uttered was met by a matching slam of derisive scorn. And so, uncle—sometimes quickly, sometimes not—would invariably give up, becoming silent.

It wasn't until much later, when the boy became a man, that he would identify a fabric to the familiar pattern. The adults, uncle included, would partake of a customary cocktail or two before dinner. In those days uncle drank vodka martinis, and after a couple of those it became apparent that it didn't matter much what his wife had to say.

On this particular occasion, the boy's aunt happened to be carrying on about "the Puerto Ricans," whoever they were, and how they were "moving in" and over-running the neighborhood, block by block. "And so what?" he thought to himself. Aunt was speaking with some urgency, however, using words to the effect that "they" were already "up to" 57th Street (aunt's house was on 66th). And it was only a matter of time before they would get to her block, "take it over" and then "everything would be ruined." The neighborhood needed to be *saved*, she firmly and passionately believed. Her forceful and emphatic final words on the subject could not be forgotten: "What is America coming to? They need to be *stopped!*" Well, this was a whole lot for a little boy to contemplate.

Both the rear and side "yards" in that neighborhood were strictly concrete, separated typically by 3 or 4 foot chain link fence. Adjoining aunt's rear yard was the rear yard of the neighbor on the next street, which was probably 65th. The neighbor had the same yard configuration, concrete and chain link fence. Along the rear property lines, sometimes there were two separate fences, the fence of one running directly parallel to the fence of another, a matter of only inches apart. It looked silly and kind of tacky, even to an unsophisticated little kid.

The boy had already learned that everything in New York City was done in haste. There was never much time for contemplation or reasoned thought, so it seemed. You were aggressive. You struck first. You asked questions later. Passive conduct was not well tolerated. And this time would be no different. In the house behind aunt, he learned that there was a family which had recently moved in. There was a boy his age, named Manny. That was an odd, unfamiliar name. That's because Manny was Puerto Rican, the kind of Puerto Rican, no doubt, who aunt had been warning about.

After dinner had ended and the kids were free to go out and "play," about the only thing the boy contemplated, as he ran through the back door into the yard and picked up a rock, was its properties. Sharp and angled, and it would skip nicely off the concrete ground, increasing the chances of success. It wasn't exactly like skipping a stone on a pond, but in Brooklyn it would have to do. A rounded shape was better for a blunt force, direct hit. That was for when one was up close.

And so the rock fights began, and continued on those Sunday visits, like it was part of the kids' entertainment program to which they actually looked forward. The kids never told the adults about the rock fights.

But how could they have missed the action? The boy tried with all his talent and God-given strength (fortunately, he did not have much of either) to strike Manny with a rock right between the eyes. He assured himself that he was doing but his own small part to "save" the neighborhood. Although time after time the boy missed the target, he kept chucking away persistently. It seemed there were always plenty of rocks around.

Thankfully, no one ever got hurt, although to this day the boy can never forget the look of fear on Manny's face, as he hurled a rock in Manny's direction. Perhaps, Manny saw the look of fear on his face, too. Manny would skillfully dodge the dangerous projectile, pick up one of his own, his wiry frame slinging one back, in turn. Manny's resilience was impressive.

But it had never occurred much to the boy, the family discussion which *must* have been going on at the dinner table in Manny's house. Surely, "they" were like his family, each having left the respective old country (the boy's had left a bit earlier) for the opportunities which the new country afforded, and which hard work provided. On reflection, Manny's family had to be thinking many things, first and foremost, that there were a bunch of lunatics living behind them. They would not be intimidated, nor would they back down. They must naturally defend themselves, come what may.

The boy was sure Manny's family knew, or sensed, that America was a good and decent place, with lots of good and decent people, that maybe these crazy nuts who happened to live behind them were surely not representative of the masses. In time, if those nuts didn't lose their twin vices of prejudice and hatred, both would be buried in the soil with them, hopefully sooner rather than later. But in a strange twist, the problem was that these crazies were not Manny's family, but *his* family.

Today, of course, his thought process is completely different, transformed from what it was back then. But surely the type of behavior described above is typical of the human condition, at least for some, probably many, in the melting pot which defines the US mid-Atlantic region. The phrase "not in my backyard," NIMBY for short, pertains to a lesson which by now should be familiar: "Don't change *my* world in a manner that threatens *my* status quo, and thereby compromises *my* reasonable pursuit of happiness." The take away value, as we see, can be quite real and literal.

***

A promised land, yes, that's what America is. The hardy first immigrants from centuries past had come for a variety of reasons, not the least of which was to flee religious persecution and poor economic conditions in their prior homelands. It seems that the predominant Roman Catholic sect of Christianity was having a field day over in Europe persecuting with little mercy their recalcitrant Protestant brethren. This precipitated the latter's flood to the New World, seeking only religious tolerance. Over here, the ordinary citizen is reminded to this day that the US was founded on *Protestant* Christian principles.

The *Mayflower* had set sail from England destined for America in 1620, carrying 102 passengers, 20 to 30 crew members and 2 dogs. A group of Puritans, together with an equal number of a wing of the new Puritan movement, called Pilgrims (or Separatists), comprised the "passenger" list. Its destination was the mouth of the Hudson River, in what is now New York City, where the passengers had received generous land grants from the king. But the ship was blown off course and with the combination of poor weather landed in Plymouth, Massachusetts. [342]

The famous story highlights two interesting points. First, since the arrival of the passengers was at an unfamiliar location beyond their charter, it appears that they were not only some of the earliest but also the first *illegal* immigrants. Did they have to be sent back to do the whole trip over again in legal fashion? Of course not. Second, once free from religious persecution here, they would use that new freedom curiously. Turning the tables, they would interject their *own* brand of intolerance and exclusion on successive generations of immigrants, especially their former Roman Catholic oppressors. Sometimes memories can be extremely long. Revenge is not exactly a Christian principle, but it is uniquely human. So instead of tolerance and inclusion, there would be intolerance and exclusion.

Today, roughly 35 million people, more than 10% of the total US population, claim to be *Mayflower* descendants. [343] How did it get this way? In 1790 the US population totaled just under 4 million, under the first census that the new constitution provided for. Of that number, 3/5 of the white population were English, 1/5 were Scottish or Irish and 1/5 of the entire population were African American slaves. The census asked just 5 questions: the number of free white males over 16 years old, free white males under 16, free white females, other, and number of slaves. The new US government contained only 75 post offices nationwide. In hindsight, the population seemed quite small, but it was growing rapidly. By 1800 the number of states had grown to 16 and the total population by more than 35% to 5.3 million. [344]

In 1845 the US actually fought a war over immigration—with Mexico. The immediate cause of the Mexican-American War was the US annexation of the state of Texas into the Union. The underlying reason was related. At the time there was as an unstoppable flow of American pioneer citizens, surging west and south across the Mississippi River over and down into Spanish Texas. Before the divisive war had ended, the US army had marched right through the gates of Mexico City, where it received a friendly, welcome cheer from the local inhabitants.

But the 1848 treaty that ended the conflict saw a US withdrawal northward to the natural border of the Rio Grande River, setting the present southern and western border of Texas with Mexico. The stated rationale was that the US did not want to extend the offer of US citizenship to *all* Mexicans. In the aftermath of the war, the size of the US was increased by a full 1/3. The Mexican territory, together with Texas, would net all or part of 10 additional new states, including the crown jewel of California. At the same time, Mexican-Americans north of the border were reduced to second class US citizens in a world where intolerance and exclusion for them would continue to be the de facto law of the land.

The ordinary citizen is made to understand that Texas must be one attractive place to settle. In the mid-19th century it was overrun by US immigrants from the north and east. But at the turn of the 21st century Texas and the old Mexican territory which includes the US southwest are being overrun by Mexican immigrants from the south. Along the stretch of desert border to the Pacific, many US citizens are hesitant to attempt to accommodate the influx, as they had once been accommodated. There are some, in fact, who would go so far to say that America is justified to build a wall to seal them out. This vision is hardly portrayed as a large tent with a welcome mat.

In the history textbooks, the ordinary citizen will typically find the term "immigration" linked to the term "nativism" and not in a positive way. In truth, the terms are at opposite ends. The phrase "nativism backlash" refers to citizens who are ardent opponents of immigration. To these citizens, it's about those already here, and preserving their way of life, rather than continuing America's rich tradition of affording the same opportunities to new immigrants. Perhaps these citizens have forgotten where *they* came from and that *they* were once immigrants, too.

There's another strange big word floating around out there in this realm: xenophobia. Quite simply, xenophobia is a fear and hatred of strangers or foreigners or of anything that is strange or foreign. [345] When it comes to the laws of human nature and US immigration policy in particular, the terms nativism, nativism backlash and xenophobia are unfortunately all in the mix.

The Industrial Revolution portended the next great wave of immigration, this time from southern and eastern Europe, as contrasted with the earlier wave from Western Europe. Ethnic groups like the Polish, Italians, Greeks and, increasingly, Jews, were *different* than prior immigrants. They *looked* different, spoke different languages and had vastly different cultures than the new "native" Americans, who had earlier pushed aside the true native American culture. They were also unskilled. T.R. had marveled in his time at both the numbers and energy of the American immigrant factory worker, upon whom the base of the new industrial economy rested but without whom there would have been no industrialization.

But nativism backlash again reared its ugly head, intolerance and exclusion slamming the golden door shut. In 1882 Congress suspended Chinese immigration for a period of 10 years, drastically restricting the rights of the Chinese already in the US. [346] Many were employed in the construction of the newly completed trans-continental railroad. By the 1920s Congress limited immigration to 3% and then 2% of each nationality residing in America. [347] "Closing the door" became a contributing cause of the Great Depression. Politicians had failed to see that the overall lack of demand was partly the result of shutting off the lucrative immigrant *market* for such things as housing and durable goods. Unfortunately, as with many of the Great Depression's contributing factors, this was not identified and understood until later.

255

In the late 18th century the #1 occupation in the US had been farming. In the late 19th century manufacturing grew to become first. But by the late 20th century the service industry had become the primary US occupation.

At the same time, the Immigration Act of 1965 ended the immigration-limiting European quota system of the 1920s, opening the floodgates of immigration to other countries, many from the so-called "third world" which embodied people of color. Some say the new law was designed to bring in more whites to the country. In reality, it had the opposite, *unintended* effect. Today, 1 in 5 immigrants is Mexican, fulfilling a critical need to perform a whole host of new occupations in the proliferating service industries, while 1 in 4 immigrants is Asian. The law is consequently understood to be one of the high water marks of late 20th-century American liberalism, although not perhaps what the liberals had intended. [348]

According to the US Census Bureau, at the time of this writing the total US population stood at about 314,000,000 people and counting. For 2009, the last year of available statistics on the subject, the total fertility rate in the US was estimated to be 2.01 children per woman, which is statistically below the sub-replacement fertility threshold of 2.1. However, the US population growth rate is among the highest in the industrialized countries, since the US has higher levels of immigration.

On the other hand, European countries such as France and Germany have population rates which are relatively stagnant. Not surprisingly, both have below-replacement fertility rates in combination with highly restrictive immigration policies. As a result, they are struggling to retain their cultures, developed over the centuries, as a matter of survival in the face of changing demographics.

Latin Americans, or Latinos as they are sometimes called, are the fastest growing ethnic group in the US. Some look to be white, others black. And they are also all shades of color in between. Defying simple generalization, they are mainly identified as, first, Spanish-speaking and, second, Roman Catholic. Latinos make up about 13% of the US population. It is estimated to be fully 50% by the year 2050. Most recently, US immigration numbers have finally surpassed those from the Industrial Revolution era. This places today's era at the apex in terms of immigrants as a percentage of the total US population.

As a result, the US is becoming the first advanced industrial nation, in which *every* resident will be a member of a minority group. Although the number one ethnicity in the US remains white (German American) according to the most recent census [349], each demographic statistic today portends the changing face of America. Immigration, and *specifically* Latino immigration, is transforming American society for the better, since we are shifting from bi-racial (i.e.: black and white) to multi-racial. At the forefront, Latino immigration is driving the issue through the force of sheer numbers. Consequently, it is an excellent environment to facilitate the practice of tolerance and inclusion in our daily lives.

***

From immigration, the lens of the ordinary citizen shifts to the delicate subjects of race and religion. Ten years following the *Mayflower*, a prominent landholder named John Winthrop organized what would become a 20,000 strong great migration to New England by 1642. Before landing, Winthrop delivered a sermon entitled "A Model of Christian Charity," in which he had asserted: "We must consider that we shall be as a City upon a Hill; the eyes of all people are upon us." However, does today's America seem like a City upon a Hill, as the metaphor suggests? Or is it more like a gated community trying to divert its eyes from those in need? [350]

The historical context is sobering. Over a period of 350 years, some 10 million blacks would be transported to the Americas. This fact stands as a testament to the greatest forced migration of a people against their will in the history of Western Civilization. Consider that when Thomas Jefferson wrote the Declaration of Independence, nearly 50% of the inhabitants of his home state of Virginia, fully 500,000, were African American. Yet, the interpretation of his political writings in those days seemed to ignore that particular demographic reality.

A recent film depicts Washington's crossing of the Delaware on Christmas night of 1776 and the ensuing Battle of Trenton. The film and the valiant struggle it represented are emotionally moving, but the eerie feeling about this version of history is that there are no blacks in it. No black civilians, no black soldiers, no black slaves or body servants—just white people bravely and busily creating a new nation. [351] Similarly, the popular TV show, *Happy Days*, depicting life in the 1950s good old days, also has no black characters. The "other side of

257

the coin" is not be depicted, almost as if it doesn't exist. Perhaps, it is wishful thinking.

Indeed, Jefferson's own writing indicates that his earliest memory was of being carried on a pillow by one slave riding on horseback to the day he was lowered into the earth in a coffin made by another. Yet, he found it impossible in his domestic culture to effectively denounce, let alone attempt to eradicate, the institution of slavery, in a life cushioned by the subjugation of others. [352]

In 1807 the slave trade was legally abolished in the US, which only seemed to make slave "breeding" more desirable and profitable to their white overlords. In the mid-19th century, the question lingered on what to do with the African American slaves, if freed. Many in the South favored a mandate to simply send them back to Africa. The nation of Liberia in western Africa was founded, but only for those who wished to return to a part of their ancestral homeland. But the plan was scuttled, when it became understood that African Americans liked it here, too, and weren't going anywhere again, involuntarily.

Yet following the conclusion of Civil War hostilities, Frederick Douglass, perhaps the most famous black abolitionist, noted in 1882 that the newly freed slave "was free from the individual master but a slave to society. He had neither money, property nor friends." [353]

At the turn of the 20th century, with black codes stifling the economy of the South, a steady trickle of African Americans left the South in search of jobs in northern cities. But the public mood was still such that when T.R. extended the first invitation to a black man, Booker T. Washington, to a White House dinner, he was publicly lambasted for his troubles. [354] This was at a time when statistics showed that black lynchings in the South were still at a rate of approximately 100 per year. [355]

By 1918, near the end of World War I, a "Great Migration" had led half a million southern African American citizens north to the "Land of Hope." Following World War II, President Harry Truman desegregated the US military in 1948, accepting the challenge to advance what was described as the "Double V" campaign. As applied to African Americans, it was said to be a double victory over racism both in Europe's Nazi Germany and at home in the US. After all, it was their blood, too, which had spilled over the battlefields of Europe. They had *earned* the right to the same sort of progress at home. Symbolically, Truman was the first president to issue a formal invitation to the NAACP (National Association for the Advancement of Colored People) to receive a White House address. [356]

But when both World War II and Korean War GI veterans returned to civilian life, neighborhoods which had been ethnically diverse prior to the war (everyone had been poor) became problematical. These problems degenerated into violence, rioting and looting in places like Los Angeles, California and several other major northern cities in the mid-1960s. A federal commission was appointed by President Lyndon Johnson to determine the cause of the race riots and unrest.

One of the core findings of the commission was that the federal government had engaged in unfair and discriminatory loan practices. For example, in important matters of employment, education and housing especially, federal low interest loans under the GI Bill were made available for white applicants only, as an incentive to flee to the "safety" of the suburbs, where a better quality of life awaited. Black veterans were illegally denied equal treatment under the law. [357]

The conclusion of the federal commission was that the riots were the result of poverty, police brutality, poor schools, poor housing, attributed to "white racism" and its heritage of discrimination and exclusion. The equation was a simple one: no education, no job, no housing and no political power equaled no hope. [358] Following the riots of the 1960s, America's suburbs became more white and its cities more black. This phenomenon occurred as much in the North and on the West Coast (Newark, Detroit, Chicago, Philadelphia, Trenton, Camden, Cleveland, Oakland and Los Angeles) as in the South (Atlanta and Charlotte).

Today, the ripple effects of these federal discriminatory loan practices were still being felt. For example, many white families could still rely upon the equity from the federally subsidized homes purchased by their ancestors in the 1950s to help get them through the Great Recession of 2008. But for blacks there would be no similar nest eggs, as families of color continued to struggle in percentage numbers which are skewed when compared to national averages.

Of course, exclusionary policies and discrimination practices were not confined to African Americans. One of the first chronicled examples of nativism backlash led to the creation of a political party, the "Know

Nothings." A massive wave of German and Irish immigration after 1845 led to outbursts of anti-foreign, anti-Catholic sentiment. Capitalizing on deep-seated Protestant antagonism, nativists charged that Catholics were responsible for a sharp increase in poverty, crime and drunkenness. Further, Catholics were subservient to a foreign leader, the Pope. The party's name was drawn from the stock answer given to a question about the memberships' workings. They replied, "I know nothing."

Following the Civil War, California and Oregon refused to ratify the 15th amendment, [359] for the reason that, if the vote were given to blacks, it would have to be extended to Chinese as well. The new California Constitution had specifically denied the Chinese the right to vote or work for a corporation.

During Reconstruction, the Ku Klux Klan grew into a terrorist organization, in the name of "preserving white civilization." Although broken up by three enforcement acts of the Grant administration, the KKK was re-born in the 1920s, standing for "100% pure Americanism," limiting its membership to white, native born Protestants. But in the end, poor leadership coupled with the absence of a political program destroyed it.

During World War II, a national poll showed that a majority of Americans actually preferred a Nazi victory in Europe to racial equality at home. Why? Americans feared in part that the persecuted Jews would arrive here upon *our* shores.

In the years before and following the Civil War, black Christian churches were constructed exclusively in the South, since Southern white churches refused blacks from participation. Similarly, Roman Catholic universities began to sprout, because the elite northeastern Ivy League universities (which were predominantly Protestant) had excluded them as well. The demographic statistics of T.R.'s Harvard College 1880 graduating class are quite telling. Suffice to say it was not the picture of diversity or inclusion. Of the 171 graduates there were no blacks, foreign students, Boston Irish, Italians, Swedes or Latin Americans, no one with a name ending in *i* or *o*. There were exactly 3 Roman Catholics. [360]

Today, the Roman Catholic Church *says* it stands for the principle of inclusion. But in reality, it appears to have written the book on intolerance and exclusionary practices. Other than the Ten Commandments, which have stood as a constant down through the millennia, a majority of the man-made rules which came later are not very user-friendly. On the contrary, they seem arbitrary, self-serving and designed to perpetuate an earthly, material well-being of a select group of men first and foremost.

A primary example, still preached today, is that the Roman Catholics hold the *only*, exclusive key to the kingdom of heaven. This continues to perplex, in view of the great religious and political upheaval brought about by the *Protestant Reformation*, as if it had never taken place.

A second example stems from the dubious principle that only the people who *know* Jesus Christ can be considered for admission to heaven. Seemingly, this would summarily exclude the vast majority of the peoples of Eastern Civilization (for example, China and India, between them containing almost half the world's population). These examples begin to strain the credibility of Christian teaching.

A final example is the church's long-standing tradition of excluding women, which seemingly defies the laws of nature by any reasonable measure. The theory is that certain men "chosen" by God and who they call "priests" are compelled to lead a life of celibacy that demands a one-on-one relationship with God. It is a theory which makes for an *unnatural* existence.

But the reasoning, while superficially plausible, is generally false, when there are other stated explanations for celibacy. First, it is understood that the church uses the marriage prohibition to control its priests, since a parish belongs to the people and to the church, not just one family, whose business had become priesthood. This rationale has facilitated the gathering and keeping of certain property under the church's umbrella, thereby eliminating the problem of denigration of the sacramental life. One thing, however, is clear. The prohibition against marriage is human law, not divine law, meaning that it can change. [361]

But the end result has not been without serious tragic human consequences, which were clearly foreseeable. Amongst the religious clergy, the insidious crimes of child sexual abuse and pedophilia continue, seemingly unabated. In the increasingly familiar pattern, when a "problem" is discovered, the offending priest is quietly transferred to another parish. Thereafter, it is business as usual, on the guise that there are new *internal* reporting requirements, introduced to adequately address the problem. And the cycle is permitted to repeat itself. So much for transparent conduct.

Many ordinary citizens are of the mind that both the offending priest and the hierarchy which is aware of the conduct but does nothing to stop it (this is referred to in legal terms as an "accessory after the fact") are the perpetrators of criminal conduct. But the punishment to the offender appears to be not jail but, rather, promotion. [362]

***

Ben Franklin had a superb view of religion. He noted that there were certain essentials common to every religion. Among them were the existence of God;

> that he made the world and govern'd it by his Providence; that the most acceptable Service of God was the doing Good to Man; that our souls are Immortal; and that all Crime will be punished and Virtue rewarded either here or hereafter.

But Franklin observed that these essentials would invariably become more or less mixed by humans with "other articles," which were "without any tendency to inspire, promote or confirm morality." This would serve "principally to divide us and make us unfriendly to one another." But to the extent that religious worship predisposed ordinary citizens to do good things, then religion was itself an admirable thing. [363]

Which is the true religion? Is it any of the three main religions of Western Civilization: Judaism (star), Christianity (cross) or Islam (crescent)? After all, they all have very much in common, being from the same seed.

What do Muslims really want? According to some, Islam is the new menace, the way communism was the menace during the 20th century Cold War. While it is true that America loves its heroes, we love our villains, as well. Some say Islam is to be feared, because it is a movement to take over the world and impose an involuntary, harsh brand of religious martial law (Sharia law) upon all ordinary citizens. This, we are told, is what the terrorists want in the end. But it appears to be but an extreme, simplistic view, in much the same way as there is such a thing as an extreme Christian, or an extreme Jewish (Zionist) view.

Madeline Albright tells an interesting story, which was included in an 18th century German drama, *Nathan the Just*:

> The story is about a special ring that conveys to its owner both the respect of his peers on Earth and the favor of God. The ring was handed down from generation to generation, going always to the most virtuous son .... . The system worked well until in one generation there were three sons of equal virtue. The father solved the problem by arranging for an artisan to make two duplicate rings so perfect that no one could tell the difference

262

between them and the original. As his life ebbed away, the father gave each son a ring and cautioned all three to act as if theirs were the true ring, as indeed it might be. The sons soon fell to quarreling about whose ring was genuine, and the matter was submitted to a judge. With the judge's guidance, they agreed that the only solution was for each son to believe in his own ring and to remain worthy through moral action, while admitting the existence of other possibilities. [364]

A colleague and good friend relates a very deep and personal story. He had been a Christian, his father a man of the cloth. He once attended one of those "Bible schools," a pejorative term for an institution of higher learning, typically in the South, which "jams" religion (Christianity) "down the throats" of their students. He said that it was a harsh brand of Kool-Aid served. There was no healthy dialogue of the scriptures; no questions permitted, no individual interpretation, absolutely no deviation from the script of the officials who ran the school. The students' role was simply to listen, absorb and become indoctrinated.

He said the experience was so dominating, so psychologically harmful, the intent to control and brainwash his mind so intense, that he chose to leave Christianity. He then converted to Islam. He explained simply that Islam is a more peaceful place, no doubt an attraction to more than just a few. He is a kind, hard-working, loving man, not to be feared, even remotely. He is not the picture of a terrorist. What ordinary citizen does not love the great Muhammad Ali? Do we recall that Ali is but an earlier Christian-turned-Muslim, as well?

As a nation founded by Christians, the ordinary citizen is familiar with the term Judeo-Christian ethic. Some have said that all Muslims really want is just for their own their rich, cultural heritage to be acknowledged by the other two great Western religions. To Muslims, it may be mostly about wanting to be part of the larger conversation: a subtle shift, perhaps, from a Judeo-Christian ethic, to a slightly larger tent that is more tolerant and inclusive, encompassing a Judeo-Christian-Islamic ethic.

***

And finally, the lens of the ordinary citizen turns to some recent currents rippling through American society today, from the "New Right" to the phenomenon of the "Tea Party."

The presidential election of 2000 between Democrat, Al Gore, and the eventual election winner, George W. Bush, was bitterly contested, explosively charged and even litigated, its outcome decided by the US Supreme Court for the first time in US History. [365] Mr. Bush had carried more states (30 to 20 + D.C.) and the electoral college (271 to 266) but came up short in the popular vote. Mr. Gore tallied 48.4% to Mr. Bush's 47.9% of the votes cast. This came out to a margin of only about 540,000 votes out of a more than 101 million then-record ballots cast. It was not exactly a mandate.

Mr. Bush had campaigned on a pledge of "compassionate conservatism." This was well within the familiar Republican Party mantra of smaller government, lower taxes, individual initiative and increased military defense spending. But less than 8 months into his presidency his best laid plans were dashed by the events of "9/11," which changed all that. The US mainland had been attacked by a foreign invader for the first time in its history. The enemy uncertain, or at least not fully understood, an immediate ban on commercial air traffic followed, which lasted for several days. During this time, the skies over the US would be patrolled by NATO aircraft and military fighter jets for the first time in its history.

Once again, the time had come where a balance would have to be struck between civil liberties and national security. The Patriot Act was enacted the following month. But these events marked the emergence of a new and complex challenge to national security. This challenge was said to be *different*, because, unlike the godless communists, the new enemy claimed to be involved in holy work. [366]

As a consequence, the "New Right" took over, a group of wealthy, right wing Christian zealots who some say effectively hijacked the Republican Party. The main architect of the so called New Right, Neoconservative ("Neocon") movement, was presidential advisor, Karl Rove. [367] Henceforth, the Bush "43" administration was to receive its orders directly from God, pursuing initiatives which were purely "faith based." Conveniently, the Neocons had a direct and exclusive communication link with heaven.

On the other side of the political aisle, Madeline Albright had made an interesting and compelling case in her reflections on history. Leaders who proclaim they have God on their side typically lead their civilizations into times of great turmoil. In turn, Bill Clinton had stated that one of the dangers of the argument that God is on *our* side is that since God can never be wrong, the position can never take into consideration any alternative possibilities.

At the same time, the Neocons moved aggressively to crack down on and censure political dissenters under the guise of the Patriot Act. The right to political dissent is identified under Federalist No. 10 [368] as a necessary prerequisite under the US Constitution. Henry David Thoreau had written that civil disobedience was at times a *duty*. [369] The conduct of the Bush/"43" administration was thus seen by many as dangerously reminiscent of the desperate attempt of the High Federalists to hold onto political power in the late 1790s. Not coincidentally, this was the period immediately prior to Thomas Jefferson's Revolution of 1800, in an election where Jefferson received exactly 0 electoral votes from states both north and east of the Delaware River.

Some Neocons even went so far as to create and monitor a watch list of the most dangerous professors in America, who were being attacked for a "far left interpretation of US History" and "criticizing American foreign policy and the Bush administration." [370] This occasions great admiration for the founding fathers with regard to the 1st amendment freedom of expression. It seems that, initially, their intent had not been to keep religion out of government, but rather, to keep government out of religion.

The initial Bush/"43" administration plan was to degrade the forces of al Qaeda, the terrorist group, which was then suspected for planning and carrying out the "9/11" attacks (the responsibility for which was later admitted), and displace its harborer, the Taliban, from Afghanistan.

But the plan was expanded in a controversial twist. Suspected of having weapons of mass destruction (WMD), neighboring Iraq was also felt to be a safe haven for terrorists. Consequently, national security necessitated regime change against Iraq's once favored dictator, although no WMD were ever found. The US struck back with a mighty "shock and awe" military campaign in a prime example of conservative gunboat diplomacy. But unlike Desert Storm in 1991, a "coalition of the willing" organized under UN authority by then-President Bush/"41," the 2003 Iraq War was prosecuted absent UN authority. [371]

On being asked whether his father would approve of the 2003 US invasion of Iraq, Mr. Bush said, "You know, he is the wrong father to appeal to in terms of strength. There is a higher father I appeal to." Moreover, prior to announcing his candidacy for the White House, Mr. Bush had confided to evangelicals deep within his party's religious base, "I believe God wants me to be President." [372]

265

For this reason, perhaps, the Neocon movement appeared to harbor a deep suspicion of the empirical basis of science in general. As the argument goes, when the government is called upon to get involved, many rank and file Republicans see only a liberal political agenda. Accordingly, initiatives based on faith would replace "science based" initiatives. In so doing, the "answers seem to come from God" or "from corporate cronies who know the right answer before the research is done." [373]

The examples were numerous: from advocating Adam & Eve creationism in public schools (today they call it "intelligent design") over the scientific theory of evolution; to a rejection of the overwhelming scientific basis of global warming; to the further rejection of the benefits of stem cell research. The holy war message was consistent, basic and to the point, featuring a fear of Muslims and an exclusionary intolerance for all things Islamic. The events of "9/11" didn't help. Skillful deployment of the politics of fear whipped a conservative religious base into frenzy, effectively locking down the forces of government under its control.

Even more troubling was the fact that the voices of the scientists were also being suppressed. A research scientist on global warming was asked if he believed the Bush/"43" administration was censoring what he could say to the public. The scientist offered the following response: "Or they're censoring whether or not I can say it. I mean, I say what I believe if I'm allowed to say it." [374]

With a de-regulated, sinking economy, hemorrhaging debt and spiraling downward toward depression, the ordinary citizen turned away from the Neocons in the election of 2008. In a cartoon analogy, it was as if the voters swooped in to snatch them from a train racing toward the cliff's edge just before it careened over. In its place President Barack Obama's message of hope, a relief train, was embraced. Perhaps a bridge to the future did appear to look like a more promising alternative than the status quo.

***

But the Neocon influence appears to be far from dead. The two terms of President Bush/"43" were sufficient to permit two key conservative appointments to the US Supreme Court. This included the 2005 appointment of the new Chief Justice, John Roberts, whose confirmation was largely viewed as being bipartisan, highly unusual in this age of divided government. [375] Moreover, his relatively young age of 50 at the time of lifetime appointment signified that he is in line to lead the high court potentially for a couple of generations. The influence of the Neocon movement appears, then, to have "retired" into the judiciary as a stronghold. There, its remains are to be preserved at least in part and fed from the US Treasury to tamp down the business of progressive reform, as Jefferson had once lamented.

As a result, the US Supreme Court is now said to be 5-4 conservative leaning. Despite conservative denouncement of "judicial activism," a controversial 2010 decision of the high court deserves mention. The high court found that corporate funding of independent political broadcasts in candidate elections cannot be limited, since to limit that spending would violate the 1st amendment. The ruling was a jolt to those lawyers and lawmakers who have been battling to curtail the corrupting influence of money in the political system. Some say that the high court's decision has created an unwelcome new path for wealthy interests to exert influence on the democratic election process. [376]

Following its defeat in the election of 2008, the Republican Party engaged in the healthy process of re-examining its political priorities. Rescued from destruction and safely on the relief train, it had the opportunity—the luxury in fact—to relax and catch its breath. What it had just been through, and put the nation through, was indeed traumatic. Once the room stopped spinning, there would be time for a shave, shower and a hot meal. It could re-group. It would thereafter re-double effort on the elusive goal of smaller government. After all, this had been the stated goal at the inception of the Bush/"43" administration. In the meanwhile, previous efforts to ban abortion in the US would be abandoned.

Consequently, entering the 2010 Congressional midterm elections, the Republican Party was re-energized through its conservative base. The phenomenon of the Tea Party had been born. Beginning as a "headless" movement, not attached to either party, it quickly began to flex its new vocal cords, finding a home among conservative Republicans on the political stage. Its main platform seemed a familiar one in Republican Party circles going back at least several decades: to reduce the size of the federal government—and curtail its involvement in the daily lives of ordinary citizens—by shrinking its budget. The Tea Party cited effective examples of a federal government continuing to grow unchecked and out of control, among them the financial bail out of Wall Street and the newly enacted national health care law.

The message resonated. The 2010 midterm elections served as a backlash to President Obama, as they had similarly set back Presidents Reagan in 1982 and Clinton in 1994 before. Some say that this time it was as a direct result of the Tea Party. In one evening the Republican Party would re-capture the US House of Representatives in an election that just about put Republicans on equal footing with the president's party. Republicans would also re-claim a significant number of state governorships, important in positioning for the presidential election of 2012. Through its new ally, the Tea Party, the Republican Party had claimed another "mandate" to reduce the size of government. [377]

In the summer of 2011 the Tea Party utilized its influence to effective end in the political imbroglio surrounding raising the nation's federal debt ceiling. The timing, however, was interesting. History had reflected that Congress previously raised the federal debt ceiling some 37 times since 1980 (17 times under Mr. Reagan, 6 times under Mr. Bush/"41," 4 times under Mr. Clinton, 7 times under Mr. Bush/"43" and 3 times under Mr. Obama). [378]

It was a high stakes game of political brinkmanship, the Tea Party using the threat of US government default as a political weapon. Treasury officials warned that the failure to act to raise the national debt ceiling, which the Reagan administration had claimed was a matter of "routine housekeeping," would have calamitous consequences. Democrats even quoted Mr. Reagan's words that the failure to act would result in consequences which were "impossible to predict and awesome to contemplate." [379] Others, however, contradicted the conservative icon, expressing "no doubt that we will not lose the full faith and credit of the United States," that the failure to act would presumably be of little consequence. [380]

Tea Party advocates utilized what was described as a harsh, "cuts only" approach to negotiation, a necessary condition precedent before they would agree to raise the debt ceiling. In the process, and as President Obama pointed out, the Tea Party had flatly rejected a "balanced approach" which had been utilized previously by former Presidents Reagan, Bush/"41" and Clinton. This balanced approach featured a combination of spending cuts and tax increases, requiring the wealthiest

Americans and biggest corporations to pay their fair share by giving up tax breaks and special deductions. [381] In fact, many of the leading Congressional Republicans who voted in favor of the Tea Party's "cuts only" approach had also voted in *favor* of the previous spending binges of Mr. Obama's Republican predecessors. [382]

When a budget deal was finally hammered out, it was not without consequences. The nation's credit rating had been downgraded by one of the major national credit rating agencies for the first time in US History. [383] As a result, financial markets both in the US and around the world continued to wobble.

In the aftermath of the Congressional battle, both sides were left bruised and exhausted. But President Obama was conciliatory and inclusive. "The reason I am so hopeful about our future—the reason I have faith in these United States of America—is because of the American people," the president said. And although individual opinions can and do differ, the president identified what has always made America great, and distinguishes us from the others: "It's because of their perseverance, and their courage, and their willingness to shoulder the burdens we face—together, as one nation." [384]

***

Many ordinary citizens would sleep better at night were they to understand that the Tea Party movement was just about cutting federal spending and the size of government. Interestingly, the Tea Party's *stated* platform sounds quite similar to the Bush/"43" agenda for compassionate conservatism at its inception. Which, given how that particular political movement turned out, should give the ordinary citizen pause.

What does the Tea Party *really* want? Is it only about shrinking the size of government? Or is there *more* to it than that? Does the movement have an *unstated* agenda, which is but a poorly kept secret? Some current events may present the ordinary citizen with but a hint. One example, in particular, is informative. In the words of Lindsay Graham, the respected moderate US Senator, R-SC, known for crossing political lines to get things done:

> 'Everything I'm doing now in terms of talking about climate, talking about immigration, talking about Gitmo is completely opposite of where the Tea Party movement's at.' ... On four occasions, Graham met with Tea Party groups. The first, in his Senate office, was 'very, very contentious,' he recalled. During a later meeting, in Charleston, Graham said he

challenged them: 'What do you want to do? You take back your country—and do what with it? ... Everybody went from being kind of hostile to just dead silent.' [385]

Another example, subtle as it may appear, is the movement among some Congressional Republicans to eliminate funding for National Public Radio (NPR). Congress had passed the Public Broadcasting Act of 1967, which President Lyndon Johnson signed into law, creating NPR. Millions of listeners have come to rely upon NPR, which receives about $90 million in federal funding annually. But the Congressional Budget Office calculated that the net savings from defunding the network would be zero. Some say the proposed legislation is no more than an ideological attack on NPR, masquerading as a fiscal issue. For it is well known that Republicans have long been critical of NPR, accusing it of having a liberal bias.

In a final example, in working towards final passage of the new national health care law, President Obama had said that all options were on the table, except the status quo, which was no longer working. And as the president had said, Republicans simply offering to do "nothing" was indefensible. Since the system was in need of reform, it was the correct approach. Against the advice of many experts, including some of his closest advisers, the president pushed the issue to the center, braving great political risk.

His perseverance was rewarded. In March 2010 a triumphant President Obama signed into law his landmark national health care overhaul better known to the ordinary citizen as Obamacare, saying it enshrined "the core principle that everybody should have some basic security when it comes to their health care." [386] The passage of this signature legislation had escaped every American leader that has tackled the issue dating back to T.R. more than 100 years ago.

While the new law is subject to evolving regulations, its main benefits were not designed to kick in until 2014, *after* the 2012 presidential election. Among the important benefits include the elimination of an insurance company's previous right to deny coverage on the basis of pre-existing conditions, the ability of a child to remain on his or her parents' family insurance plan to age 26, and documented cost savings of $1.3 Trillion spread over a 20 year period, according to the nonpartisan Congressional Budget Office (as compared to an "alternative" model where "nothing" was done).

Republicans and Tea Party activists nonetheless wish to "repeal and replace" the law, believing, rightly or wrongly, that their success in the 2010 midterm elections was a mandate to do so. But when asked what their "replace" law should look like, they can cite no additional benefits which the new law does not already contain. They are completely lacking on specifics. [387]

There are yet other examples of what appears to be a hidden agenda: from union stripping bills through the elimination of the right to collective bargaining; to attempts to "block grant" Medicare; to restricting access to the voting booth to those with a valid driver's license or state picture ID card on the guise of a disingenuous claim of previous voter fraud (designed to make it harder for students, the sick and disabled, people of color, all of whom typically vote the Democratic ticket) [388]; to making it difficult, if not impossible, for a woman to get a legal abortion [389]; to implementing mandatory drug tests for citizens receiving public assistance [390]; to opposing same sex marriage laws; to declaring war on the EPA and the provisions of the Clean Water Act. [391]

These examples provide a preview of the *real* agenda. The results of the 2010 midterm elections may be analogous to a play in a football game. An offensive lineman moves before the ball is snapped. The official throws the yellow penalty flag, blows the whistle and a false start is enforced. The offense re-huddles. When the offense re-sets, the play formation does not change. It consists of a *moral* agenda, so indicative of the Neocon religious movement which has effectively infiltrated the Tea Party. [392] The two ideological cousins, the evangelicals and the Tea Party, seem to have fused into a new force which may be more appropriately described as the "Teavangelicals." [393]

A favorable result in the 2012 presidential election would have signaled a green light to run the play. Fortunately, the Teavangelicals were turned back. But machinations quickly turn to 2016, 2020 and beyond. Should the Teavangelicals ever be permitted to run their play, what the ordinary citizen may experience is an orchestrated movement designed to "repeal" virtually every aspect of F.D.R.'s New Deal social safety net. It is a huge undertaking, understood to be a reverse social engineering project of revolutionary magnitude. And "replace" with what?

The *real* "Teavangelical" agenda appears to begin and end with the same basic principle. It envisions an unregulated system of capitalism with a select few private individuals sitting atop. [394] This is coupled with a strong national military to facilitate the transportation of goods and services and to protect investments in furtherance thereof. Period. The social safety net is systematically eliminated. It's every man for himself in a land where every man is slave to a wealthy few. [395]

It is big government, only Tea Party style. Unfortunately, it is best suited to serve the rich man who lives on an *exclusive* island than the masses living in an *inclusive* democracy. It is a bridge to the past, genuflecting before the foot of that runner already across the finish line, while the masses remain tethered to the starting block. And coming as it does less than a handful of years following the disastrous, failed priorities of the Neocons, attempting to target and obstruct the Obama administration as the scapegoat, the agenda is audaciously brazen.

In what is seen as an increasingly narrow vision of the democratic ideal, the theory of American capitalism favors materialism and material accomplishment first and foremost. To protect material interests, it champions the legal protection of property rights, corporate and special interests over the interests of human welfare. It also tends to favor cementing private material gains in perpetuity. This gradually and unacceptably concentrates equality of opportunity which is supposed to be available to all citizens into the hands of fewer and fewer individual beneficiaries of special privilege.

Over the succeeding generations, the rules of the game have been tweaked to support a class of numerically small but extremely wealthy conservative citizens. If the rules can never be modified to correct inequities by the very same government that created those rules, the formula will continue to favor growing economic disparity and class division.

And so it is little wonder why the Teavangelicals want less government. When government attempts in good faith to call a foul and change the rules, government is portrayed as the evil. Finally, claiming the moral high ground, it is said that both the existing plan and its material beneficiaries have the blessing of God. Therefore, no effective impediment can be placed in their path. Their victory is complete.

But the Teavangelical agenda contains at least two critical flaws. First, any platform which favors property rights over human welfare by definition fails the basic litmus test of adherence to the disinterested ethical obligation to serve others before self. Teavangelicals are unable to effectively reconcile that a Christian God, in fact, stands for the opposite claim. And second, the main interest which binds Teavangelicals together is selfishness. So when they are attacked, they divide their energies into individual fits of independent, self-possessed despotism and are thereby degraded.

***

On occasion, a situation occurs which provides a glimpse of what American society might look like in a future world where ordinary citizens live in perpetual subjugation to their Teavangelical "brethren." Might a bit of room be allotted for tolerance and inclusion in the rich man's continuing obsession to acquire even greater material wealth? [396] Don't count on it.

A final story may best serve to illustrate the point. Angry over the proposed national health care bill prior to its passage, some demonstrators, mostly Tea Party activists outside the US Capitol shouted "nigger" at US Rep. John Lewis, D-GA, civil rights icon. Lewis was nearly beaten to death during an Alabama civil rights march in the 1960s. The protesters also shouted obscenities at other members of the Congressional Black Caucus, lawmakers said. "They were shouting, sort of harassing," Lewis said. "But, it's okay, I've faced this before. It reminded me of the '60s. It was a lot of downright hate and anger and people being downright mean."

But it didn't stop with racism. Protestors also used a slur as they confronted US Rep. Barney Frank, D-MA, an openly gay member of Congress (Frank also happens to be left handed and Jewish) [397] A writer for the Huffington Post said the crowd called Frank a "faggot." Frank told the Boston Globe that the incident happened as he was walking from the Longworth office building to the Rayburn office building, both a short distance from the US Capitol. Frank said the crowd consisted of a couple of hundred people and that they referred to him as "homo."

Frank told the Globe:

> I'm disappointed with the unwillingness to be civil. I was, I guess, surprised by the rancor. What it means is obviously the health care bill is proxy for a lot of other sentiments, some of which are perfectly reasonable, but some of which are not. [398]

The previous discussion provides a useful springboard from which to launch into our final topic on Paris 1919, or tomorrow.

Chapter 13
Paris 1919, or Tomorrow

The way I see it, he said
You just can't win it
Everybody's in it for their own gain
You can't please 'em all
There's always somebody calling you down
I do my best
And I do good business
There's a lot of people asking for my time
They're trying to get ahead
They're trying to be a good friend of mine

I was a free man in Paris
I felt unfettered and alive
There was nobody calling me up for favors
And no one's future to decide
...
If I had my way
I'd just walk through those doors
And wander
Down the Champs-Elysees
Going cafe to cabaret
Thinking how I'll feel when I find
That very good friend of mine

- from the song, *Free Man In Paris*,
by Joni Mitchell (1974)
available on the *Court and Spark* collection

***

One beautiful spring Florida morning, a gentleman's pursuit of happiness was interrupted by a loud noise that sounded like an explosion. If a gas line somewhere had ruptured, there would be consequences for anyone in proximity. His visiting mother-in-law rushed outside. "Did you hear that noise?" she posited. "I wonder if that was the space shuttle re-entering the atmosphere."

It was true that by chance the shuttle was scheduled to land around mid-day, Discovery's last voyage, a nostalgic moment for the space shuttle program of nearly 30 years. Only two more shuttle missions were planned, until the program would be scrapped, to pave the way for the next generation of future space exploration.

The sky was blue, the weather conditions clear, puffy high clouds dotting the horizon. The gentleman looked up into the sky in the general direction he thought the shuttle was heading. It was about as un-scientific as one could get. All of a sudden, he spotted a shiny, silver white object streaking from behind a cloud. It looked like no bird or plane he had ever seen before, faint yet clearly visible to the naked eye. A neighbor, who had come outside to see, assured him from past experience that it was, in fact, the shuttle. The bird snuck back in behind a cloud, peeked out again for a brief moment. Then, it was gone.

What does it mean when a maverick father scribbles in his adolescent son's grammar school graduation book the words "Aim higher!"? Was father talking about a gun? Was he referring to son's career? Aspirations? His dreams? Was he referring to the quality of son's friendships? Business relationships? His life? Could father have been warning son at such a tender age to refuse to let "The Man" do his thinking for him, regardless of the politics, the same idea Clarence Thomas had rejected?

Perhaps it is all of the above. The most cherished people act in the other person's best interest, not their own. It may not be what an ordinary school teacher does, but it is what the very best teachers do. The trick is to surround oneself with those kinds of people, and then stick to them like glue. But if it is hard enough to find one of these Good Samaritan types, it is all but impossible to find any glue around when you need some. Like the space shuttle, once they're gone, they're gone.

Are we ordinary humans capable not only of aiming higher but also achieving real, meaningful progress? Then-US Senator, Barack Obama, has expressed similar sentiments:

> I wonder, sometimes, whether men and women in fact are capable of learning from history—whether we progress from one stage to the next in an upward course or whether we just ride the cycles of boom and bust, war and peace, ascent and decline. ... From the promenade above Jerusalem, I looked down at the Old City, the Dome of the Rock, the Western Wall, and the Church of the Holy Sepulcher, considered the two thousand years of war and rumors of war that this small plot of land had come to represent, and pondered the possible futility of believing that this conflict might

somehow end in our time, or that America, for all its power, might have any lasting say over the course of the world. [399]

Oliver Wendell Holmes, Chief Justice of the US Supreme Court, where he served for nearly 30 years (1902-1932), has offered similar sentiments from a more ordinary perch. Best known for his concise, forceful opinions, which were full of vigor, substance and meaning, Mr. Justice Holmes remains one of the most celebrated and widely quoted justices in history. On the eve of his 59th birthday, before he had been appointed to the high court, he spoke at a dinner given to him by the lawyer's bar, summing up his years on the Supreme Judicial Court of Massachusetts:

> I ask myself, what is there to show for this half lifetime that has passed? I look into my book in which I keep a docket of the decisions of the full court which falls to me to write, and find about a thousand cases, a thousand cases, many of them upon trifling or transitory matters, to represent nearly half a lifetime....
>
> Alas, gentlemen, that is life.... We cannot live our dreams. We are lucky enough if we can give a sample of our best, and if in our hearts we can feel that it has been nobly done.
>
> 'This must be the epilogue to any honest pilgrim's progress.' [400]

Before reflecting upon the possibilities of tomorrow, we would be well served to consider a diversion. Watching the simple behavior of puppies at play can be an interesting form of entertainment. Acknowledging the *object* of their behavior in a larger context can be enlightening. Are we able to learn anything from these creatures, who have never read a book? Give them a bone to play with, and they'll squabble over it. But it is usually more playful than serious. In a short while, the two former combatants can be found sound asleep, snuggling close with one another. They seem secure in the knowledge that their treasure will keep, that warmth and closeness mean so much more to them.

By contrast, when two humans decide they want the same thing, whatever the object, they will both cling, rigidly determined that each is right, and has a greater entitlement. But has either of the puppies asleep at our feet lost the treasure he tried so hard to keep? No, it lays but a few feet away, not a treasure, but an object of play. What is their contentment? Perhaps, it is the friend who plays this game with them, yet is still willing to snuggle, over and over again. And why cannot humans be the same way? Why can we not learn the great lesson here: that things are not precious, it is the friendships that are dear. For what good will this thing do, this precious bone, if in the end we find ourselves left completely alone? [401]

277

Human beings have intellectual capacity, the ability to reason; communicate verbally, some on a high level. Scientists say this distinguishes and elevates humans from domesticated animals, like dogs and cats. That being the case, what is it about *possession* of a bone that makes human beings different, but not necessarily better, than man's best friend?

***

At the outset of college US History classes, students do not typically appreciate that the subject involves a basic working knowledge of European and World History, too. That is to say, does the ordinary citizen ever wonder how this "status quo" we keep talking about came to be the "status quo?" When we know where we've been, it's easier, and more interesting, to contemplate where we may be going.

For example, World Wars I and II involved civil war conflict originating in Europe. In each case, the US had been dragged in reluctantly, against its will, Great Britain and Germany the predominant players. Although the cause of World War I remains a topic of some controversy, a few salient facts would make the events which transpired seem clearer, although the following explanation is admittedly simplistic.

At one time, the Roman Empire stretched north and west to the Straight of Gibraltar through what is now The United Kingdom (England, Scotland, Wales and Northern Ireland). After a time, their physical resources stretched, the Romans withdrew to concentrate their defenses on the European mainland. A hardy, free spirited people from the mainland, the Saxons, together with tribes of Angles and Jutes, then either invaded or migrated, filling the power vacuum. The Saxons were a confederation of Old Germanic tribes, the modern-day descendants of which are considered to be ethnic Germans, Dutch or English. It is understood that Saxon raiders had been harassing the southeastern shores of Britain for centuries prior. This paved the way for the Germanic settlement and takeover of southern Great Britain by these tribes.

Consequently, the term Anglo-Saxons is used typically to describe the invading Germanic tribes in the south and east of Great Britain from the early 5th century AD, and their creation of the English nation, to the Norman conquest of 1066. The name "England" originates from the tribe of Angles, their whole nation coming to Britain, leaving their former land empty. From this patchwork, one thing appears rather certain: Anglo-Saxons have *both* German and British Isle bloodlines, with a sprinkling of Dutch.

But as between the ethnic Germans remaining on the mainland versus those who had left for the isles, the seeds of rivalry had apparently remained. Human nature dictating that memory for such actions is rather long, these maneuverings would remain the subject of an unsettled score. In fact, the rumor of a second invasion of Britain by Germany was alive and well in the two decades immediately prior to World War I. A provocative 1903 novel had sounded a warning of the dangers of invasion across the North Sea. It was dismissed at the time, with its author, as pure bunk. [402]

Subsequent to the Saxon conquest, Sir Francis Drake defeated the Spanish Armada in an epic 1588 naval battle to secure Britain's place of dominance in Western Civilization. As a result, and tracing the rise and decline of past maritime powers, a simple theory was developed. National greatness and commercial supremacy were directly related to supremacy at sea. [403] The nation possessing the strongest navy would control the world's shipping lanes, creating conditions for favorable economic trade and thereby securing colonial riches. The balance of power would remain that way until the period following World War II in or about 1945 to 1948, when Great Britain ceded the torch of leadership to the US.

In the years prior to World War I, Great Britain, France and the US each maintained "mercantile" colonial possessions, which existed more or less exclusively for the benefit of the mother countries. By expanding the markets for their industrial bases, this enabled the continued growth of their economies. Germany, on the other hand, had no significant colonial possessions, although possessing its own formidable industrial juggernaut along the banks of the Rhine River, every bit the match of its western counterparts. But in the absence of colonies, the German economy could not grow and was destined to stagnate.

With Great Britain at the top of the pyramid, and uninterested in sharing its colonial empire, Germany understood that the only way to achieve the growth it needed was to build its military strength. A challenge to British naval supremacy became inevitable. The British goal was to maintain supremacy on the high seas. Conversely, Germany's goal was to break British world domination, so as to lay free the necessary colonial possessions for the central European states, which needed to expand. [404] This is how one ends up with a civil war, European style, shooting match. This was also the stuff of World War I, two dogs fighting over a bone, the dogs, however, connected this time by blood.

The stakes could not be understated. The various British colonial possessions had familiar names like India, Australia, New Zealand, Egypt and Canada. In combination with the territories of the British Isles, at its height in 1922 following World War I, the British Empire, including its colonial territories, would encompass almost a quarter of the world's land surface, the largest physical empire in history. It was said that the sun never sets on the British Empire.

As World War I dragged on toward stalemate, all sides in effect would become physically exhausted. A psychological *break* would lead the participants to conclude that what remained of the pre-war order and its values had finally fractured and fallen apart. Machine guns, one of the new, efficient weapons made possible by the industrial age, could not erase memory. But they made memory irrelevant. [405]

Germany had calculated with painstaking scrutiny that by way of naval blockade it could starve Great Britain into submission, before the US entry into the war and naval power could have a material impact. But the Germans badly miscalculated the Americans' ability to quickly mobilize and enter the playing field. The rapid American entry, enabled by its own powerful industrial base and a ready-to-fight navy, would tip the balance in favor of Allied Britain and France.

The US President, Woodrow Wilson, convinced the Axis Powers, led by Germany, to give up the fight, that there would be "peace without victory." Steam whistles blared, punctuated by church bells and car horns. Major US cities throbbed, as air-raid sirens, fire crackers, brass bands and even cow bells added to the cacophony. [406] The Great War was at an end. The Germans put down their weapons and went home, awaiting an invitation to participate at the peace table. But the invitation never came.

***

In the spring of 1919 the victors gathered at the Palace of Versailles just outside of Paris, France to set the peace terms, in what would become famous as the Treaty of Versailles. The five victorious Allied

Powers were lead by David Lloyd George (Great Britain), Clemenceau (France) and the American President, Woodrow Wilson (US). The 4th and 5th "other" victorious powers were Italy and Japan, in that order. In Wilson's case it was the first trans-ocean voyage of a sitting US President while in office. The goal was to set upon a new world order, to change the lines on the map, six months that changed the world. [407]

Every aspiring people able to make the trip came to this world stage, nationalistic fervor at a pitch, seeking democracy and self-determination. Advocating his League of Nations to protect free trade among and the world security of nations, President Wilson would garner the Nobel Piece Prize in 1920. [408]

Like Germany, the USSR was not invited to the peace table, either. Its signing of an armistice with Germany and quitting the war in 1917 during the communist Bolshevik Revolution had occasioned a serious breach of trust with the other victorious Allies. Moreover, its communist uprising was not taken very seriously at the time, largely dismissed as another case of "old-fashioned Russian imperialism in new clothing." [409]

Despite President Wilson's strong support of the League of Nations, built around the interdependence of democracy, free trade and liberty, the US Congress failed to ratify the Treaty of Versailles. Absent its foremost world military power, the League was ultimately doomed to failure. The US Congress rejected the Treaty of Versailles, because it did not wish to place US soldiers on foreign soil and under foreign command to protect the territorial integrity of "other" nations. President Wilson issued a grim warning, ultimately proven to be accurate. The failure of the US to participate in the League of Nations would lead to another war within a generation.

With Germany metaphorically tied up in the basement of the Versailles palace, the USSR not invited and the US leaving for home, these developments left Great Britain and France alone at the peace table to divvy up the spoils. It was like leaving two mischievous kids alone in a candy store with no one at the cash register. But with actions there would come to be consequences.

The pertinent events of World War I brought an end to three major empires: Czarist Russia, Austro-Hungarian and Ottoman. The communist proletariat uprising that replaced Czarist Russia would endure from its Soviet birth until its fall in 1991. Austria and Hungary became fully separate countries. The Ottoman Empire constituted in large part what the world knew then as parts of North Africa, the Middle East, the Arabian Peninsula, Mesopotamia and Persia. The names were more reminiscent of Biblical than present times. Great Britain and France retained large swaths under their exclusive dominion and control.

New countries would be formed in the war's aftermath. Two countries came into being: Czechoslovakia and Yugoslavia. Poland, which had been "carved up" by Russia, Prussia and Austria between 1772 and 1795, was reunited as an independent country. In the Baltic region, Finland gained complete independence from Russia, while Estonia, Latvia and Lithuania became independent countries.

The Turkish War of Independence would defeat an attempted Greek military conquest and form the new Republic of Turkey. Its capital, Istanbul, was re-named from Constantinople of the old Roman Empire. [410] Turkey has been a huge success in maintaining its Islamic credentials within the framework of a secular democracy. Its government respects that citizens have a variety of religious practices, beliefs and traditions, and neither infringes upon the various individual beliefs nor imposes one set of religious beliefs upon any unwilling citizen. For these reasons, Turkey is geographically, strategically and symbolically important, stretching across two continents from southeastern Europe into western Asia.

Long planned by Great Britain and France from the early days of World War I, the balance of the former Ottoman Empire was "partitioned." Though not completed at Versailles, the partitioning facilitated the creation of the modern Arab world. The League of Nations granted the United Kingdom mandates over Mesopotamia and Palestine and Jordan. Out of the former, the nation of Iraq was conceived, while part of the Arabian Peninsula became what are today Saudi Arabia and Yemen. The League of Nations granted France a Mandate for Syria and Lebanon, two additional new nations, and another for the southern tip of Indochina, where France had existing colonial interests. [411] Subsequently, the US would come to know this area well as the tiny nation of Vietnam.

A few of the old Middle East names remained, like Egypt and Palestine, the latter at least for the time being. While Iran, formerly Persia, was never formally "colonized," its rich history nonetheless was marked by significant Russian and British counterbalancing influences. The question of which of those two countries could maintain world supremacy in an ongoing competition, including control of the Middle East, was described by one historian as "the Great Game." [412]

Great Britain had maintained three specific war goals. First, it sought to secure control of the most important strategic communication line in the Allied war zone, Egypt's Suez Canal, although it was the French who had built it. This would facilitate troop movement from India, Australia and New Zealand to the European front. The second goal was to secure the oil refinery (at this point only an imperial outpost) found at the Persian Gulf's head, in Mosul (today, southern Iraq). A final priority was to establish a foothold on the other side of the Sinai Desert at Gaza, then Jerusalem and northern Palestine. [413]

In the case of Jerusalem and the later formation of the State of Israel, it had begun in 1917 with the Balfour Declaration. By that document, the British government announced a formal statement of policy, favoring the establishment in Palestine of a national homeland for the Jewish people. Great Britain pledged its best efforts to facilitate the achievement of this object, with the following condition: "it being clearly understood that nothing shall be done which may prejudice the civil and religious rights of existing non-Jewish communities in Palestine."

Jerusalem was the British Empire's so called missing link. Geographically, it was the key strategic midpoint of its existing colonial possessions, located as it was between Egypt and Suez to the west on the road to India and Australia to the east. Even a cursory review of a map would betray this obvious detail, potentially critical in military terms. It was argued that Britain's future success depended upon Palestine becoming a buffer state inhabited by a friendlier people. [414]

But there was infinitely more to it than that, according to some. Control of Jerusalem involved a religious component which was felt to drive British foreign policy. Guided by scripture, many Puritans had believed that the Messiah's second coming would be hastened by restoring the Jews to their native land and converting them to Christianity. But the future return to the holy land remained a vision "until the ideology of 19th century Europe converted it into a contemporary political program." Although there was no single reason for Britain's evolving Palestine policy, that Britain was to be the chosen instrument for the return of the Jews to the holy land struck a responsive chord in British public opinion. [415]

At Versailles, Britain's mandate for Palestine paved the way for creation of the new Jewish state. However, by 1948, following the World War II German blitzkrieg, Great Britain was knocked down and exhausted. At midnight on the very day that the British Mandate for Palestine expired, Israel declared its independent sovereignty on former Palestinian land. The American President, Harry S. Truman, recognized the new Jewish state in 11 minutes, barely enough time for the two cables to cross the vast oceans which separate the two nations. [416] The torch of Western Civilization had been passed. The US remains Israel's staunchest ally in the Middle East region to the present day.

In the case of Iraq, recall that the British navy's conversion to oil during World War I had provided the critical military advantage over the German navy, which was still using coal. Consequently, absent its own domestic source of oil, Great Britain's "Mandate for Iraq" was, purely and simply, a plan to implement a foreign policy initiative whose goal was to secure a safe, abundant domestic oil supply. First and foremost, the oil would be used to power the royal navy in continued military domination of world shipping lanes.

The administration of the plan facilitated a secure supply of Arabian oil over land to Western Europe. Britain identified the lines of the Tigris and Euphrates Rivers as the most favorable supply routes from the cities of Mosul and Basra. Britain then struck upon a set of arbitrary lines around the physical arrangement, through which it could administer both efficiently and productively, and called it "Iraq."

Suffice to say the local inhabitants were not consulted. Consequently, it mattered not in the least to Britain that the new nation would have a Shiite Muslim population in the south and east, Sunni Muslims in the west, and the nomadic Kurds in the north. The latter group also had a significant population north of the arbitrary border, in southern Turkey. As between the Shiites and the Sunnis, the Sunnis were the decided minority, so Britain decided to arm and provide them with the local ruling authority under the mandate. Some called it "nation building 101." [417]

These three disparate groups had little in common otherwise, with claims of Holy War made as early as 1920, when Muslim leaders began to organize an insurgent effort. A fatwa (religious ruling) was then issued, which pointed out that it was against Islamic law for Muslims to countenance being ruled by non-Muslims. Muslim leaders thereafter called for a jihad (holy war) against the British.

And then there was Japan. [418] Lost in the shuffle of World War I was the fact that Japan's navy had loyally patrolled the shipping lanes of the Pacific Ocean for the Allies in unmolested fashion. This had permitted Great Britain and the US to team up on Germany in the Atlantic theatre. By way of metaphor, it might be helpful to think of the physical arrangement of the countries involved in the war as "books." Holding them in place as "bookends" were the remarkably similar island nations of Great Britain situated to Europe's west and Japan to Asia's east.

Both were comprised of hardy, industrious (some go so far as to say even aggressive), educated peoples, possessing formidable manufacturing bases and world class navies. Consequently, each had vast economic capabilities. Japan possessed still greater economic potential. Each boasted historically proven power in war and was seen as a truly unsinkable aircraft carrier. But the Achilles heel was that neither was blessed with an abundance of natural resources, especially oil.

Japan was the sole Allied Power whose people were not ethnically white. And so, the yellow people had made one simple request to acknowledge its part in the Allied victory: a clause on racial equality. President Wilson refused. A significant component of Wilson's power had come from a predominantly "white" political base in California. At the time, Californians were lawfully segregating the minority Japanese American population in separate schools and other public places. It was the same manner in which blacks were legally segregated in the South in the days of separate but equal. President Wilson could not agree to Japan's request, to the extent that it meant compromising his political base. [419]

So, instead, the Allies made a "concession" to Japan, turning over one of Germany's only pre-war colonial possessions, China's Shantung province, which Japan had liberated from Germany during the war. It was said to be a "dagger in the heart of China," a country not involved in the war.

The Axis Powers, led by Germany, were summoned only *after* the terms were decided upon and then simply to receive them. It was neither what Germany was promised by President Wilson nor expected. While President Wilson had called for lenient monetary reparations and self-determination, Britain and France wanted to punish Germany to ensure that it would never be able to provoke war again. In the end, the best the American president could do was compromise to scale back Britain and France's appetite. Germany was ordered to pay harsh monetary reparations, which it could never hope to re-pay, saw a significant portion of the motherland carved up and its further colonial possessions given away.

From these events, the ordinary citizen can plainly observe a couple of factors which were at work at Versailles. First, the framework did set up a new world order, which would be tested but remain secure, more or less, over the next almost 100 years to the present. Second, the mistakes conceived there sowed the seeds of discord for several military conflicts which were to follow.

Germany would rise up again, a new government convincing its people that the old had duped them into wrongly believing it had lost World War I. But if it had lost, then why were there no conquering troops parading through the streets of Berlin? Had Germany's defeat merely been orchestrated as a hoax to empower its successor government, the Weimer Republic? Would the coming World War II Battle of Britain signal the onset of a second Germanic invasion? And who would be the acknowledged superior master race: Arians? Anglo-Saxons? In any case, it was not going to be the Jews.

For its part, Japan did not care to be treated like a snubbed inferior at Versailles, the China concession notwithstanding. Nor did Japan care for expanded US colonial encroachment in its formerly exclusive domain, in places like China, the Philippines, Midway Island and Hawaii. In fact, Japan's own dreams of expansion clashed with the twin pillars of US Far Eastern policy: preserving the "Open Door" for trade and protecting China's territorial integrity.

Neither did Japan care to be at the heel of the US, when it came to the procurement of a secure oil supply. Why should Japan have to beg America for oil? Great Britain certainly did not have that problem. Only one generation later, World War II, the second European civil war, would unite Nazi Germany and Imperial Japan as formidable allies in a second game of world conquest.

Following World War II, with the US recognition of Israel, the victorious Allies were successful in physically removing the "Jewish problem" from Europe and relocating it back to its Middle East ancestral roots. No longer considered terrorists, insurgents or guerillas, the successful Jewish fighters in the Middle East would henceforth be known as "freedom fighters." The nation of Palestine would cease to exist, as the world had known it.

Meanwhile, China's own civil war progressed toward an outcome by late 1949. Grappling with internal dissension, should the Chinese choose Western capitalism? Soviet communism? Or should they choose their own, yet to be formulated economic model? One thing was becoming apparent, however. China's unease for the West had been growing, based upon the West's undue reliance on individualism, competition and the fallout from the European civil wars. [420] Ultimately, China would embark upon a new, previously untested brand of communism, the devil it didn't know over the devil it did.

The People's Republic of China, a new communist state conceived in the image of the Stalinist USSR, cast a second ill-boding shadow over the mainland of Asia. The defeated Chinese "Nationalist" forces, in turn, retreated and removed to Formosa, a small island which lies off China's southeast coast. Taiwan, its more familiar name, is considered a separate political entity, known formally as the Republic of China. It is claimed by communist China but defended by the US in a complex political status arrangement unresolved by the Chinese civil war.

In summary, world events as such and US History in particular have largely flowed from what did and did not take place, and what was allowed and not allowed to take place, as a result of actions at Versailles in 1919. The status quo had been set.

***

And so, where does that leave us today? The discussion must begin with China, the 800 pound gorilla in the room. Although sometimes overused, that expression is not an understatement in this instance. With a population of almost 1.4 billion people, China contains about 20% of the world's population. In the aftermath of a break with the Soviets in the 1960s, China is presently undergoing its own industrial revolution, recently surpassing Japan as the world's 2nd largest economy (the US economy is still first). Its experiment with "market reforms" behind the veil of state communism continues.

If China follows the path the US took during its own Industrial Revolution, a military build up will ensue. It may well be time for a formidable new world power to start acting the part. For one thing, China is understood to be expending significant resources into developing a ballistic missile system which specifically targets US aircraft carriers. Those carriers, strategically positioned around the world, help the US to maintain control of world shipping lanes. They remain key to US commercial supremacy, national greatness and security in the present world order. [421] This is a perilous sign.

Economically, it is also well understood that the US is a debtor nation, China owning the great majority. As the US continues to overspend, China continues to buy our debt obligations. But what if China were to stop buying? Although China has not historically been a nation bent on world conquest, it certainly appears that political conditions will come to reflect the reality of conditions on the ground.

Next, it's always enigmatic to touch upon the Middle East "puzzle." Israel has claimed Jerusalem as its capital and insists that a shared arrangement of any kind is not feasible. The Palestinian people are physically divided, some living in the somewhat lawless Gaza Strip, from which Israel withdrew in 2005. Others are living under an arrangement of forced occupation by the Jewish state along the West Bank of the Jordan River. [422] Now it is the Palestinian people who are said to be the terrorists. [423] Will they ever be known as freedom fighters?

A "road map" for peace was first unveiled in 2002. It consists of a plan to resolve the Israeli-Palestinian conflict, calling for an independent Palestinian state living side by side with Israel in peace. Proposed by the US, the European Union, Russia and the UN, it appears to be a vision with a starting point. [424]

What are America's "interests" in the Middle East? Is it about the US commitment to Israel? Is it about secure oil flow to help meet our economic dependency? Or is it both? Is it also about promoting democracy and human rights in the surrounding nations of this important yet volatile region? The recent popular uprisings in Egypt, with the ouster of its 30+ year dictator, portend the winds of change in what has been called the Arab Spring. So do similar popular uprisings in Libya. Ensuing political unrest has followed in Bahrain, Yemen, Saudi Arabia and Tunisia.

Some have said and the US has long feared that extremist Islam is the motivating force in the Middle East. They point with good reason to the theocracy in Iran, which followed its own Islamic Revolution in 1979. With Iran's religious rulers cracking down on popular dissent, perhaps

Iran is but an isolated case and should be judged accordingly. But it certainly does appear that a re-shuffling of the deck in the predominantly Islamic world may be about nothing more than the natural yearning of peoples, in this case especially their own women, to be free. [425] Importantly, the unfolding events have the potential significance to re-shape the world map in a manner not seen since Versailles in 1919.

For example, following the toppling of its former dictator in 2003, the idea of an "Iraqi revolution" seems absurd, given the arbitrary nature of Iraq. The indigenous population is no more "Iraqi" than we Americans are from Mars. Perhaps, we are on the brink of a peaceful transition to a new world order that includes a theoretical new USSI (United States of Shiite Islam), replacing the previously drawn lines within ethnic and religious tolerances. Indeed, that area would appear to take on the physical configuration of a large "Shiite crescent" in portions of what are present day Iran and Iraq. [426]

Does the US have the resources and will to dictate terms in far away places, or have those days come and are they long gone? Or should we simply act as an integral part of the world community, as the world expects us to act, and not as its master? And shouldn't these peoples have their own say, which would be a first in modern times, in a bid for self-determination? Don't *we* want the same things *they* want? Has the ordinary citizen ever been challenged to consider the Jewish question, and the calling of a people for a homeland, with freedom and security, from the perspective of the Islamic peoples?

In his own time, President Lincoln had spoken of summoning the better angels of our nature. Fifty years later, T.R. spoke of the "peace of righteousness," setting forth these reflections:

> There can be nobler cause for which to work than the peace of righteousness; and high honor is due those serene and lofty souls who with wisdom and courage, with high idealism tempered by sane facing of the actual facts of life, have striven to bring nearer the day when armed strife between nation and nation, between class and class, between man and man shall end throughout the world. Because all this is true, it is also true that there are no men more ignoble or more foolish, no men whose actions are fraught with greater possibility of mischief to their country and to mankind, than those who exalt unrighteous peace as better than righteous war. The men who have stood highest in our history, as in the history of all countries, are those who scorned injustice, who were incapable of oppressing the weak, or of permitting their country, with their consent, to oppress the weak, but who did not hesitate to draw the sword when to leave it undrawn meant inability to arrest triumphant wrong.

> All this is so obvious that it ought not to be necessary to repeat it. [427]

Shortly after he had been sworn in, President Obama made a speech in which he emphasized the following:

> We uphold our most cherished values not only because doing so is right, but because it strengthens our country and keeps us safe. Time and again, our values have been our best national security asset—in war and peace; in times of ease and in eras of upheaval. [428]

What is America's role in the global economy of the 21ˢᵗ century? We've highlighted and analyzed the obvious foreign policy hot spots. Is our commitment to individual expression within a larger collective social identity as US citizens confined simply to other US citizens? Or should our commitment to human welfare and dignity in the democratic ideal extend to all humans, regardless of national boundaries?

Perhaps a number of developing countries today do not dislike the US *because* we are a democracy—but rather because we only *masquerade* as a democracy. Perhaps the political rhetoric tells them that the moral prestige of the man behind the curtain may be lacking—that he has little regard for the inhabitants of his own house. Actions may speak louder than words.

***

How do we keep our American core values in a state of perpetual progress? Fortunately, the founding fathers left the ship with a precise yet sophisticated system of navigation. Over the succeeding generations, the problem of forming a more perfect union came to be simplified to one main consideration: whether and when to *steer* the ship (Hamilton)—or simply to *drift* (Jefferson).

The stated goal has never varied much, an equality of opportunity for all citizens, regardless of status, with special privileges to none. When that equality was at risk, it was time to steer. Once achieved, it was time to leave it alone and drift. The aim was "a better quality of human nature effected by a higher type of human association." Its foundation was "mutual confidence and fair dealing." [429]

But some say Hamilton was guilty of over-steering, to the extent that his capitalist system is dogged by the ill effects of preferred status, unscrupulous competition and selfish materialism. Others say Jefferson's fundamental principle gave rise to an indiscriminate individualism, fatal "to both the essential individual and the essential social interest." Over-drift was akin to abandoning ship.

Yet liberty and equality of opportunity, each a desirable principle, are often at odds. Insofar as equal rights are freely exercised, they are bound to result in inequalities, made to be perpetual. The "marriage," which the free exercise of equal rights is designed to consecrate between liberty and equality, "gives birth to unnatural children, whose nature it is to devour one or the other of its parents."

Consequently, the principle of equality of opportunity cannot be "confined to the merely negative task of keeping individual rights from becoming in any way privileged." It must go further. The nation's task in its collective capacity must progress to a selection among the "various prevailing ways of exercising individual rights" those which contribute to national and individual integrity." [430]

As a threshold matter, whether and when to steer the ship demands a national consensus. But when does an issue become national, requiring centralized action? To be sure, there were those in the 19th century who believed that human bondage was merely a local issue which failed to meet the threshold. Others in the 20th century believed similarly in the throes of economic depression. When is the line crossed wherein action in one's own best interest is in fact unreasonable?

Such is the suspicion of reasonable men to subject themselves to the corruptive and abusive effects of political power unacceptably concentrated. Better to stall and prostrate the legitimate legislative function with a jammed circuit board of competing economic special interests. Better yet to neuter the executive function, while decrying the judiciary to stick to legal interpretation and refrain from activist law making.

Perhaps human nature is such that there will be those who deem the ship to be in a safe port, sheltered from the storm, where steering is altogether unnecessary. Just as soon as there will be others who, with a sense of alarm, see the same ship as careening toward a direct confrontation with rocky shoals or the Titanic iceberg. Perhaps there can be no effective reconciliation between these contrasting visions. All the while, the pendulum swings back and forth. We steer, then drift. The process repeats itself. Each cycle brings us arguably closer to a more perfect union.

Individuals should enjoy as much opportunity and freedom from interference as is necessary to the efficient performance of their work. The making of fortunes has been of the utmost benefit to the whole economic engine, contributing greatly to economic efficiency and productivity. They have been overpaid, but it has been earned. Individuals must continue to be encouraged to earn distinction by abundant opportunity and with cordial appreciation. The rule is of the utmost social value and must be retained.

But individualism is threatened when forced into a common mold, as when the ultimate measure of value is the same, and is nothing but its results in cash. The pressing need is to discredit a democracy of indiscriminate individualism and promote one of selected individuals obliged constantly to justify their selection, as, for example, by adhering to a broader standard, which includes the disinterested, ethical obligation. In truth, individuality cannot be dissociated from the pursuit of a disinterested object. [431]

To the extent that the rule has tended to create a powerful yet limited class whose object is to hold and increase the power it has gained, should it be perpetuated? Should individuals be permitted to outlast their own utility? Or must individual distinction continue to be earned? Hostility is not dependent upon the existence of advantageous discriminations for a time, but upon their persistence for too long a time. Put another way, can economic power at least be detached in some measure from its individual creator?

Take the inheritor of a fortune, who has an opportunity thrust upon him, an economic privilege which he has not earned and for which he may be wholly incompetent. Individual ability is rarely inherited with the money. But by virtue of that power he is primed to exploit his fellow citizens, whose own opportunities are thereby diminished. His position bestows upon him a further opportunity to increase his fortune without making any individual contribution to social character of the nation.

The money which was a source of distinction to its maker becomes a source of individual demoralization to its inheritor. His life is organized for the purpose of spending a larger income than any private individual can really need. In time it can hardly fail to corrupt him. As a consequence, the social bond upon which the political bond depends is loosened. The result is class envy on one side, and class arrogance or contempt on the other, unity coming at a cost of a mixture of patronage and servility.

In the present context, the promise of economic freedom and prosperity has exhausted its supply of natural opportunities. Its redemption, attempted unsuccessfully by T.R. in 1912, fully 100 years ago, may prove to be beyond the patience, the power and the wisdom of the American people and their leaders. But if the promise is not kept, democracy, as it familiar to us, will no longer exist. [432]

What a wage earner needs, and what the interests of a democratic society require, is a constantly higher standard of living. If it is to earn the wage earner's loyalty, a democracy must recognize the legitimacy of his demand, and make the satisfaction of it the essence of its public policy.

Many say we have passed the point of critical mass where the drift of indiscriminate individualism requires the increasing control of property in the public interest. A more scrupulous attention to federal responsibility naturally follows the concentration of corporate and individual wealth, dedicated only to the further proposition of perpetuating its gains.

Unless American independence emancipates itself from its traditional illusions, its spirit vanishes. Perhaps the American people understood this if only instinctively by the 2008 election, choosing to seat a leader who has begun a new chapter in the process of steering once again.

But it doesn't necessarily have to be either all steer or all drift. The two principles can and should peaceably co-exist, working together if not always in perfect harmony. Each, however, must make a legitimate concession to the other. Both the individual and national interest must sacrifice their extreme elements for the joint benefit of individual distinction and social improvement. The two principles must become subordinate to the higher principle of human welfare.

However, it can be expected that the privileged classes will be hospitable only to those reforms which spare their privileges. But their privileges cannot be spared, to the extent that rational ideas may achieve any decisive influence in their political life. The consequences would be the cultivation of contempt for intelligence, the excessive worship of tradition and complacent social subserviency. [433]

It would be intriguing to view the vexing problem of inequality of opportunity through the lens of human welfare ahead of any other legitimate interest. The goal would secure the benefits of the existing organization, while casting the net of opportunity over a larger social area.

Conservative principles, traditions and national history require only the gradual alteration of adverse social conditions in the name of progress. Perhaps a people can best exhibit its common sense so clearly as to be contemporary without breaking the ties of historical anchorage. To move too suddenly by uprooting any essential element of the national tradition would come at a severe penalty, as ordinary citizens discovered when they decided to cut slavery out of their national composition.

It is assumed the people wish to escape the need to regain their health by means of another surgical operation. They must then consider carefully how much of a reorganization of traditional institutions, policies and ideas are necessary to achieve a new, more stable national balance. They must also consider that any disloyalty to democracy by way of national policy will in the end be fatal to national unity. [434] The following section will undertake such an exercise.

***

Does a black man who argues that the test of equality of opportunity must be based on *need*, and *not solely* on race, ethnicity or gender, make him insensitive to black civil rights? The response of Clarence Thomas is telling, struck as he was by how easy it had been for sanctimonious whites to accuse him of not caring about civil rights. He said that accusing a black man of not caring about civil rights "was as ludicrous as a well-fed man lecturing a starving person about his insensitivity to world hunger." [435]

It is understandable why many blacks are uncomfortable with Clarence Thomas' outside the box views. "He is not one of us," they say. But the record of black oppression over the many centuries is without historical equal. Maybe it's not that Clarence Thomas is wrong. After all, he's a smart man who stood up for what he believed in. Perhaps, his thoughts in this regard are just many years ahead of his time.

Education.

If the democratic ideal is the moral and societal progress of human association to a higher purpose, then the sure way to get there is through education. But American intelligence as expressed through freedom of thought has still to issue its own Declaration of Independence. [436]

Once justified to protect freedom of expression inside the classroom, the concept of tenure for school teachers has been grossly perverted from its original benign intent. What was conceived as a means to preserve freedom of expression inside the classroom has evolved into an obstruction thrown in the path of government to protect the most incompetent from lawful discharge. While freedom of expression must continue to receive the strongest of protections, the state must retain the right to discharge incompetent teachers. A merit system based on prudent, common sense guidelines would balance the benefits of standardized test taking's objective measurement against the value of true learning.

Recognizing good intentions, adherence to the disinterested ethical obligation, can only be achieved through the disciplinary training of the individual. This implies a popular realization that our experiment in democratic political and economic organization was founded partly on unique temporary conditions and partially flawed and outdated theories. The great value of a revised experiment in collective purpose would derive from intellectual enlightenment and moral emancipation. It would require the sacrifice of cherished interests and traditions in the name of submission to more fundamental responsibility and a much larger infusion of disinterested motives into the American system.

The bondage from which ordinary citizens need emancipation is from the easy-going and habitual conformity of their own intellectual and moral traditions. By reducing temptations and increasing opportunities, both economic and as derived from the disinterested improvement of human welfare, a revised experiment would contribute to individual freedom. [437]

Toward the end of his life, Jefferson received a request from a distant schoolmaster for a piece of his handwriting. He responded:

> Now what man is free? The wise man who rules himself, afraid neither of poverty, death or prison; who has enough strength to check his passions and scorn honors; who is self sufficient, who offers to external accident no hold and whom chance cannot catch unaware. [438]

Legislative and Judicial Reform: Local vs. National.

Much of the utility of popular democratic government has devolved to the national level as the repository of important questions. This is due to no particular virtue of the federal system. Rather, it is a peculiar vice to ask state or local government to regulate matters beyond their effective jurisdiction. [439] However, a unique benefit of local government is that mistakes typically do not imperil national security. This enables local governments to act as crucibles of experimental democracy. With local grassroots support, the most successful of these experiments can serve as a model for federal reform.

But the layering of local government at municipal, county, school and state levels tends toward resulting redundancies. And it also tends to be a most effective way to dole out patronage. To check this, overlapping services such as police, first aid and public works must be consolidated to the appropriate government level. Defined benefit pension and health insurance perks for elected officials and public service employees must be eliminated. In their place should be substituted defined contribution plans as exist competitively in the private sector.

Lawmakers on the national level, in particular, seem to be crying out for help with the difficult task of legislating transparently in the public interest. Certain conclusions may be drawn about the umpiring when the 400 richest Americans are able to settle in with more wealth than the bottom 150 million combined. And the conclusions are not all positive.

It appears rather obvious that the corruptive forces of money are being used to prostrate honorable public servants from acting in the public interest. Special interests for private gain have effectively accomplished this through the transformation of legislative office from a position of public trust to an individual prize. [440] It is said that the main role of a legislator these days is solely to insulate corporations from complying with the laws. At the same time, while special interests remain subtle and inconspicuous, the ugliness of greed is exposed. Society's unrest naturally follows.

Meanwhile, a coefficient of legislative inertia and weakness is to some extent the expansion of executive and judicial power, which is compelled to fill the void. Left to their own devices, these complimentary branches in a system of checks and balances sometimes overreach into the legislative sphere, throwing the separation of powers into harmful imbalance. Allegations of imperial presidency as to one branch and judicial activism as to the other foster mutual mistrust, distracting from the primary mission to achieve meaningful equality of opportunity.

It takes a significant amount of time, and stealth, to amass the present level of wealth concentration. In turn, calm deliberation permits the lens of the ordinary citizen to focus as it should on what Congress, the legislative branch, has done to ameliorate the disparity. If the answer is "nothing," then it becomes compelling that something has to change. Consider it a moral issue which can no longer be secondary.

As applied to its lawmaking body, America simply has been unable to come to grips with the self-interest component of concentrated economic power on the human condition. Over time, corruption of the umpire has carved out a chasm which is morally indefensible. This confounds the quest to complete our great unfinished business—achieving equality of opportunity. A candid assessment of the American condition serves up the root cause.

But no matter how diligently we strive to create a more perfect union, collecting things and changing money remain the great motivation which obscures life's true purpose. Sideshows in the political process have a tendency to swallow substance, reducing important questions to a partisan, smallness debate on the proper size of government. At the same time, entrenched status quo interests spread dollars around systematically, muddying the water so that change becomes all but impossible. To check this, we must move beyond a traditional analysis affixed to economic cycles of boom and bust, war and peace. To progress meaningfully from one stage to the next in an upward course, we must aim higher.

Then how best to do this? One might say, "If the lawmakers don't perform, throw them out and replace them at the next election with those who will perform." If only apportioning equality of opportunity more equitably under the law were to be so easy. Those monopolizing opportunity would never agree to change the myriad of laws necessary to do so. And the monopolizers have sufficient power to ensure that these laws would never be changed. Therefore, it is folly to attempt changing these laws directly.

Rather, the way to end the indignities is to give the ordinary citizen the power to put them to an end. The power comes from the ballot box. But the ordinary citizen already has the right to vote. Then how? Make the ordinary citizen's vote constructively more powerful to elect lawmakers who are accountable to the public interest. The ordinary citizen will then be liberated to do the rest himself. Do this and equality of opportunity is bound to improve over time. [441]

How then can the ordinary citizen's vote be made constructively more powerful to reasonably check the self-interest component of the federal lawmaker? How can the ordinary citizen participate more effectively in the management of his government? Put another way, since concentrated economic power rules, how can we limit big money in politics? How can we re-direct emphasis away from the traditional measure of American success on a strictly material basis, moving the ancient principle of service to the center? Is it even possible to apply the service model on a secular, political level? [442]

The solution accepts the plain reality that the omnipresent "influence" which Jefferson identified cannot nor should it be eliminated. It can, however, and must be reasonably checked. This can be accomplished by insulating lawmakers from the pressures and corruptive influences of special interests in today's money-craving, material society. If the incentive for self-interest is effectively contained, chances are much improved that lawmakers will serve the people's business, for they will be left with little choice. The very idea of service can be made to mean service—and only service—once again.

The good news is that a sound, practical solution appears to be available. It is not complicated. Consider the following proposal, which contains three components.

The *first* component is tied to the front end of legislative service. Our democratic system was designed for voters to choose their legislators at the ballot box. But lawmakers have long chosen their voters in a self-serving *custom* by drawing arbitrary, movable lines around voting districts to make them "safe" from challenge by the other side. It's opposite the way it's supposed to work in a representative democracy and therefore must be abolished. [443]

By way of example, in the 2012 midterm elections, Democrats received over 1.4 million more votes for the US House of Representatives than Republicans. Yet Republicans won control of the House by a margin of 234 to 201 [444], using their distorted majority to frustrate the popular will on a range of important issues. This is not democracy, certainly not the way the founding fathers envisioned it. But both parties are culpable. Both share equal blame.

The system has evolved such that in the 2014 Congressional midterm elections, relatively few incumbents will actually face realistic challenges. The drawing of legislative districts so tightly in their favor to suit the pleasure of each party's ideological base serves two efficient but self-serving, undemocratic ends. First, the possibility of ouster is seen as being remote. Second, the incentive for compromise in crafting national legislation is greatly reduced. Put another way, primary candidates must pander to their party's extremist elements. To the frustration of the ordinary citizen, and the mainstream at the center line, the concept of partisan gridlock results.

Moreover, Republicans now seek to extend and advance this system of cherry picking constituents to the presidential electoral college. The scheme, initiated so that the loser of the popular vote could more easily win key states and the presidency, is an undesirable threat to representative democracy and must be strongly resisted. [445]

The *second* component addresses the lawmaker's seat, once in office and serving. That seat must be restored to a position of public trust from the anomaly of a fully evolved individual prize. A place of profit must be restored to a post of honour—meaning a post of *service*—as originally designed.

How can this best be accomplished? We can start by denying the lawmaker *any* privilege which is not the right of every citizen—in a broad range of issues from working conditions to compensation to health care to retirement. A lawmaker must be barred from voting on any proposed legislation which may affect his or her family members personally. Special interest perks must be eliminated by use of a bright line. This component will provide more than enough incentive, urgency and assurance that any disparity which needs fixing will be fixed. The US Congress must no longer be maintained, nor should any legislative body, as an exclusive, closed door establishment paradise for its members.

Additionally, how can we best accomplish the goal of redirecting lawmakers to conduct the people's business, instead of just stalling? The US Senate was designed to cool the passions of the majority House of Representatives, as by analogy boiling hot tea is cooled by transfer from pot to cup and saucer. [446] It was not designed to be a wall. But since the time of the founding fathers, the filibuster has added an "unconstitutional dimension" to hijack the very heart of the legislative process. Through the filibuster, a senator can talk indefinitely relative to a proposed measure to keep it from ever coming to a vote.

The filibuster has been described as a peculiar institution responsible in large part for Congress' failures, "purely and simply an undemocratic technique to permit rule by a minority." It has delayed, for decades in certain instances, passage of social legislation by the House and desired by a majority of Americans. [447] The technique serves to transform the Senate from a moderating force into an impregnable barrier, blocking the rising demand for social justice. [448] The result effectively transforms a designed cooling period into a protracted ice age. Consequently, its unrestricted use must be abolished. [449]

Another lingering structural problem involves a lawmaker's right to serve indefinitely, for unlimited term or duration, in many instances for life. This brings us to the final component.

Third, on the back end of legislative service, George Washington's precedent of *executive* term limit must be extended on a constitutional basis to the *legislative* branch. If lawmakers are made to understand that they are out after a time certain—returned to private life with strict, transparent limitations on future economic dealings at government expense—they will possess little incentive but to act conscientiously in the affairs of the people. Their perpetual concern about re-election

300

as a distracting self-interest proposition and corruptive force will have been effectively removed.

In both the House of Representatives and the Senate, a limitation of 12 years in elected office is suggested as a flexible starting point for discussion. Likewise, consideration should be given in the *judicial* branch for appointment to the US Supreme Court for a single term not to exceed a proposed duration of 20 years, forsaking lifetime appointment. Those who come to view their place in the federal government as a hereditary or privileged entitlement will be removed by the regular operation of law, so that fresh, new, ordinary blood can renew the people's fight.

T.R. did not believe

> that any man should ever attempt to make politics his whole career. It is a dreadful misfortune for a man to grow to feel that his whole livelihood and whole happiness depend upon his staying in office. Such a feeling prevents him from being of real service to the people while in office, and always puts him under the heaviest strain of pressure to barter his convictions for the sake of holding office. A man should have some other occupation ... to which he can resort if at any time he is thrown out of office, or if at any time he finds it necessary to choose a course which will probably result in his being thrown out, unless he is willing to stay in at cost to his conscience. [450]

Steering this proposal into law will serve to render a legislative seat more responsive to the will and strengthened vote of the ordinary citizen and not to concentrated economic power. Consequently, lawmakers will regain their rightful place as the *impartial* umpire in the affairs of the people's business set on a level playing field.

This proposal does, however, contain one catch. And it is a major catch. Unfortunately, lawmakers cannot reasonably be expected to legislate away in regular session privileges they have devised, perfected and come to expect and enjoy for themselves by tradition over the course of more than two centuries. This is to be anticipated in the context of human nature's important lesson—that reasonable people will act reasonably in their own best interest.

To implement change for the greater good, we must provide favorable conditions without the constraints of today's competing, partisan ideologies. It is apparent that these reforms simply cannot be accomplished, therefore, absent a national constitutional convention called specifically for this purpose. Delegates to the convention must be pledged solely to the great unfinished business of the nation, not to partisan, special or self-interest. Does the ordinary citizen possess the courage to meet this challenge?

Health care.

The 2010 national affordable health care legislation, an admirable and remarkable achievement that has confounded the attempts of a century's worth of leaders, must be given the chance to succeed. This is true, since many of the law's key provisions do not become effective until 2014 and later. Additionally, the plain fact of the matter is that a significant number of the millions who will be able to obtain health insurance coverage for the first time are ordinary citizens of color. What doesn't work should be scrapped and modified where necessary. Let's continue to experiment and improve until we get it right.

Immigration.

While some say that our borders are not secure enough, especially our southern border with Mexico, the fact is that our borders have been rather porous for decades. Perhaps the ongoing movement to secure our borders is a good place to start. But against the wishes of some, our borders simply cannot be sealed off by constructing walls with the cost expensed to the national credit card, as we've done in a business-as-usual manner for the past 30 years.

A recent Arizona law permits law enforcement to investigate immigration status incident to a "lawful stop, detention, or arrest." However, to the extent that the due process part can come later, it is inconsistent with American core values.

But securing our borders must be part of a comprehensive reform package, including holding businesses accountable if they deliberately hire and exploit undocumented workers illegally. It must also include demanding responsibility from the people living here illegally (estimated at around 11 million) to acknowledge that they broke the law and are ready to do what is required to comply. [451]

During the 2013 session proposed federal legislation along these lines passed the US Senate with bipartisan support. But the legislation was blocked in the House and effectively killed by a Republican majority which claimed its authority through gerrymandered districts. [452]

Taxation.

A sure way to reduce income disparity and broaden wealth distribution is through the constitutional power to tax. Do we wish to prohibit corporations from becoming too big to fail, or reduce their size if they are already too big? Then we should utilize a meaningful, graduated tax against excess profits. Do we wish to discourage the payment of obscene compensation packages to corporate executives? Then income paid over a certain amount should no longer be considered a legitimate corporate deduction. The savings can go to ensuring that all workers on the pay scale's lower end receive a living wage.

A graduated tax cannot be meaningful, however, where loopholes are used to destroy its basic intent. So a vital component would require that loopholes be closed. Revenue should flow to education and infrastructure investments to promote opportunity for millions to lift themselves into the middle class. The question of whether we have the political will may be overshadowed by our nation's certain demise for failure to act.

The present federal tax code, both individual and business, must be simplified. The relative popularity of a so-called "flat tax" system has ebbed and flowed through the various economic cycles, as has the idea of a consumption based national sales tax.

The main benefit of a flat tax system lies in its administrative simplicity. Not surprisingly, however, opposition comes from both ends of the spectrum. The wealthy and large corporations can afford to pay high priced professionals (CPAs, accountants, tax attorneys) to find loopholes so that in many instances they pay little or no taxes at all. On the other end, the poor and much of the lower middle class pay little or no income taxes. Neither situation is completely fair.

A flat tax, equitably based, requires all to pay a certain minimum percentage of income, without loophole or deduction. A graduated rate applies to higher income levels. There is no distinction between earned versus unearned income. Both are subject to the flat tax.

Others advocate a wealth tax. It's an intriguing idea. Wealth demands legal protection of material assets, in proportion to its concentration in individual and corporate hands. The affluent require this protection to greater degree than the middle class, so why shouldn't the wealthy pay more for the added protection they get? The theory is the more wealth possessed, the greater the need that it should be taxed, regardless of income considerations.

In fact, this model serves as the basis by which financial services firms are compensated for managing money in the private sector. Typically, firms require the individual or entity to pay an annual fee in a percentage range between .50% to 1.0% for "assets under management," regardless of trading activity. With annual returns approximating low double digits, clients have little cause for complaint.

As a mode of equitable and fairer taxation, why not apply the private sector model as a function of the costs of government for wealth protection? The federal government can effectively use this model to reflect "assets under the protection of US law." A minimum dollar exemption should be included to protect the base of the middle class.

Similarly, the inheritance laws must subject all property bequeathed or placed in trust for the benefit of heirs above a certain amount to a stated minimum percentage tax, without loophole or deduction.

Energy.

If it is true that our economic dependence on foreign oil is a greater threat to national security than any threat from terrorism, real or perceived, then we must change. The time is now. Perhaps of utmost importance to our well-being as ordinary citizens is the creation of a coordinated national energy policy. Eliminating our dependency on foreign oil will make the US safer and the world both safer and cleaner. Stewardship of the environment is not an issue of mere convenience. It is rather a moral issue.

Let's begin by accelerating our transition in leading the world to a clean energy economy, which has great potential to create new "green" industries and thousands of American jobs. Let's incentivize innovation which is committed to the process, not vested oil company interests. The Obama administration supports these initiatives. Let's be wary of permitting the large energy companies to harvest domestic natural gas reserves through the chemical process of fracking, until the long-term environmental consequences are better understood and can be more safely addressed.

Let's do it in conjunction with putting ordinary citizens back to work rebuilding our nation's aging electricity grid, energy distribution and delivery channels, understanding that the spending is both a stimulus and an investment in our future. And let's do it by memorializing T.R.'s theme, articulated more than 100 years ago, of conservation as a "National Duty."

Criminal Justice and Corporate Governance.

It is time to re-think the policies of who gets jailed and who gets rewarded. Nearly 40 years and $1 trillion since its inception during the Nixon administration, are we any closer to winning the so-called war on drugs? [453] Is the rationale still defensible? Stated differently, do we still *need* the war on drugs—and the bloated civil and military bureaucracy that go with it? Or is it time to recognize its obsolescence and concede that the fixation is misplaced?

What is the message to be distilled from the fact that blacks comprise just 13% of America's population [454] but almost 50% of its prison population? Or that nearly 1 out of 13 African American adults have been disenfranchised? Or that America comprises less than 5% of the world's population but incarcerates nearly a quarter of all prisoners on earth? [455]

Does it make good sense to jail low level perpetrators of "victimless" crimes such as simple marijuana possession or use? Is society served by the present arrangement? [456] At the same time, a silent but creeping epidemic of still perfectly legal prescription drug abuse is perpetrated by so-called "pill mill" doctors and their clientele. [457] If it is rampant on the street, how rampant might be prescription drug abuse in back rooms on places like Wall Street?

Since the Vietnam and Cold Wars are now over, why not scale back the war on drugs and prosecute a new war on poverty? Through reform of the nation's drug laws, the savings can be re-directed in part to fund a domestic Marshall Plan. This would create millions of jobs for ordinary citizens living in or near poverty to re-build our cities, schools, highways, railways and other necessary 21st century infrastructure.

A revision of the nation's drug laws, coinciding with the *substantial* re-allocation of resources toward crimes of violence against the person and property seems long overdue. Federal prosecutors must target "white collar" crime, successful dishonesty, unscrupulous businessmen who bilk their shareholders and investors alike, as well as those responsible for recklessly manipulating our financial system to the point of failure.

Neither can government regulators who were asleep at the switch be immune. We must strive to eliminate corruption in all forms, necessary to preserve the public's faith in capitalism.

Recently, Warren Buffett, the legendary investor, admitted that corporate boards of directors have done a poor job by private contract with business CEOs. The latter are rewarded equally for success or failure, as if success doesn't matter, a management structure that is simply not realistic. Their compensation has increased grossly in disproportion to the regular employee, who in some instances does not even receive a basic minimum health care benefit.

The idea of corporate governance does not require the federal government to have a seat with absolute veto power on every corporate board of directors. However, the compensation of upper level management must be linked by law to longer term human welfare criteria, like a decent living wage for the labor force, the security of rank and file worker retirement obligations and the potential, long-term consequences of harmful environmental degradation.

But absent the will of the private sector to govern itself from within, Congress must act. Mr. Buffett said that he didn't think CEOs should go to jail—but they should be poor if their companies fail and should not be permitted to drive Cadillacs. [458] And they, too, like the corrupt lawmaker, must be turned out.

***

It's time for closing thoughts.

The January 2009 inauguration of a new president was a day like no other. Nothing could prepare one for the experience. Crowds swarmed in all directions. It was impossible to stay together in a group of more than three or four. Security detail was impressive. And it was everywhere, highly visible, yet friendly. After all, on this day we were *all* Americans. The potency and destructive potential of some bizarre looking hand held weapons could only be imagined. Police sharpshooters stood atop the Lincoln Memorial.

People of color could be seen crying, everywhere. And for good reason. They were probably relieved more than anything else, and they were happy. The looks on the faces, the emotional outpouring, said it all. They had come a long way, their desire only for the equal rights of

306

citizenship—to be *seen* as equal—perhaps validated once and for all. Finally, it seemed, America had shaken off the terrible events of the spring of 1968 and was rousing from a deep, 40 year slumber.

As Mr. Obama was to take the oath of office and give his inaugural address, "swat" teams fanned out. Unscientifically, a small group of three decided that was their signal to rush the reviewing stand. They didn't get far. The crowd closed in. They were quickly sealed off, packed in like sardines, trapped about 1.2 million people from the front of the line. Which was not a bad seat on this day.

The sense was like being at a combined wedding/family reunion. One really didn't "know" any of the people, but somehow it was understood instinctively that these people were *all* part of a single, extended family. It was a proud, memorable day to be an ordinary American citizen. Mr. Obama had concluded his opening remarks as the nation's new 44th president. The military green helicopter appeared directly overhead on the great lawn, in the familiar and great tradition of transporting the family of the now former president out of town. The peaceful transformation of power was complete.

It was an awesome experience to behold, envied in many places throughout the world. All who attended somehow knew—that the promise of a new chapter in American History—had begun. Will President Obama answer the call of the great presidents—to influence and move us and the world to purpose he envisions? Will this new chapter take on broader meaning, pressing forward as it did in Jefferson's time with James Madison's 1808 election? Many believe that Hillary Clinton, former First Lady, US Senator (D-NY) and Secretary of State, will be the one to break the executive glass ceiling for women in 2016.

How can we meet the challenge of *our* time? Some recent spring cleaning uncovered a letter written to a boy by his parents on the occasion of his graduation from grammar school, several years ago. A passage serves as a fitting way to conclude:

> As you move forward, understand and accept that there will be times when you will stumble. During these times, especially, you would do well to recall what is important: that you know right from wrong, that you will always try to do right, that you will aim high, that you will be sensitive and try to help those around you who are less fortunate, and that you do your best. That is all.

Offered with gentle humility, there is often the opportunity for a teachable moment. *Questions*, not answers. Good, pointed questions provoke a keener, deeper insight, unlocking the art of critical thinking. "What would you do if teacher weren't here?" frames the issue on appropriate occasion. Questions which make one think provoke curiosity and the desire to learn. Socrates, the great philosopher of ancient Greece, made a pretty good living at it. Jesus Christ spoke in parables. Neither had written a book.

Of course, learning occurs not only in school but also at important moments long after those years pass into memory's dimming recesses. The idea is to continually seek improvement, to move forward through all the phases and crossroads of our ordinary yet busy lives. It's a marvel that we indeed have the capacity to analyze and retain those things found to be good and working in our lives, the courage to change what isn't and the wisdom to know the difference. All the while, we remember that we are imperfect and fallible by human nature. Perhaps this work will facilitate ordinary people to discover or rediscover the gift of learning, the joy of which should never end.

When Ben Franklin returned home after participating in the secret deliberations to draft the US Constitution, he was said to have had an inquisitive exchange with a Philadelphia woman:

"What have you made for us, Dr. Franklin?" the woman had wanted to know.

"A republic, madam, if you can keep it," Franklin replied.

Franklin understood that democracy was not forever assured—that active, informed citizenship would be required not only to keep but also to help it evolve. [459] The challenge of ordinary citizenship, then, is to promote progressive ideas towards the improvement of our democratic ideal, regardless of the politics, regardless of the political party. That means solving the crisis of achieving meaningful equality of opportunity for all citizens, not just the wealthy or privileged few. [460]

Yes, the challenge seems daunting. But can it be any more daunting than that facing the New Dealers who descended upon the grimness of Washington in the national fear and despair of 1933?

For the best of them, the satisfaction lay

in some deep sense of giving and sharing, ... rooted in the relief of escaping the loneliness and boredom of oneself, and the unreality of personal ambition. The satisfaction derived from sinking individual effort into the community itself, the common goal and the common end. This is no escape from self; it is the realization of self. [461]

Yet despite the New Deal's accomplishment, 35 years later, what had really changed, if anything? "For the many," said Robert Kennedy, "roots of despair all feed at a common source. ... Our gross national product ... measures everything, in short, except that which makes life worth while." [462]

With eyes closed, picture a small child who is attracted to a piano. As the child bangs on the keys, the piano generates an odious assembly of noises, a piercing blare of discordance. Yet how different is this familiar sound from a cacophony of voices which represents the ebb and flow of ordinary citizens engaged in the great continuing American experiment in democracy?

Do we understand that the sound is the product of individual voices crying out collectively, if not together, in the shadows? Do we recognize that some are weak, some are strong, some have been crying out for a long time? Do we know why it takes so long to hear some of them? Do we possess the sensitivity to accept that these voices belong to thinking, feeling human beings, who also must be looked upon with a spirit of empathy? Finally, will we discharge our collective, disinterested ethical obligation to act selflessly—with kindness toward the voices of need?

In the end, will we ever hear pleasant harmony? Perhaps not. But our efforts come from faith—and will produce a seed of satisfaction, knowing that the lives of the less fortunate are made just a little bit better. That is the plain duty of citizenship. We will be welcomed and permitted to dwell happily and honorably among the ordinary people as one of their own. In a life of service, some say the return can only be modest. But many others will know the reward cannot be greater.

Acknowledgments

I definitely did *not* do this alone. Many important people helped me through the rough patches and over the hurdles. They deserve proper credit for a journey which has led to this place.

My parents stressed formal education which brought me in touch first with liberal arts and then the law. Brian Zychowski encouraged my intellectual progression and plunge into teaching. Mark Lender actually hired me to teach. John Silva and Larry Landau supplied pearls of wisdom which were transformed into timeless lessons. Tom McManus was the first to encourage me to write a book and nurtured the process. Bill Maione provided inspiration.

A work of this nature—to try to get it right—became a daunting responsibility. Jackie Garnett and Cari Burkard, trusted co-editors in chief, supplied editorial brilliance both for style and substance. Those who donated a generous amount of their time to read and critique evolving drafts—and/or constructively challenged my vision—include Paul Forti, Patrick Stasolla, Rob Moran, Nick Monaghan, Mira Blythe, Brian Corey, Bob Fatovic, Lynda Bochetto-Sutter, Christopher Starr, John Verrier and Cory Eider. Barbara Bingham, my publisher, is the gem who offered many useful suggestions and supplied the finishing touches, making this the best book it could be.

Last but not least, my wife, Joyce, and son, Anthony, tolerated me through all this to the end. Their sacrifice was substantial.

For any who were inadvertently left out I accept full and total responsibility. Likewise, any errors in the text are due solely to my own shortcomings, which are humbly conceded. Mr. Justice Holmes was correct when he said that we cannot project our best at all times—that we are lucky enough if we can give but a sample—in our hearts nobly done. I can sleep knowing this standard has been met.

Thank you one and all.

Notes

INTRODUCTION

1   Bill Moyers has said our democracy depends upon maybe just a few such independent voices.

Source: The Rachel Maddow Show, *CNBC*, interview with Bill Moyers, July 14, 2011.

2   Maddow introduces Moyers as "the big thinker among all us," the founding organizer of the Peace Corps, press secretary to President Lyndon Johnson for four years, a journalistic veteran of Newsday, of CBS News, and of many award-winning PBS series, including "Bill Moyers Journal."

McCullough, David, John Adams (1991), at p. 68.

3   Nagel, Paul C., John Quincy Adams (A Public Life, A Private Life) (1997), at p.90.

4   Roosevelt, Theodore, An Autobiography (1913), at p. 17.

5   Miller, Merle, Plain Speaking, An Oral Biography of Harry S. Truman (1974), at p 111.

6   Grant, Ulysses S., Personal Memoirs of U.S. Grant (Volume One) (1885), at p. 1.

7   Roosevelt, An Autobiography, supra, at p. 251.

Abraham Lincoln was similarly drawn to Gen. Grant for the same reasons.

8   Maynard, W. Barksdale, Woodrow Wilson (Princeton to the Presidency) (2008), at p. 68.

9   Id., at p. 136.

10   Radio story as broadcasted on National Public Radio (NPR), October 7, 2010.

11   President Thomas Jefferson, *First Inaugural Address*, delivered March 4, 1801.

See also Malone, Dumas, <u>Jefferson the President, First Term, 1801-1805</u> (Volume Four) (1970), at p. 18-19. The italics in the quote were retained from the source material.

Malone's <u>Jefferson and His Time</u>, six volume series on the life of Thomas Jefferson was awarded the Pulitzer Prize in 1975.

12   <u>Id</u>. See also Malone, <u>Jefferson the President, First Term, 1801-1805, supra</u>, at p. 19-20.

13   McCullough, <u>John Adams, supra</u>, at p. 650.

CHAPTER 1.
AN IMPORTANT LESSON IN THE MOST USEFUL
"SCIENCE OF HUMAN NATURE"

14   McCullough, David, <u>Truman</u> (1992), at p. 571.

15   Miller, <u>Plain Speaking, supra</u>, at p. 395.

16   McCullough, <u>Truman, supra</u>, at p. 463.

17   Miller, <u>Plain Speaking, supra</u>, at p. 70.

18   McCullough, <u>Truman, supra</u>, at p. 325.

19   See <u>John</u> 2:13-17.

20   Franklin, Ben, <u>The Autobiography</u> (1791).

The source material is taken from Franklin, <u>Autobiography, Poor Richard and Later Writings</u>, The Library of America edition (1997).

21   <u>Id.</u>, at p. 573-605.

22   <u>Id.</u>, at p. 657.

23   <u>Id.</u>, at p. 644-645.

For an excellent discourse of the various virtues as identified and articulated throughout the course of the human condition, see also Bennett, William J. (editor), <u>The Book of Virtues</u> (1993) and the accompanying illustrated <u>Children's Book of Virtues</u> (1995), which together constitute a treasury of great moral stories.

To be sure, virtue's antagonist lives on through its opposing state of moral depravity or corruption, habitual defects or shortcomings, otherwise known as vices. We find examples of these in the vices more commonly known as ambition, pride, greed, vanity and fear, among others.

24 Miller, John C., <u>Alexander Hamilton</u> (1959), at p. 46.

25 <u>Id.</u>, at p. 114.

26 Miller, <u>Alexander Hamilton, supra</u>, at p. 199.

27 <u>Id.</u>, at p. 46.

28 President Andrew Jackson, *Veto Message to Congress*, July 10, 1832. President Jackson made these remarks relative to the re-chartering of the Bank of the United States (the "BUS").

29 Merton, Thomas (editor and foreword), <u>The Way of Chuang Tzu</u> (2004), at p. 72.

30 <u>Id.</u>, at p. 112-114.

CHAPTER 2. FLYING UNDER THE RADAR

31 McCullough, <u>Truman, supra</u>, at p. 43-44.

32 Freeman, Douglas Southall, <u>R.E. Lee</u> (Volume 1) (1935), at p. 432-437.

Freeman's four volume series on the life of Robert E. Lee was awarded the Pulitzer Prize when it was released in 1935.

33 <u>Id.</u>, at <u>Volume 4</u>, p. 215-222.

34 <u>Id.</u>, at <u>Volume 3</u>, p. 241-245.

35 Smith, Jean Edward, <u>Grant</u> (2001), at p. 77-88.

36 <u>Id.</u>, at p. 90-93.

37 <u>Id.</u>, at p. 286-289.

38 Smith, <u>Grant, supra</u>, at p. 295.

The quote is from Adam Badeau, a former newsman, who had become U.S. Grant's military secretary.

39 Roosevelt, Theodore, "Citizenship in a Republic," Speech at the Sorbonne, Paris, April 23, 1910.

40 Morris, Edmund, Colonel Roosevelt (2010), at p. 47.

41 Matthew 5:15-17.

42 President Franklin D. Roosevelt, *First Inaugural Address*, delivered March 4, 1933.

43 George H. W. (Herbert Walker) Bush was the 41st President of the United States. His son, George W. Bush, was the 43rd President. To keep them separate and for ease of reference, therefore, I defer to the somewhat familiar method of distinguishing them. The father will be hereafter referred to as President Bush "41" and his son President Bush "43."

44 More commonly known as the "Patriot Act", the USA PATRIOT Act was proposed by the US Congress and signed into law by President Bush "43" on October 26, 2001. The title of the act is a ten letter acronym (USA PATRIOT) that stands for:

Uniting (and) Strengthening America (by) Providing Appropriate Tools Required (to) Intercept (and) Obstruct Terrorism Act of 2001.

45 The quote is excerpted from Plato's Republic.

46 *New York Times Magazine*, July 4, 2010, at p. 44.

47 Malone, Jefferson the President, First Term, 1801-1805, supra, at p. 26.

48 Jefferson, Thomas, *Letter to Thomas Cooper Washington*, "Noiseless Course," November 29, 1802.

49 Jefferson, Thomas, Secretary of State, *Opinion on the Constitutionality of a National Bank*, as addressed to President George Washington, February 15, 1791.

50 Kent, Christopher, D.C., tribute to, *The Power of 10*. "Total Solution" seminar, sponsored by the Chiropractic Leadership Alliance, September 6-9, 2001.

51 In 1845 Thoreau embarked on a two-year experiment in simple living, moving to a small, self-built house on forested land around the shores of Walden Pond, Massachusetts. During this time, he ran

into the tax collector, who asked him to pay six years of delinquent poll taxes. When Thoreau refused, due to his opposition to the Mexican-American War and slavery, he spent a night in jail.

The experience left a strong impact, prompting lectures on "The Rights and Duties of the Individual in Relation to Government." These were later revised into an essay entitled *Resistance to Civil Government* (better and more commonly known today as *Civil Disobedience*).

CHAPTER 3. A FEW OF MY FAVORITE THINGS: US HISTORY (PART 1)

52 McCullough, Truman, supra, at p. 326.

53 Id., at p. 349.

54 McDougall, Walter A., Promised Land, Crusader State, The American Encounter with the World Since 1776 (1997), at p. 23.

McDougall's book won the Pulitzer Prize for History when it was published in 1997.

55 Id., at p. 23-24.

56 Quote is from then Virginia Congressman Light-Horse Harry Lee, at the funeral of George Washington on December 26, 1799.

See also, Malone, Dumas, Jefferson and the Ordeal of Liberty (Volume Three) (1962), at p. 442-443.

57 The full version of George Washington's last will and testament can be readily found at http://gwpapers.virginia.edu/documents/will/text.html. An excellent, recent biography on the Father of our Country can be found at Ellis, Joseph J., His Excellency (2004).

58 Jefferson, Thomas, *Letter to Spencer Roane*, September 6, 1819.

See also, Malone, Jefferson the President, First Term, 1801-1805, supra, at p. 26-27.

59 Id., at p. 23.

60 Remini, Robert, The Course of American Freedom (Volume Two) (1981), at p. 235-236.

Remini is widely acclaimed as the pre-eminent scholar on Andrew Jackson living today. His biography of Andrew Jackson consists of three volumes. The third of Remini's three volume series on the life of Andrew Jackson was awarded the Pulitzer Prize in 1984.

In 2005, Remini was appointed the Historian of the United States House of Representatives.

[61] Id.

[62] Phillips, Donald T., Lincoln on Leadership (1991), at p.40.

[63] Id., at p. 53.

[64] Donald, David Herbert, Lincoln (1995), at p. 135-136.

[65] In the presidential election of 1860, the national vote tally was as follows:

Candidate	Party	Popular Vote	Electoral Vote	Voter Participation
Abraham Lincoln	Republican	1,865,593 (39.8%)	180	81.2%
Stephen A. Douglas	Democratic	1,382,713 (29.5%)	12	
John C. Breckenridge	Democratic	846,356 (18.1%)	72	
John Bell	Union	592,906 (12.6%)	39	

[66] Grant, Julia Dent, The Personal Memoirs of Julia Dent Grant, edited by John Y. Simon (1975), at p. 113.

[67] President Abraham Lincoln, Second Inaugural Address (excerpted from), delivered March 4, 1865.

[68] See Matthew 7:1. In that verse Jesus Christ spoke thus:

"Judge not, that you be not judged.
for with what judgment you judge, you will be judged;
and with the same measure you use, it will be measured back to you.

"And why do you look at the speck in your brother's eye,
but do not consider the plank in your own eye?

"Or how you can say to your brother,
'Let me remove the speck out of your eye';
*and look, a plank **is** in your own eye?*

"Hypocrite! First remove the plank from your own eye,
and then you will see clearly to remove
the speck out of your brother's eye.

...
"Therefore, whatever you want men to do to you,
do also to them, for this is the Law of the Prophets."

CHAPTER 4. LENSES, FILTERS AND WALLS

69   Sinclair achieved his popularity in the first half of the 20th century. While a member of the Socialist Party for nearly 30 years, his particular creed was described as being romantic, old-fashioned with a utopian flavor. In 1906 he published *The Jungle*, which "exposed the horrors of the meatpacking industry and helped bring about the Pure Food and Drug Act." He left the party to run for governor of California in 1934 on the Democratic ticket but was roundly defeated. In his career he wrote nearly a hundred books as an "amiable scourge of the capitalist system." See Schlesinger, Arthur M., Jr., The Politics of Upheaval (1960), at p. 111-122.

70   Kurlansky, Mark, Cod: a Biography of the Fish That Changed the World (1997).

71   For the seminal work on the history of oil, see Yergin, Daniel, The Prize (1991).

72   Jefferson, Thomas, *Letter to Dr. John Manners*, "Classification on Natural History," February 2, 1814.

73   With respect to the idea that each of our perceptions is different, the Rorschach inkblot test is a noted psychological test, in which subjects' perceptions of what they see in basic inkblots are recorded and then analyzed using psychological interpretation. Developed in the 1960s, the test is still used today by some psychologists to examine a person's personality characteristics and emotional functioning, although researchers continue to raise questions, mainly over the objectivity of testers.

74 Malone, Dumas, <u>Jefferson and the Rights of Man</u> (Volume Two) (1951), at p. 175.

75 Malone, Dumas, <u>The Sage of Monticello</u> (Volume Six) (1981), at p. 104.

76 <u>Id.</u>, at p. 323.

77 President Thomas Jefferson, *First Inaugural Address, supra.*

See also Malone, <u>Jefferson the President, First Term, 1801-1805, supra</u>, at p. 22.

78 <u>Id.</u>, at p. 252.

79 <u>Id.</u>, at p. 488.

80 Malone, Dumas, <u>Jefferson the Virginian</u> (Volume One) (1948), at p. 106-7.

81 Malone, <u>Jefferson and the Rights of Man, supra,</u> at p. 110.

82 <u>Id.</u>, at p. 109.

See also, Jefferson, Thomas, <u>The Jefferson Bible, The Life and Morals of Jesus of Nazareth</u> (Beacon Press edition, 1989; originally published 1904).

83 Malone, <u>Jefferson the Virginian, supra,</u> at p. 106.

84 Malone, <u>Jefferson and the Rights of Man, supra</u>, at p. 175.

85 Malone, <u>Jefferson the Virginian, supra,</u> at p. 107, 109.

86 Jefferson, Thomas, *Letter to Peter Carr*, August 120, 1787.

87 Jefferson, Thomas, *A Summary View of the Rights of British America* (1774).

88 Malone, <u>The Sage of Monticello, supra</u>, at p. 199.

89 <u>Id.</u>, at p. 499.

90 <u>Id.</u>, at p. 198.

91 Malone, <u>Jefferson and the Rights of Man, supra</u>, at p. 466-7.

92 Jefferson, Thomas, *Letter to John Adams*, "The Natural Aristocracy," October 28, 1813.

93 Malone, Jefferson and the Rights of Man, supra, at p. 460.

94 See Matthew 6:24. The full verse reads:

You Cannot Serve God and Riches

No one can serve two masters; for either he will hate the one and love the other, or else he will be loyal to the one and despise the other. You cannot serve God and mammon.

The Merriam-Webster dictionary defines "mammon" as "material wealth or possessions especially as having a debasing influence" and the reference is sent back to the above Bible quotation.

95 Schlesinger, Arthur M., Jr., Robert Kennedy And His Times (Volume One) (1978), at p. 198.

Schlesinger writes that Robert Kennedy felt organized corruption, *not* communism as expressed in the popular media, to be the enemy within.

96 According to NASA website feature: *China's Wall Less Great in View from Space,* January 24, 2011.

97 Source: Jewish Virtual Library as accessed at www.jewishvirtuallibreary.org.

98 Morris, Edmund, Theodore Rex (Volume Two) (2001), at p. 234.

99 Radio story as broadcasted on NPR, March 25, 2011.

100 For example, during the 2011 MLB season the payrolls of the 3 highest teams average $179.2M (the New York Yankees first at $202.7M, the Philadelphia Phillies second at $173M and the Boston Red Sox third at $161.8M). By contrast, the payrolls of the 3 lowest teams average $40.7.M (the Kansas City Royals last at $36.1M, followed by the Tampa Bay Rays at $41.1M and the Pittsburgh Pirates at $45M). Source: *USA Today.*

101 In 2011 the salaries of New York Yankee players Alex Rodriguez, CC Sabathia and Mark Teixeira were $32M, $24.2M and $23.1M, respectively, for a total of $79.3M. This exceeded the payrolls of 12 of the 30 teams in MLB. Source: *USA Today.*

CHAPTER 5. DISTINGUISHING THE
WHEAT FROM THE CHAFF

[102] Thomas, Clarence, My Grandfather's Son, a Memoir (2007), at p. 140-141, 150.

[103] For an excellent discussion of the Thomas-Hill controversy from the perspective of Thomas, see Id., at p. 241-283.

[104] Remini, Robert, The Course of American Empire (Volume One) (1977), at p. 14-21.

[105] Id., at p. 136-42.

[106] Id., at p. 255-297.

[107] Remini, The Course of American Freedom, supra, at p. ix.

[108] Id., at p. 154-155.

[109] Remini, The Course of American Empire, supra, at p. 414.

[110] Remini, The Course of American Freedom, supra, at p. 366.

[111] Remini, The Course of American Empire, supra, at p. 1.

[112] Remini, The Course of American Freedom, supra, at p. 381.

[113] Remini, The Course of American Empire, supra, at p. 1-2.

[114] Andrew Jackson, note to his trusted colleague, former Vice President, and ultimate successor in office, the new President of the United States, Martin Van Buren, March 30, 1837.

[115] Hirshson, Stanley P., The White Tecumseh (1997), at p. 3-7.

[116] Id., at p. 17-83.

[117] Sherman, William T., Memoirs of General Sherman (Volume One) (1875), at p. 202-14.

[118] Hirshson, The White Tecumseh, supra, at p. 181.

[119] Sherman, Memoirs of General Sherman, Volume One, supra, at p. 255.

[120] Grant, Personal Memoirs of U.S. Grant, Volume One, supra, at p. 315.

121 Sherman, Memoirs of General Sherman, Volume Two, supra, at p. 109-110.

The catchphrase of the Democratic Party opposition to Lincoln in the 1862 Congressional midterm elections leading to the presidential election of 1864 had in fact been "the Constitution as it is and the Union as it was." Waugh, John C., Re-Electing Lincoln (1997), at p. 12.

122 Sherman, Memoirs of General Sherman, Volume Two, supra, at p. 344.

123 Id., at p. 347-351.

124 Durkin, Joseph T., S.J., General Sherman's Son (1959), at p. 139.

125 Hirshson, The White Tecumseh, supra, inside preface, *inscription*.

126 Id., at p. 206.

CHAPTER 6. EQUAL ACCESS TO THE AMERICAN ECONOMIC OPPORTUNITY STRUCTURE

127 127 Donald, Lincoln, supra, at p. 121. Of course, Congress consisted *only* of men at the time.

Lincoln mentioned one great exception in John Quincy Adams, the former president, who was one of only two former Presidents to do so (Andrew Johnson later served in the US Senate in the post-Civil War era). According to Lincoln, JQA was "distinguished alike for his rocklike integrity and his implacable hatred of slavery." He was elected to the House of Representatives, serving Massachusetts for eight consecutive terms from 1831 until his death in 1848.

128 Thomas, My Grandfather's Son, a Memoir, supra, at p. 74-77.

129 The "slave codes" typically stated the following:

1. A slave, like a domestic animal, could be bought, sold, and leased.
2. A master had the right to compel a slave to work.
3. Slaves were prohibited from owning property.
4. Slaves were prohibited from testifying against whites in court.
5. Slaves were prohibited from making contracts.
6. Slave marriages were not recognized by law.
7. Slavery was lifelong and hereditary.
8. Any child born to a slave woman was the property of her master.
9. Slaves were forbidden to strike or use insulting language toward white people.

10. Slaves were forbidden to hold a meeting without a white person present.
11. Slaves were forbidden to leave plantations without permission.
12. Whites and free backs were prohibited from teaching slaves to read and write, gamble with slaves, or supply them with liquor, guns or poisonous drugs.

130 The law of "separate but equal" and so-called "Jim Crow" laws to legalize racial separation, enforced more strictly in the South, came to the ordinary citizen courtesy of the US Supreme Court case of Plessy vs. Ferguson. 163 U.S. 537 (1896).

131 "Separate but equal" was overruled by the US Supreme Court by the case of Brown vs. Bd. of Education of Topeka, KS, 347 U.S. 483 (1954).

132 Thomas, My Grandfather's Son, a Memoir, supra, at p. 130-132.

133 Id., at p. 61-63.

134 Wilkins, Jefferson's Pillow, supra, at p. 105.

135 Id., at p. 141.

136 Id., at p. 142.

137 In his film, *Park Avenue: Money, Power and the American Dream,* Academy Award-winning filmmaker Alex Gibney makes a contention that America's richest citizens have "rigged the game in their favor," and created unprecedented inequality in the United States which has accelerated over the past 40 years. As a result, upward mobility is increasingly out of reach for the poor.

The statistic is consistently cited by Robert Reich, presently a Professor of Public Policy at the University of California at Berkeley.

Previously, Mr. Reich served as Secretary of Labor in the Clinton administration. *Time Magazine* named him as one of the ten most effective cabinet secretaries of the 20th century.

138 Id.

[139] For an excellent, fully thorough discussion of the shift in US domestic and foreign policy during this time, see McDougall, Promised Land, Crusader State, The American Encounter with the World Since 1776, supra.

[140] The term "Gilded Age," which was commonly given to the era, comes to us in borrowed form from the literary world of fiction. For a highly entertaining tale of greed and political corruption in post-Civil War America, see Twain, Mark, and Warner, Charles Dudley, The Gilded Age: a Tale of Today (1873).

[141] Nasaw, David, Andrew Carnegie (2006), at p. 589, 653.

[142] Id., at p. 737.

[143] Durkin, General Sherman's Son, supra, at p. 123.

[144] Caro, Robert A., The Years of Lyndon Johnson: The Path to Power (Volume One) (1983), at p. 36-39.

The Years of Lyndon Johnson consists of a four volume biography of America's 36th president. The third volume, Master of the Senate (2002) was awarded the Pulitzer Prize for Biography or Autobiography. A fifth and final volume is also in the works.

[145] Ms. Perkins was instrumental in the construction of a "permanent system of personal security through social insurance." See Schlesinger, Arthur M., Jr., The Coming of the New Deal (1959), at p. 298-301.

[146] Morris, Theodore Rex, supra, at p. 233, 351.

[147] T.R.'s policies were extended through the presidential administration of Woodrow Wilson (1912-1920) by way of the advancement of Wilson's "New Freedom" political agenda.

[148] Roosevelt, An Autobiography, supra, at p. 259-60, 268-69, 342.

[149] Id., at p. 228.

150 Of course, in this context it would be negligent to omit the failed uprising to defeat the stated US policy of the "Open Door." In 1900 a group of Chinese nationalists, known as Boxers, called for the expulsion or death of all westerners in China. But a joint European and American "rescue force" crushed the local resistance. The so-called Boxer Rebellion had failed.

151 McDougall, <u>Promised Land, Crusader State, The American Encounter with the World Since 1776, supra</u>, at p. 120.

152 Roosevelt, <u>An Autobiography, supra</u>, at p. 748.

153 <u>Id.</u>, at p. 401-411.

154 The nomenclature, "First European Civil War" and "Second European Civil War," was used throughout in the seminal work on 20th century US foreign policy, entitled Acheson, Dean, <u>Present at the Creation: My Years in the State Department</u> (1969). It is understood that the book remains the teaching authority of choice in at least one Ivy League university.

155 A recognized authority which contains a most detailed and thorough accounting of World War I, from the initial German planning in the 19th century, to the war's inception, and finally to Germany's surrender, is found in Keegan, John, <u>The First World War</u> (1998). British accounts of the war are said to be the most thorough, detailed and exhaustive, since the other main players were pre-occupied with either assessing the damage, picking up the pieces or other matters.

156 Yergin, <u>The Prize, supra</u>, at p. 167-183.

157 Hoover, Herbert, speech accepting the Republican presidential nomination, Palo Alta, California, August 11, 1928.

See also, Schlesinger, Arthur M., Jr., <u>The Crisis of the Old Order</u> (1957), at p. x, 88-89, 128-129. The first of a three volume series under the title of <u>The Age of Roosevelt</u>, the book was the winner of both the Bancroft Prize and the Francis Parkman Prize in 1958.

158 <u>Id.</u>, at p. 155.

159 <u>Id.</u>, at p. 160-161.

160 <u>Id.</u>, at p. 178, 180.

161 <u>Id.</u>, at p. 181.

162 Schlesinger, <u>The Coming of the New Deal, supra</u>, at p. 87.

163 <u>Id.</u>, at p. 269.

164 Smith, Jean Edward, <u>FDR</u> (2007), *inscription*.

165 The "whole impression" was "of an honest anxious man faced by an impossible task—humanizing capitalism and making it work," of F.D.R. as a

> trustee for those in every country who seek to mend the evils of our condition by reasoned experiment within the framework of the existing social system.
>
> If you fail, rational choice will be gravely prejudiced throughout the world, leaving orthodoxy and revolution to fight it out.
>
> But, if you succeed, new and bolder methods will be tried everywhere, and we may date the first chapter of a new economic era from your ascension to office.

For an excellent big picture overview of the task at hand, the methods used and the stakes involved, see Schlesinger, <u>The Politics of Upheaval, supra</u>, at p. 645-657. The quoted language is found at p. 655-656.

166 Through the decades, some have criticized F.D.R., calling him a socialist and the New Deal socialistic. But the New Deal's aim, according to F.D.R., was simply to multiply the number of American shareholders. "Is this socialistic?" the president asked with a hearty laugh. See Schlesinger, <u>The Coming of the New Deal, supra</u>, at p. 315, 320.

Now in its 9th working decade, the social safety net represents a continuous responsibility of government for human welfare. It is understood to contain four main anti-poverty, risk-managing components.

The first component is the New Deal's lynchpin, the Social Security Act of 1935, including the Truman administration's subsequent "Fair Deal" augmentations. Coupled with Social Security is the legal right of every worker to join a union of his or her own choosing under NLRA.

The second component involves government assistance for the poor. According to Milo Perkins, the program's first administrator, the initial program from 1939-1943 built a practical bridge across the chasm "with farm surpluses on one cliff and under-nourished city folks with outstretched hands on the other." In 1961, it was renewed and renamed as the Food Stamps Program. By 1996, the program was replaced with the aforementioned block grants to states. In 2008, the name was changed to the current Supplemental Nutrition Assistance Program (SNAP), and funds could also be used to provide recipients with education and training, career pathways and other public benefit programs. A USDA summary statistical report indicated that almost 47 million people used SNAP in 2012, up from 26 million in 2007, a 177% increase. That's roughly 15% of the total US population today.

The third component added in 1965 is Medicare/Medicaid, a program of financed health care for older Americans and for persons in poverty, including the Bush/"43" administration's 2006 prescription drug augmentations.

The fourth and most recent component set into place in 2010 is the new Obamacare health care reform overhaul. Conceived as another cornerstone onto bedrock, it consists of basic security in health care for all Americans.

167 Id., at p. 179-181. Of course, by 1932 it was apparent that the stimulative potential of traditional, natural opportunities afforded via abundant, free land for western migration and new industries like the railroad and automobile no longer existed, as they once had. Economic maturity thus called for a rational national plan.

168 Id., at p. 11-12.

169 Id., at p. 10.

170 Schlesinger, The Crisis of the Old Order, supra, at p. 449-450.

171 "Involving many States and the future lives and welfare of millions," the president said, the TVA "touches and gives life to all forms of human concern." A lifelong proponent called it "the most wonderful and far-reaching humanitarian document that has ever come from the White House." Schlesinger, The Coming of the New Deal, supra, at p. 321-324. See also Schlesinger, The Politics of Upheaval, supra, at p. 373-384.

172 The "Second New Deal" was said to commence in 1935. With a strong push from the U.S. Supreme Court, F.D.R.'s administration

was compelled to move away from reliance on centralized planning for a directed economy under the constitution's commerce clause. The move was to a mixed or compensated, de-centralized economy which promoted increased private competition. In short, "The First New Deal characteristically told business what it must do. The Second New Deal characteristically told business what it must not do." While the goal remained reflation through monetary policy and fairer income distribution, the effective tools were the constitutional powers of taxation and expenditure. Id., at p. 392, 396-400.

173 "Nothing in the politics of the New Deal was more daring," Schlesinger relates, "then (sic) the project of combining in the same party the descendants of the slaveholders and the descendants of slaves." Robert L. Vann, the publisher of the influential *Pittsburgh Courier*, the largest black paper in Pennsylvania, was put in charge of the 1932 Democratic state campaign. "My friends, go home and turn Lincoln's picture to the wall," Vann told black voters. "That debt has been paid in full." Id., at p. 425-438.

174 Schlesinger, The Crisis of the Old Order, supra, at p. 134.

175 Acheson, Present at the Creation, supra, at p. 730.

176 Id., at p. 3, to Note at p. 740.

177 Id., at p. 730-731.

178 McCullough, Truman, supra, at p. 352.

179 For a superb, detailed academic work on this subject, see generally Beisner, Robert L., Dean Acheson: A Life in the Cold War (2006). Acheson never strayed from the view that Europe itself was the great prize worth fighting for in the Cold War. All US foreign policy actions could be safely viewed through this prism, including the defense of South Korea (and thereafter Formosa), seen as an initial test of western resolve.

The brilliant idea of "double containment" lay in adding and boxing in West German (and Japanese) power to the west while simultaneously boxing out Soviet expansionism. Id., at p. 644.

When asked to name his proudest achievement, President Truman replied: "We completely defeated our enemies and made them surrender. And then we helped them to recover, to become democratic, and to rejoin the community of nations." Id., at p. 642-643.

180 Id., at p. 646, 654.

181 Id., at p. 645.

182 McCullough, Truman, supra, at p. 467.

183 Robert Kennedy delivered the victory speech in the Embassy ballroom of the Ambassador Hotel, Los Angeles, CA on the evening of June 4, 1968.

184 Sirhan Sirhan, the assassin, was born in 1944 in Jerusalem, Mandatory Palestine, which at the time was still under British administration, carved out of Ottoman Southern Syria following World War I. He is a Jordanian citizen who strongly opposes Israel, currently serving a life sentence in a California federal prison. The assassination was thought to be the first major incident of political violence in the US stemming from the Arab-Israeli conflict in the Middle East.

185 Like George Washington before him, President Dwight D. Eisenhower issued ominous warnings to America about possible future concerns for the citizens of America. In his 1960 Farewell Address, President Eisenhower noted, in particular, that the "military industrial complex"—an alliance between government and business—could threaten the nation's democratic process. As Eisenhower had remarked earlier in his presidency:

Every gun that is made, every warship launched, every rocket fired signifies, in the final sense, a theft from those who hunger and are not fed, those who are cold and not clothed.

186 Schlesinger, Arthur M., Jr., Robert Kennedy and His Times (Volume Two) (1978), at p. 734-756.

187 Id., at p. 45-48, 64.

188 Id., at p. 816. The reference in the citation is to Dr. King only, but Muhammad Ali's credentials on this subject are also beyond question.

189 The source of this famous quotation is traced to Theodore Parker. A graduate of Harvard College (1831) and the Harvard Divinity School (1836), Parker was said to be a reforming minister of the

Unitarian Church and leading abolitionist, whose sermons also inspired Abraham Lincoln.

190 Dr. Martin Luther King, Jr., speech delivered at the Mason Temple (Church of God in Christ Headquarters), Memphis, Tennessee, April 3, 1968.

191 President Johnson had stated that

> I knew from the start that I was bound to be crucified either way I moved. If I left the woman I really loved—the Great Society—in order to get involved with that bitch of a war on the other side of the world, then I would lose everything at home. ... And I knew that if we let Communist aggression succeed in taking over South Vietnam ... that would shatter my Presidency, kill my administration, and damage our democracy.

See Schlesinger, Robert Kennedy and His Times (Volume Two), supra, at p. 774.

192 Id., at p. 818.

193 This followed immediately on the news of the Tet Offensive in the early days of 1968, which, Schlesinger said, "changed everything." Tet manifested the acute level of deception by the Johnson administration, and, according to a textbook used at West Point, was labeled an "intelligence failure ranking with Pearl Harbor." Id., at p. 879.

194 "Literally," Schlesinger said, "this was not true. He meant that his brother had been involved." Robert Kennedy's own role had, in fact, been limited. Id., at p. 745-747, 760, 807.

195 Id., at p. 779-780. The speech, given at the University of Cape Town on June 6, 1966, was said to be Robert Kennedy's greatest.

196 Id., at p. 408, 430, 817-825.

197 Id., at p. 939.

198 Id., at p. 825, 834.

199 Id., at p. 836.

200 Id., at p. 930.

201 Morris, Edmund, Dutch: A Memoir of Ronald Reagan (1999), at p. 3.

202 Sen. Goldwater's political theories were set forth in his book, entitled The Conscience of a Conservative (1960).

203 President Ronald Reagan, speech at the Brandenburg Gate near the Berlin Wall on June 12, 1987, commemorating the 750th anniversary of Berlin.

204 Perlstein, Rick, "The Southern Strategist," *New York Times Magazine*, December 30, 2007.

See also, Caro, Robert A., The Passage of Power (Volume Four) (2012), at p. 452-465. The term "Southern Strategy" had previously described the efforts of the Democratic Party to openly block civil rights reform legislation in the era spanning the end of Reconstruction in 1876 through 1964.

The secrecy component, that is, supporting civil rights enforcement in the open but opposing it behind closed doors, did not come to the forefront until the Republican Party picked up the torch in the years after 1964.

205 See testimony of Hugh Davis Graham, Holland McTyeire Professor of American History, Vanderbilt University, given before the US House of Representatives, Committee on the Judiciary, Subcommittee on the Constitution, April 3, 1995.

206 Hutchinson, Earl Ofari, "The Great Racial Surprise of the Reagan Presidency," Pacific News Service *AmericanRenaissance.com*, June 2007.

207 Id.

208 As to Mr. Obama's anecdotes of history and human nature written from the perspective of a then-US Senator, D-IL, see the best selling book, Obama, Barack, The Audacity of Hope (2006).

209 Corporate Average Fuel Economy (CAFÉ) standards are regulations of the federal government intended to improve the average fuel economy of cars and light trucks sold in the US in the aftermath of the 1973 Arab oil embargo.

210 With little or no chance of Congressional support and so bypassing Congress, President Obama boldly announced in June 2013 that his administration would use executive powers, among other things, to limit the carbon dioxide that power plants could emit. By stretching the intent of the 1970 Clean Air Act which was not written with climate change in mind, the aim is to substantially reduce

greenhouse gas emissions in an effort to minimize the damaging effects of climate change.

The formal action was to order the Environmental Protection Agency to begin devising an emission control plan. Experts say, however, that by acting now the Obama administration "will be lucky to get a final plan in place by the time he leaves office in early 2017." See Gillis, Justin, "Obama Puts Legacy at Stake with Clean-Air Act," *The New York Times*, June 25, 2013.

CHAPTER 8. NEEDS VS. WANTS

[211] 211 *The Sunday Star-Ledger*, Section 1, at p. 12-13, February 10, 2008.

[212] Franklin, Benjamin, *Speech in the Constitutional Convention*, June 2, 1787.

[213] Franklin, Benjamin, *Letter to Robert Morris*, December 25, 1783.

[214] Franklin, Benjamin, The Compleated Autobiography (compiled and edited by Mark Skousen) (2006), at p. 336-37.

[215] The term "establishment paradise" is a phrase borrowed from Boris Yeltsin in describing the inner workings of the Soviet Politburo, the governing body and Central Committee of the Communist Party prior to the fall of the USSR. See Yeltsin, Boris, Against the Grain (1989), at p. 137.

[216] Remini, The Course of American Freedom, supra, at p. 189-90.

[217] Jackson, Andrew, *First Presidential Message to Congress*, December 8, 1829.

[218] Miller, An Oral Autobiography of Harry S. Truman, supra, at p. 350.

[219] Id., at p. 351, 354.

[220] A second defined pension benefit formula for a younger state worker, now in his early forties, is said to take the average of the worker's annual salary from the three highest years of the prior five years, then multiply that number by the sum of the total number of years of service divided by the number 60. A relatively miniscule worker contribution has also been added.

For the younger state worker the calculation is 25/60 = .42 or 42% of $175,000.00. This formula yields a slightly lower dollar figure than the calculation for the current retiree, requiring the younger worker to put in an additional 5 years (or 30 years of service) to get to 50%.

221 Among these are the following: fraud; unilateral mistake; impossibility; that the legislature had committed an act which itself is deemed *ultra vires* (exceeded the scope of its authority, since prior legislatures were unaware that they were creating a property right that the Citizens would not have the ability to honor in subsequent years); or that the old retirement system law is subject to *nullification* in the public interest. The latter would be under the familiar states' rights theory. Yes, it's the same Old South pre-Civil War argument, previously rejected as applied "up" to the federal government but which might gain some traction as applied "down" from the state government level to a public labor union.

222 Smith, FDR, supra, at p. 387.

223 Id., at p. 313-316.

224 Id., at p. 315.

The latter quote was reported in *The New York Times*, March 12, 1933.

225 Gov. Christie's methods of ascent to state and national prominence have raised questions which may keep him otherwise occupied, as the "Bridgegate" scandal investigation unfolds. See MacGillis, Alec, "Chris Christie's Entire Career Reeks; It's Not Just the Bridge," *The New Republic*, February 12, 2014.

226 Delli Santi, Angela, "New Jersey Anti-Union Bill Approved, Governor Chris Christie Signs Into Law," *Huffington Post*, found at *huffingtonpost.com*, August 10, 2011.

227 Magyar, Mark J., "Handing Christie an Easy Win (Why did the Democratic leadership line up behind the governor on pension and healthcare reform for public employees?)," *NJ Spotlight*, found at *njspotlight.com*, June 27, 2011. The source claims to be "an online news service providing insight and information on issues critical to New Jersey, with the aim of informing and engaging the state's

communities and businesses. We are nonpartisan, independent, policy-centered and community-minded."

CHAPTER 9. THE NEED FOR CHANGE ...

228 Acheson, <u>Present at the Creation, supra</u>, *inscription.* The quote is attributed to Alphonso X, the Learned, 1252-1284, King of Spain.

229 Wooden's teams won 7 consecutive NCAA championships and 10 in 12 seasons, which included a record men's winning streak of 88 games and 4 perfect 30-0 seasons.

230 For an excellent analysis as to the causes of the financial crisis, see Leonhardt, David, "Heading Off the Next Financial Crisis," *New York Times Magazine*, March 25, 2010.

231 Cooper, Helene, "Obama Signs Overhaul of Financial System," *New York Times*, July 21, 2010.

The article reports that in response to the 2008 financial crisis that tipped the nation into the worst recession since the Great Depression, President Obama signed a sweeping expansion of federal financial regulation. But within minutes of the bill's passage, several Wall Street groups were leveling criticism at the new regulations, as was The Business Roundtable, the US Chamber of Commerce and other business organizations.

The substance of the law is said to subject more financial companies to federal oversight and regulates many derivatives contracts, while creating a consumer protection regulator and a panel to detect risks to the financial system. However, a number of the details have been left for regulators to work out, "inevitably setting off complicated tangles down the road that could last for years."

Before signing the legislation, Mr. Obama remarked that "because of this law, the American people will never again be asked to foot the bill for Wall Street's mistakes." Mr. Obama said that "There will be no more taxpayer-funded bailouts. Period."

From our discussions on the history of the financial industry in this country, the ordinary citizen is, however, expressing a great deal of frustration and doubt, in attempting to take Mr. Obama at his word.

232 The direct source quote is the following: "He that will not apply new remedies must expect new evils; for time is the greatest innovator." -Francis Bacon. See Schlesinger, The Politics of Upheaval, supra, *inscription.*

233 See Story, Louise, "Income Inequality and Financial Crises," *New York Times Magazine*, August 21, 2010. In the article, the author cites to David A. Moss, an economic and policy historian at the Harvard Business School, who has spent years studying the phenomenon of income inequality. Mr. Moss has hypothesized that growing disparity between the rich and poor is not only harmful to the people on the bottom but also creates serious risks to the world of finance, where many of the richest earn their great fortunes.

In fact, as he studies the financial crisis of 2008, Mr. Moss says that another crisis may be brewing. When he accepted the suggestion of a colleague that he overlay two different graphs—one plotting financial regulation and bank failures, and the other charting trends in income inequality—he was surprised that the timelines danced in sync with each other. Specifically, income disparities between rich and poor widened, as government regulations eased and bank failures rose.

"I could hardly believe how tight the fit was—it was a stunning correlation," he said. "And it began to raise the question of whether there are causal links between financial deregulation, economic inequality and instability in the financial sector. Are all of these things connected?"

234 The US unemployment rate stood at 8.5% of the work force by way of statistical data through December 2011. Generally, economists see "full" employment (defined as), at an unemployment rate of 3% unemployment for persons 20 and older, 4% for person age 16 and over, of the available work force. That puts the number of unemployed who are seeking work at somewhere between 15.5 million and 18.6 million.

Source: US Department of Labor, Bureau of Labor Statistics.

235 In a CBS news national television interview, which aired on *60 Minutes* in March 2009, Chairman Bernanke opened the halls of the Federal Reserve to film cameras and the curious eye of the general public for the very first time. Mr. Bernanke reassured a

wary public that he had not only the necessary formula but also the tools to combat the Great Recession of 2008. Asked when the recession would end, the Chairman replied:

> It depends a lot on the financial system. The lesson of history is that you do not get a sustained economic recovery as long as the financial system is in crisis. We've seen some progress in the financial markets, absolutely. But until we get that stabilized and working normally, we're not gonna see recovery. But we do have a plan. We're working on it. And I do think that we will get it stabilized, and we'll see the recession coming to an end probably this year. We'll see recovery beginning next year. And it will pick up steam over time.

236 Jefferson, Thomas, excerpt from *Letter (from Paris) to William Smith*, November 13, 1787.

237 Jefferson, Thomas, excerpt from *Letter (from Paris) to James Madison*, September 6, 1789. Jefferson did not simply pluck this number out of thin air. Rather, he devised a formula to determine when constitutions ought to expire based on the average life expectancy of men.

238 Panel 4 on the Jefferson Memorial monument in Washington, DC. The full quote from the original text was from Jefferson, Thomas, *Letter to H. Tompkinson (a/k/a Samuel Kercheval)*, July 12, 1816. It may be found at Malone, The Sage of Monticello, supra, at p. 348.

239 *Noblesse Oblige*, the term of art, is a French phrase literally meaning "nobility obliges."

240 Roosevelt, An Autobiography, supra, at p. 249-50.

241 Morris, Theodore Rex, supra, at p. 504.

242 Id., at p. 504, 507.

243 Morris, Edmund, The Rise of Theodore Roosevelt (Volume One) (1979), at p. 729-730.

The first of Morris' three volume series on the life of Theodore Roosevelt was awarded the Pulitzer Prize and the National Book Award in 1980.

244 Roosevelt, An Autobiography, supra, at p. 320, 353.

245 Morris, <u>Theodore Rex, supra</u>, at p. 508.

246 Roosevelt, <u>An Autobiography, supra</u>, at p. 347-348.

247 <u>Id.</u>, at p. 348.

248 <u>Id.</u>, at p. 353.

249 Morris, <u>Colonel Roosevelt, supra</u>, at p.88-92.

250 <u>Id.</u>, at p. 154.

251 <u>Id.</u>, at p. 93.

252 <u>Id.</u>

253 <u>The Promise of American Life</u> was published by the political philosopher, Herbert Croly, in 1909. Many of its ideas were said to derive from T.R.'s 1908 *Special Message to Congress*.

254 La Forte, Robert S., "Theodore Roosevelt's Osawatomie Speech," *Kansas Historical Quarterly*, Summer, 1966 (Vol. 32, No. 2), at p. 187.

255 Roosevelt, Theodore, speech at Osawatomie, Kansas, August 31, 1910.

By the late summer of 1932, during the depths of the Great Depression, Franklin D. Roosevelt, presidential candidate, lamented equality of opportunity's extinction. The industrial plant was built out, the last frontier reached. There was essentially no more free land to which those thrown out of work could go for a new start. The immigrant was no longer invited. The independent business man was running a losing race, the ordinary citizen provided but a drab existence. Wealth concentration, left unchecked, was steering a course toward economic oligarchy controlled by approximately a dozen corporations and perhaps a hundred men who controlled them. See Schlesinger, <u>The Crisis of the Old Order, supra</u>, at p. 424-425.

256 Many people, including this author, have labored under the assumption that the rich hated T.R., and F.D.R., on the simple charge of turning their backs on them. But Schlesinger writes that Joseph Kennedy, father of the Kennedy men and himself a rich man,

identified a more penetrating charge. The elder Kennedy felt that F.D.R. exposed once and for all "the popular myth that business success was a guarantee of civic virtue." The rich man's "material position" had not been harmed, "but his moral prestige is gone." See Schlesinger, <u>Robert Kennedy and His Times (Volume One),</u> <u>supra</u>, at p. 12.

257 Morris, <u>Colonel Roosevelt, supra</u>, at p.153-157.

258 <u>Id.</u>, at p. 198.

259 <u>Id.</u>, at p. 209.

260 <u>Id.</u>, at p. 94.

261 <u>Id.</u>, at p. 211.

262 <u>Id.</u>, at p. 212.

263 <u>Id.</u>, at p. 221-227.

264 Excerpted from Theodore Roosevelt's *New Nationalism Speech*, supra.

265 Morris, <u>Colonel Roosevelt, supra</u>, at p. 230, 237, 651 (Note).

266 <u>Id.</u>, at p. 243-244, 247-248, 654-655 (Note).

267 <u>Id.</u>, at p. 257, 658 (Note).

Pleading guilty to T.R.'s shooting, with qualifications, Schrank was committed to the hospital for the criminally insane and remained there until his death on the anniversary of his first vision of the ghost of McKinley thirty-one years earlier.

268 <u>Id.</u>, at p. 251.

269 In the presidential election of 1912, the national vote tally was as follows:

Candidate	Party	Popular Vote	Electoral Vote	Voter Participation
Woodrow Wilson	Democratic	6,293,454 (41.9%)	435	58.8%
Theodore Roosevelt	Progressive	4,119,538 (27.4%)	88	
William H. Taft	Republican	3,484,980 (23.2%)	8	
Eugene V. Debs	Socialist	900,672 (6%)	-	

[270] Morris, Colonel Roosevelt, supra, at p. 639 (Note).

[271] Id., at p. 237.

[272] Id., at p. 651 (Note).

[273] Caro, Robert A., Means of Ascent (Volume Two) (1990), at p. 410.

Despite love for the law but a deep reluctance for politics, Coke Robert Stevenson also had a storied career in Texas state politics. A Democrat, Stevenson was the only 20th century Texas politician to serve as Speaker of the Texas House of Representatives, Lieutenant Governor, and then Governor, the latter position which he held from 1941 to 1947.

A staunch states' rights conservative, Stevenson was nonetheless painted as a liberal in the contentious, controversial 1948 campaign for election to a US Senate seat won by his opponent, Lyndon Johnson. Johnson's special interest money had purchased the election, but when even that was insufficient, many believe that Johnson had in effect stolen it through voter fraud, a charge widely acknowledged as accurate today. Following the election Stevenson retired to the simple lifestyle of a Texas rancher.

Like many leading men of his era, Stevenson became increasingly disenchanted with the Democratic Party. This signaled a major national political shift, a conservative movement away from expanded government assistance in favor of individual initiative and personal responsibility which resonates to the present day. The movement's advocacy of small, frugal, debt-free government, however, remains elusive as a practical matter.

[274] Excerpted from Theodore Roosevelt's New Nationalism Speech, supra.

[275] "A chicken in every pot and a car in every garage" is the complete quote, attributed to then-candidate Herbert Hoover's 1928 election campaign. It epitomized the mass psychology characteristic of the "Roaring '20s."

[276] Yergin, The Prize, supra, at p. 213.

277 Schlesinger, The Politics of Upheaval, supra, at p. 620.

278 School desegregation would have to await another decade and a new president. In 1962, James Meredith sought enrollment as the first black student in the University of Mississippi, with the full support of the Kennedy administration.

On the one hand, Ross Barnett, the white Mississippi governor, opposed Meredith's enrollment. He appeared on statewide television and said that "We will not surrender to the evil and illegal forces of tyranny." For his part, Meredith said he believed he had "a Divine Responsibility to break white Supremacy in Mississippi, and getting in Ole Miss was only the start." Meredith succeeded, with the assistance of federal troops, graduating in 1963.

The question arises —was it worth the cost? According to Meredith:

I believe that I echo the feeling of most Americans when I say that 'no price is too high to pay for freedom of person, equality of opportunity, and human dignity.'

Meredith said later that had Richard Nixon been elected in 1960 he might not have applied. See Schlesinger, Robert Kennedy and His Times (Volume One), supra, at p. 330-331, 338.

279 In 1951 Dean Acheson, Secretary of State, had said the following about the French predicament in Indochina:

At this time we began an effort—a frustrating and unsuccessful one—to get our friends to see and face the facts in Indochina. France was engaged in a task beyond her strength, indeed, beyond the strength of any external power unless it was acting in support of a dominant local will and purpose.

280 Nelson D. Rockefeller was the grandson of John D. Rockefeller, the Standard Oil founder and chairman. In a distinguished career, he served as the Governor of the state of New York from 1959 to 1973. In 1974, then-president Gerald Ford appointed him vice president of the United States in the aftermath of the Watergate scandal which brought down the presidency of Richard M. Nixon.

281 Brinkley, Douglas, Gerald R. Ford (2007), at p. 114-115.

282 Tupac Shakur, the iconic black rapper, captured the feeling in his 1992 classic hip hop song, *Changes*:

Instead of a war on poverty
They got a war on drugs
So the police can bother me

283 In July 2013 President Obama told the nation that

Trends that have been eroding middle class security for decades, technology that makes some jobs obsolete, global competition that makes others movable, growing inequality and the policies that perpetuate it—all those things still exist. And in some ways the recession made them worse. Reversing these trends must be Washington's highest priority. It sure is mine. But over the past couple of years in particular Washington has taken its eye off the ball. An endless parade of distractions and political posturing and phony scandals shift focus from what needs to be done.
...

(R)epealing Obamacare, gutting critical investments in our future, threatening to default on the bills this country has already racked up or shutting down the government just because I'm for keeping it open? None of those things add up to an economic plan.

The president acknowledged that the income gap is fraying the social fabric of the nation. "I will seize any opportunity I can find to work with Congress to strengthen the middle class, improve their prospects, improve their security," Mr. Obama said. But he added that

I'm not just going to sit back if the only message from some of these folks is no on everything, and sit around and twiddle my thumbs for the next 1,200 days.
...

(T)here's not an action that I take that you don't have some folks in Congress who say that I'm usurping my authority. Some of those folks think I usurp my authority by having the gall to win the presidency.

Source: President Obama's *Your Weekly Address*, www.whitehouse. gov, July 27, 2013; Calmes, Jackie and Shear, Michael D., "Obama Says Income Gap Is Fraying U.S. Social Fabric," *The New York Times*, July 28, 2013.

284 In the mid-1990s, as part of reform of the welfare system to significantly increase its work requirements, federal funds under SNAP were also "block granted" to the individual states. This means that states receive a fixed amount that is largely insensitive to recessions and inflation. Accordingly, since the block grant began, its real value is down 30%.

Source: Bernstein, Jared, "Lessons of the Great Recession: How the Safety Net Performed," *The New York Times*, June 24, 2013. Bernstein was the Chief Economist and Economic Adviser to Vice President Joe Biden from 2009 to 2011 in the Obama Administration.

Presently, this same block grant strategy on poverty is considered to be a fixture of conservative policy to be applied to Medicare/

Medicaid. To be sure, during the presidential election of 2012, Republicans campaigned on a promise to "privatize" Medicare in what they said was an effort to reduce its costs. Democrats, however, saw it as a veiled attempt to eliminate the popular program.

285 With respect to voting rights, a significant Republican victory was recently achieved. A 5-4 ruling by the conservative U.S. Supreme Court struck down the heart of the 1965 Voting Rights Act in <u>Shelby County vs. Holder</u>, 570 <u>U.S.</u> ____ (2013). Essentially, the Court ruled that Congress improperly relied on stale "coverage formula" data to determine which state governments need to get approval from the federal government before changing their voting laws.

Source: Liptak, Adam, "Supreme Court Invalidates Key Part of Voting Rights Act," *The New York Times*, June 25, 2013. See also Schwartz, John, "Between the Lines of the Voting Rights Act Opinion," *The New York Times*, June 25, 2013; Riley, Theresa, "The Fight to Protect Voting Rights in Texas," *Moyers & Company*, category: "Connecting the Dots," billmoyers.com, July 13, 2013.

286 In simple terms, as the author understands it, the term "cap and trade" means essentially that the free market permits industries to buy and sell the right to pollute, in this case carbon emissions. Originally, it was a conservative Republican idea dating as far back as the 1980s with the environmental problem of acid-rain-causing sulfur dioxide. An extremely effective cap and trade system was then put into place by Republican President Bush "41." Recently, it has been adopted by the Democrats, prompting the Republicans essentially to abandon and now oppose it.

See Lowell Feld NRDC Action Fund, "Remember, Cap-and-Trade Was Originally a Free-Market, Conservative Idea," *Blue Virginia*, July 1, 2010.

287 During the 1980 Republican presidential primary, candidate George H. W. Bush coined the term "voodoo economics" in reference to fellow candidate Ronald Reagan's economic policies. That is to say, before Bush/"41" became Mr. Reagan's vice president, he viewed his eventual running mate's economic policies somewhat

less than favorably. He also viewed Mr. Reagan's aggressive Cold War rhetoric on the use of military power as "dangerous."

288   In September 1981, at the time of President Reagan's first fiscal budget, the federal debt totaled just under $1 Trillion ($997,855,000). By September 1993, however, the federal debt had mushroomed more than four-fold to almost $4.5 Trillion ($4,411,488,883,140).

During President Clinton's two terms in office, the federal debt increased at a much more moderated pace, to a figure that was *only* just over $5.8 Trillion by September 2001.

But the presidential administration of President Bush/"43" seemed to make the other previous spenders pale by comparison. During his two terms in office, representing the annual fiscal budgets from September 2001 to September 2009, the federal debt more than doubled to a staggering figure of over $11.5 Trillion. Moreover, at its inception the new presidential administration of Barack Obama was compelled to address an economy which most economists agreed was on the brink of another Great Depression. Mr. Obama's projected federal budget deficit was around $800 Billion, even before he had taken the oath of office.

Mr. Obama's predicament did not include federal spending programs which carried over to the new administration, passed by Mr. Obama's predecessor. Specifically, the Troubled Asset Relief Program (TARP) is a program which was signed into law by President Bush/"43" on October 3, 2008 to purchase assets and equity from financial institutions to strengthen the US financial sector. It was a component of the federal government's measures to address the subprime mortgage crisis.

Additionally, this did not include the American Recovery and Reinvestment Act of 2009 (ARRA), commonly known as the Stimulus Act. ARRA was an economic stimulus package enacted by the 111th US Congress in February 2009 and signed into law by President Obama on February 17, 2009, less than one month after he took office. The primary objective was to save and create jobs almost immediately through emergency spending measures in place of the private sector, which had essentially ceased to function. Secondary objectives were to provide temporary relief programs for those most impacted by the recession and invest in infrastructure, education, health, and so called "green" energy. The approximate cost of the economic stimulus package was estimated to be $787 Billion at the time of passage.

When added to the projected deficit, additional emergency spending from the stimulus law meant that the Obama administration faced a first year deficit of $1.6 Trillion, before it had even "spent" a dollar on its own watch.

Like a good sport, Mr. Obama addressed the situation somewhat lightly. He noted that the other party had spent the prior 8 years making a huge mess, then handed him only a broom to clean it up. His critics then complained that he wasn't sweeping properly. "Here, let me show you how to hold the broom," Mr. Obama mimicked his critics. The references, not only to the scale of the problems but also to the racial overtones he faced, were not to be lost on the ordinary citizen.

The most fascinating period, however, was the presidency of Andrew Jackson from 1829 to 1837. He inherited a federal debt of $58 Million and *reduced* it to $33,000 (that's 33 *Thousand* dollars) by 1835. No wonder the Bank of the United States hated him.

Source: Congressional Budget Office

[289] Smith, FDR, supra, at p. 351.

"If I have anything to say about it," F.D.R. explained, "it will always be contributed, and I prefer it to be contributed, both on the part of the employer and the employee, on a sound actuarial basis. It means no money out of the (US) Treasury." See Schlesinger, The Coming of the New Deal, supra, at p. 308.

[290] The topic is covered in admirable detail in Moynihan, Daniel Patrick, Pandaemonium (1993).

Both political parties completely missed the instability in the region as far back as the 1970s. In fact, Henry Kissinger, while still Secretary of State, had warned that "for the first time in our history we face the stark reality that the (Communist) challenge is unending." Id., at p. 145, 166-167.

Ten years before the Soviet Union collapsed, however, then US Senator Moynihan, D-NY, stood almost alone in predicting its demise. As the intelligence community proclaimed the enduring strength of the Moscow regime, Moynihan, focusing on ethnic conflict, argued that the end was at hand. He argued and was ultimately proven to be correct that "the vertical category of nationalism has proven far more powerful than the horizontal category of (economic) class consciousness." Id., at p. 125.

291 For an insightful discourse, including a litany of examples, see Bradley, Bill, The New American Story (2007). The particular example cited can be found at p. 246-248.

From a historical perspective, the broader context reveals a tumultuous trade off. On the one hand, Republican administrations of Harding/Coolidge/Hoover (1920s), Eisenhower (1950s) and Bush/"43" (2000s) were certainly understood to mean well in the ideological expression of liberty via individual initiative and enterprise. Yet left strictly to their own devices, they would devolve ultimately to a damaging personification of individual excess. As the pendulum swung back sharply in the other direction, each compensatory social safety net enactment followed.

With the passage of Obamacare in 2010 (discussed in a later chapter), as with the enactment of Medicare in 1965 and Social Security in 1935, there is little wonder that the Republican Party's dominant, conservative right wing base is in a dither about the "liberal" President Obama. The familiar cry can be heard once again of an impending end to American life as we know it. Strictly from the lens of the class interest of business, Republicans may be "right" once again. But, fortunately, government under order of the New Deal is about the larger, class interest of the nation. For the dispossessed in all their ordinary colors, shapes and sizes, the social safety net does begin to speak rather well of a democratic society in relation to its citizens.

292 The federal legislation is called the Medicare Prescription Drug, Improvement, and Modernization Act, also called the Medicare Modernization Act or MMA (2006).

293 Morris, Colonel Roosevelt, supra, at p. 198.

294 Excerpted from Theodore Roosevelt's New Nationalism Speech, supra.

[295] Morris, Colonel Roosevelt, supra, at p. 271.

CHAPTER 11. MORAL ISSUES: WHEN ARE THEY "SECONDARY?"

[296] Maynard, Woodrow Wilson. supra, at p. 218.

[297] Id., at p. 163.

[298] See Humphrey, Hubert H., The Education of a Public Man (1976), at p. 132-144.

[299] Gov. Jim McGreevey, a Democrat, served as New Jersey's 52nd governor from January 15, 2002 until he resigned from office on November 15, 2004.

Since leaving the governorship, McGreevey has reportedly earned a master of divinity degree, and hopes to be accepted as a candidate for the priesthood in the Episcopal Church. His decision came, he says, in the dark days following his resignation. He sought comfort in Catholicism, his childhood faith. At the same time he sensed that his previously closeted existence, and what he calls "the total mess of my life," was at least partly caused by Catholic teaching that condemns homosexual behavior as sinful.

Source: Vitello, Paul, "Out of Politics and Closet, McGreevey Pursues Dream to Join Clergy," *The New York Times*, May 16, 2011.

[300] A regional newspaper, The *Star-Ledger* of Newark, NJ also reported the nation's first openly gay governor earns $17,500 per annum and has been an executive in residence since Nov. 1, 2007.

The public university job requires McGreevey to work up to 15 hours a week and helps the 53-year-old continue to accrue credits in the state pension system, the corruption within which has been alluded to elsewhere in this work, at length. McGreevey said everyone is entitled to their own perspective and he didn't pick a state job because of the retirement benefits.

See de Vries, Lloyd, "Ex-N.J. Gov. McGreevey Now Teaches Ethics," *CBS News, Politics*, April 19, 2007.

[301] In fact, it is widely understood that Abraham Lincoln is the most written about person in history right after Jesus Christ.

302 Most ordinary citizens are unaware that the official title of Harriet Beecher Stowe's 1852 book is <u>Uncle Tom's Cabin: or, Life among the Lowly</u>, nor that it was the second most widely read book of the 19th century. Holding the number one spot is the Holy Bible.

303 <u>Id.</u>, at p. 250.

304 Today the number remains more or less unchanged at an even 1.0%.

Source: US Census Bureau.

305 "Teacher's Guide," *Harriett Beecher Stowe Center*, p. 7.

306 Dixler, Elsa, <u>(A Guide to) Harriett Beecher Stowe's *Uncle Tom's Cabin*</u>, Barron's Educational Series, Inc. (1985), at p. 57. The source material indicates that this account has appeared in 28 books written between 1890 and 2008.

307 The US Supreme Court case of <u>Dred Scott vs. Sandford</u> may be found at 60 <u>U.S.</u> 393 (1857).

308 McDougall, <u>Promised Land, Crusader State (the American Encounter with the World since 1776), supra</u>, at p. 82.

309 Donald, <u>Lincoln, supra</u>, at p. 268-269.

310 The idea that the South saw the *moral* issue of slavery as *secondary* is generally attributed to the famous Lincoln-Douglas debates of 1858, the stakes being an Illinois US Senate seat. Lincoln had won the Republican Party's nomination for the seat, which put him head-to-head in a race with the powerful US Senator, Stephen A. Douglas, an incumbent, who was running for a third term as a Democrat. A series of seven debates between Lincoln and Douglas in towns across Illinois ensued over the next 10 weeks.

The debates attracted national attention for several reasons. First, Douglas had enjoyed a reputation as the "Little Giant" of the Democratic Party and its best stump speaker. Together with Henry Clay, he had been one of the key figures behind the Compromise of 1850. The national debate over slavery was also reaching a boiling point. Responding to the fervor, journalists accompanied the candidates, writing detailed articles and offering editorial commentary that was unprecedented in American political history to that point. Consequently, the whole country watched the debates unfold.

Lincoln had boldly announced that slavery was simply immoral and had to be dealt with forthrightly by Congress. For Lincoln, slavery violated the fundamental assertion of the Declaration of Independence that all men are created equal, arguing that its continued existence and support ran counter to the wishes of the founding fathers. Ultimately, only the power of the federal government could resolve the issue by extinguishing slavery from the nation. Although Lincoln contended that there existed no constitutional way of interfering with slavery where it presently existed, he believed that it should not be allowed to expand westward. For him, the matter was a question of right and wrong, with Douglas indifferent to a moral wrong.

Douglas met the challenge by trying to portray Lincoln as a radical abolitionist, disagreeing with Lincoln's claim that the founding fathers had opposed slavery. Douglas pointed out that many of them, including George Washington and Thomas Jefferson, had owned slaves. He played down the moral issue, saying that the power to decide about the existence of slavery should be dealt with on the local level. And he argued that slavery would never be able to survive outside of the South for simple economic reasons in any case. He warned the nation not to try to judge political issues on moral grounds, lest emotions spill over into civil war. Ultimately, Douglas argued that the issue came down to conflicting ideologies: a view of the nation as a confederacy of sovereign and equal states vs. a federalist empire of consolidated states.

311 Thomas, My Grandfather's Son, a Memoir, supra, at p. 100-101.

312 Id., at p. 137-8.

313 Korematsu vs. United States, 323 U.S. 214 (1944).

314 Morris, Theodore Rex, supra, at p. 99-100.

315 "Guantanamo Bay's Peculiar History," Public Broadcasting Station (PBS), week of May 19, 2006, updated July 28, 2006.

316 Hersh, Seymour M., "Torture at Abu Ghraib," The New Yorker, May 10, 2004.

317 Morris, Theodore Rex, supra, at p. 100-101.

318 Buschschluter, Vanessa, "The Obama Approach to Interrogation," *BBC News*, January 29, 2009.

319 Angle, Jim, "Critics Say Obama's Torture Ban Undermines Vow to Protect America," *Fox News*, May 1, 2009.

320 AP News, "Bush Visit to Geneva Canceled After Protest Threat," *CBS News, World*, February 5, 2011. Mr. Bush discusses in his 2010 book, Decision Points, the subject of whether his administration had authorized the use of torture.

According to a story by *CNN: Politics, Interrogation*, which ran on November 5, 2010, Mr. Bush took responsibility for giving the go-ahead for waterboarding terror suspects. According to excerpts from the book, Mr. Bush stated the following:

The choice between security and values was real.
…
CIA experts drew up a list of interrogation techniques. ... At my direction, Department of Justice and CIA lawyers conducted a careful legal review. The enhanced interrogation program complied with the Constitution and all applicable laws, including those that ban torture.

There were two that I felt went too far, even if they were legal. I directed the CIA not to use them. Another technique was waterboarding, a process of simulated drowning. No doubt the procedure was tough, but medical experts assured the CIA that it did no lasting harm.

321 Source: EnergyLiteracy.org.

322 Moyers, Bill, "Chris Hedges on Capitalism's 'Sacrifice Zones,'" interview with Chris Hedges, *www.smirkingchimp.com*, July 24, 2012.

Chris Hedges and graphic artist and journalist, Joe Sacco, collaborated on a book entitled Days of Destruction, Days of Revolt (2012). It is an unusual account depicting daily life in four centers of 21st century contemporary American poverty and desolation.

323 McCain-Obama Presidential Debate 1, September 26, 2008.

324 Weitz, Dr. Richard, "The U.S. Military and Bahrain," *Second Line of Defense, (Delivering Capabilities to the War Fighter)*, February 24, 2011.

325 Morris, Theodore Rex, supra, at p. 514-517.

326 Id., at p. 223, 231.

327 Yergin, <u>The Prize, supra</u>, at p. 715.

328 Source: *EnergyLiteracy.org., supra.*

329 Take the recent case of the 2010 BP oil spill disaster (BP is a British company, standing for British Petroleum) in the Gulf of Mexico. The accident and resulting explosion killed 11 workers on the offshore oil platform and injured 17 others. Oil spewed unchecked for almost 3 months and released some 4.9 million barrels into the Gulf, in an environmental accident of catastrophic proportions, whose effects may not be known for decades. BP executives performed the requisite *mea culpas*, and after a time offshore production and drilling operations were allowed to resume.

Subsequently, however, it was discovered that the major US oil companies were still submitting plans to receive new government drilling permits, using the old technology from the failed blowout preventer which had caused the accident. Moreover, although BP had submitted no new permit applications directly, it did submit them indirectly through its differently named subsidiaries.

The upshot is that the rigs today are no safer than before the accident. The oil companies and US government regulators simply cast blame on each other.

Source: The Rachel Maddow Show, *CNBC*, (segment: Deepwater oil drilling permits issued with no "real life testing of equipment"), March 24, 2011.

330 News story: "Historic Hudson River Cleanup to Begin After Years of Delay, But Will General Electric Finish the Job?," *National Resources Defense Council (NDRC)*, March 23, 2007.

331 In 1980 Congress passed the Superfund Act, which regulated hazardous waste sites and the conditions for their clean up. Superfund is the common name for the Comprehensive Environmental Response, Compensation, and Liability Act (CERCLA).

332 See Wilson, Richard, "How Wal-Mart Is (Mis)Shaping the Global Economy," *American Educator* (The Professional Journal of the American Federation of Teachers), Volume 31, No. 1, Spring 2007, at p.34.

[333] Moyers, "Chris Hedges on Capitalism's 'Sacrifice Zones,' " interview with Chris Hedges, supra, *www.smirkingchimp.com*.

[334] Smith, Hendrick, "When Capitalists Cared," *The New York Times*, op-ed section, September 2, 2012.

[335] Moyers, "Chris Hedges on Capitalism's 'Sacrifice Zones,' " interview with Chris Hedges, supra, *www.smirkingchimp.com*.

[336] Schlesinger, The Coming of the New Deal, supra, at p. 90, 94.

[337] Drucker, Jesse, "Romney 'I Dig It' Trust Gives Heirs Triple Benefit," *Bloomberg.com*, September 27, 2012.

[338] During the 2012 election campaign, candidate Romney created quite a national stir when he made some inopportune comments at a closed-door Republican fundraiser on May 17, 2012. Meant strictly for private consumption, as fate would have it the cat got out of the bag. Video was captured and published by *Mother Jones* on September 17, 2012 and subsequently replayed on what seemed like a near constant loop on cable news in the lead-up to the November election. Among other things, Mr. Romney in his remarks said that

There are 47 percent of the people who will vote for the president no matter what. All right, there are 47 percent who are with him, who are dependent upon government, who believe that they are victims, who believe that government has a responsibility to care for them, who believe that they are entitled to health care, to food, to housing, to you name it. That's an entitlement. And the government should give it to them. And they will vote for this president no matter what. And I mean, the president starts off with 48, 49, 48—he starts off with a huge number. These are people who pay no income tax. Forty-seven percent of Americans pay no income tax. So our message of low taxes doesn't connect. And he'll be out there talking about tax cuts for the rich. I mean that's what they sell every four years. And so my job is not to worry about those people—I'll never convince them that they should take personal responsibility and care for their lives.

Mr. Romney's rationale for his position that it was fair for him to pay a lower effective tax rate than his secretary was that entrepreneurs like him were job creators and that a lower tax rate was required to create jobs. But the national employment statistics, at least since 1960, consistently fail to support Mr. Romney's claim.

339 Moyers, "Chris Hedges on Capitalism's 'Sacrifice Zones,' " interview with Chris Hedges, supra, www.smirkingchimp.com.

340 Are Democratic presidents better than Republican presidents at job creation? Former President Bill Clinton said as much—forcefully, in his speech at the Democratic National Convention in Charlotte, NC on September 5, 2012:

> Since 1961, for 52 years now, the Republicans have held the White House 28 years, the Democrats 24. In those 52 years, our private economy has produced 66 million private sector jobs. So what's the jobs score? Republicans 24 million, Democrats 42 (million).

In the packed convention hall, it was said to be one of the night's biggest applause lines. "Partisans are free to interpret these findings as they wish," wrote Pulitzer Prize winning PolitiFact.com, "but on the numbers, Clinton's right. We rate his claim True."

Source: "Bill Clinton says Democratic presidents top Republican presidents in job creation," *Tampa Bay Times*, www.politifact. com'truth-o-meter/statements, September 6, 2012.

341 One of the early masters in the burgeoning field of transparency and corporate social responsibility, specifically in business and academic organizations, is Tom McManus, co-editor of the *Journal of Management Development*, a publication that provides an international communications medium for those working in management development whether in industry, consultancy or academia. Mr. McManus is also recently assistant professor at The City University of New York and adjunct assistant professor in the MBA program at the Frank G. Zarb School of Business at Hofstra University, where he teaches business ethics, and has written extensively on the subject.

CHAPTER 12. TOLERANCE AND INCLUSION: ARE THEY MERELY WORDS?

342 Philbrick, Nathaniel, a conversation with, as told to Aldrich, Ian, "Why the Pilgrims Still Matter," *Yankee Magazine*, November 2006, p. 125-127. Philbrick is a National Book Award-winning author of <u>Mayflower: A Story of Courage, Community, and War</u> (2006).

343 <u>Id.</u>, at p. 125.

344 Source: US Census Bureau.

345 Source: Merriam-Webster Dictionary.

346 These restrictions were a part of the Chinese Exclusion Act of 1882.

347 The Emergency Quota Act (1921) and the National Origins Act (1924).

348 The other two were the Voting Rights Act of 1965, which enforced the right of African Americans to vote, and the Medicare/Medicaid Act, which financed health care for older Americans and for persons in poverty as part of President Lyndon Johnson's Great Society.

When the president signed the Immigration Act of 1965 at the foot of the Statue of Liberty, he stressed the law's overall symbolic importance:

This bill that we will sign today is not a revolutionary bill. It does not affect the lives of millions. It will not reshape the structure of our daily lives, or really add importantly to either our wealth or our power. Yet it is still one of the most important acts of this Congress and of this administration (as it) corrects a cruel and enduring wrong in the conduct of the American nation.

The president from Texas was not being uncharacteristically modest, saying only what his advisors and "experts" had told him. But the myriad potential consequences of the new law, little noted at the time and ignored by most historians for decades, were appreciably misjudged by the president's experts.

Source: "The Immigration Act of 1965 (Intended and Unintended Consequences of the 20th Century)," *America.gov*, April 3, 2008.

349 The US Census Bureau defines white people as those "having origins in any of the original peoples of Europe, the Middle East, or North Africa." The term "Caucasian" is used interchangeably with "White." Like all official US racial categories, "White" has a "Not Hispanic or Latino" and a "Hispanic or Latino" component, the latter consisting mostly of White Mexican Americans.

An interesting discussion of German immigration, specifically, can be found at Bradley, Bill, Times Present, Times Past, supra, at p. 319-327.

According to the most recent US Census Bureau figures, German Americans (16.5%), Irish Americans (11.9%), English Americans (9.0%), Italian Americans (5.8%), Polish Americans (3.3%), French Americans (3.1%), Scottish Americans (1.9%), Dutch Americans (1.6%), Norwegian Americans (1.5%), Swedish Americans (1.4%), Scotch-Irish Americans (1.2%), Russian Americans (1.0%), Welsh Americans (0.7%), Portuguese Americans (0.4%) and Armenian Americans (0.075%) in the aggregate make up more than half of the White population. Whites constitute the majority, with 80% (66% non-Hispanic Whites and nearly all 14% Hispanic) or 75% (65.4% non-Hispanic and 9.6% Hispanic) of the US population. Some 60 million Americans, nearly one fifth of the total US population, claim British ancestry.

[350] Albright, The Mighty and the Almighty, supra, at p. 89.

[351] Wilkins, Jefferson's Pillow, supra, at p. 4.

[352] Id., at p. 4-6.

[353] See "Freedom, A History of US," Segment 6 titled "Jim Crow," *pbs.org*.

[354] Morris, Theodore Rex, supra, at p. 52-55.

[355] Id., at p. 47.

[356] In the last several decades of the 20th century through the present, however, the "Great Migration" appears to have reversed itself. Preliminary 2010 US Census figures reveal an ongoing and dramatic return of blacks to the South. The former Confederate states now hold 57 percent of the black population, up from 55 percent 10 years before and 53 percent in 1990 and the highest percentage since 1960. The share of African American growth in the South, census figures show, was the highest since 1910, when about 90 percent of blacks lived in the South.

Source: Jonsson, Patrik (staff writer), "2010 Census Showcases America's Great Racial Seesaw," *The Christian Science Monitor*, March 25, 2011.

[357] Beginning on July 15, 2007 *The Star-Ledger*, a regional newspaper out of Newark, NJ, published an interesting and provocative series on the 40 year anniversary of the riots, which took place in the

Watts section of Los Angeles, as well as the major northern US cities, including Chicago, Detroit, Milwaukee, Washington, D.C. and Newark. The riots were not confined to the US, however. Great Britain and South Africa also experienced race riots during this time.

358 The riots had begun in 1965, due to mounting civil unrest, continuing for three successive summers. President Lyndon Johnson had appointed the commission on July 28, 1967, while rioting was still in progress. Upon signing the order establishing the commission, the president asked for answers to three basic questions about the riots: "What happened? Why did it happen? What can be done to prevent it from happening again and again?"

The commission's final report, named the Report of the National Advisory Commission on Civil Disorders, or Kerner Report, was released on February 29, 1968, after seven months of investigation. The 426-page document became an instant best-seller, with over two million Americans purchasing copies. Its basic finding was that the riots resulted from black frustration at lack of economic opportunity. Dr. Martin Luther King, Jr. critiqued the report a "physician's warning of approaching death, with a prescription for life."

The report's most infamous passage warned, "Our nation is moving toward two societies, one black, one white—separate and unequal." The report berated federal and state governments for failed housing, education and social service policies, also aiming some of its sharpest criticism at the mainstream media: "The press has too long basked in a white world looking out of it, if at all, with white men's eyes and white perspective."

The Johnson administration had the report analyzed, however, and dismissed its recommendations on budgetary grounds. See Schlesinger, <u>Robert Kennedy and His Times (Volume Two), supra,</u> at p. 883, Note 21.

359 As part of Reconstruction "package" following the Civil War, three new amendments to the US Constitution were ratified by the states. The 13th amendment memorialized Lincoln's Emancipation

Proclamation, while the 14th amendment forbade a State from depriving "any person of life, liberty or property without due process of law" or denying "the equal protection of the laws." The 15th amendment, enacted in 1870, provides as follows:

The rights of citizens of the United States to vote shall not be denied or abridged by the United States or by any State on account of race, color or previous condition of servitude.

See Bradley, <u>Times Present, Times Past, supra</u>, at p. 328.

360 McCullough, David, <u>Mornings on Horseback</u> (1981), at p. 198-199.

361 Dr. Chris Bellitto is the resident expert on Roman History, Greek History and the History of the Papacy, serving as associate professor and chair of the History Dept. at Kean University. Dr. Bellitto was kind enough to weigh in on the question of how it was that marriage came to be forbidden in the Roman Catholic Church. His response follows:

The prohibition against marriage is what's known as human law, not divine law—that is, it can change and in fact the RC church has married priests. Clearly, the early church had proto-priests and proto-bishops who were married; I say "proto" because it took several centuries for these offices to start looking like what we think of today.

Over time, as a practical matter, it seemed to make sense that a clergy unburdened by a family would be more available to his congregation. Some of this was linked with an extreme *contemptus mundi* that wanted clergy to be focused exclusively on spiritual matters. You still get a bit of this in the Eastern and Greek Orthodox churches where priests can marry, but bishops can't because the latter are married to their dioceses and wear a ring to prove it.

But we know, as a matter or course, that for the first millennium of church history, many (most?) priests were married—if only because local, regional, and general church councils again and again said they shouldn't be. They must have been, or else why repeat the prohibition? This was known as concubinage, but it's not that negative: marriage even for the laity isn't a sacrament as such until the Middle Ages. You lived together and got a blessing when you could pick one up.

Around 1050, with the start of the papal revolution centered around Gregory VII (1073-1085), we get stronger prohibitions with teeth that say priests can't marry and, indeed, part of the problem was that priests were deeding the local church vestments, vessels, etc. to their eldest son as a cobbler did with the family business, regardless of whether the son had a vocation or not. So you get a denigration and sloppiness of the sacramental life.

This was a spiritual reform at bottom—but not only. Gregory also wanted to pull the church out of its cozy relationship with the state and claimed the right to name bishops and abbots who would, in turn, name local clergy to this or that parish. It became a control issue, sure, but also a fair enough one: a parish belongs to the people and to the church, not just one family whose business had become priesthood. This could be viewed as an attempt of the church to amass property, but for my money that's unfair: there were worthy goals at work.

For some "synthetic, textbook-style citations," Dr. Bellitto would refer the reader to Lynch, Joseph H., The Medieval Church: A Brief History (Longman, 1992), at p. 72-83, 126-29, 136-50 and Tellenbach, Gerd, The Church in Western Europe from the Tenth to the Early Twelfth Century, trans. Timothy Reuter (Cambridge Medieval Textbooks, 1993), at p. 26-37, 75-90, 122-34, 157-84.

362 The foregoing example is of Cardinal Bernard Francis Law, Archbishop of Boston. On December 13, 2002 Fox News ran a story of a report from Vatican City that Cardinal Law, under fire for his role in the sex abuse scandal that rocked the Roman Catholic church in the US, resigned as the Archbishop of Boston, his resignation accepted by then-Pope John Paul II. At the time, Law was the highest-ranking church figure brought down by the sex abuse scandals embroiling the American church.

Law had been accused of having shuffled from parish to parish priests, who were accused, often repeatedly, of sexually abusing minors. The crisis in Boston was touched off by Law's admission that he reassigned a former priest, John Geoghan, despite accusations of sexual abuse. It quickly spread to other dioceses, as Catholics demanded greater accountability from their leaders.

The release of thousands of pages of the Boston Archdiocese's personnel files suggested that Law had covered up sexual abuse committed by priests in his Archdiocese, producing some of the most shocking revelations in the scandal associated with the Archdiocese. Among the worst cases, the papers documented a priest "beating his housekeeper, another trading cocaine for sex, a third fathering two children and then abandoning the mother, a fourth claiming to be the second coming of Christ to lure teenagers training to be nuns into having sex, and a fifth allegedly molesting a boy on 21 consecutive nights during a cross-country trip."

On May 27, 2004 WCVB-TV, the ABC local Boston affiliate, reported that the Vatican had announced that Cardinal Law had been *promoted* to a job overseeing a church in Rome. The Vatican statement said that Pope John Paul II named Law archpriest of the Basilica di Santa Maria Maggiore in Rome, one of four churches under direct Vatican jurisdiction. Law's responsibility extended to the financial management of that church, succeeding an 82-year-old Italian cardinal. It was said to be largely a ceremonial position reserved for retired prelates.

Facing enormous payments in settlements with sex-abuse victims, the Boston Archdiocese and the Vatican considered whether the Archdiocese should declare bankruptcy to protect itself from creditors. The Archdiocese settled with most claimants for $86 million. In June 2004 much of the land around the Archdiocese of Boston headquarters and chancery in Brighton were sold to Boston College, a Roman Catholic university run by Jesuit priests, in part to raise money for legal costs associated with scandal in Boston. As a footnote, the author had graduated from Boston College in 1980 with a degree in liberal arts.

Following the death of Pope John Paul II in April 2005, Law was said to be celebrating masses on a regular basis to celebrate the life of John Paul II. He is currently 79 years old, four years older than 75, the age at which diocesan bishops and assistant bishops are requested to offer their resignation to the Pope. But, the Pope can indefinitely delay acceptance of such resignations.

As to the involvement of another key player, Cardinal Timothy F. Dolan of New York, see Goodstein, Laurie, "Dolan Sought to Protect Church Assets, Files Show," *The New York Times*, July 2, 2013.

363 Franklin, The Autobiography, supra, at p. 642, 656.

364 Albright, The Mighty and the Almighty, supra, at p. 280-281.

365 The allegation of partisan decision making by the judicial branch of government was perhaps never more intense than in the wake of the decision in Bush vs. Gore, 531 U.S. 98 (2000), when a divided 5-4 US Supreme Court relied on innovative readings of the US

Constitution to resolve the 2000 presidential election dispute in favor of the more conservative candidate.

The outcome of the election between Vice President, Al Gore (Democrat), and Texas Governor, George W. Bush (Republican), turned on a razor thin victory for Mr. Bush in the state of Florida. Trailing by a few hundred votes, the Gore campaign requested hand recounts of ballots in four Democratic counties, arguing that manual inspections might lead to the discovery of legal votes that were inadvertently uncounted by the vote tabulating machines. The strategy of the Bush campaign was to mobilize all political resources and sympathetic office holders to block all efforts at hand recounts. At the time, Mr. Bush's brother, Jeb, was Florida's governor.

After the Florida Supreme Court ruled that state law required a statewide manual recount of all ballots in which a machine failed to register a vote for president, the federal case of Bush vs. Gore ensued. Less than a day later, the five most conservative justices on the US Supreme Court issued an emergency injunction halting this recount, explaining that the review of these ballots threatened "irreparable harm to (Mr. Bush), and to the country, by casting a cloud upon what he claims to be the legitimacy of his election." The four dissenters responded that "counting every legally cast vote cannot constitute irreparable harm."

After oral arguments were held, on December 12 the same five justices ruled that no more recounting could take place. They noted that the Florida Supreme Court did not articulate a more specific standard for determining a legitimate vote than the statutory standard of "clear intent of the voter," and this made it possible that identical ballots would be treated differently in different parts of the state. This, they said, violated the equal protection clause of the 14th Amendment.

They did not explain what this innovative interpretation might mean more generally for vote counting in American elections, or even how it applied to the original vote totals in the state of Florida, where balloting and counting practices varied widely from county to county. Instead, the majority said simply, "our consideration is limited to the present circumstances, for the problem of equal protection in election processes generally presents many complexities."

While under a different set of circumstances it might have been possible to send the case back to the Florida Supreme Court so that it might create a more explicit counting standard, the majority announced that it was *their belief* that the state of Florida intended to resolve all disputes by December 12, so that the state would benefit from a federal law that ensured the state's electoral college votes would not be challenged in the Congress. Since the decision was handed down on the evening of December 12, the majority invoked this deadline in support of their conclusion that there was no time left to count votes in Florida.

Each of the four dissenters wrote separately to argue that the US Supreme Court had no business interfering in this presidential election dispute, stressing that these issues were more properly addressed by the state of Florida and then Congress, if necessary. The dissenters also emphasized that the majority's opinion was inconsistent with the previously expressed views of those justices on equal protection and federalism.

The practical effect of this decision was to declare Mr. Bush the president-elect. Mr. Gore conceded the election the following day. While the majority insisted that its intervention was an "unsought responsibility," the most frequently cited language in the opinion belonged to Justice Stevens, who lamented that the actual loser of this presidential election was "the Nation's confidence in the judge as an impartial guardian of the rule of law."

Source: *The Oxford Companion to the Supreme Court of the United States*, edited by Kermit L. Hall, Oxford University Press.

366 Albright, The Mighty and the Almighty, supra, at p. 154.

367 For an informing and engaging discussion on how the political machine of the Republican Pyramid of the New Right had developed, see Bradley, Bill, The New American Story, supra, at p. 259-266.

368 The *Federalist Papers* are a series of essays or political commentaries, arguing for the ratification of the US Constitution. Federalist No. 10 was written by James Madison and is perhaps one of the most famous of the *Federalist Papers*. Federalist No. 10 addresses the issue of how to guard against "factions," or groups of citizens, with interests contrary to the rights of others, or the interests of the whole community. It is here that the right to dissent is championed.

Madison argued that a strong, large republic in federation would be a better guard against those dangers than smaller republics, as, for instance, the individual states.

369 The reference is specifically to Thoreau's infamous *Duty of Civil Disobedience* (1849). The essay makes the argument that a citizen should not permit any government to overrule or shrink his or her conscience, and that citizens have a duty to avoid allowing such acquiescence to enable the government to make them the agents of injustice.

370 Bradley, The New American Story, supra, at p. 263.

371 On February 6, 2003, Secretary of State, Colin Powell, appeared before the UN, attempting to prove the urgency for that body to entertain a resolution to engage in a war with Iraq. The presentation failed to change the fundamental position of the UN Security Council, including France, Russia, China and Germany, although Powell succeeded in hardening the overall tone of the UN towards Iraq.

In March 2003 the US government announced that diplomacy had failed and that it would proceed with a "coalition of the willing" to rid Iraq under Saddam Hussein of weapons of mass destruction the US had insisted it possessed. The 2003 invasion of Iraq began a few days later.

Prior to this decision, there had been much diplomacy and debate amongst the members of the UN Security Council over how to deal with the situation. Prior to 2002, the UN Security Council had passed 16 resolutions on Iraq and in 2002 passed Resolution 1441 unanimously. Resolution 1441 stated that Iraq was in material breach of several prior UN resolutions but would be given "a final opportunity to comply with its disarmament obligations" that had been set out in several previous resolutions.

In 2003, the governments of the US, Great Britain and Spain proposed another resolution on Iraq, which they called the "eighteenth resolution." This proposed resolution was subsequently withdrawn, when it became clear that several permanent members of the UN Security Council would thereby veto it by casting "no" votes on any new resolution.

On September 16, 2004 Kofi Annan, UN Secretary General, speaking subsequently on the US invasion of Iraq, said, "I have indicated it was not in conformity with the UN Charter. From our point of view, from the charter point of view, it was illegal."

372 Albright, The Mighty and the Almighty, supra, at p. 160.

373 Bradley, The New American Story, supra, at p. 252-253.

Unfortunately, the record of the Bush/"43" administration is replete with examples, from the uncontroverted scientific phenomenon of global warming, the uncontroverted scientific benefits of stem cell research and the rejection of Darwin's theory of evolution in favor of "intelligent design."

374 See "Rewriting the Science (Scientist Says Politicians Edit Global Warming Research)," segment which aired on *60 Minutes, CBS News* on March 19, 2006. A follow up story was written on July 30, 2006, from which the quote was extracted.

375 The nomination of Mr. Roberts, who was born in Buffalo, New York and later raised in Indiana, was approved by the Senate Judiciary Committee by a vote of 13–5, with Senators Joe Biden, Richard Durbin, Dianne Feinstein, Ted Kennedy and Charles Schumer, casting the dissenting votes. Subsequently, Mr. Roberts was confirmed by the full Senate by a margin of 78–22. All Republican Senators and the one Independent voted in favor, while the Democrats split evenly, 22–22. Historically, Mr. Roberts was confirmed by what was a narrow margin for a Supreme Court justice.

However, all three subsequent confirmation votes have been even narrower: Samuel Alito of New Jersey in 2006 (58-42); Sonia Sotomayor of New York in 2009 (68-31); and Elena Kagan of Massachusetts in 2010 (63-37).

376 See Citizens United vs. Federal Election Commission, 558 U.S. 310 (2010).

Note the contrast of this judicial opinion with the temperament of F.D.R.'s New Deal. "The concentration of economic power in all-embracing corporations," F.D.R. proclaimed in a 1936 campaign speech, "does not represent private enterprise as we Americans cherish it and propose to foster it. On the contrary," he continued, "it represents private enterprise which has become a kind of private government, a power unto itself—a regimentation of other people's lives. ... The struggle against private monopoly is a struggle for, and not against, American business. It is a struggle to preserve individual enterprise and economic freedom." Schlesinger, The Politics of Upheaval, supra, at p. 631-632. It should surprise few that the rich hated F.D.R., as they do President Obama today.

The dissent had found an ally on the Supreme Court in the Hon. Sandra Day O'Connor, until she stepped down from the high court in 2006. The justice who replaced her, Samuel Alito, a conservative, joined the 5-4 majority in the decision.

Source: Mosk, Matthew, "O'Connor Calls Citizens United Ruling a 'Problem,'" *ABC News*, January 26, 2010.

[377] "Republicans Capture House in Historic Wave, Claim 'Mandate' to Shrink Government," *Fox News*, November 3, 2010.

[378] "Raw Data: Comparison of Past Debt Ceiling Increases," *Fox News.com*, July 26, 2011.

[379] McAuliff, Michael, "Ronald Reagan Hailed by Liberals in Debt Fight," *Huffington Post*, July 20, 2011.

The article points out remarks by President Reagan which Democrats were quick to circulate throughout Washington, D.C. during the debate:

The full consequences of a default or even the serious prospect of a default by the United States are impossible to predict and awesome to contemplate. Denigration of the full faith and credit of the United States would have substantial effects on the domestic financial markets and the value of the dollar in exchange markets. The nation can ill afford to allow such a result.

Mr. Reagan had also made a radio address on September 26, 1987 in which he criticized those who would attempt to score political points out of wrangling over raising the federal debt ceiling. Mr. Reagan's full quote was as follows:

Congress consistently brings the government to the edge of default before facing its responsibility. This brinkmanship threatens the holder of government bonds and those who rely on Social Security and veterans benefits. Interest rates would skyrocket. Instability would occur in financial markets, and the federal deficit would soar. The United States has a special responsibility to itself and the world to meet its obligations. It means we have a well earned reputation for reliability and credibility—two things that set us apart from much of the world.

364

380 Ward, Jon, "Debt Ceiling Debate: Michele Bachmann Says Washington Is 'Deceiving' American People," *Huffington Post*, July 28, 2011.

The story contains a curious side light. When asked about reports that her husband's Christian counseling clinic has advised homosexuals to try to change their sexual orientation—commonly referred to as "reparative therapy," US Rep. Michele Bachmann, R-MN, reportedly had a "ready dodge."

"I am extremely proud of my husband," she said. "But I am running for the presidency of the United States. My husband is not ... I am more than happy to stand for questions on running for president."

381 President Barack Obama, *Address by the President to the Nation*, July 25, 2011.

382 "US Congress Votes Database," *The Washington Post–Postpolitics*, August 22, 2011.

383 "U.S. Loses AAA Credit Rating from S&P," *Fox News*, August 6, 2011.

384 President Barack Obama, *Remarks by the President, State Dining Room*, August 8, 2011.

385 Draper, Robert, "Lindsey Graham, This Year's Maverick," *The New York Times Magazine*, July 1, 2010.

386 The Patient Protection and Affordable Care Act (PPACA) is a federal statute that was signed into law by President Obama on March 23, 2010. This Act and the accompanying Health Care and Education Reconciliation Act of 2010 (signed into law on March 30, 2010) made up the health care reform of 2010. The laws focus on reform of the private health insurance market, providing better coverage for those with pre-existing conditions, extending eligibility for coverage of younger Americans on their parents' plans until the age of 26; improving prescription drug coverage under Medicare and extending the life of the Medicare Trust fund by at least 12 years.

387 In fact, during an August 2013 White House press conference President Obama noted that "The one unifying principle in the Republican Party at the moment is making sure that 30 million people don't have health care," referring to the number of people

who will have health insurance as a direct result of the law. "Why is it that my friends in the other party have made the idea of preventing these people from getting health care their holy grail? Their number one priority?"

The president chuckled as he reminisced about the previous Republican position. Republicans at least used to say they would replace the law with a better health care proposal. But now? Not anymore. The president continued:

There's not even a pretense now that they're going to replace it with something better, The notion is simply that those 30 million people, or the 150 million who are benefiting from other aspects of affordable care, will be better off without it. That's their assertion. Not backed by fact. Not backed by any evidence. It's just become an ideological fixation.

Source: Bendery, Jennifer, "Obama: Republicans' 'Unifying Principle' Is Denying Health Care to 30 Million People," *http://www.huffingtonpost.com*, August 9, 2013.

[388] For example, in April 2011 the state of Kansas became the 10th state to pass a voter ID bill. The bill was passed by a Republican governorship on the basis of the generous estimate of the Secretary of State, who indicated that there have been just 221 incidents of voter fraud in the state in the last 14 years—a rate of just more than 0.0002% of all voters.

Reminiscent of the now illegal poll taxes of the 1950s and early 1960s, the bill threatens to disenfranchise 620,000 voters in Kansas and will cost thousands or even millions of additional taxpayer dollars. Since a majority of African Americans in Kansas do not hold drivers' licenses, the new law figures to have the greatest effect on that demographic group, who voted for Barack Obama in record numbers in the election of 2008.

The Secretary of State attempted to push through a second bill that would allow all parts of the legislation—requiring both a photo ID and proof of citizenship—to take effect *before* the 2012 election. Despite overwhelming support for the initial bill, the Kansas Senate rejected the Secretary's second measure in bipartisan fashion. In response to the defeat, the Secretary put the change at the top of his legislative agenda for the next year and commissioned a task force dedicated to "reviewing the (current) law and developing forms, policies and regulations to implement it before the 2012 election cycle."

389 Following the election of 2008, the Republicans *said* it wasn't about being opposed to abortion anymore, that they were giving up that objective in favor of the objective of a smaller federal government. But in 2010 the number of anti-abortion bills had climbed to 39. In 2011 Republican controlled state governments have enacted a surge of anti-abortion legislation. So far this year 80 such anti-abortion bills had been passed, trending significantly above historical norms. The methods vary, ranging from de-funding programs in areas such as Planned Parenthood, to requiring right to life counseling prior to considering a request for abortion services, to writing new regulations just applicable to abortion clinics.

For example, the state of Kansas (again, I'm afraid) has stepped up its war on abortion providers, this time by granting new powers to shut down Kansas' clinics. Here's how it works. A 2011 law permits the secretary of the state's health department to write new regulations just for abortion clinics. And then, that official also gets to enforce those regulations. If the state's abortion clinics do not meet those new regulations, he can shut them down.

So, some arbitrary new regulations were drafted, about the exact size and number of the janitorial closets, bathrooms, their location and numbers and the kind of lighting the clinics had to have. The regulations were tighter and more specific than Kansas has even for hospitals.

Two days after the clinics received a copy of the new regulations, state inspections began to see if they complied. Of course, no clinic had met the new licensing rules. A federal judge, however, has issued an injunction prohibiting these new regulations from taking effect.

Source: The Rachel Maddow Show, *CNBC*, June 30, 2011; Martel, Frances, "Maddow: If Tea Party Isn't Socially Conservative, Why Have Abortion Laws Shot Up?," *mediaite.com*, July 13, 2011.

390 In the state of Florida, Gov. Rick Scott's brand of Tea Party Republican, big, intrusive government has also expanded the role of the state to include mandatory drug tests for Florida residents receiving public assistance. There is no requirement of probable cause or even reasonable suspicion, just any citizen who is getting

assistance. Neither is there a requirement for those receiving other forms of assistance, such as scholarship aid, or the employees of corporations receiving state tax incentives, or state contractors. Gov. Scott said that "Studies show that people on welfare are higher users of drugs than people not on welfare."

Gov. Scott's forced drug testing plan went into effect in July 2011. The preliminary results? *The Tampa Tribune* reported that the state's own numbers from the new program showed that about 2 percent of welfare applicants are failing the drug tests so far. But a study by the Office of National Drug Control Policy demonstrated that just over 8 percent of all Floridians use illegal drugs.

Source: The Rachel Maddow Show, *CNBC*, August 24, 2011.

Here's the kicker, though. The mandatory drug tests for Florida residents receiving public assistance are being performed under an exclusive contract by the state with a company that is controlled by Gov. Scott's spouse. Although this arrangement is impermissible in many states on illegal conflict of interest grounds, it is not, however, illegal in Florida, which Gov. Scott has pointed out in his defense.

Gov. Scott's ignominy preceded his conduct while in the Florida governor's mansion. Back in 1997, Scott "was forced to resign as the head of a company that pled guilty to massive amounts of systematic fraud, including 14 felonies, leading to a historic $1.7 billion fine." His resignation as CEO came less than four months after the US Department of Justice inquiry became public and before the level of fraud became known. On his campaign website, Scott had admitted his company paid $1.7 billion in fines as part of a federal settlement concerning fraudulent health care billing. The settlement was executed in two phases, the first in 2000 and the second in 2002. In a related civil lawsuit which claimed that his company breached the terms of a communications contract, Scott exercised his 5th amendment privilege against incrimination on some 75 separate occasions.

Source: "Rick Scott, Former Healthcare CEO, Faces Questions About Past, *St. Petersburg Times*, May 20, 2010; "Does Rick Scott Invoking the Fifth Amendment Imply Guilt?," *St. Petersburg Times*, October 12, 2010.

391 The reference here is to the energy and natural gas industry's effort to harvest natural gas from an abundant underground supply understood to be within the geographical confines of the lower 48 states. One businessman in particular, T. Boone Pickens, a trained geologist and billionaire hedge fund manager of BP Capital, LLC, has been lobbying for a congressional bill that would provide incentives to trucking companies that switch to 18-wheelers that run on natural gas instead of oil. Mr. Pickens has said that if the nation's fleet of 18-wheelers were converted from diesel fuel to natural gas, the savings alone in crude oil would make a significant dent in the nation's dependence on foreign oil. He says that part of the problem for why it isn't happening is related to burdensome federal government regulation.

The problem is an environmental one. The natural gas is understood to be contained within shale rock deep beneath the earth's surface. In a process known as fracturing, or "fracking," chemicals and sand are first mixed with vast quantities of water. Then, under high pressure the mixture is blasted into the shale rock in a process which releases the natural gas. On a mass scale, the energy companies have not demonstrated the long-term environmental safety of the procedure on vital ground water supplies. The effect has not been determined, nor has safety data been presented.

The energy companies, it is supposed, just want federal regulators and the American people to "trust" them that the procedure is safe, refusing to demonstrate environmental safety through the disclosure of any supporting empirical data. The harvesting of natural gas by this process promises either to provide the US with a relatively clean domestic source of energy or degrade rural areas and poison drinking water supplies, depending on whom you ask.

392 In late May 2011, Rick Perry, three term Texas governor, told a group of East Texas business leaders that he was "called to the ministry" at age 27, suggesting that the governor's office was his pulpit and that God put him "in this place at this time to do his will."

Source: Burns, Alexander, "Rick Perry 'called' to the 'pulpit,'" *politico.com*, July 14, 2011.

On August 6, 2011, Rachel Maddow showcased some of the more controversial views of those around Gov. Rick Perry's Aug. 6 Christian prayer summit in Houston, Texas. In a series of video clips, a few of the event's sponsors and official endorsers are shown preaching some rather bazaar messages. Among them, they preach that the Statue of Liberty is a "demonic idol," Oprah Winfrey is the "precursor of the Antichrist," Hitler was God's plan to get the Jews to go to Israel and the decline in the Japanese stock market was the result of the Emperor having sex with the sun goddess. Gov. Perry dismissed questions about the religious views of his prayer partners, saying the "focus ought to be on the day of prayer and fasting, not the sponsors."

A few days later, Gov. Perry announced that he was entering the 2012 Republican primary race. Within about a week of that announcement, he surged into the lead, according to national polls conducted in late August 2011.

In his recent book, Fed Up! (2010), Gov. Perry hinted that certain federal entitlement programs, like Social Security, Medicare and Medicaid and unemployment insurance, are "unconstitutional." In defense of his book, candidate Perry, however, has now backtracked, his staff exhorting that the book was not meant to be representative of his views. To the ordinary citizen, saying that something is unconstitutional sounds like a proposal to get rid of it.

Further, in remarks on health care at the Carolinas Hospital System in the Pee Dee region of South Carolina, candidate Perry told gathered health care professionals that if he is elected president, on his first day in office, "There will be an executive order on that desk that eliminates as much of Obamacare as I can have done with an executive order" and that he will work with Congress to repeal the rest.

Source: Shepherd, Shawna CNN Political Producer, "Rick Perry: Immigration Is a 'Federal Responsibility,' " *krdo.com*, August 19, 2011.

393 Wayne Slater, columnist and senior political writer with *The Dallas Morning News*, is understood to be the first to use the term "Teavangelical." Mr. Slater has covered Texas politics for more

than 20 years. The way he explains it, the religious right (i.e., the evangelicals) and the Tea Party are often viewed as separate groups. However, that is not exactly accurate. He further explains that there are libertarian-minded Tea Party advocates who care only about fiscal issues. There are also social conservatives for whom abortion, gay marriage and religious expression are of primary importance. "But there is considerable overlap. Many social conservatives embrace the Tea Party agenda. Call them "Teavangelicals."

In Mr. Slater's view, abortion and homosexuality, as well as spending and debt, are moral absolutes for these Teavangelicals. "Out-of-control spending and over-taxation are as wrong and immoral as stealing." In an extension of the familiar conservative mantra, "programs that don't encourage personal responsibility aren't just bad, they're morally wrong," as well.

Source: Slater, Wayne, *The Dallas Morning News*, August 2, 2011. See also Slater, Wayne, "Texas Faith Blog: When Is It Okay to Apply Moral Absolutes to Public Policy?," *Austin Presbyterian Theological Seminary, austinseminary.edu*, August 3, 2011.

394 In the aftermath of the 1929 Great Depression, prominent American socialists had complained that the New Deal was no more than a blind experiment in "political pragmatism," an opportunistic "form of self-deception which could issue in only one result." It had been shown, they argued, that capitalism produced depression and war. And the New Deal's attempt to preserve it, especially unregulated capitalism, meant fascism. There could be no other result, no way in which capitalism could "be 'reformed' into giving decent or efficient results." Of course, an over-regulated, government planned economy produced the opposite extreme, communism. See Schlesinger, The Politics of Upheaval, supra, at p. 168-175.

395 The 1930s Spanish civil war formed the backdrop to Ernest Hemingway's classic novel, *For Whom the Bell Tolls*. The war pitted the extremist elements of communism to the left and fascism to the right against each another in a setting which would presage the events of World War II. One poignant exchange between Primitivo,

a communist freedom fighter, and Robert Jordan, an American sympathizer, followed:

Primitivo: But surely the big proprietors and the rich will make a revolution against such (income and inheritance) taxes. Such taxes appear to me to be revolutionary. They will revolt against the government when they see that they are threatened, exactly as the fascists have done here.

Robert Jordan: It is possible.

Primitivo: Then you will have to fight in your country as we fight here.

Robert Jordan: Yes, we will have to fight.

Primitivo: But there are not many fascists in your country?

Robert Jordan: There are many who do not know they are fascists but will find it out when the time comes.

Primitivo: But you cannot destroy them until they rebel?

Robert Jordan: No. We cannot destroy them. But we can educate the people so that they will fear fascism and recognize it as it appears and combat it.

Id., at p. 224.

396 "It is easier for a camel to pass through the eye of a needle than for a rich man to enter the kingdom of God." – Matthew 19:24; Mark 10:25; Luke 18:25.

How might billionaire individuals such as Rupert Murdoch and the Koch brothers attempt to justify their rather dubious conduct alongside this particular Biblical quotation? Each man is understood to be among the richest in the world.

Murdoch is the Australian American global media baron and the Chairman and CEO of News Corporation, the world's second-largest media conglomerate. In 1953, he became managing director of News Limited, inherited from his father. Murdoch acquired troubled newspapers in Australia and New Zealand during the 1950s and 1960s, before expanding into the UK in 1969. He moved to New York in 1974, expanding into the US market, and became a US citizen in 1985. By 2000 News Corporation owned over 800 companies in more than 50 countries with a net worth of over $5 billion.

Murdoch has been listed three times in the *Time 100* as among the most influential people in the world. He is ranked as the 13th most powerful person in the world in The World's Most Powerful People list, published by *Forbes* in 2010, with a personal net worth of $7.6 Billion.

In July 2011 Murdoch faced allegations that his companies had been regularly engaged in the illegal practice of hacking the phones of private citizens, including the cell phones of deceased victims of "9/11." He also faces police and government investigations into bribery and corruption in the UK and FBI investigations in the US.

The Koch (pronounced *coke*) family is most notable for control of Koch Industries, the second largest privately owned company in the US. Fred C. Koch was born in Texas, the son of a Dutch immigrant. He started the family business in the 1920s, developing a new method for refining heavy oil into gasoline. In 1927, Koch developed a more efficient thermal "cracking" process for turning crude oil into gasoline. This process led to bigger yields, higher octane and helped smaller, independent oil companies compete. The larger oil companies filed some 44 different lawsuits against Koch, Koch winning all but one. That verdict was later overturned when it was revealed that the judge had been bribed.

The Koch brothers, David H. and Charles G., are two of four sons of inherited wealth who have funded conservative and libertarian policy and advocacy groups in the US. The Koch family foundations have given more than $100 million to think tanks like the Heritage Foundation and the Cato Institute, as well as more recently Americans for Prosperity. Americans for Prosperity and Freedom Works are Koch-linked organizations that have been involved in the Tea Party movement.

397 TV interview with Leslie Stahl, segment which aired on *60 Minutes*, *CBS News* on December 14, 2008.

398 "Racism, Homophobia Dominates Tea Party Protest Over Health Care Bill," as reported on AlterNet.org, March 22, 2010.

[399] Obama, The Audacity of Hope, supra, at p. 322.

[400] Acheson, Present at the Creation, supra, quoting Mr. Justice Holmes, at p. 725.

[401] Author not identified, "Puppies at Play," *Pet Pages* (Sarasota, Manatee, DeSoto & Charlotte counties), 2011 edition, at p. 124.

[402] See Childers, Erskine, The Riddle of the Sands (1903).

[403] Credit for this theory is generally attributed to Alfred Thayer Mahan, a graduate of the US Naval Academy. After 30 years of service and appointment to the staff of the Naval War College in Newport, RI, Captain Mahan authored his world-shaking book, Influence of Sea Power (1890).

The book was said to be extremely influential with T.R. in shaping US naval preparedness for participation in world affairs at the turn of the 20th century.

[404] The views expressed herein are generally adopted and condensed from Acheson, Present at the Creation, supra.

[405] Morris, Colonel Roosevelt, supra, at p. 462-463.

[406] Id., at p. 545.

[407] For a superb historical discussion of the inter-relationships of the various forces that came together at Versailles, see MacMillan, Margaret, Paris 1919: Six Months that Changed the World (2001). The author is the great-granddaughter of David Lloyd George, the British Prime Minister in attendance.

[408] It was the second such award given to a sitting US President (Theodore Roosevelt being the first in 1906 for mediating the end of the war between Russia and Japan, and Barack Obama's recent award in 2009 being the third and latest). President Jimmy Carter won the 2002 award, but this was, of course, more than 20 years after his presidential administration had ended.

The 2009 Nobel Peace Prize was awarded to Barack Obama "for his extraordinary efforts to strengthen international diplomacy and cooperation between peoples." Given in the first year of Mr. Obama's presidency, the award was criticized as undeserved, premature and politically motivated. Mr. Obama himself said that he felt "surprised" by the award and did not consider himself worthy, but accepted it nonetheless.

Source: Nobelprize.org

It may have been more about the world breathing a collective sigh of relief, acknowledging gratefully that the US had turned away from hasty decisions and unilateral military action. Although well intentioned, these prior decisions were based upon fear instead of foresight. In its place was set forth a spirit of international cooperation, based on core human values as articulated by Mr. Obama, and not America's attempt to justify a need, such as securing an oil supply. From an historical, world perspective, the fact that the award went to Mr. Obama may simply have been symbolic that he happened to be in the right place at the right time.

409 MacMillan, Paris 1919: Six Months that Changed the World, supra, at p. 227.

410 The "I" in Istanbul most certainly stands for Islam. The city of Istanbul had become the capital of the Ottoman Empire after its capture from the Romans in 1453, but was transformed quickly from a bastion of Christianity to a symbol of Islamic culture.

Today, Istanbul is the largest city in Turkey and the third largest city proper in the world with a population of 13 million, also making it the largest metropolitan city proper in Europe and the second largest metropolitan area in Europe by population. It extends both on the European and Asian continents, the only metropolis in the world which can claim that designation.

411 Vietnam's Ho Chi Minh was a tiny, frail, thin splinter of a man, gentle and always respectful in public. Even after he had come into sole power in North Vietnam, he steadfastly avoided all the usual trappings of authority, favoring the simple shorts and sandals worn by Vietnamese peasants. Sure of who he was, and certain of his place in Vietnamese history, he had no desire to impress others with his position. Minh considered rich people to be selfish, since their wealth *had* to be gained at the direct expense of others. As one

authority explained, "the idea remains with the Vietnamese that great wealth is anti-social. It is not a sign of status, but of selfishness."

Minh was studying in Paris when World War I ended and world leaders came to Versailles for the peace conference. He wanted to meet President Wilson, to plead for independence (from France) for his country. He had no wife, no children, no friends, only a cause: self-determination for his own people. Wilson ignored his request, mistaking him for a cook. While Vietnam remained France's colony, Minh moved on—farther east and further left. Disillusioned with France and socialism, Minh traveled to Moscow, where Lenin had declared war against imperialism. There, Minh embraced communism.

In 1945, borrowing passages from the American Declaration of Independence, Minh declared Vietnamese independence. Following the end of World War II, Vietnam became a pawn in Cold War politics, with France in the South and Minh in the North. By 1956, France had been ousted from North Vietnam. Peace talks were held in Geneva between the French and the North. Elections to re-unify Vietnam were proposed. But the South refused, backed by US President Eisenhower.

Mr. Eisenhower also withheld information as to just how corrupt the French backed administration in South Vietnam actually was. Among other acts of malfeasance, in the guise of land reform, the Roman Catholic church was permitted to take land from Vietnamese peasants, who just so happened to be Muslim, and grant the land to their Vietnamese Christian peasant counterparts.

The US involvement over the next 20 years is well documented and beyond the scope of this work, the US, however, agreeing to "substitute" for the defeated France on the infamous "domino" theory of communism. The Vietnam War, which ended in failure in 1975, is the first war that the US has actually come out on the losing end. As we now know, although Vietnam was finally unified, the "domino" theory proved to be invalid.

[412] Fromkin, David, A Peace to End All Peace (Creating the Modern Middle East, 1914-1922) (1989), at p. 26-27.

[413] Keegan, The First World War, supra, at p. 218-221, 415.

[414] Fromkin, <u>A Peace to End All Peace, supra</u>, at p. 268-272.

[415] <u>Id.</u>

[416] McCullough, <u>Truman, supra</u>, at p. 614-620.

[417] The seminal work on the history of oil, including the British "Iraq Mandate," is covered in exhaustive detail in Yergin, Daniel, <u>The Prize, supra</u>.

[418] Theodore Roosevelt had earlier warmed to that "warlike little power" to check Russian menacing into the Philippines. See Morris, <u>Theodore Rex, supra</u>, at p. 229.

T.R. had also noted the role of the white (Anglo-Saxon) man in advancing society and Western Civilization:

> During the prior three centuries, the spread of the English-speaking peoples over the world's waste spaces has been not only the most striking feature in the world's history, but also the event of all others most far-reaching in its importance. Morris, <u>The Rise of Theodore Roosevelt, supra</u>, at p. 474-477.

He noted, however, assistance from the Russians in this regard and observed presciently that the Russians were and would remain a formidable, positive force for good, as long as they did not fall under the sway of the looming false promise of communism.

As to Japan, T.R. had also presciently noted as early as 1905:

> In a dozen years the English, Americans and Germans, who now dread one another as rivals in the trade of the Pacific, will have each to dread the Japanese more than they do any other nation.... I believe that Japan will take its place as a great civilized power of a formidable type, and with motives and ways of thought which are not quite those of the powers of our own race. My own policy is perfectly simple, though I have not the slightest idea whether I can get my own country to follow it. I wish to see the United States treat the Japanese in a spirit of all possible courtesy, and with generosity and justice.... If we show that we regard the Japanese as an inferior and alien race, and try to treat them as we have treated the Chinese; and if at the same time we fail to keep our navy at the highest point of efficiency and size—then we shall invite disaster. Morris, <u>Theodore Rex, supra</u>, at p. at p. 397.

With respect to the Chinese, T.R. was making reference to US domestic treatment of the Chinese as well as in China as a consequence of the "Open Door" policy.

[419] MacMillan, <u>Paris 1919: Six Months that Changed the World, supra</u>, at p. 306-321.

420 <u>Id.</u>, at p. 322-344.

Of course, certain events which occurred *between* the two European Civil Wars didn't help the West's cause, either. One event in particular deserves mention here. Pre-occupied with the fallout from the economic chaos brought on by the Great Depression, the US was unable to continue effective military protection of China under the "Open Door" policy. Japan promptly took advantage of the situation. In 1931, seeking to acquire large parts of China, Japan staged an incident in the Chinese province of Manchuria, then invaded China in 1937, in the process slaughtering more than 300,000 innocent Chinese. It is a singular event which China has not forgotten to the present day.

421 In fact, US naval power is presently understood to be in a particularly vulnerable state, as experienced only on two occasions previously. The first was at or about the time of Germany's U-boat sinking of the Lusitania in 1915, which, in part, drew the US into World War I in 1917. The second was in the decade of the 1930s, during the era of the Great Depression, when America was pre-occupied with other matters. The Japanese attack on Pearl Harbor followed in December 1941.

422 For an interesting assessment of the situation from a humanitarian standpoint, see Carter, Jimmy, <u>Palestine: Peace Not Apartheid</u> (2010) a *New York Times* Best Seller book. Carter is one and the same Jimmy Carter, the 39th President of the United States. Critical response to the book is said to be mixed.

423 In 2005 world leaders met, considered, but failed to agree on a working definition for the term "terrorism," proposed by UN Secretary General, Kofi Annan. "The main issue was whether actions taken to resist occupation should be considered 'terrorism,' if they result in the death or injury of noncombatants."

See Albright, <u>The Mighty and the Almighty, supra</u>, at p. 276, footnote.

424 See Otterman, Sharon, "MIDDLE EAST: The Road Map to Peace," *Council on Foreign Relations*, February 7, 2005.

Direct "final settlement" peace talks between the parties have begun under the auspices of US Secretary of State John Kerry against what many suggest are insurmountable odds. See Gordon, Michael R. and Rudoren, Jodi, "Kerry Achieves Deal to Revive Mideast Talks," *The New York Times*, July 19, 2013.

425 According to Shimon Peres, the 90-year-old president of Israel:

The great and intriguing debate in Egypt today is about ... whether to give women freedom or not. It is here that the Arab Spring will be judged. President Obama asked me who I think is preventing democracy in the Middle East. I told him, 'The husbands.' The husband does not want his wife to have equal rights. Without equal rights, it will be impossible to save Egypt, because if women are not educated, the children are not educated. People who cannot read and write can't make a living. They are finished.

Source: Bergman, Ronen, "Shimon Peres on Obama, Iran and the Path to Peace," *The New York Times*, January 9, 2013.

426 The nations where Shiite Muslims form a dominant majority are Azerbaijan, Iran, Bahrain and Iraq, a plurality in Lebanon and large minorities in Turkey, Afghanistan, Pakistan, Kuwait, Saudi Arabia, India, the United Arab Emirates and Syria. The physical shape of these countries put together does in fact resemble a crescent moon or a half moon.

427 Roosevelt, An Autobiography, supra, at p. 392.

428 The speech, entitled *Protecting our Security and our Values*, was given at the National Archives Museum, Washington, D.C., May 21, 2009.

429 Croly, Herbert, The Promise of American Life (1909), at p. 166.

430 Id., at p. 188-190.

431 Id., at p. 410-411.

432 Id., at p. 198-206.

433 Id., at p. 234, 279.

434 Id., at p. 266-270.

435 Thomas, My Grandfather's Son, supra, at p. 202.

436 Croly, The Promise of American Life, supra, at p. 421.

437 Id., at p. 406-409, 426.

438 Malone, The Sage of Monticello, supra, at p. 199. Jefferson, Thomas, *Letter to Amos J. Cook,* January 21, 1816, quoting Chinard, Literary Bible, at p. 120-121.

439 Croly, The Promise of American Life, supra, at p. 356-357.

440 An historical overview is detailed in Robert A. Caro's ground breaking work, Master of the Senate (2002). By way of example, Caro cites Henry Adams' 1880 description of the United States as "a government of the people, by the people, for the benefit of Senators." See p. 27-30. This was before the direct election of Senators occasioned by the 17th Amendment to the US Constitution, ratified in 1913. If anything, direct election may have made the issue more transparent but certainly no less prevalent.

441 See Caro, Master of the Senate, supra, at p. 888-889.

Caro attributed the 1957 turning point in the civil rights movement to US Senate majority leader Lyndon Johnson's basic idea to "Just give Negroes the vote and many of these problems will get better … ." Looking at the idea even with the benefit of hindsight does nothing to diminish its visionary quality.

The Civil Rights Act of 1957, primarily a weak, toothless voting rights bill aimed at registering eligible African American citizens of the South, would presage the epic federal civil rights legislation of the 1960s during the Kennedy/Johnson years.

442 For an interesting discussion of man's individual freedom as secured by the Christian principle of justice in political form and its refutations of socialism, see Durkin, General Sherman's Son, supra, at p. 177-184.

443 On the federal level, the practice is popularly known as "gerrymandering," or setting electoral districts that attempt to establish a party's political advantage by manipulating geographic boundaries to create partisan advantaged districts. The practice dates back to the early 1800s and was named for Elbridge Gerry, the Massachusetts governor who resorted to the practice by signing a bill that redistricted the state to aid his party.

For current examples of gerrymandering in action, see "Redistricting, New York Style," *The New York Times*, http://documents.nytimes.com/redistricting-games-in-new-york%20?ref=editorials. See also as source document: http://s3.amazonaws.com/nytdocs/docs/210/210.pdf, November 11, 2009.

444 Wang, Sam, "The Great Gerrymander of 2012," *The New York Times*, February 2, 2013.

For an analysis of how voting districts are being made more "safe, lily-white" as the nation is becoming more racially diverse, see Friedman, Thomas L., "Our Democracy Is At Stake," *The New York Times*, October 1, 2013.

445 Nichols, John, "Three Strategies to Block the Gerrymandering of the Electoral College," *The Nation*, January 25, 2013.

446 Caro, Master of the Senate, supra, at p. 9.

447 Id., at p. 385, 446.

The quote is attributed to the liberal US Sen. Hubert H. Humphrey, Jr., D-MN, upon his election to the Senate in 1948. Humphrey would later serve as Vice President during Lyndon Johnson's administration.

448 Id., at p. 83, 92, 105.

449 In a historic move that was said to substantially alter the balance of power in Washington, the US Senate in November 2013 voted, in fact, to abolish the super majority 60 vote filibuster requirement concerning presidential nominees to executive and judicial appointments. That means a return to the democratic process of a simple majority for Senate confirmation.

The US Constitution gives a president the right to nominate top executive officials and name judges and is silent about the ability of a Senate minority to stop them. Although the practice barely existed before the 1970s, Senate Republicans for the first five years of the Obama administration have refused to allow confirmation votes on dozens of perfectly qualified candidates nominated by the president for government positions. They also have effectively nullified entire federal agencies by denying them leadership and "abused Senate rules past the point of tolerance or responsibility."

Republicans blocked Obama administration nominees "not because they object to the qualifications, but because they seek to undermine the very government they were elected to serve," according to Senate majority leader Harry Reid, D-NV. "For the first time in the history of our republic, Republicans have routinely used the filibuster to prevent President Obama from appointing an executive team and from appointing judges," Reid noted. "The need for change is so, so very obvious."

President Obama remarked that nearly 30 presidential executive nominees had been filibustered during his presidency, compared with 20 such cases previously in all of history. "In each of these cases," the president said, "it's not been because they opposed the person ... it was simply because they opposed the policies the American people voted for in the last election."

The change will not affect legislation or appointments to the US Supreme Court. But the vote may lead to broader filibuster changes that could finally spell an end to logjams that have prevented important legislation from reaching votes.

Source: Editorial, "Democracy Returns to the Senate," *The New York Times*, November 21, 2013; McCarthy, Tom, "Senate Approves Change to Filibuster Rule After Repeated Republican Blocks," *theguardian.com*, November 21, 2013.

[450] Roosevelt, An Autobiography, supra, at p. 42.

[451] President Obama gave a major speech on the subject of Comprehensive Immigration Reform at the American University School of International Service, Washington, D.C. on July 1, 2010. The full text of that speech can be viewed at *www.whitehouse.gov*, Office of the Press Secretary.

[452] See Parker, Ashley and Schmidt, Michael S., "Boehner Rules Out Negotiations on Immigration," *The New York Times*, November 13, 2013.

[453] In 1972 the US prison population stood at 300,000. By 2014 it had climbed to 2,300,000. Can America kick its addiction to incarceration? See Frontline–"Locked Up in America," *Public Broadcasting*

Station (PBS), two films airing April 22, 2014 and April 29, 2014. Link: http://www.pbs.org/wgbh/pages/frontline/locked-up-in-america/#prison-state.

454 Most recent population figures according to the 2010 US Census Bureau.

455 For a scorching indictment of the racialized war on drugs, see Alexander, Michele, <u>The New Jim Crow: Mass Incarceration in the Age of Colorblindness</u> (2010).

456 In August 2013 Attorney General Eric H. Holder, Jr. delivered a speech in San Francisco announcing a major shift in federal criminal justice policy. Prosecutorial discretion would henceforth be used to circumvent certain mandatory minimum sentences for low-level, drug related "victimless" offenses. The move is intended to curb soaring taxpayer prison costs and address chronic unfairness in the justice system. Mr. Holder on behalf of the Obama administration declared what many have long argued, justifying his decision in both moral and economic terms:

> … too many Americans go to too many prisons for far too long and for no good law enforcement reason. … Although incarceration has a role to play in our justice system, widespread incarceration at the federal, state and local levels is both ineffective and unsustainable. … It imposes a significant economic burden … and it comes with human and moral costs that are impossible to calculate.

Source: Savage, Charlie, "Justice Dept. Seeks to Curtail Stiff Drug Sentences," *The New York Times*, August 12, 2013.

457 See Laughlin, Meg, "Doctor Says Conviction Saved Him" and "An 'Innocent Fool,' or Just Guilty," *St. Petersburg Times*, June 26, 2011.

458 Mr. Buffett's remarks were the subject of a *CNBC* television interview with news reporter, Becky Quick, on March 2, 2011.

459 Wilkins, <u>Jefferson's Pillow, supra</u>, at p. 139-140.

460 On August 28, 2013 President Obama gave a speech on the 50th anniversary of Dr. King's march on Washington. Almost five years into his presidential term he reminded the ordinary citizen that his eye remains on the ball, as he strives to mold America to a purpose he boldly envisions:

> In some ways, though, the securing of civil rights, voting rights, the eradication of legalized discrimination—the very significance of these

victories may have obscured a second goal of the march, for the men and women who gathered 50 years ago were not there in search of some abstract idea. They were there seeking jobs as well as justice—not just the absence of oppression but the presence of economic opportunity. For what does it profit a man, Dr. King would ask, to sit at an integrated lunch counter if he can't afford the meal?

This idea that—that one's liberty is linked to one's livelihood, that the pursuit of happiness requires the dignity of work, the skills to find work, decent pay, some measure of material security—this idea was not new.
...

Dr. King explained that the goals of African-Americans were identical to working people of all races: decent wages, fair working conditions, livable housing, old age security, health and welfare measures—conditions in which families can grow, have education for their children and respect in the community.

What King was describing has been the dream of every American. It's what's lured for centuries new arrivals to our shores. And it's along this second dimension of economic opportunity, the chance through honest toil to advance one's station in life, that the goals of 50 years ago have fallen most short.

The president continued:

... the measure of progress for those who marched 50 years ago was not merely how many blacks had joined the ranks of millionaires; it was whether this country would admit all people who were willing to work hard, regardless of race, into the ranks of a middle-class life. The test was not and never has been whether the doors of opportunity are cracked a bit wider for a few. It was whether our economic system provides a fair shot for the many ... . To win that battle, to answer that call—this remains our great unfinished business.

The full text of the speech can be found at http://www.washingtonpost. com/politics/transcript-president-obamas-speech-on-the-50th- anniversary-of-the-march-on-washington/2013/08/28/0138e01e- 0ffb-11e3-8cdd-bcdc09410972_story.html.

In March 2013 Pope Francis, who became the first non-European pontiff in 1,300 years, also got into the act in another encouraging sign for the ordinary citizen. In an 84-page document known as an apostolic exhortation, the Pope set out a platform for his papacy.

In it he attacked unfettered capitalism as "a new tyranny," calling for an overhaul of the financial system and warning that economic inequality and unequal distribution of wealth inevitably leads to violence. Absent a solution to that problem, "no solution will be found for the world's problems or, for that matter, to any problems." Francis attacked the "idolatry of money," urging politicians to "attack the structural causes of inequality" and strive to provide work, healthcare and education to all citizens.

Francis also called upon the affluent to share their wealth:

Just as the commandment 'Thou shalt not kill' sets a clear limit in order to safeguard the value of human life, today we also have to say 'thou shalt not' to an economy of exclusion and inequality. Such an economy kills.

"How can it be that it is not a news item when an elderly homeless person dies of exposure," the Pope asked, "but it is news when the stock market loses 2 points?"

"I prefer a Church which is bruised, hurting and dirty because it has been out on the streets," the Pope wrote, "rather than a Church which is unhealthy from being confined and from clinging to its own security."

Source: O'Leary, Naomi, "Pope Attacks 'Tyranny' of Markets in Manifesto for Papacy," *Reuters.com*, November 26, 2013.

461 Schlesinger, <u>The Coming of the New Deal, supra</u>, at p. 19.

462 Kennedy, Robert F., "Topics: 'Things Fall Apart; the Center Cannot Hold …'," *The New York Times*, February 10, 1968. His piece focused on "the malaise of the spirit" in America.

One month later, Kennedy was asked by the friends of Cesar Chavez, the Mexican American civil rights activist, labor leader and co-founder of the United Farm Workers union, to attend a Mass of Thanksgiving in California. The Mass was to mark the end of Chavez's fast in penance for violence provoked by his union's struggle for survival. Too weak to speak, Chavez's speech was read for him:

When we are really honest with ourselves, we must admit that our lives are all that really belong to us. So it is how we use our lives that determines what kind of men we are. It is my deepest belief that only by giving our lives do we find life. I am convinced that the truest act of courage, the strongest act of manliness, is to sacrifice ourselves for others in a totally nonviolent struggle for justice. To be a man is to suffer for others. God help us be men.

Schlesinger, <u>Robert Kennedy and His Times (Volume Two), supra</u>, at p. 884.

Bibliography

Acheson, Dean, <u>Present at the Creation: My Years in the State</u>
<u>Department</u> (1969)

Albright, Madeline, <u>The Mighty and the Almighty</u> (2006)

Beisner, Robert L., <u>Dean Acheson: A Life in the Cold War</u> (2006)

Bennett, William J. (editor), <u>The Book of Virtues</u> (1993) and the
accompanying illustrated <u>Children's Book of Virtues (1995)</u>

Bradley, Bill, <u>Times Present, Times Past (a Memoir)</u> (1996)
<u>The New American Story</u> (2007)

Brinkley, Douglas, <u>Gerald R. Ford</u> (2007)

Caro, Robert A., <u>The Years of Lyndon Johnson (Four Volumes)</u>:
<u>The Path to Power (Volume One)</u> (1982); <u>Means of Ascent</u>
<u>(Volume Two)</u> (1990); <u>Master of the Senate (Volume Three)</u>
(2002); <u>The Passage of Power (Volume Four)</u> (2012)

Childers, Erskine, <u>The Riddle of the Sands</u> (1903)

Croly, Herbert, <u>The Promise of American Life</u> (1909)

Donald, David Herbert, <u>Lincoln</u> (1995)

Durkin, Joseph T., S.J., <u>General Sherman's Son</u> (1959)

Ellis, Joseph J., <u>His Excellency</u> (2004)

Franklin, Ben, <u>The Autobiography</u> (Library of America publisher)
(1791)
<u>The Compleated Autobiography</u> (compiled and edited by
Mark Skousen) (2006)

Freeman, Douglas Southall, <u>R.E. Lee (Four Volumes)</u> (1935)

Fromkin, David, <u>A Peace to End All Peace (Creating the Modern</u>
<u>Middle East, 1914-1922)</u> (1989)

Grant, Ulysses S., <u>Personal Memoirs of U.S. Grant (Two Volumes)</u>
(1885)

Grant, Julia Dent, The Personal Memoirs of Julia Dent Grant, edited by John Y. Simon (1975)

Hays, Greg (introduction and notes), Meditations of Marcus Aurelius (2002)

Hemingway, Ernest, For Whom the Bell Tolls (1940); The Old Man and the Sea (1952)

Hirshson, Stanley P., The White Tecumseh (1997)

Humphrey, Hubert H., The Education of a Public Man (1976)

Jefferson, Thomas, The Jefferson Bible, The Life and Morals of Jesus of Nazareth (Beacon Press edition, 1989; originally published 1904)

Keegan, John, The First World War (1998)

Kurlansky, Mark, Cod: a Biography of the Fish That Changed the World (1997)

MacMillan, Margaret, Paris 1919: Six Months that Changed the World (2001)

Malone, Dumas, Jefferson and His Time (Six Volumes): Jefferson the Virginian (Volume One) (1948); Jefferson and the Rights of Man (Volume Two) (1951); Jefferson and the Ordeal of Liberty (Volume Three) (1962); Jefferson the President, First Term, 1801-1805 (Volume Four) (1970); Jefferson the President, Second Term, 1805-1809 (Volume Five) (1974); The Sage of Monticello (Volume Six) (1981)

Martin, James Kirby; Roberts, Randy; Mintz, Steven; McMurry, Linda O.; Jones, James H., America and its Peoples, Volume 1 to 1877, Volume 2 from 1865 (fifth edition, 2003)

Maynard, W. Barksdale, Woodrow Wilson (Princeton to the Presidency) (2008)

McCullough, David, Mornings on Horseback (1981)
Truman (1992)
John Adams (2001)

McDougall, Walter A., Promised Land, Crusader State, The American Encounter with the World Since 1776 (1997)

Merton, Thomas (editor and foreword), The Way of Chuang Tzu (2004)

Miller, John C., Alexander Hamilton (1959)

Miller, Merle (editor), Plain Speaking, an Oral Biography of Harry S. Truman (1974)

Morris, Edmund, The Rise of Theodore Roosevelt (Volume One) (1979); Theodore Rex (Volume Two) (2001); Colonel Roosevelt (Volume Three) (2010)
Dutch (A Memoir of Ronald Reagan) (1989)

Moynihan, Daniel Patrick, Pandaemonium (1993)

Murrin, John M.; Johnson, Paul E.; McPherson, James M.; Gerstle, Gary; Rosenberg, Emily S.; Rosenberg, Norman L.. Liberty, Equality, Power, a History of the American People, Volume I: to 1877, Volume II: since 1863.(concise fifth edition, 2008)

Nagel, Paul C., John Quincy Adams (A Public Life, A Private Life) (1997)

Nasaw, David, Andrew Carnegie (2006)

Newfield, Jack, RFK: a Memoir (1969)

Obama, Barack, The Audacity of Hope (2006)

Phillips, Donald T., Lincoln on Leadership (1991)

Remini, Robert, Andrew Jackson: The Course of American Empire (Volume One) (1977); Andrew Jackson: The Course of American Freedom (Volume Two) (1981); Andrew Jackson: The Course of American Democracy (Volume Three) (1984)

Roosevelt, Theodore, An Autobiography (1913)

Schlesinger, Arthur M., Jr., The Age of Roosevelt (Three Volumes): The Crisis of the Old Order (Volume One) (1957); The Coming of the New Deal (Volume Two) (1959); The Politics of Upheaval (Volume Three) (1960)
The Imperial Presidency (1973)
Robert Kennedy and His Times (Two Volumes) (1978)

Sherman, William T., Memoirs of General Sherman (Two Volumes) (1875)

Smith, Jean Edward, Grant (2001)
FDR (2007)

Stowe, Harriet Beecher, Uncle Tom's Cabin: or, Life among the Lowly (1852)

Thomas, Clarence, My Grandfather's Son, a Memoir (2007)

Thomas, Evan, Robert Kennedy, His Life (2000)

Waugh, John C., Re-Electing Lincoln (1997)

Wilkins, Roger, Jefferson's Pillow (2001)

Winik, Jay, April 1865 (2001)

Yergin, Daniel, The Prize (1991)

Yeltsin, Boris, Against the Grain (1989)

Index

Marshall, Thurgood 91, 117
Mary, the Blessed Mother 66
Mason and Dixon's line 56
Mayflower, Compact 42, 120, 253,
    257, 353
McCarthy, Joseph 2
McClellan, George 103
McGreevey, Jim 225, 347
McKinley, William 132, 199, 200, 216
Medicare/Medicaid 211, 219, 220,
    271, 328, 342, 343, 346, 354,
    365, 370
Meditations 41
Meredith, James 341
Mexican-American War 101, 254, 317
Military-industrial complex 148, 157
Minh, Ho Chi 207, 209, 375
Missouri Compromise 54
Mitchell, Margaret 57, 133
Mohammed 41
Morgan, J.P. 128
Moyers, Bill 313
Moynihan, Daniel P. 345
Muhammad Ali 150, 263, 330
Muir, John 238
Murdoch, Rupert 64, 372
Mussolini, Benito 47
NAACP 259
Napoleon 33
National Environmental Policy Act
    (NEPA) 210
National Labor Relations Act (NLRA)
    142, 327
National Public Radio (NPR) 270,
    313, 321
Nativism 131, 255, 259
NATO 147, 264
Neocons (Neoconservatives) 264, 266,
    267, 271
New Deal 140, 142, 147, 153, 168,
    172, 177, 182, 183, 194, 205,
    271, 309, 325, 327, 328, 329,
    345, 346, 352, 363, 371, 385
New Orleans, Battle of 96
New Right 247, 263, 264, 361
New World 18, 65, 253

New Zealand 136, 280, 283, 372
NIMBY 252
Nixon, Richard 2, 209, 210, 341
Nobel Piece Prize 281
Noblesse oblige 188
Norton, Mary 173
Nullification, theory 50, 55
Obama, Barack 45, 93, 155, 156, 182,
    205, 211, 220, 235, 237, 266,
    268, 269, 270, 272, 276, 290,
    304, 307, 332, 333, 335, 342,
    344, 345, 346, 350, 364, 365,
    366, 374, 375, 379, 381, 382,
    383
O'Connor, Sandra Day 133, 364
Old World 18
OPEC 238
Open Door Policy 135, 286, 326, 377,
    378
Outsourcing 240, 241
Paine, Thomas 43
Pakistan 237, 379
Palestine 282, 283, 284, 287, 330, 378
Panama Canal 135, 136
Parcells, Bill 90
Parker, Theodore 330
Patriot Act 28, 49, 234, 264, 265, 316
Pearl Harbor, Hawaii 47, 65, 135, 143,
    331, 378
Pelosi, Nancy 133
Pension formula, NJ 169
Peres, Shimon 379
Perkins, Frances 133
Perkins, Milo 327
Perry, Rick 369, 370
Pharisees 7
Philippines 135, 234, 235, 286, 377
Pickens, T. Boone 369
Pilate, Pontius 7
Plato 28, 30, 41, 111, 316
Plutarch 3, 41
Pocahontas 132
Poland 282
Polk, James 100
Pope, Clement VII 42
Pope, Francis 384

Printed in the USA
CPSIA information can be obtained
at www.ICGtesting.com
LVHW021653091123
763115LV00098B/1213/J